Cultural Atlas of
MESOPOTAMIA
and the Ancient Near East

Project Manager Graham Bateman
Editor Michael March
Cartographic Manager
Olive Pearson
Cartographic Editor Sarah Rhodes
Picture Editor/Art Researcher
Linda Proud
Index/Proof Reading
Angela Mackeith
Design Adrian Hodgkins
Production Clive Sparling

 AN EQUINOX BOOK

Advisory Editor Nicholas Postgate

Additional contributions by
Dominique Collon (pages 72–73)
and Georgina Herrmann
(pages 156–157)

Planned and produced by
Equinox (Oxford) Ltd, Musterlin
House, Jordan Hill Road, Oxford
OX2 8DP, England

Facts On File, Inc.
460 Park Avenue South
New York NY 10016
USA

Facts On File Limited
Collins Street
Oxford OX4 1XJ
United Kingdom

**Library of Congress
Cataloging-in-Publication Data**

Roaf, Michael.
    Cultural atlas of Mesopotamia and
    the ancient Near East/Michael Roaf.
        p.   cm.
    Includes bibliographical references
    and index.
    ISBN 0-8160-2218-6
    1. Iraq—Civilization—To 634.
    2. Middle East— Civilization—
    To 622.   I. Title.
DS69.5.R63 1990   90-3429
935—dc20   CIP

A British CIP catalogue record is
available from the British Library.

Facts On File books are available at
special discounts when purchased in
bulk quantities for businesses,
associations, institutions or sales
promotions. Please call our Special Sales
Department in New York at
212/683-2244 (dial 800/322-8755 except
in NY, AK or HI) or in Oxford
0865/728399.

Origination by Scantrans, Singapore

Filmset by Hourds Typographica,
Stafford, England

Printed in Spain by Heraclio
Fournier SA, Vitoria

10 9 8 7 6 5 4 3 2 1

Frontispiece Delegations of subject
peoples to Xerxes, Apadana staircase,
Persepolis.

Cultural Atlas of
MESOPOTAMIA
and the Ancient Near East

by Michael Roaf

Facts On File
New York • Oxford

CONTENTS

Site Features

King Lists

List of Maps

CHRONOLOGICAL TABLE

all dates are approximate

	BC 12,000	7000	4000	3000
ARCHEOLOGICAL PERIOD	EPIPALEOLITHIC	NEOLITHIC		EARLY BRONZE AGE
NORTHERN MESOPOTAMIA		Aceramic Neolithic — Hassuna / Samarra / Halaf — Ubaid	Gawra — Uruk	Ninevite 5
SOUTHERN MESOPOTAMIA		Ubaid	Uruk	Early Dynastic / Royal Cemetery of Ur

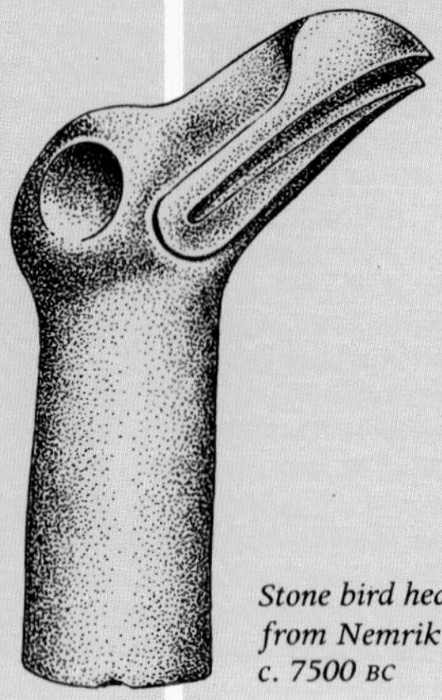

Stone bird head from Nemrik c. 7500 BC

Susa A bowl c. 4000 BC

Stone statue from Khafajeh c. 2500 BC

(vertical labels: FIRST FARMERS / PROTO-NEOLITHIC)

	BC 12,000	7000	4000	3000
LEVANT/PALESTINE	Natufian	Pre-Pottery Neolithic B — Halaf / Ubaid	Nahal Mishmar hoard / Uruk colonies	Egyptian influence
IRAN/THE GULF	Sea level rising	Mesopotamian influence / Ubaid pottery	Susa A / Uruk influence	Proto-Elamite
ANATOLIA		Chatal Huyuk		Early Transcaucasian
CULTURAL AND TECHNOLOGICAL DEVELOPMENT	Hunting and gathering / Domestic dog / Farming / Mud-brick / Weaving / Early copper / Small bands	Plow / Irrigation / Boats / Baked brick / Temples / Pottery / Faience / Cast copper / Stamp seals / Villages	Donkey / Sledges / Wheel / Monumental architecture / City walls / Lost-wax casting metal vessels gold, silver, lead arsenical copper / Cylinder seals / Writing / Cities	Camels (in Iran) / "the Flood" / Palaces / Metal axes and daggers / Tin bronze / Developed cuneiform script / City states

8

MIDDLE BRONZE AGE   **LATE BRONZE AGE**   **IRON AGE**

Akkadian	Old Assyrian	Mittani	Late Assyrian		Persian rule
Third Dynasty of Ur	Shamshi-Adad	Middle Assyrian			
	Mari letters				

Akkadian	Isin–Larsa	Kassite	Late Babylonian	Assyrian domination	Neo-Babylonian
Third Dynasty of Ur	Old Babylonian	Middle Babylonian			Persian rule

Bronze and silver stag from Alaca Huyuk c. 2300 BC

Faience mask from Tell al-Rimah c. 1350 BC

Horse head on a relief from Dur-Sharrukin c. 710 BC

Stele from Neirab near Aleppo c. 600 BC

Head of blue paste from Persepolis c. 450 BC

Ebla	Egyptian influence	Egyptian rule	Israel	Assyrian conquests	Babylonian and Persian rules
Amorite invasions	Hyksos	Sea peoples	Judah		
		Amarna letters Israelites	Phoenician, Aramaean and Neo-Hittite states		Exile and return of the Jews
		Mittani			
		Hittite conquest			

Old Elamite	Old Elamite	Middle Elamite	Medes	Medes	Medes
Godin III	Godin III				Achaemenid
Dilmun	Dilmun	Arrival of Iranian tribes	Urartian and Assyrian invasions	Assyrian invasions	Persians

Alaca Huyuk tombs	Old Assyrian trade	Hittite	Urartians	Lydians	Median and Persian conquests
	Old Hittite	Arrival of Phrygians	Phrygians		

Horses	Horse bits	Camels		Cotton	
	Chariots	Chickens			
	Spoked wheels		Cavalry		
Ziggurats	Icehouses				
		Glass Glazed pottery		Coins	
		Iron smelted		Brass	
	Early alphabet			Aramaic	
Empires					

INVASION OF ALEXANDER

PREFACE

From the end of the last Ice Age until the emergence of the civilizations of Greece and Rome the most advanced societies lived in the Near East. It was here that the fundamental transition from hunting and gathering to farming first took place. Here also, were the first temples and cities, the first metalworking, the first writing, the first kingdoms, the first empires. The heartland of the ancient Near East was Mesopotamia, the fertile plains watered by the Tigris and Euphrates rivers. At different periods the power of the various Mesopotamian kingdoms extended far beyond the lowland plains, making contact with neighboring regions, which also made important contributions to the civilization of the ancient Near East. The aim of this book is to describe the highlights of human achievement in Mesopotamia and the ancient Near East against the background of the geography of the region.

The period covered lasted for more than 10,000 years ending with the conquest of the Near East by Alexander. During that time the local populations experienced huge social changes. At the beginning of the period, small bands of people supported themselves by hunting, fishing, scavenging and gathering plant food. By the end of it, there were empires ruling almost the whole civilized world. To emphasize these crucial historical developments the text follows a chronological framework. Almost all the present knowledge of the ancient Near East (except for the biased accounts in the Bible and by the Greeks who deal with the latest periods) has been resurrected by archeologists over the last century and a half. The early chapters of the book cover the periods before the invention of writing, when the material remains left by the early inhabitants of the Near East provide the basic evidence. In later periods, more abundant textual sources have been recovered and the scope of the investigation extends to historical events and personalities.

How much archeologists and ancient historians have been able to reconstruct is remarkable, given the remoteness of the period and the fragmentary nature of the evidence on which our understanding of the past is based. There are, of course, many gaps in the story and many questions still unanswered, but the outline is now clear and modern civilization's debt to the ancient Near East is undeniable. Much that is taken for granted in the modern world has its origins in the ancient Near East: foodstuffs, building bricks, wheeled vehicles and the use of a written language all derive from developments described in these pages.

At intervals throughout the book, special topics are featured, starting with modern methods of archeological excavation. Other features include subjects as diverse as the origins of writing and the art of hunting. The major archeological sites of the ancient Near East are also described and illustrated in individual features.

The intention at all times has been to make the material accessible to the nonspecialist reader, and technical language has been avoided whenever possible. Furthermore authorities are not cited even for the most controversial statements. The short bibliography at the end of the book is intended to act as a guide toward further reading rather than as the source for any particular statement. The glossary of terms also includes further information about problems of terminology and chronology.

The study of the ancient Near East is still in its infancy. It is only 150 years since the unearthing of the sculptures of the Assyrian palaces and the first decipherment of the Babylonian cuneiform script. Every year brings new discoveries that increase our knowledge and correct our preconceptions. Much basic research work still remains to be done, and investigations currently under way will undoubtedly change accepted views.

The locations of many ancient places are uncertain and the boundaries of kingdoms are often conjectural. As it has not been possible to indicate all the various possible alternatives in the maps, the most probable locations have generally been chosen. In some cases, it has been possible to indicate how reliable an identification may be, in others it has not. Furthermore, basic elements of the ancient geography, such as the courses of the rivers and the coastline of the Gulf, are still the subject of much debate. The reader should, therefore, be aware that the views expressed in this book offer an interpretation of present knowledge.

It is a pleasure to thank the Advisory Editor, Nicholas Postgate, for his many suggestions and St. John Simpson for reading and improving the text and for assisting with the captions and the bibliography. I am also greatly indebted to Dominique Collon and Georgina Herrmann for writing the special features on Cylinder Seals and Ancient Ivory, subjects on which they are the leading experts, and to John Curtis, David Hawkins, Jane and Robert Killick, Roger Moorey, Trevor Watkins and other Near Eastern archeologists who have helped with specific matters. The editorial team at Equinox (Oxford) Ltd has contributed greatly to the quality of the publication and I am extremely grateful to them for the skillful work they have done. Finally I owe an enormous amount to my family, Susan, Christopher and Richard, for their unfailing love and support.

Michael Roaf

Opposite The wedges of the cuneiform script carved over the relief sculpture from a 9th century BC palace at Kalhu.

Archeology of the Near East

Most of our knowledge of the ancient Near East has been gained in the last 150 years through archeological fieldwork. In the 19th century the main concern of archeologists was the discovery of works of art to display in the museums of Europe. Since then archeology has become a scientific discipline that requires years of professional and academic training. Carefully devised techniques of excavation and recording ensure that the maximum amount of information is recovered. But imagination and luck can also play their part.

The excavation of an archeological site is a complex operation, requiring the cooperation of numerous specialists. As well as the director in overall control of the project there will be archeologists who supervise and record the digging, surveyors who make plans of the buildings discovered, photographers, draughtsmen, registrars who record the objects found, and conservators who are responsible for consolidating and repairing fragile or broken objects. On a typical excavation, literally hundreds of thousands of pieces of broken pottery, fragments of flint, discarded animal bones and so on have to be examined and recorded. Increasingly, soil scientists, metallurgists, chemists, geologists, computer programers and statisticians are coming to the archeologists' aid.

As well as excavating sites, archeologists will also try to reconstruct the ancient surrounding landscape. Surface survey, in which the visible traces of ancient civilization within an area are recorded, is a valuable way of discovering the history of settlement of a region, and indeed of selecting a site to be excavated later.

One of the archeologist's most pressing concerns is to date what has been found. By a careful examination of the different deposits, it is possible to work out the order in which they were laid down. The shape of the artifacts used in a particular region evolved over time and by arranging them in chronological sequence they can serve to date the context where they were discovered. In the Near East, decorated pottery vessels provide the chronological framework for the study of past cultures. In some cases, dates can be derived from historical sources that can be fixed with reference to astronomical events such as eclipses. Otherwise, scientific techniques such as tree-ring or radiocarbon dating may give an estimate of the age of an object.

One of the most characteristic features of the archeology of Mesopotamia is the abundance of texts written, for the most part, on unbaked clay tablets. Half a million cuneiform tablets have been recovered from archeological sites in the Near East, many of which have not yet been published. Many more tablets are still buried under the ground.

Archeological investigations are expensive and there are few projects that have had sufficient funds to achieve the highest standards. The rapid agricultural and industrial development programs that are now being undertaken in the Near East present a further problem, destroying hundreds of ancient sites each year. Although some of the governments of these countries are aware of the problem and have financed large-scale rescue projects in advance of building major dams on the rivers, more and more sites are destroyed each year and their evidence is lost for ever.

Right Excavations in progress at Tell Mardikh. In the middle of the picture is a mud-brick wall on stone foundations. The right-hand end of this wall was removed by a large pit, which is indicated by the thick black lines in the edge of the trench. Ideally, a site should be excavated by peeling off the latest layers first, before tackling the earlier levels. However, this is a slow, difficult and expensive way of working. It can be more cost-effective to dig down quickly and determine what has been dug through by examining the section of the trench.

Left Tell Khuera in northern Syria. Excavations have to be carefully planned to enable the best use of resources. Today's archeologists have very precise aims in mind and they attempt to solve specific problems. Lengthy discussions between the team members determine the place to work, but because they cannot yet see beneath the ground the results are often unpredictable.

Above Excavating with a small pick and a paintbrush, a Syrian workman at Tell Mardikh (ancient Ebla) collects pieces of pottery, which are placed in a black rubber basket. The pottery is then washed, studied and recorded. By noting where each type of pottery was found, it is possible to establish a detailed picture of the development of different pottery styles.

Below The easiest way to recover carbonized plant remains is to throw the earth that has been dug up into a large container of water and to stir it so that the carbonized seeds float to the top. These can then be skimmed off through a set of graded sieves and left to dry before being sorted and identified.

Below Sieving to ensure a representative sample of the artifacts is essential for quantitative studies to be carried out. If the soil is sandy, dry sieving is feasible, but if the soil is more lumpy then wet sieving, first dissolving the soil in water, may be the better method. Only selected samples are sieved.

Above Archeologists collecting artifacts and planning their positions on a site in the Jordanian desert. In the countryside many archeological sites are difficult to recognize. These include the temporary camp sites of nomadic sheepherders, sites used for flint-knapping and sites that have been completely eroded by the wind, leaving behind the stone artifacts buried there.

Below Cleaning and consolidation of a group of statuettes from Ain Ghaza in Jordan, belonging to the Aceramic Neolithic period (c. 7000 BC). They were made out of mud on a reed framework and were very fragile. The statues were removed as a single piece and taken to the laboratory where they were carefully cleaned and impregnated with a chemical consolidant to preserve them.

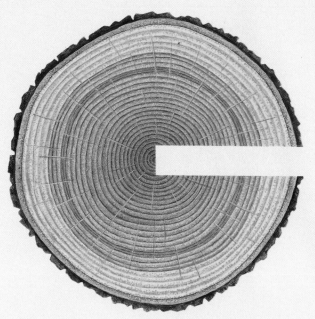

Below Tree-ring dating, or dendrochronology. The thickness of the annual growth rings of trees depends on the weather. A sequence of years has a distinct pattern of thick and thin rings. By starting with living trees, sequences going back more than 9,000 years have been calculated. The patterns of rings of an ancient piece of timber can be matched against the sequence to ascertain the date of the timber. However, the pattern differs by region. When the pattern for the Near East has been worked out, this will be an extremely valuable dating method. Tree-ring dating has been used to calibrate radiocarbon determinations.

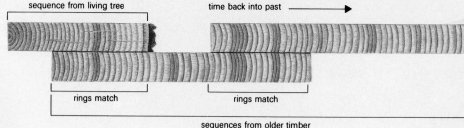

Right Part of the calibration curve for converting radiocarbon determinations to calendar years. Radiocarbon dating provides an objective time-scale for measuring the age of objects. Living plants and animals absorb carbon dioxide from the atmosphere, which contains the radioactive Carbon-14 isotope. This decays at a constant rate, with a half-life of 5,750 years. This means that every 5,750 years a dead object loses half its Carbon-14 atoms. The amount of Carbon-14 that remains in the object can be measured to give a radiocarbon determination of its age. This determination is given in the form 4,500 ± 100 b.p., meaning that the average value is 4,500 radiocarbon years before AD 1950 with a standard error of 100 years due to statistical variation in the measurements. As the amount of Carbon-14 in the atmosphere has not remained constant with time, the radiocarbon determination must be calibrated to give the age in calendar years. The calibration curve was made by testing tree-ring-dated timber and shows that radiocarbon determinations are too recent by up to 1,000 years. For example, a radiocarbon determination of 4,500 ± 100 b.p. corresponds to a calendar date between 3360 and 2930 BC with a probability of 2 out of 3, or between 3520 and 2910 BC with a probability of 19 out of 20. For the sake of simplicity all the dates in this book have been converted to calendar years and are given as the average value of the interval.

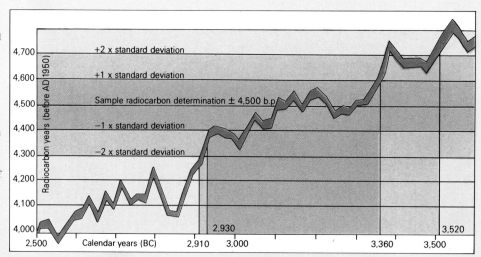

Below In excavation the earth is loosened using a large pick and removed with a spade or hoe before being taken away in baskets to be dumped. Increasingly, human labor is being supplemented by mechanical equipment such as wheelbarrows, conveyor belts and dumper trucks. For more precise excavation, such as tracing the faces of mud-brick walls or floors, a small pick and trowel are more effective. For very delicate cleaning of fragile objects or skeletons, knives or scalpels, cocktail sticks, dental picks and paint brushes are used, but each archeologist has his or her own collection of tools.

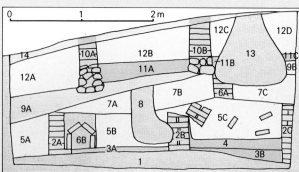

Above The excavation of a Near Eastern *tell* is often a complex process requiring great skill on the part of the excavator, who has to distiguish between the different deposits. Early deposits will be underneath or cut by later ones. Through careful observation of the stratigraphy, the correct sequence of deposits can be determined. If a later pit has gone unnoticed or the natural layers have been incorrectly identified, objects from different periods will be muddled, possibly leading to faulty conclusions.

Layers numbered in order of deposition from the earliest to the latest
1 Natural soil 2A,B,C Mud-brick walls 3A,B Floors going with 2A,B,C 4 Later floor going with 2B and 2C 5A,B,C Fill of rooms when the walls collapsed including sections of fallen wall and mud-bricks 6A Mud-brick wall 6B Mud-brick tomb in grave dug beneath floor 7A,B,C Fill of rooms 8 Grave dug from a level that has been eroded away 9A,B Layers of silt washed down from the top of the site 10A,B Mud-brick walls on stone foundations 11A,B,C Floors going with walls 10A and 10B 12A,B,C,D Fill of rooms 13 Grain storage pit dug from level now eroded away 14 Silting from the top of the site Level I 2-5 Level II 6-7 Level III 8 Level IV 10-12 Level V 13 Layers deposited when the site was not occupied 1, 9, 14.

PART ONE
VILLAGES

EARLY FARMERS (12,000-7000 BC)

The distant past

The evidence from the past is fragmentary. Only a few features of human activity are preserved in the archeological record. Large areas remain unknown and unknowable. Yet those traces that have survived suggest that in some ways people have been the same for thousands of years. For instance, we ascribe the same emotions and motivations to prehistoric humans that we ourselves have today. These characteristics, which distinguish us from our animal cousins, developed at some point on the long ladder of evolution. Indeed, many human characteristics also find parallels in the animal kingdom. For example, ants farm caterpillars and aphids, they live in cities, and like humans their social roles change according to the circumstances. Yet no other species has the variety of skills that humans have developed. Whereas animals have

systems of communication that can convey a limited amount of essential information, human speech can communicate a vast range of seemingly trivial as well as indispensable knowledge. Some animals can make and use simple tools, but we rely on tools so much that we could not survive without them. Both speech and toolmaking are transmitted through culture, that is they are learned from previous generations.

The success of culture as a means of survival was apparent in the widespread distribution of human colonies by the beginning of the Upper Paleolithic period, more than 35,000 years ago. The popular image of stone-age people dressed in skins, living in caves and wielding clubs is rather one-sided. Indeed, they lived mostly in small bands and survived by gathering roots, berries, leaves and grubs, only supplementing their diet by hunting

The spread of agriculture in the Old World
Barley and wheat were first domesticated shortly before 9000 BC and for some time arable farming was confined to the hills around Mesopotamia. Over the next two millennia it spread to the southeast of the Caspian Sea and to the west of the Indus valley and by 5000 BC had been introduced into Europe, Egypt and the whole of the Indus region, with, very probably, animal-drawn plows being used and irrigation practiced. In north China and southeast Asia new crops of millet and rice were being domesticated. Within another 2,000 years arable farming had become the normal way of life for the Old World, though animal herders still exploited the habitats of Russia and Africa.

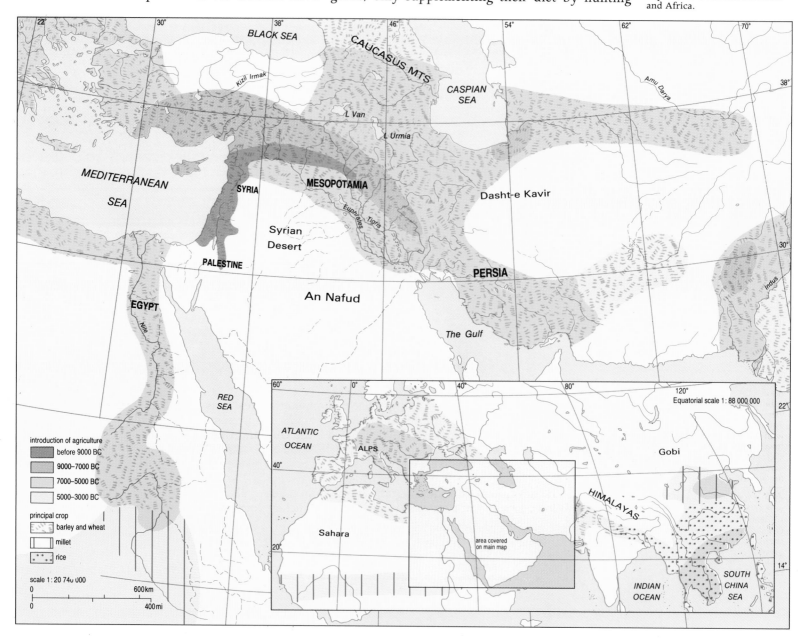

introduction of agriculture

- before 9000 BC
- 9000–7000 BC
- 7000–5000 BC
- 5000–3000 BC

principal crop

- barley and wheat
- millet
- rice

scale 1: 20 740 000

0 — 600km
0 — 400mi

Equatorial scale 1: 88 000 000

area covered on main map

working, pottery and stone carving. Gradually, new forms of social organization developed, leading, more than 5,000 years ago, to the emergence of cities, ruling classes, established religion and writing—the standard ingredients of modern civilization. From the Near East the agricultural and urban ways of life passed to Europe, where, through the Greeks and Romans, they formed part of modern civilization. In other regions of the Old World where farming developed, the connection with the Near East is less clear, though very probably the concept of agriculture ultimately came from there. Agriculture and complex forms of social organization also sprang up independently in the Americas a few thousand years later, but the Near Eastern developments, being the earliest and ancestral to modern civilization, have particular significance.

Geography of the region

The supply of food, the basic requirement for human settlement, depends on the environment and the local geography. The Near East has been called the land of the five seas, being encircled by the Mediterranean, the Black Sea, the Caspian Sea, the Gulf and Red Sea. The seas, however, have been a less important influence on human settlement in the region than the land. There is a great diversity of landscapes in the Near East, from the marshes of southern Iraq through the basalt desert of Jordan and Syria to the snow-covered mountains of Iran. Each environment supports different vegetation and imposes different methods of subsistence on its inhabitants. Of the few shared geographical features in the region, the only significant one is the lack of rainfall in the summer months. The variety of habitats in close proximity allowed different ways of life to exist in constant contact with each other, a factor that may have led to a cross-fertilization of ideas and stimulated the remarkable technological, scientific and social advances of the ancient Near East.

Geology

Two hundred million years ago the two ancient continental landmasses, Gondwanaland and Laurasia, which together with the ocean basins made up the earth's crust, started to break up and to move toward each other. Between them lay the Tethys Sea with thick layers of marine sediments. As the continents collided they split into several smaller coastal "plates" whose movements relative to each other created the main geographical features of the modern Near East. As the Arabian plate moved under the Iranian plate it was forced down, to form the Gulf and the Mesopotamian lowlands, through which the Tigris and Euphrates rivers flow. The same movement pushed up the steep parallel ridges of the Zagros mountains to the northeast of Mesopotamia. The Taurus mountains of southern Turkey formed in a similar way, by the African plate moving under the Turkish plate. The Red Sea was created by the spread of the Arabian and African plates, splitting the Arabo-Nubian massif, which had formed part of the ancient continent of Gondwana. The same movement of the Arabian plate to the north also formed the rift valley from the Gulf of Aqaba north along the Wadi Arabah, as well as the Dead Sea and the Jordan valley.

Above The contrast between the rugged mountains and the fertile plains filled with sediments brought down by the spring floods is found throughout the region where wheat and barley were first domesticated. Here the Taurus mountains, still covered with snow in the late spring, tower over an upland valley in Cilicia in southern Turkey. The mountain slopes provide grazing for sheep and goats while cereals and vegetable crops are grown in the flat fields. This region lies within the zone where there is sufficient rainfall for dry farming, but irrigation increases the yields and extends the growing season so that more than one crop per year can be raised.

larger animals. This way of life, which has been observed throughout the world, proved effective for hundreds of thousands of years and is still found in many regions today. About 12,000 years ago, however, as the sea level was rising at the end of the last Ice Age, people in the Near East discovered a new way of obtaining food. It involved the cultivation and subsequent domestication of plants and animals and is now so widespread that it is difficult to imagine any other basis for human existence. The development of farming in the Near East was followed by its rapid spread into Europe, Africa and Asia. Within a few thousand years the bands of hunter-gatherers, whose way of life had developed over many millions of years, were replaced by settled villagers.

The introduction of farming brought about other important changes. Houses became a permanent feature of village life, while settlers explored new materials and new technologies, such as metal-

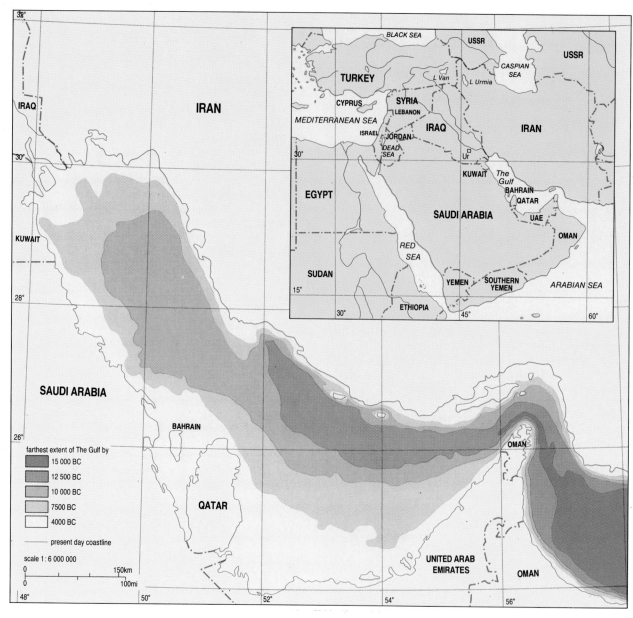

The advance of the sea after the last Ice Age
In 15,000 BC sea levels throughout the world were about 100 m lower than they are today. By about 4000 BC they had reached present-day levels. For most of the Near East this would have submerged only a narrow coastal strip, but in the Gulf everything was flooded. The Tigris and Euphrates with the other rivers coming from the mountains of Iran flowed through the area of the Gulf, the river banks providing suitable habitats for hunter-gatherers. Unfortunately, any trace of such occupation is submerged beneath the waters of the Gulf, buried under sediment layers brought down by the rivers. The lakes and inland seas (Lake Urmia, Lake Van, the Caspian Sea and Dead Sea and others) had higher water levels than today and the interior basins of Turkey, Iran and Arabia may have had extensive marshes and lakes. Since 4000 BC the sea level has varied by only 1–2 m, but such small changes, combined with local subsidence and silting caused by the rivers, could have made great differences to the coastline. Many scholars think that the head of the Gulf reached much farther inland, perhaps as far as the city of Ur in about 2000 BC.

The precise boundaries of the plates are still uncertain but their complex interaction has created numerous points of structural weaknesses where earthquakes and volcanoes are common and in certain places rocks of volcanic origin, such as basalt and obsidian (volcanic glass), cover large areas. Most of the surface rocks in the Near East are sedimentary, either formed under the sea as limestones or made of redeposited eroded rocks such as sandstones and mudstones. This process has continued to the present day, with much of the Arabian peninsula covered by sand dunes and many of the river valleys and inland basins filled with alluvial silt eroded from the mountains and deposited by the rivers. Only along the western edge of the Arabian peninsula and in Sinai, and in occasional exposures in the mountains of Iran and Turkey, are earlier, igneous rocks (containing valuable minerals) easily accessible.

The landscape
As a result of these geological processes and the more recent effects of water, wind and ice, the landscape of the Near East is very varied. To the north, in Turkey and Iran, plateaus bordered by mountain ranges rise some 2,000 meters above sea level. In Turkey two main ranges run from east to west, the Pontus mountains near the Black Sea and the Taurus mountains near the Mediterranean Sea. Between these ranges the Turkish plateau, which is more than 500 meters above sea level, slopes up from west to east. In eastern Turkey the mountains coalesce and join the two main mountain ranges of Iran: the Elburz in the north, which runs along the southern shore of the Caspian Sea, and the Zagros range, which runs from the northwest to the southeast and separates the Mesopotamian lowlands from the Iranian plateau. These mountains reach heights of about 4,000 meters and the tallest peaks, which are, in fact, extinct volcanoes, rise even higher. They include Mount Ararat (5,125 meters), where today Turkey, Iran and the Soviet Union meet, Mount Savalan (4,810 meters), Kuh-i Taftan on the Pakistan border (4,040 meters) and—highest of all—Mount Demavand in the Elburz mountains in northern Iran (5,605 meters). In the center of the Iranian plateau are two vast inhospitable deserts, the Dasht-i Kavir and the Dasht-i Lut.

South of the mountainous regions of Turkey and Iran the landscape is less savage, as the steep mountain ranges give way to the plains of Mesopotamia. From the Gulf in the southeast the land rises slowly to the northwest, following the course of the Euphrates river until it turns north and enters

Above right The banks of the Euphrates in Syria. The Euphrates and Tigris rivers leave the mountains of eastern Anatolia to flow in narrow valleys through northern Mesopotamia. South of the dry-farming zone, crops grow in the river valleys and flocks of sheep and goats graze on the extensive steppe lands. In spring, when the snows melt in the mountains of Turkey and Iran, the Tigris and Euphrates rivers rise several meters and become raging muddy torrents of immense violence. At other times, the rivers flow more gently and the waters are clear.

Right Sheep and goats graze in the Lar valley in the Elburz mountains in northern Iran. Spring comes later to the snow-covered mountain valleys of Iran and Turkey than to the lowlands. In summer, tribes of nomadic pastoralists take their herds up into the mountains, where the grazing is still lush after the vegetation has turned brown in the hotter, drier regions. This way of life may go back to prehistoric times but it has left little trace in the archeological record.

the Taurus mountains, having risen only 400 meters over a distance of 1,200 kilometers. The lower part of the Mesopotamian plain is almost flat, being formed by silt brought down by the Euphrates, Tigris and other rivers from the mountains to the north and east. In the upper part of Mesopotamia the landscape is rolling plains.

Along the Mediterranean coast of Syria, Lebanon and Palestine are more mountain ranges. The highest peaks are in the Lebanon, in places reaching more than 3,000 meters above sea level. Here the topography is varied, with the upland zone split by the north–south fault that now forms the Jordan valley, the Dead Sea (some 300 meters below sea level) and the Wadi Arabah valley leading to the Red Sea.

More mountains run parallel to the Red Sea on the Arabian peninsula. The Hejaz range at the northern end of the Red Sea is more than 2,000 meters high, while the Asir mountains in Yemen at the southern end of the Red Sea rise to 3,500 meters. From there the land slopes down gradually to reach the Mesopotamian plains and the Gulf coast. The mouth of the Gulf, however, is marked by the high mountains of Oman, which exceed 3,000 meters.

Sea-level changes

The relief has been forming for hundreds of thousands of years, but an important change occurred with the end of the last Ice Age. During the Ice Age huge icefields covered the polar regions, trapping part of the waters of the oceans and reducing the

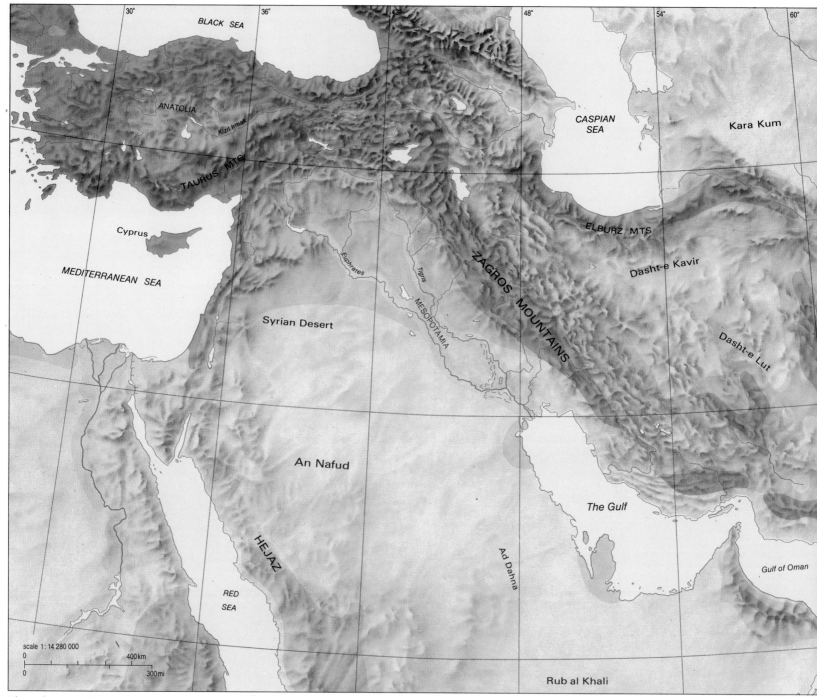

scale 1 : 14 280 000

| 0 | 400 km |
| 0 | 300 mi |

The vegetation of the Near East

This map shows the natural vegetation of the Near East, that is, how the vegetation would be if left alone, without human interference. The vegetation depends to a great extent on the pattern of rainfall. Large areas of the Near East receive so little rain that the land is desert and unsuitable for human settlement. On the fringes of the deserts extending into the foothills the natural vegetation is steppe, where grasses and low shrubs grow, and on the mountain slopes are wooded regions. The populated areas of the past are the same as those where people live today. For this reason, scientists believe that over the last 10,000 years there have been no great changes in the climate and vegetation apart from those caused by human interference with the natural environment through overgrazing, deforestation and agriculture.

Climate of the Near East

The winds from the west bring rain to the Near East. It falls where the winds first hit the hills and mountains. Many inland areas are situated in a "rain shadow", such as the region to the east of the Caspian Sea, and the Arabian desert, and these receive less rain. Almost all the rain falls in the winter months and, except along the coasts of Turkey and of the Caspian Sea, there is no rainfall between June and September. The temperature in the Near East increases toward the south and decreases with altitude. There is a considerable difference between the summer and winter temperatures. Near the coasts the difference is about 15°C but it rises to more than 25°C in the mountains. Much of the higher land of Iran and Turkey is under snow in winter.

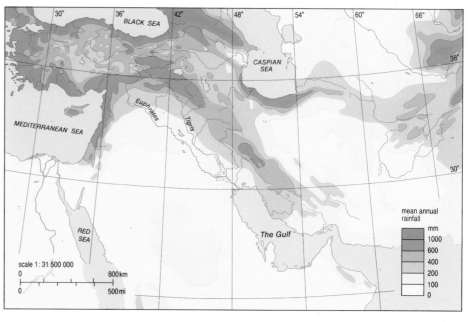

scale 1 : 31 500 000

| 0 | 800 km |
| 0 | 500 mi |

mean annual rainfall

| mm |
| 1000 |
| 600 |
| 400 |
| 200 |
| 100 |
| 0 |

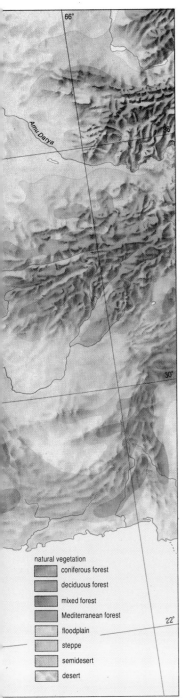

natural vegetation

coniferous forest
deciduous forest
mixed forest
Mediterranean forest
floodplain
steppe
semidesert
desert

sea level by more than 100 meters. Then, about 16,000 years ago, the sea level started to rise. Most of the seas surrounding the Near East shelve steeply down, so that the resultant changes in the coastline were not great. The Gulf, however, is shallower and there the rivers fed from the runoff from the Taurus and Zagros mountains reached the sea much sooner than they had done earlier. The flat alluvial plains of southern Mesopotamia and the Egyptian Delta were created after the sea had reached approximately its modern level. The sea level rose rapidly, at times exceeding 1 meter in a century, and reached its present level in about 4000 BC. It has remained within 1 or 2 meters of this since then. One effect of the steep rise is that the evidence for early occupation in the Gulf region and in southern Mesopotamia is buried beneath thick sediments. For the early periods therefore it is necessary to look at areas where the landscape has changed less and where the occupations are more readily accessible.

Climate and environment

The sources of evidence for the climates of ancient times are many and varied. For example, the relative proportions of the two oxygen isotopes O^{16} to O^{18} in the sea are an indication of the amount of water held in the polar ice caps and hence of global temperatures. Similarly, thick sedimentary deposits reveal increased river flow, which may be the result of greater rainfall. One of the most useful techniques is the identification of the pollen grains from flowering plants preserved in the sediments of ancient lakes. From these it is possible to build up an idea of the changing vegetation. Although there is no final agreement on how to interpret these results, which seem to vary from region to region, a rough picture emerges.

As the ice sheets retreated and the seas rose, the temperature increased rapidly, rising almost 10° Celsius between 12,000 and 8000 BC, before reaching a maximum of 1° or 2° Celsius above present levels. During the Ice Age the northern mountain zone had had largely steppic vegetation and a cold, arid climate. Afterward, as the climate became warmer and moister, thick forests grew, so that by about 6,000 years ago oaks and other trees covered the slopes of the Zagros and Taurus mountains, as

they do today. Farther south too, the dry and cold conditions of the Ice Age yielded to a warmer, moister climate, allowing the growth of more trees. However, by about 11,000 BC the rainfall had become less and large areas once again reverted to steppe or desert.

During the last 10,000 years the climate and the vegetation of the Near East have been broadly similar to conditions there today. Four distinctive zones formed bands across the area. The mountain zone, where deciduous and coniferous trees grew with varying mixtures of oak, pine, cedar and juniper, experienced cold wet winters and dry summers. In the foothill zone, extending along the Mediterranean coast and the foothills of the Taurus and Zagros mountains, the winters were mild and moist and the summers warm and dry. The vegetation was fairly open Mediterranean forest, with oak, pine and terebinth trees, and grasses that included the wild varieties of early domesticates such as barley and wheat. A steppe zone along the eastern and southern margin of the foothills and on the Iranian and Turkish plateaus had mild dry winters and hot dry summers, supporting open, almost treeless, grassland. Finally, the desert zone in the interior of Arabia and Iran had mild dry winters and hot dry summers, but virtually nothing grew there. The boundaries between these regions have shifted with small changes in climate, but the general pattern has remained the same even though changes in water courses, the drying up of lakes and springs and the movement of sand dunes have probably caused local changes. Moreover, during the last 10,000 years human intervention through overgrazing, deforestation and interference with the natural water courses has increasingly changed the environment.

The presence of permanent water supplies created particularly favorable habitats, which though they did not occupy large areas, were very important to early human beings. These included the sea and lake shores, with their rich stores of marine and aquatic life (both animal and vegetable), the river valleys and spring-fed oases, where thickets of tamarisk and other trees and bushes thrived, and swamps, where near the head of the Gulf the wild ancestors of the date palm tree probably flourished.

The Near East was also rich in land-based animals. Herds of gazelle, fallow deer, wild ass and wild cattle roamed the steppes. Red deer, roe deer, wild sheep and wild goats were more common in the mountains while wild boar thrived in damp conditions. Preying on these animals were jackals, wolves, bears, lynxes, hyenas, cheetahs, leopards, tigers and lions. Smaller mammals included foxes, hares, wildcats, hedgehogs and different species of rodents. Two surprising absentees were the camel and the horse, which, having disappeared during the Ice Age, did not reappear until the third millennium BC. Amphibians and reptiles were common, including tortoises, snakes, lizards and frogs, while from the rivers, lakes and seas came many varieties of fish and shellfish. There was a wealth of birdlife in the region, including numerous migrant species, as the Mediterranean coast and the head of the Gulf lie on the main migration routes from Russia to Africa. Of the larger birds, ostriches, bustards, partridges, ducks and geese were a useful food source.

mean annual temperature

°C
25
20
15
10
5
0

scale 1: 31 500 000

0   800 km
0   500 mi

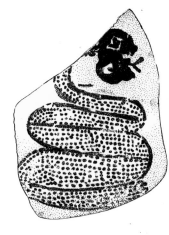

Left An oasis in western Syria. The provision of water can transform the barren waste of the Near East into fertile land where orchards and gardens thrive. The water may come from rivers or springs. If the water source dries up, the area will once again become desert.

Early settlements in the Near East

After the end of the last Ice Age, people established settlements where they could exploit the naturally occurring wild varieties of wheat, barley and other plants and hunt animals. Most of these sites lay within the area where barley and wheat grow wild today, which is limited to the south because of the available rainfall. The large number of sites discovered in Palestine reflects both the intensity of archeological work in this area and the importance of the region in the Epipaleolithic period (c. 18,000–9300 BC). In the following Proto-Neolithic period (c. 9300–8500 BC) it is probable that wheat and barley were already domesticated.

Above and above right Prehistoric pottery was often decorated with paintings of animals and birds. The animals were normally wild rather than domestic and chosen partly for their decorative effect. Wild sheep and ibex were very popular. The representations are often so stylized that the particular species cannot be identified. The snake (above), dating to the 6th millennium BC, shows the typical primitive method of representation, with the body seen in profile and the head from above. The skidding leopard (*above right*) comes from Luristan in western Iran and dates to the 4th millennium BC.

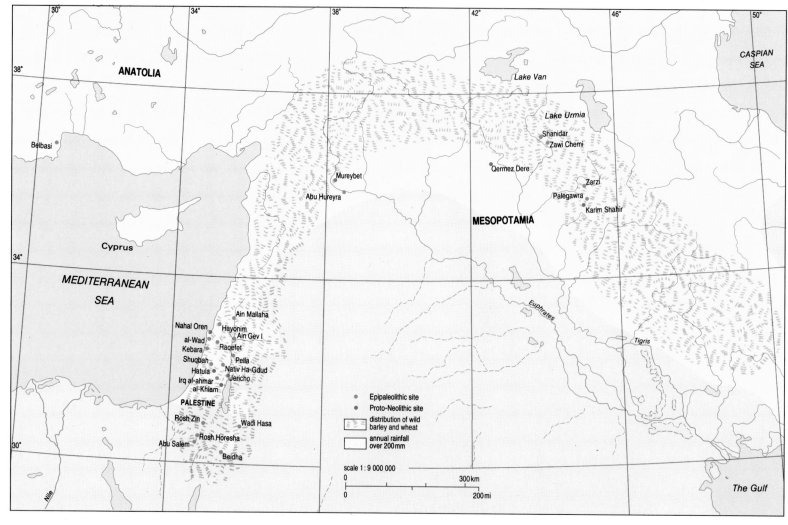

ANATOLIA

CASPIAN SEA

Lake Van

Lake Urmia

Shanidar
Zawi Chemi

Qermez Dere

Zarzi

Palegawra
Karim Shahir

Belbasi

Mureybet

Abu Hureyra

MESOPOTAMIA

Cyprus

MEDITERRANEAN SEA

Euphrates

Tigris

Ain Mallaha
Nahal Oren   Hayonim
al-Wad   Ain Gev I
Kebara   Raqefet
Shuqbah   Pella
Hatula   Nativ Ha-Gdud
Irq al-ahmar   Jericho
al-Khiam

PALESTINE

Rosh Zin
Wadi Hasa
Abu Salem
Rosh Horesha
Beidha

Nile

The Gulf

- ● Epipaleolithic site
- ● Proto-Neolithic site
- ▭ distribution of wild barley and wheat
- ▭ annual rainfall over 200mm

scale 1 : 9 000 000

0 — 300km
0 — 200mi

The origins of agriculture

During the millions of years in which people survived by hunting, scavenging and gathering, they had made great technological advances. With the emergence of anatomically modern human beings (*Homo sapiens sapiens*) the pace of progress accelerated, leading to the colonization of all the continents by no later than 20,000 BC. People's increasing ability to control their environment showed in improved and more elaborate flint-working techniques, in more settled occupation and in more complex social behavior such as ceremonial burial rites and paintings on cave walls, dating from about 30,000 BC. These skills were necessary prerequisites to adopting agriculture as a way of life.

As hunter-gatherers people had exploited plants and animals, but made little attempt to look after them. Obviously any predator that allowed its main source of food to dwindle would itself be in danger of extinction. In fact, from early on humans had attempted limited forms of cultivation by leaving alone young animals and small fish and by protecting selected species. Proper domestication, however, implies that the plants or animals are themselves dependent on people for their survival. In the early stages of agriculture people cultivated wild species of plants and animals. But over succeeding generations, through selective harvesting and sowing of plants and selective breeding of animals, changes occurred and new varieties and breeds emerged. Some of these changes, which are recognized in plant remains and animal bones found on archeological sites, serve to distinguish

wild from domesticated varieties and breeds. However, the identification and interpretation of animal and vegetable remains is a matter for experts, who do not always agree about their findings.

The collection of seeds and bones has been a regular part of archeological excavation only during the last 40 years. Before that, archeologists relied on noticing changes, such as in the method of making stone tools, to distinguish between periods. In the Early Stone Age, tools were made by chipping and flaking but in the Neolithic period (Late Stone Age) grinding and polishing were used. Other changes were recognized as occurring at roughly the same time. These included settlement sites with houses, the use of pottery vessels, and the burial of the dead in cemeteries. (Although similar sequences of development occurred in India, China, Africa and America, the earliest were in the Near East.)

It is interesting to speculate why farming developed at this time. During the cold and warm periods that alternated with the earlier Ice Ages agriculture should have been possible sooner. However, it was only after the latest Ice Age that human groups had a sufficiently developed social and technical infrastructure to take advantage of the opportunity afforded by the climate and geography. In particular, the use of language, which developed between 100,000 and 20,000 years ago, would have been crucial in communicating information and passing it on from generation to generation.

The spread of farming and animal husbandry
Remarkable advances were made in the Aceramic Neolithic period (c. 8500–7000 BC). Plants and animals were domesticated, large settlements housing hundreds of people grew up and industry in the form of metalworking and lime-plaster manufacture began on a large scale. The settlements still lay within the region of rainfed arable farming but now extended into the wooded mountains and onto the Turkish and Iranian plateaus. While most settlements depended on cereal cultivation, there were still some that survived as hunter-gatherers. During this period the emphasis on Palestine that was evident earlier is less marked.

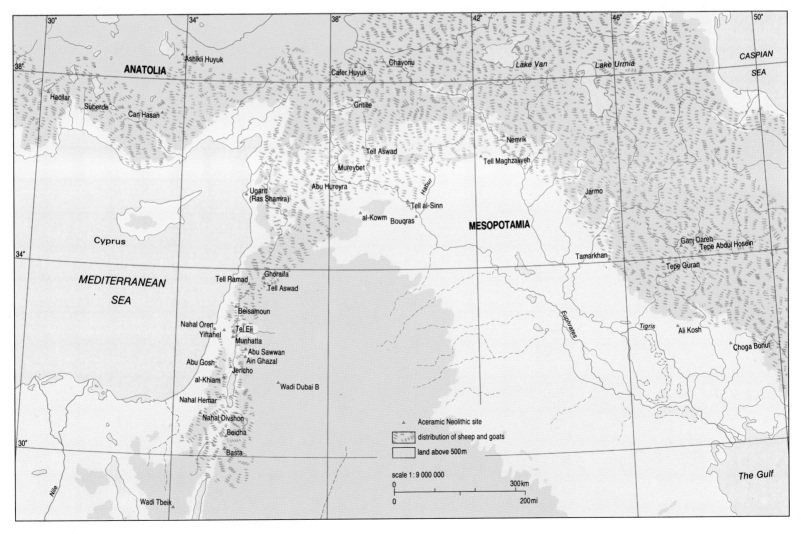

However, the reasons that first attracted stone-age people to cultivate plants and raise livestock were arguably different from those that perpetuated that way of life. According to recent studies, farmers work harder than hunter-gatherers to obtain enough food to survive and agriculture does not provide easier or more abundant supplies. Against this, a more settled life, with the possibility of larger social groups, offered the advantages of reduced child mortality, as mothers did not have to move with the tribe, and through agriculture, more direct control of the food supply. There were also unforeseen opportunities within the agricultural way of life which eventually resulted in its adoption in all but the most remote and the least hospitable areas of the world. For example, sheep, which were probably bred at first for meat, skin and bones, also became a useful source of milk and wool through selective breeding.

Early settlements in the Near East

The transition from hunter-gatherer to farmer in the Near East is most apparent in the Levant and Palestine. Over the last 40 years, archeologists, in the course of intense fieldwork, have excavated numerous early sites in Israel, compared with only a few in other Near Eastern countries. Despite the unevenness of this research, this region does seem to have been crucial for the development of agriculture.

The first habitation sites in the Near East were either caves or temporary open-air camps or work areas. Following the last Ice Age, more permanent settlement sites became common, as evidence from the Kebaran period in Palestine (from about 18,000 to 11,000 BC) shows. At Ain Gev I, a site on the eastern shore of the Sea of Galilee, dated about 15,000 BC, the foundations of what had probably been a round dwelling hut contained stone slabs and a stone mortar for grinding grain, as well as sickle blades that had the characteristic sheen caused by reaping cereals or reeds. The Kebaran people also hunted wild animals and often went after particular species. For example, nearly three-quarters of the bones found at Nahal Oren on Mount Carmel belonged to gazelle, whereas at Wadi Madamagh, near Petra, more than 80 percent were from wild goats.

The presence of grinding stones, however, shows that plants and cereals formed an integral part of their diet. Cereal grains are very nutritious but are protected by an indigestible husk. To make them edible, the husk was removed by roasting, before cooking the grain at a low temperature with water to form a type of porridge, or the grains were ground up to make flour, which was then mixed with water and baked at a high temperature. The sickles, made out of several flint blades set in a wood or bone handle, may have been used to reap wild cereals, though cutting the stems risked scattering the seeds, and so plucking the ripe grain by hand was probably more efficient. Similar types of flint working have been found in the contemporary cultures in Turkey and in the Zagros mountains but there is no comparable evidence for plant food preparation.

The Natufian period

The Natufian culture, which lasted from about

Left It has been suggested that the fierce wild cattle were originally domesticated for religious reasons or for their meat, hides, bones and horn. But early in the Neolithic period cattle were probably kept for their milk and for use as draft animals. Oxen (neutered bulls) are still widely used today for plowing, harrowing, threshing, and for pulling carts.

Above Cereal cultivation involved new technological processes that included reaping and milling, using flint sickle blades and grindstones, some of which have been preserved on archeological sites. Other activities such as winnowing, which used wooden tools and took place away from the settlements, have left little trace in the archeological record.

11,000 to 9300 BC, was more widespread than the Kebaran. It extended throughout Palestine and the Levant and related sites have been found on the Euphrates in Syria and further east. In the Natufian period the archeological evidence for the adoption of cereals as a major element of the diet is much clearer. Grindstones, hearths and storage pits have been uncovered at Natufian sites along with the burned seeds of wild two-row barley and wild einkorn wheat, and of other wild food plants such as acorns, lentils, chickpeas and peas.

Besides having tough husks, which are closely attached to the seed and can only be removed by roasting or by pounding, wild cereals also have a brittle rachis (central axis) which breaks very easily, causing the seed to scatter and making harvesting difficult. Once people had learned to sow and harvest grains, they preferred varieties with a tougher rachis. This is one of the criteria used to distinguish domesticated from wild varieties of cereals.

Two species of wild wheat were found in the Near East: einkorn wheat and emmer wheat, which may have arisen as a natural hybrid of einkorn with another species of wild grass. Through selective harvesting and planting, both einkorn and emmer wheat produced domesticated varieties. The modern hexaploid wheats were probably derived from domesticated emmer wheat through hybridization with another wild grass. Varieties

The Neolithic Village

Village life in the Near East does not appear to have changed greatly between the Neolithic period and the late 19th century, though our knowledge of the early period is based largely on the remains of stone or bone tools and the ruins of buildings, as organic materials are seldom preserved. In the extremely dry conditions of the cave of Nahal Hemar, near the Dead Sea, a wider range of material has survived, including textile and basketry fragments and wooden tools and beads. The textiles, in particular, show a surprisingly high level of technical ability. Some finds hint at the religious life of the time, but the rich heritage of dance and myth is now beyond our grasp.

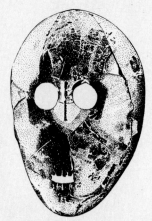

Left This painted stone mask from Nahal Hemar may have been used in some ritual ceremony. Some scholars think that the finds at Nahal Hemar belonged to a temple or other religious institution.

Below The earliest houses were round huts sunk into the ground, like this one from Qermez Dere in northern Iraq, dating to the Proto-Neolithic period. They were more than just places of shelter and played a central role in the spiritual life of the community. The stone and plaster pillar and the placing of human skulls on the floor of the abandoned building are indications of the kinds of rituals enacted in the house.

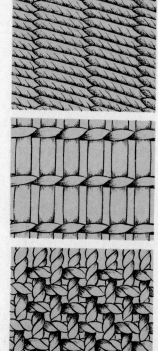

The earliest evidence for textile manufacture comes from the Aceramic Neolithic period. In the cave of Nahal Hemar, material was made by twisting pairs of flax (linen) weft threads round the warps. Where the twisted threads are separated this is called spaced twining (*above center*); otherwise it is called close twining (*top*). Impressions on clay from Jarmo show that normal weaving (tabby weave) (*above*) was also known at this period.

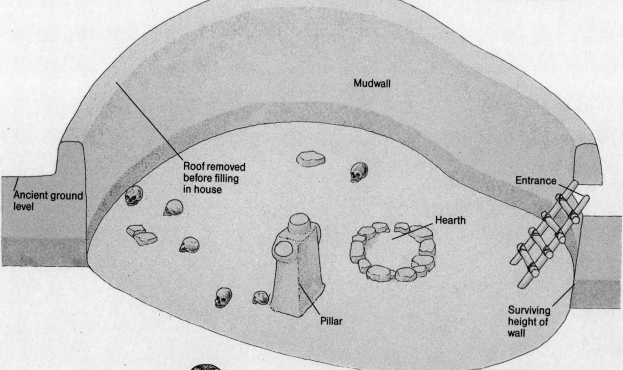

Mudwall

Roof removed before filling in house

Ancient ground level

Hearth

Entrance

Pillar

Surviving height of wall

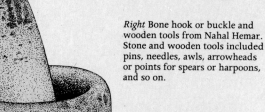

Right Stone mortar and pestle from Jericho. It had a wide variety of uses, from food preparation to grinding pigments. Similar stone vessels were used from the Natufian to the Islamic periods.

Right Bone hook or buckle and wooden tools from Nahal Hemar. Stone and wooden tools included pins, needles, awls, arrowheads or points for spears or harpoons, and so on.

Below A sickle from Nahal Hemar with flint blades fixed into a wooden haft using bitumen as a glue. It may have been used for cutting reeds.

may also be distinguished by whether the husks, or glumes, stick to the seeds (hulled or glume wheats) or whether they are easily removed (naked or free-threshing wheats). Barley, too, has hulled and naked varieties as well as varieties that have either two or six rows of seeds in each head. Not surprisingly, the naked or free-threshing varieties were generally preferred to the hulled kinds.

It is often possible to tell from their shape whether grains of wheat or barley belonged to wild or domesticated species, but with other edible plants this difference is less easy to recognize. The wild varieties of legumes such as lentils, vetches and peas, fruit such as figs, apples and pears, nuts such as acorns, almonds and pistachio are almost identical with the domesticated varieties though these have become larger over the years. Many food plants only occasionally leave traces in the archeological record. Leafy plants like cabbage, lettuce, spinach, onion and garlic, and fleshy plants such as melons, cucumbers and mushrooms are only seldom found in archeological excavations and the history of their cultivation can only be guessed at. For these reasons, archeologists have concentrated their attention on the cereals. On present evidence, the cereals were among the earliest domesticated plants, but it is likely that legumes were harvested and cultivated at about the same time.

The cereals also differ from much other plant food in that they can be stored for long periods, provided that they are kept dry and free from insects or rodents. Grain can also be heated or parched to prevent germination. These properties of cereals allow a delayed return on the energy invested in their collection, so that grain can act like money, having an accepted standard of value and a medium of exchange. The storage and, later, cultivation of grain thus allowed the possibility of wealth accumulation, promoting the development of a society in which status was based on wealth.

The Natufian people collected wild cereals and other plants, but perhaps also "cultivated" them to protect them from predators and may have even planted some wild varieties. The worn-down teeth of Natufian skeletons have been attributed to the grit in their diet from the extensive use of grindstones in the preparation of plant food. The ratio of strontium to calcium in their bones is similar to that in the bones of herbivorous animals rather than carnivores, suggesting that the bulk of their diet was made up of plants.

The inhabitants of many Natufian sites also hunted particular species of wild animal. At al-Wad and Nahal Oren 80 percent of the animal bone recovered belonged to gazelles and at Abu Hureyra on the Euphrates (possibly the end of the gazelle's natural migration route) 65 percent of the bones were gazelle bones. At Beidha, near Petra in southern Jordan, goats were the main game animal, while the bones found at Ain Mallaha in the Jordan valley included gazelle's (44 percent) as well as those of roe deer, fallow deer and boar, and a few from wild cattle, goats, foxes, hyenas and hares. The remains of birds, fish, snails, mussels, snakes, tortoises and rodents were also found at Ain Mallaha, though it is unlikely that all of these served as food.

As with plants, the process of domestication affected animals, so that over generations differences in the bones enable zoo-archeologists to distinguish wild from domestic varieties. Other signs of domestication include the presence of animals outside their natural habitats, size differences, changes in the composition of flocks and changes in the proportions of different species. Some of these differences, however, were not solely due to domestication but might also have been caused by changes in climate. After the last Ice Age, many animals became smaller, perhaps in order to cope with the warmer climate, though domestication also seems to have favored smaller animals.

The animal bones found on Natufian sites were predominantly those of wild species. At Ain Mallaha and Hayonim terrace to the southwest, however, archeologists measured a set of bones that were smaller than those of the modern wolf and probably belonged to "man's best friend"— now shown to be the oldest too—the domestic dog. From the same period at Ain Mallaha, about 10,000 BC, an old woman was found buried with a 3–5 month-old puppy. Although it was not possible to tell whether the skeleton was that of a wolf or a dog, the animal clearly enjoyed a close relationship with the woman. Many animal bones from Natufian sites, unlike those from earlier periods, showed signs of having been chewed, another indication of the presence of dogs. Since the bones of dogs were relatively rare, however, they were probably kept not for food but to help with the hunting. A dog's jawbone was also found in the cave of Palegawra in northeastern Iraq. This has been assigned to the slightly earlier Zarzian culture

Below Two varieties of wild wheat are found in the Near East, namely einkorn wheat and emmer wheat. The latter may have arisen as a natural hybrid of einkorn with species of wild goat grass. Through selective harvesting and planting, both einkorn and emmer wheat produced domesticated varieties and it is from the domesticated emmer wheat that the modern hexaploid wheats were probably derived by hybridization with another wild goat grass. Varieties may be distinguished on the basis of whether the husks or glumes stick to the seeds (hulled or glume wheats) and those where the husks are easily removed (naked or free-threshing wheats). Only hard, bread and club wheat were naked or free-threshing. Wild plants had brittle ears that broke before or during harvesting, while in domesticated varieties the ears remained attached to the plant, which was an advantage during harvesting. In the earliest stages of agriculture the seeds would not have been modified and so could not be distinguished from wild varieties.

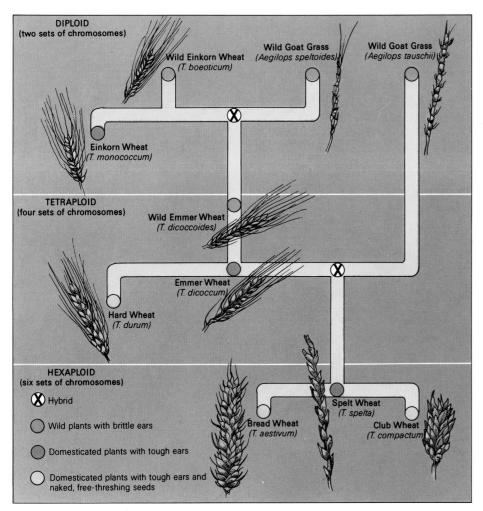

DIPLOID (two sets of chromosomes)

Wild Einkorn Wheat (T. boeoticum)

Wild Goat Grass (Aegilops speltoides)

Wild Goat Grass (Aegilops tauschii)

Einkorn Wheat (T. monococcum)

TETRAPLOID (four sets of chromosomes)

Wild Emmer Wheat (T. dicoccoides)

Emmer Wheat (T. dicoccum)

Hard Wheat (T. durum)

HEXAPLOID (six sets of chromosomes)

Ⓧ Hybrid

● Wild plants with brittle ears

● Domesticated plants with tough ears

○ Domesticated plants with tough ears and naked, free-threshing seeds

Spelt Wheat (T. spelta)

Bread Wheat (T. aestivum)

Club Wheat (T. compactum)

of about 11,000 BC, but it is likely that it belonged to a later period. Whether people of the Natufian period herded animals and cultivated plants is a subject of disagreement among experts, but there is insufficient evidence to prove that this was so.

Patterns of Natufian settlement

Wild cereals still grow in the Near East and in the few weeks when the grain is ripe a family can gather enough grain to last a year. The difficulty of moving grain supplies, however, and the need for heavy equipment such as grindstones would have favored permanent settlements in Natufian times. Settlements were either occupied throughout the year or just at certain times of the year. Villages or camps were situated in the areas where wild cereals grew and other, more temporary campsites were set up elsewhere for the purposes of hunting. Settlement sites were sometimes in the open and sometimes on terraces outside caves and rock-shelters. In the open, the buildings were simple, round huts whose roofs were supported by wooden posts. Often they were sunk more than a meter into the ground to make them easier to build and improve the insulation. The huts generally had a hearth and the floors were paved with stones. Those at Ain Mallaha were between 3.5 and 5 meters in diameter. They were frequently rebuilt and probably were inhabited throughout the year. The remains of nine huts have been found, but originally there were probably fifty or more housing a community of 200 or 300 people, much larger than the size of modern hunter-gatherer bands, which average about 30 people.

Some human skeletons have been discovered beneath the floors of the huts, but other burials took place away from the buildings. There were some individual graves and others contained several skeletons. Funerary gifts were rare but items of personal ornament were common, including shell and bone beads used for head coverings, necklaces, bracelets and anklets.

Natufian contemporaries

The cultures in the Zagros mountains and the foothills are less well known than the Natufian and only a few sites have been investigated. The flint tools found in the Zagros sites are similar to those found in the Levant and belonged to hunting and gathering communities who exploited a wide variety of plants and animals. However, the use of ground stone tools and the move to open settlements possibly occurred a little later than in the west. Evidence from Zawi Chemi, an open-air site in northeastern Iraq dating to about 10,000 BC, suggests that the inhabitants used grinding stones and lived in circular huts. Also, as in the Natufian of the Levant, burials contained personal ornaments. A cemetery belonging to this period that was uncovered in the Shanidar Cave, famous for the much earlier Neanderthal skeletons, contained 26 graves, including that of a child with 1,500 small beads around its head and a woman's grave that had a knife with a bone haft and a flint blade set in bitumen. The skeletons of adults buried in Shanidar Cave were often accompanied by those of small children, in what is thought by some to have been a form of human sacrifice.

An intriguing find from Zawi Chemi was a pile of

Left Although there have been occasional finds of burials from earlier times, in the Natufian period disposal of the dead outside houses or in caves became common. No offerings or items of equipment were left with the corpse to suggest that the people of the time thought that they should provide for the needs of the deceased in the afterlife. A number of skeletons, however, still had their personal ornaments such as necklaces, as in this grave from al-Wad (Mugharet el-Wad) on Mount Carmel. The body was buried in a contracted position, while round the head was placed a headdress that included rows of shell beads from the Mediterranean Sea.

bones consisting of the skulls of 15 goats and the bones of 17 or so large birds of prey, mostly white-tailed sea eagles. The vast majority of the bird bones belonged to the wings, some of which were still joined together. Marks on the bones showed that the wings had been cut off, suggesting some magic ritual that involved dressing up in bird wings and goat heads. Similar scenes are shown in wall paintings at the much later site of Chatal Huyuk.

The Proto-Neolithic period

In the Levant the period following the Natufian is known as Proto-Neolithic or Pre-Pottery Neolithic A. Proto-Neolithic sites are less common than those of the Natufian or the succeeding Aceramic Neolithic (or Pre-Pottery Neolithic B) periods. Perhaps this was because overexploitation of the land together with lower rainfall reduced the natural food supply, leading to a decrease in the size of the population and later encouraging reliance on cultivated plants and herded animals.

The most impressive remains of this period were found at Jericho in the Jordan valley. By about 9000 BC a settlement had grown up near an abundant spring, the inhabitants living in round huts measuring about 5 meters across. These, like earlier Natufian huts, were partly sunk into the ground and entry was by a short passageway with steps leading down. The walls were of handmade bricks with rounded tops, made out of mud dried in the sun. This is the earliest known example of the use of mud-brick, which is still the standard building material of the Near East. Mud-brick has many advantages. It is readily available, cheap to make and easy to use. It is also structurally sound and a good insulator. It is, however, easily eroded by running water and needs careful annual mainten-

Below Mud-brick. Mud is a most versatile building material. Walls can be built out of layers of mud, or the mud can be fashioned into bricks and dried in the sun before use. The earliest bricks, from the Proto-Neolithic period, were modeled by hand and had a flat base and rounded top.

Brickmakers in Jericho in the Aceramic Neolithic period produced longer bricks, pressing their thumbs into the top to make a herringbone pattern, which provided a key for the mud mortar. Elsewhere, bricks were by this time being made in a mold.

Right Village in northwestern Iran. Throughout most of the Near East today, as in the past, houses are made of mud-bricks and have flat roofs. The walls and the roofs are coated with plaster made of mud and straw. When the buildings fall down or are abandoned the roof timbers are removed but the rest of the structure is left to form a small, flat mound of mud. Over the centuries rebuilding on the same site has resulted in high mounds being formed. Most of the archeological sites in the Near East are made out of the debris of many levels of buildings. Sometimes the mounds that contain the remains of important cities reach heights of more than 50 m, though those belonging to villages are only a few meters above the surrounding fields.

Left and below To make mud-bricks mud, chopped straw and water are mixed together and allowed to steep for some days. The straw stops the brick from cracking as it dries. Sometimes gravel or other material is used instead of straw. The brickmaker takes a lump of mud and presses it into a square or rectangular mold. The bricks are then left to dry in the sun for several weeks. For this reason mud-bricks are normally made in summer after the harvest, when there is little danger of rain and when straw is available. The shape and size of mud-bricks varied from period to period and thus the type of bricks in a building can sometimes help to determine its date.

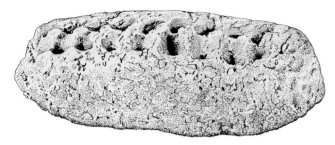

ance. For these reasons, mud-bricks were not re-used, when a building fell into ruin, but the site was leveled and a new building built on top. As building succeeded building, a mound formed to produce the typical archeological site found in the Near East. In Arabic, this is called a *tell*, in Persian a *tepe* and in Turkish a *hüyük*. Some twenty-five building levels from the Proto-Neolithic period were identified at Jericho, forming a mound 10 meters high.

During this period a large stone wall and a stone tower attached to the interior face of the wall were built over the remains of some of the huts. The tower stood on the west side of the site and the remains of the wall have been found to the north and to the south. If the wall enclosed the whole settlement but not the spring on the east, Jericho covered some 3 to 4 hectares. Estimates of its population range from 400 to 3,000, but most probably about 1,500 people lived there. Building the wall, which was made of more than 10,000 tonnes of stone, required not only a large labor force but also considerable political will and organization. Its purpose—and that of the tower—are unclear. At first, they were thought to be a defence against possible invasion, but equally plausibly the walls and ditch were a protection against flooding.

Evidence for domesticated plants has also been found in Proto-Neolithic Jericho. This includes six grains of two-row hulled barley and two grains of emmer, as well as legumes and fig pips. However, until these seeds have been radiocarbon-dated or

Jericho

The site of ancient Jericho (Tell al-Sultan) lies in the Jordan valley some 200 meters below sea level. Jericho is now remembered as the city where Joshua blew his trumpet and the walls came tumbling down, but it was an important city long before and long after the Israelite invasions in the late second millennium BC. The prosperity of Jericho depended on the abundant spring on the east side of the site. The earliest occupation lies deeply buried beneath later remains and has been investigated in a few areas only. These show that after settlement in the Natufian period, it was an important center in the Proto-Neolithic (Pre-Pottery Neolithic A) and Aceramic Neolithic (Pre-Pottery Neolithic B) periods and throughout the Bronze Age.

Below In the Proto-Neolithic period Jericho was surrounded by a stone city wall and a ditch cut into the rock. The settlement of round huts covered an area of 3 ha and probably contained some 1,500 people. Jericho showed a precocious development, and no other site of this period approached it in size. Only in the following Aceramic Neolithic period did other sites become as large or as complex.

Left In the Aceramic Neolithic period at Jericho the dead were commonly buried beneath the floors of the houses with their skulls removed. The removal of the cranium was probably carried out after the flesh and sinews had decayed, as the lower jaw was normally left with the rest of the skeleton. Some of the skulls found under the floors had had their features modeled in plaster and the eye sockets filled with shells, sometimes bivalves, and in one case cowrie shells.

Right and below One of the more remarkable features of Proto-Neolithic Jericho is the stone tower attached to the inside of the city wall. The tower is 10 m in diameter and still survives to a height of more than 8 m. A doorway 1.7 m high on its eastern side leads inside to a staircase of 22 steps, each made out of a single block of stone. The city wall was repaired and rebuilt several times and a ditch 8 m wide and more than 2 m deep was cut into the rock outside the wall. The purpose that the tower served is still a matter of debate.

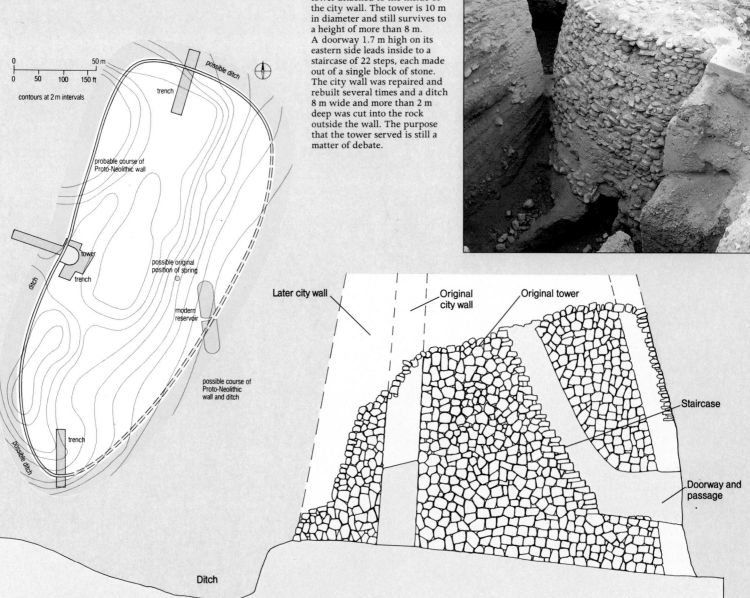

0   50 m
0   50   100   150 ft

contours at 2 m intervals

possible ditch

trench

probable course of Proto-Neolithic wall

tower

ditch

trench

possible original position of spring

modern reservoir

possible course of Proto-Neolithic wall and ditch

possible ditch

trench

Later city wall — Original city wall — Original tower

Staircase

Doorway and passage

Ditch

more have been found, the possibility remains that they were of a later date and were moved there by mice or ants (though, admittedly, this is unlikely). The animal bones found at Jericho belonged to wild rather than to domesticated species. Furthermore, the pattern of high numbers of gazelle and fewer sheep and goat was the same as in the earlier period, when hunting was practiced, and quite unlike the following Neolithic period, when sheep and goats were kept in herds. The source of wealth of Jericho is uncertain. It may have derived from cereal cultivation, using water from the abundant spring, or from trade in salt and bitumen from the Dead Sea or from its position as a distribution center for the surrounding region.

The mound of Tell Mureybet, beside the Euphrates in Syria, is a site that spans the Natufian and Aceramic Neolithic periods. It includes the remains of round or oval huts from the earlier Proto-Neolithic period as well as later Proto-Neolithic buildings, some of which were not single-roomed huts but rectangular multiroomed structures. This has been taken as a sign of increasingly complex social organization. The remains of animal bones from the Proto-Neolithic period showed that the people hunted wild ass, gazelle and wild cattle. Wild einkorn, wild barley, lentils and bitter vetch were among the plants that were consumed. Interestingly, wild einkorn does not now grow in the area, so it may have been cultivated at Tell Mureybet, but it is equally possible that the distribution of wild einkorn was not the same then as it is today.

The Aceramic Neolithic period

In the Aceramic Neolithic period (called Pre-Pottery Neolithic B and C in the Levant), which started in about 8500 BC, both the number and the size of settlements increased and they spread farther afield. By the end of the period, about 7000 BC, sites such as Tell Abu Hureyra, Ain Ghazal, Jericho, Beisamoun and Basta each occupied about 10 hectares and had populations of a thousand or more, requiring elaborate forms of social organization. However, not all the Aceramic Neolithic sites were so large. Many covered less than a hectare. Settled farming villages based on cereal-crop cultivation and domesticated animals existed on the Anatolian and Iranian plateaus and throughout the Near East. The inhabitants grew domesticated varieties of barley, einkorn and emmer wheat and, by the end of the period, cultivated flax and spelt, club and bread wheat. They kept goats, sheep and pigs and later, probably cattle also. Hunting and gathering, however, still played an important part in the economy. Some settlements, such as those in Sinai or in the Jordanian desert, show no evidence that agriculture was practiced.

In the earlier levels of sites and in temporary hunting camps, round huts were still common. However, a tendency toward more complex, rectangular structures is seen at the small site of Beidha, near Petra. Whereas the early levels had round, semisubterranean huts, the later levels had rectangular or polygonal buildings. Some of the houses had rectangular rooms measuring 5–7 by 6–9 meters with plastered floors painted brown or red. Others appear to have been foundations or basements for upper floors. One room contained beads of stone, bone and shell, another contained

horn for working and another looked as if it had belonged to a butcher.

While on most agricultural sites the buildings contained several rectangular rooms, the type of construction varied. The walls were of stone, mud or mud-bricks, some of which were handmade with thumb impressions on the top to help key the mud mortar and some were rectangular bricks made in a mold. The floors were made either of mud or of a thick lime plaster that had been polished smooth and decorated with red or brown paint. Some had substructures whose purpose was perhaps to provide damp-proofing or insulation.

At Basta, in southern Jordan, narrow channels roofed over with slabs of stone were concealed beneath the floors. Similar features, called grill-plan foundations, have been found at Chayonu in southern Turkey and at Jarmo in eastern Iraq covered by floors supported on stone or reeds. Chayonu also had a form of mosaic floor made out of small pebbles. Some of the later buildings at Chayonu had substructures made of intersecting cross walls (called cell plan foundations) and larger rooms that might have housed some ritual activities within the community.

Situated on the Euphrates near the confluence with the Habur, Bouqras is the site of a village from the end of the Aceramic Neolithic period. Some of the buildings were excavated and others near the surface became visible after an unusually wet winter. The houses were rectangular and, on average, measured 7 by 5 meters. They had about nine rooms per house, including both long and small square rooms. The buildings were close together on the same alignment with alleyways between them.

Tell Maghzaliyeh, which also dates from the later Aceramic Neolithic period, is the site of a small village that probably occupied less than a hectare. It was surrounded by a stone wall standing some 2 meters high that still exists today. Perched on a hill above a stream, the site did not need protection against flooding (unlike Jericho) and the wall was possibly intended as a defence against invaders, though there is little evidence for warfare at this period.

Burial and ritual

Methods for the disposal of the dead in the Aceramic Neolithic period differed across the region. Often, headless bodies—sometimes with the lower jaw still attached to the skeleton—were buried beneath the floors of the houses, and the skulls deposited elsewhere in groups. The separate burial of skulls was also practiced during the Proto-Neolithic period. In the Aceramic Neolithic this method was common at many sites in Palestine and the Levant and even as far afield as Hacilar, on the Anatolian plateau, and Chayonu, near the source of the Tigris. Occasionally the skulls were decorated. Some had been scraped with a sharp blade, others painted with red ocher or bitumen, and a few had shells placed in the eye sockets with the features modeled in plaster. Skulls treated in this elaborate way have been found at Jericho, Tell Ramad, Beisamoun and Ain Ghazal. The cult has been interpreted as a form of worship in which the dead ancestors, according to the belief, probably exercised a powerful influence over their descendants and had to be pacified by prayer and sacrifice.

At Chayonu three buildings associated with this ritual have been identified. One may have been used for sacrifices and another contained numerous human skulls as well as several bulls' heads. Animal skulls were also found at Ganj Dareh in the Zagros mountains and in Nemrik in northern Iraq, where they were attached to the walls of buildings. A similar practice was adopted at Mureybet in the Proto-Neolithic period and in the later shrines of Chatal Huyuk, and still continues today in the mountains of Iran.

At Ain Ghazal, in Jordan, several pits that were excavated were found to contain large male and female statues made of clay and modeled over a reed framework. Statues similar to these, which may have been used in religious rituals, were also found at Jericho and at Nahal Hemar, a cave in the Judean desert to the southwest of the Dead Sea. The cave also contained a stone mask with a human face, heads made of wood and clay, four small carved bone human heads and several skulls of adult men decorated with a net pattern in bitumen, perhaps representing plaited hair. These objects were probably associated with the local religion.

Examples of representational art have been found from the Natufian period, but they were more common in the Aceramic Neolithic. The site

Nemrik contains 15 stylized stone sculptures of birds, animals and humans. Clay figurines, particularly of women, are also common. At Bouqras a wall painting showing a row of birds has survived.

Trading links

Trade, or at least the importation of goods, was practiced long before the Neolithic period. A site in Wadi Hasa dating to about 15,000 BC contains shells that had been carried more than 100 kilometers from the Red Sea and the Mediterranean. Evidence for long-distance trade during the Aceramic Neolithic period became more apparent with the use of obsidian, a form of volcanic glass for making cutting tools. Obsidian supplemented the traditional chert and flint used in tool making. Scientific analysis has traced obsidian to its source and uncovered extensive trade networks. Most of that used in the early Near East came from the Anatolian plateau in eastern or central Turkey, but in the Aceramic Neolithic period obsidian was being used in sites more than 800 kilometers from the source. Whether, however, the obsidian was carried by professional traders, or passed from village to village, or whether trading expeditions were sent out from the major centers, is so far unclear. Shells, semiprecious stones, copper and bitumen are also found on sites far from their sources. There was

Above These remarkable clay statuettes dating from the Aceramic Neolithic period were found at Ain Ghazal, an archeological site in the suburbs of Amman in Jordan. Unlike the cult of skulls, for which evidence has been found at Ain Ghazal and on other sites of this period linking it with ancestor worship, the purpose of these images is unknown, though it was certainly religious.

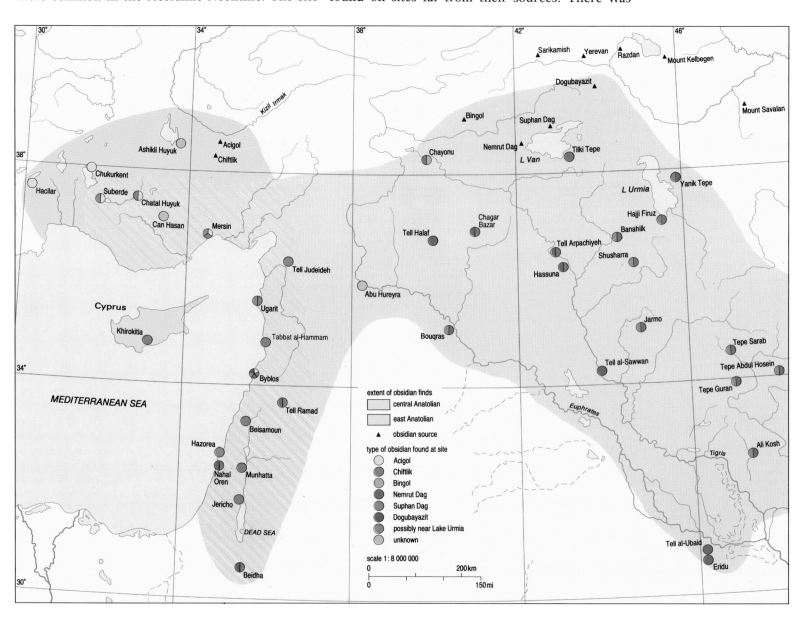

The resources of the Near East
The lowland plains of Mesopotamia were rich in fertile earth and water and produced great wealth through farming, but many materials do not occur in the plains and had to be brought there either from the mountains to the north and east or from farther afield. Good-quality timber and stones for building, metals of many kinds, gemstones, and even grindstones for making flour all came from outside the river valleys. Identifying the sources of these raw materials still requires a lot of work. Sources that are of minor importance today may have been more significant in the past, while political and economic considerations would also have helped determine which sources were exploited.

Below In the Aceramic Neolithic period, before pottery came into general use, vessels were made out of a type of lime plaster called white ware, as in this example from Abu Hureyra. Large quantities of lime plaster were also used for floors of buildings of this period. At Chayonu one building contained about 1.6 tonnes, while one at Yiftahel had as much as 6 tonnes.

Obsidian trade in the Neolithic period
Obsidian is a naturally occurring volcanic glass which was used to make very sharp cutting tools. As pieces of obsidian from different sources have different chemical compositions (some of which are very distinctive), it is sometimes possible to identify the sources of obsidian tools found on archeological sites. In the Aceramic Neolithic period the obsidian used in the Near East came from central and eastern Anatolia. Not all the sources, however, have been discovered and there is still debate about the identification of some obsidian types. The widespread distribution of obsidian indicates extensive trading links. The volume of the trade was not great, but it shows that the early settlements were not isolated and independent, but maintained contact with each other. In the 4th millennium, obsidian cutting tools were superseded by those made from copper alloys.

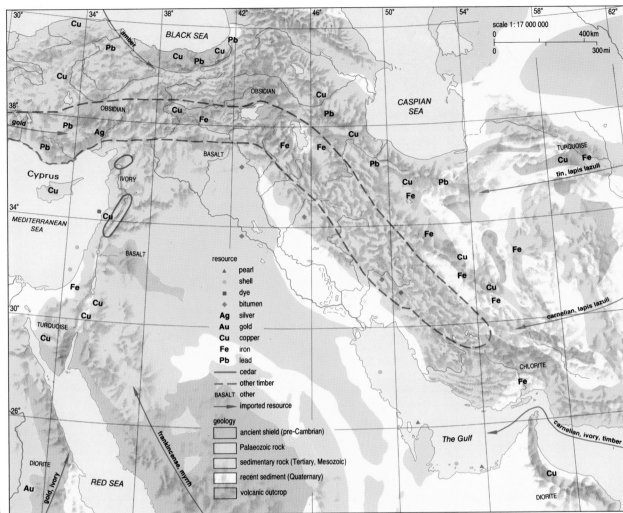

probably trade in other goods, too, such as salt, textiles, skins and other vegetable or animal products, but the evidence has not survived.

Advances in technology

Before the discovery and excavation of the cave of Nahal Hemar in 1983, a few impressions of reed matting and textiles left in bitumen or in clay, or traces in the soil that disappeared when excavated, were the sum total of what was known of the basketry, textiles and wooden objects of the period.

At Nahal Hemar the items preserved included wooden-handled sickles as well as fragments of thick mats made of bundles of rushes or grass held together with string, baskets made of coils of twisted cord coated with bitumen, and hundreds of pieces of cord varying from fine string to 10-millimeter-thick ropes. Bitumen-coated baskets and containers have also been found on other sites and carved stone vessels were common—more than two thousand fragments were found at Jarmo alone. Many carved stone bracelets have also been found on Aceramic Neolithic sites throughout the region. Other containers were made of white ware, a mixture of lime plaster and ashes, which was popular in parts of the Levant. In Mesopotamia vessels were more often made of gypsum plaster. Clay too was sometimes used for making vessels but more often for figurines. At Ganj Dareh, clay pottery vessels were found intact in a level that was destroyed by burning. The vessels had presumably been made of unbaked clay that was fired at

the time of the destruction of the village.

The making of lime plaster, used in white-ware vessels and in the fine floors of the Aceramic Neolithic houses was a process that required considerable technical skill. It needed a lot of labor and fuel as well as kilns capable of reaching high temperatures. Lime plaster is made from crushed limestone ($CaCO_3$), heated up to a temperature of 850°C for several days and then left to cool slowly to produce quick lime (CaO). It is then treated with water to produce slaked lime ($Ca(OH)_2$), which on contact with carbon dioxide will set hard. It was manufactured on a vast scale; one building at Chayonu used about 1.6 tonnes of it.

At Chayonu, which lies only 20 kilometers from the rich copper mines of Ergani Maden, archeologists have uncovered more than one hundred copper beads, pins and tools from the early levels of the site. On other sites of the Aceramic Neolithic period, however, only a few copper artifacts have been found, including an awl from Tell Maghzaliyeh (made out of copper said to come from central Iran, more than 1,000 kilometers away) and beads from Tell Ramad in the Levant and from Ali Kosh in southwest Iran. These objects are thought to have been made of naturally occurring metallic copper, not from smelted copper ore.

The precocious use of metals, public works, craft specialization, long-distance trade and the increasing importance of religion all signaled that these communities of the Aceramic Neolithic period had taken a major step on the road to civilization.

Animals

Only certain species of wild animals can be successfully domesticated. These include wolves, bezoar goats, Asiatic moufflons, wild boar, aurochs (wild cattle), wildcats and wild asses, all of which were native to the Near East and are thought to have been the respective ancestors of dogs, goats, sheep, pigs, cows, cats and donkeys. These breeds, with the addition of the chicken, are still the most common farm animals and pets throughout the world.

Information about animals in Mesopotamia comes from three sources: from excavated bones, from textual references and from pictorial representations. Studying animal bones can show not only the species, but also the sex and age of the animal and sometimes the diseases that it suffered from. The ancient texts included standard lists of animal names, as well as the economic records of temple herds, observations on animals in omens, and lists of animals that were hunted or kept by the kings in their special parks. Many animals—domesticated, wild or fantastic—were illustrated on the monuments and cylinder seals of the ancient Near East. These included elephants and flies, vultures and crabs as well as snakes, turtles and fish, though the animals most commonly shown were those of importance in Mesopotamian culture, such as lions and bulls.

Domesticated animal	Wild ancestor	Region	Date	
Dog	Wolf	Near East	c.	11,000 BC
Goat	Bezoar goat	Near East	c.	8500 BC
Sheep	Asiatic moufflon	Near East	c.	8000 BC
Pig	Wild boar	Near East	c.	7500 BC
Cattle	Auroch	Near East	c.	7000 BC
Cat	Wild cat	Near East	c.	7000 BC
Chicken	Red jungle fowl	China	c.	6000 BC
Llama	Guanaco	Andes	c.	5000 BC
Donkey	Wild ass	Near East	c.	4000 BC
Horse	Tarpan	Southern Russia	c.	4000 BC
Camel	Wild camel	?Southern Arabia/ ?Southern Central Asia	c.	3000 BC
Guinea-pig	Cavy	Peru	c.	2000 BC
Rabbit	Wild rabbit	Spain	c.	1000 BC
Turkey	Wild turkey	Mexico	c.	300 BC

Above A relief from the North Palace of Ashurbanipal (668–627 BC) at Nineveh showing a breed of mastiff kept by the Assyrians for hunting. Dogs were the earliest animals to be domesticated. Dog skeletons found in the Ubaid graves at Eridu (c. 5000 BC) have been identified as greyhounds.

Below Herds of gazelle roamed the steppes of the ancient Near East. The herd carved on this relief (detail shown) from the North Palace at Nineveh has been disturbed by a beater and flees toward the Assyrian king who lies concealed in a pit ready to shoot them.

Above A relief from the Northwest Palace of Ashurnasirpal (883–859 BC) at Kalhu showing horses being groomed and fed. Horses arrived in Mesopotamia at the end of the 3rd millennium BC. They came from southern Russia, where they had been domesticated almost 2,000 years earlier, and were used in warfare for pulling chariots. In the 1st millennium BC mounted cavalry became more important, particularly for campaigns in mountainous terrain. The acquisition of horses was one of the priorities of the Assyrian army. The breeds that were especially prized came from the mountains of northwestern Iran and from Nubia. Mules were valued as beasts of burden.

Below Baked clay head of a sheep, similar to a sandstone head found at Uruk dating to about 3000 BC. Sheep have always been the most important domestic animals in Mesopotamia. Woollen textiles were one of its main exports. Length 13.6 cm.

Below center Ivory box found in the palace of Niqmepa at Alalah (14th century BC). The missing parts of the neck and lid have been restored in wood. Ducks and geese were kept in Mesopotamia from at least 2500 BC and probably long before. Length 13.5 cm.

Left On this relief from the North Palace of Ashurbanipal at Nineveh, Arabs on their camels are fleeing from the invading Assyrian army. Camels were introduced into Mesopotamia in the second half of the 2nd millennium BC. The two-humped, or Bactrian camel came from Central Asia and made its home in the mountains of Iran, and the single-humped camel, or dromedary, probably came from the Arabian peninsula and was found in the deserts to the south. They were used for transportation but not in battle.

Above These strange beasts carved on the Black Obelisk of Shalmaneser III (858–825 BC) at Kalhu were part of the tribute of Musri (probably Egypt). The first (on the left) was called a river-ox (perhaps a water buffalo); the second may be a rhinoceros, while the third looks like some species of goat. Other animals brought from Musri were two-humped camels, elephants, monkeys and apes.

Pottery

The earliest known pottery comes from Japan and dates to the 11th millennium BC. In the Near East pottery appeared about 3,000 years later and was almost certainly an independent invention. Throughout the world, pottery is associated with settled village life, as its bulk and fragility make it unsuitable for the mobile life-style of most hunter-gatherers.

Pottery is one of the most useful artifacts for Near Eastern archeologists and fragments are found in great abundance on sites throughout the region. Pottery vessels were cheap to manufacture and easily broken. The broken pieces could not be reused, and were simply thrown away, ready to be rediscovered. Fortunately baked clay is almost indestructible and is preserved in almost all conditions. Many sites are covered with a thick layer of potsherds, left behind after the wind and rain have washed away the surface soil from the site.

A great deal of information can be obtained from studying pottery. As the chemical composition of clays used to make pots varies, the sources of the clays can often be identified by scientific analysis. Even without scientific aids, it is easy to distinguish between different types of pottery. The tempering added to the clay can be of different kinds—sand, chaff, hair and so on—and each leaves its own distinctive trace in the fabric of the vessel. The firing of the vessel can vary according to the conditions under which it takes place. In particular, the presence or absence of oxygen in the kiln chamber changes the color of the clay from red (oxidized) to gray or black (reduced). Pottery vessels came in a wide variety of shapes and sizes, from shallow saucers to huge storage jars. Some were formed by hand and built up by adding pieces of clay as pellets or as slabs or as a coil. Some were pressed in a mold, and some were shaped on a slow wheel (from about 4500 BC) or thrown on a fast wheel (after about 2000 BC). Surface treatments also varied. These included wet smoothing (being slipped with a thin liquid clay), painting with clay pigments, being burnished, incised, carved, stamped or inlaid, and, after 1500 BC, glazed.

Different techniques of manufacture and of decoration were characteristic of different regions and periods, so that pottery can be used to date a period. This is particularly useful for prehistoric times or those when written sources were not abundant. Furthermore, sherds picked up from the surface of a site can be used to date the occupation of the site and so establish changes in settlement patterns of a region through time. Pottery can also reveal trading activities and cultural influences.

Although, however, the main features of the development of pottery styles for the different regions of the Near East are known, much more research will be needed to refine the chronological sequence and to understand the details of the manufacture and distribution of ancient pottery.

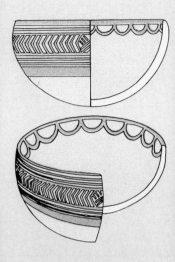

Above Scale drawings of the pottery vessels found in excavations enable archeologists to compare one vessel with another. The normal method is to view the pot from the side with one quarter removed. In this way, a single drawing can show both the outside and inside of the vessel as well as a cross-section through the vessel wall.

Left In the Ubaid period (c. 5900–4300 BC) pale pottery was decorated with dark paint. The patterns used varied over time. This is an example of the latest style, found in a grave at Ur. Diameter 23 cm.

Left Early Ubaid pottery has only been found in southern Mesopotamia. Pottery in the style of the Late Ubaid period has been discovered from the Iranian plateau to the Mediterranean. This Late Ubaid jar came from a grave at Tell Arpachiyeh near Nineveh.

Below The earliest pottery was only lightly fired and so was still quite porous. Higher temperatures for baking achieved through building more efficient kilns enabled the Hassuna-period potters to make vessels that could be used to store liquids. This pottery jar found at the site of Tell Hassuna dates to an early part of the Hassuna period, around the middle of the 7th millennium BC. It is decorated with herring-bone patterns of lines inscribed with a sharp instrument. Some later pottery has a similar design but can be distinguished by the quality of the clay.

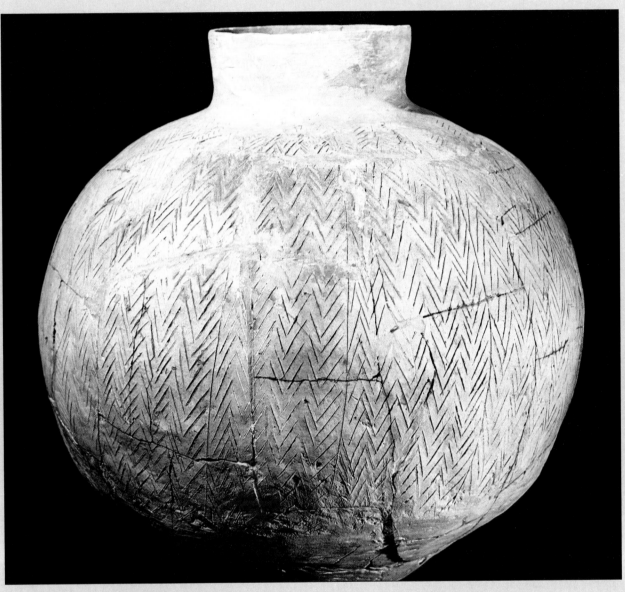

Right A Samarran-style bowl from Tell Hassuna. Samarran pottery is found in central Iraq but was also used in northern Iraq at sites where Hassuna pottery was the local ware. Samarran pottery sometimes has swirling patterns like that shown here. The bowl was broken and mended in antiquity, as is shown by the holes drilled either side of the break. Diameter 25 cm.

Far right The pottery of the Halaf period (c. 6000–5400 BC) is some of the finest produced in the Near East. An outstanding series of polychrome bowls were found in the latest Halaf level at Tell Arpachiyeh. The geometric design was painted in red, black and white. Diameter 33 cm.

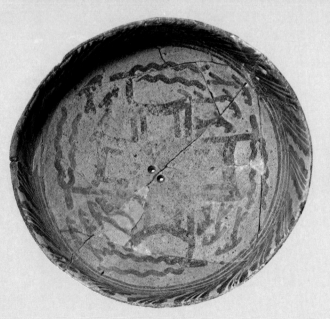

TOWARD CIVILIZATION (7000-4000 BC)

Early agricultural settlements

After the discovery and widespread adoption of agriculture and animal husbandry, different kinds of settlement arose in the Near East. Some were small agricultural villages distinguished from their predecessors by the increasing use of pottery but where otherwise the daily life was almost unchanged. Others were more sophisticated both in the objects they made and used and in their social organization. These developments culminated in the remarkable urban transformation that took place in southern Mesopotamia in the fourth millennium BC, which formed the basis for modern societies.

The early agricultural settlements of the Near East were in hilly regions and in oases, favoring areas along the rivers and on the shores of lakes and seas. The lower-lying plains, which received too little rainfall to allow cereal crops to grow, were occupied by nomadic tribes. Cereal grains stored up in a good year could enable a community to survive a disastrous harvest, but attempting to farm in areas where the rainfall was unreliable would not have been a risk worth taking when there was plenty of more productive land available. The distribution of early farming settlements was very similar to that of the dry-farming region (not using irrigation) of today. It corresponds to areas that receive more than 250 millimeters of rainfall a year, confirming that the climate has indeed changed little in the last 8,000 years.

Unlike the Egyptian Nile, which flooded in the growing season to allow cereal crops to thrive without additional rainfall, the rivers in the rest of the Near East flooded in the spring at just the wrong time of year, and cereal agriculture had to rely on rainfall. The development of irrigation by canals changed the pattern of settlement. The colonization of the fertile but drought-stricken alluvial plains gave increased yields, allowing larger settlements to thrive and eventually leading to the first cities.

The developments following the Aceramic Neolithic period up to the beginnings of urbanization span the Pottery (or Later) Neolithic and the Early and Middle Chalcolithic periods. Conventionally the Neolithic and Chalcolithic periods are divided by the Chalcolithic people's use of copper and bronze tools in addition to the tools of chipped and polished stone, which were used by Neolithic people. However, a few copper tools were already in use in the Aceramic Neolithic, and, in fact, little metal has been found on sites antedating the Late Chalcolithic period.

Small farming communities throughout the ages differed less from each other in their basic everyday life-styles than did the earliest village communities from their hunter-gatherer predecessors. Many of the features of modern society are absent among hunter-gatherer societies and had to be invented or discovered at some stage. Some charac-

teristics already existed in the earlier formative period of the Aceramic Neolithic and became more elaborate or more firmly established in the Pottery Neolithic and Chalcolithic periods. These provided the vital background from which urban life could emerge.

The Pottery Neolithic period

Pottery that had been lightly or accidentally fired is occasionally found even on sites of the Aceramic Neolithic period. In the following Pottery Neolithic period, however, it became so common that archeologists define local cultures according to the type of pottery rather than according to the types of stone tools used, which defined earlier periods. Decorated pottery is much more sensitive to changes in fashion than chipped stone and is thus a more sensitive indicator of both cultural affiliation and chronology.

Transforming pliable soft clay into hard impervious, virtually indestructible pottery by heating is an almost a magical process. It was known to the inhabitants of Chayonu and Ganj Dareh, who made pottery vessels and small figurines as early as the eighth millennium BC. In the Aceramic Neolithic period vessels were normally of stone or wood, or of basketry, sometimes covered with plaster or bitumen, or of plaster, as in the white ware of the Pre-Pottery Neolithic B. By about 7000 BC, however, pottery had become widespread throughout the Near East.

At any period the inhabitants of a region made pots in only a limited range of types and styles, enabling quite small pieces of pottery to be identified. Archeologists have learned much by comparing changes in pottery over a time in one region with other sequences of change in pottery styles from other areas. In this way, sherds of broken pottery have been used to date the sites where they were found. These results together with information on the changes in styles that took place over quite a short period can provide relative chronologies that are often more informative than radiocarbon determinations.

Similarities in pottery assemblages may indicate close connections between different groups. Pottery that was obviously imported from another area indicates trade or exchange in the pots themselves or in their contents. Studying pottery offers one of the best ways of investigating societies that existed before writing was invented and even in historical periods is a valuable aid to the archeologist.

As well as the settlements around the foothills of the fertile regions of the Near East, during the Aceramic Neolithic a few settlements had started to exploit the resources of the Turkish and Iranian plateaus, and some existed along the river valleys of Mesopotamia. From that time on the plains of Mesopotamia became more important while the Levant and Palestine, which had been the scene of

Previous pages A scene in the marshes of southern Iraq. Changes in the courses of the rivers have left large areas of the southern alluvial plain under water. The positions of the lakes have changed over the years, and although the marshes were depicted in the 8th-century BC Assyrian reliefs, their precise locations in the past have not been identified. The still waters of the lakes with their plentiful supplies of fish, provide an alternative way of life to the farming communities found elsewhere in the Near East.

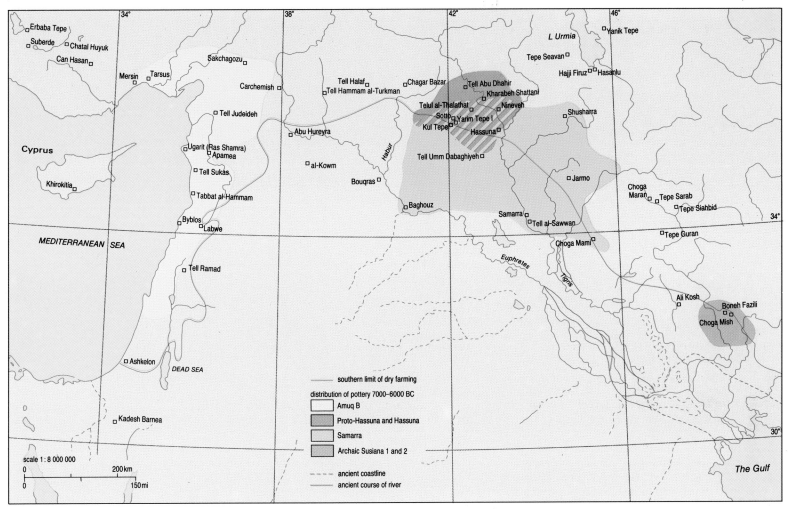

Early pottery-using cultures
In the 7th millennium the use of decorated pottery became widespread, enabling archeologists to distinguish cultural groups on the basis of different pottery styles. In the Hassuna and contemporary Archaic Susiana and Amuq B periods the plow was probably already in use, and this allowed the cultivation of large areas of less fertile land away from the moist soils utilized by earlier farmers. In the Samarra period, which partly overlapped the Hassuna period, gravity-fed canals for crop irrigation gave improved yields, permitting agricultural settlements to be established in areas outside the limits of dry farming.

remarkable changes in the earlier periods, declined in influence.

The site of Chatal Huyuk

A number of sites on the Anatolian plateau such as Hacilar, Suberde and Can Hasan III are similar in date and standard of achievement to the Aceramic Neolithic of the Levant, but none of these compares with Chatal Huyuk, which is much bigger and better preserved. The site covers over 12 hectares and the Neolithic levels are each 15 meters high. So far, the earliest levels have not been investigated, but the 14 levels that have, according to the evidence of radiocarbon determinations, cover from about 6850 to 6300 BC, close to the final Pre-Pottery Neolithic B period of the Levant. Unfortunately, in common with other archeological sites, the latest levels at Chatal Huyuk have been badly eroded.

Wall paintings

Some of the rooms on the site have remarkable wall paintings, relief figures on the walls and benches and pillars with modeled bulls' heads and horns. These were probably shrines, as having such decoration in an ordinary house would have been both odd and inconvenient. However, the number of these ''shrines'' (about a third of all the houses excavated in the sixth and seventh levels) is surprising. Either they had a purely religious function, in which case the excavated area of the site was probably a religious quarter, or they were a special type of dwelling.

The walls and floors of the houses were covered with layers of fine white mud plaster, and in one

building there were 120 of these. The plastering was possibly carried out annually (as the houses within a single level had approximately the same number of plasterings), giving an idea of the age of the buildings. In those rooms that were painted, the painted layers were separated by several layers of plain plaster, so that the paintings had probably been visible for only a short period before being covered over. Why the inhabitants sometimes painted the walls is not known, but the fact that the wall paintings have been preserved owes a lot to their being plastered over rather than allowed to decay. The paint, which was applied with a fine-hair brush, was mostly made from minerals that occur naturally in Anatolia, such as ocher, azurite, malachite, cinnabar, manganese and galena. Apart from the white or pale-cream background, the main color was red or red-brown, though yellow, black, gray, mauve and blue were also used.

Most of the painted scenes were within a single panel framed by the wall pilasters, though some of the most impressive paintings were more extensive. Some panels were painted plain red, some had geometric patterns, and others depicted scenes of people and animals. Some experts have compared the patterns with the woven rugs traditionally made in Turkey, but there is no other evidence for weaving with different-colored yarn at this date.

The most interesting paintings were representational. Some were quite naturalistic while others were more stylized. Rows of human hands, sometimes painted in reverse, were reminiscent of the art of the Upper Paleolithic, though the same motif is also found today painted on the local village

Chatal Huyuk

The site of Chatal Huyuk (Çatal Hüyük) was excavated by James Mellaart between 1961 and 1963
and produced spectacular and unsuspected results.
He uncovered a large area of a town of the seventh
millennium BC where the houses were unusually
well preserved. Some, which the excavator called
shrines, had elaborate wall paintings and modeled
reliefs, with animal skulls attached to the walls and
benches. The fantastic decoration of the ''shrines''
has led to much speculation about the nature of the
religion of the inhabitants: mother goddesses and
birth goddesses have been seen in the figurines,
the leopards and the modeled breasts stuck on the
walls, while the numerous skulls and horns of bulls
are said to represent male deities. religion was a
driving force within the society. Chatal Huyuk is
very different from the simple farming villages that
had previously been considered to typify the
period. As a prehistoric site it is still unrivaled,
though more recent excavations at Aceramic Neolithic sites such as Ain Ghazal, Abu Hureyra and
Bouqras show the antecedents of the developments
at Chatal Huyuk.

Above Baked clay figure of a fat
pregnant female in the act of
giving birth. It has been
identified as a ''birth
goddess''supported by two
cat-like animals. The figure was
found in one of the latest shrines
at Chatal Huyuk. The head has
been restored.

Right A reconstruction of part of
the settlement of level VIʙ. The
single-storey buildings were
entered from the roof. The roofs
rose up in terraces toward the
center of the settlement.

Above right A reconstruction of a
shrine in level VIA. The walls
were made of mud-bricks built
around a timber framework.
Men were buried beneath the
northeast platform and women
and children beneath the others.

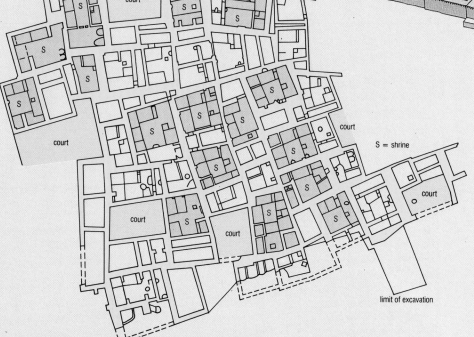

court

court

court

0   5   10 m
0   10   20   30 ft

court

court

court

court

court

court

court

S = shrine

limit of excavation

Above right A reconstruction of
the north and east walls of a
shrine in level VII. The legs of
the vultures are strangely human
and it has been suggested that
the scene shows priests dressed
up as birds with a headless
corpse between them.

Right One of a pair of painted
leopards from a shrine in level
VII. The animals had been
replastered many times and
repainted at least seven times.

Right In level VIʙ the tightly
packed houses shared their walls
with their neighbors. About half
the buildings have been
classified as ''shrines''. Between
the houses were open spaces,
formed by the remains of
derelict houses, that were used
for the disposal of garbage.
Typically, the design consisted
of a roughly square living room
that led into a long narrow storeroom, either by a low door or
through a porthole in the wall.

Below A view over the excavated houses at Chatal Huyuk. On average the houses covered an area of about 25 m², which suggests that they each accommodated a nuclear family. It has been calculated that in the whole site there would have been about 1,000 households with a population of 5,000 people. The edge of the settlement has not been investigated, so it is not known whether there was a wall round the site. The house walls themselves would have formed an obstacle to any invading force.

Above Some of the graves of adult men in the later levels contained baked clay stamp seals. These had a variety of shapes and were carved with deeply incised lines, spirals and triangles. As no impressions left by these seals on clay have been found, it has been suggested that they were used on less durable materials, such as textiles, or skins, or even for the decoration of the human body.

houses. Impressive hunting scenes decorated two of the "shrines" at different levels. In both the north wall was dominated by a huge red bull about 2 meters long, while diminutive figures wearing leopard-skin loincloths danced around. Most of the figures were male and their skin was painted red. The painting from level V, the earlier of the two levels, continued on all four walls, and included other animals such as deer, boars, wild asses, bears, wolves and lions. The scenes do not accurately depict a hunt but probably had some symbolic function, perhaps showing a festival that included dancing and animal baiting such as Minoan bull-jumping or Spanish bullfighting. A fragmentary scene from the shrine at level III, however, showed a male hunter, accompanied probably by a dog, shooting an arrow at a stag.

Another bizarre scene, which occurred three times, showed large birds and small, headless humans. Although painted in a stylized way, the birds have been identified as griffon vultures stripping the flesh from the bodies of the exposed dead. Another painting that was thought to be connected with the treatment of the dead was found at a lower level (level VI). It supposedly showed a charnel house made of reeds and matting and decorated with woven mats that had hollow-eyed skulls beneath.

Human and animal figures

Some of the walls were also decorated with reliefs modeled in mud plaster on a framework of reeds, like the Pre-Pottery Neolithic B statues from Ain Ghazal, Jericho and Nahal Hemar. These reliefs were sometimes painted, showing human and animal figures, animal heads and female breasts. The seven human figures in relief were each about a meter high and were frontal with arms and legs sticking out horizontally on both sides. One fine example was painted with a crazy network of orange, red and black lines. The faces, hands and feet of all the figures were damaged, perhaps because they had been decorated with some valuable material that was reusable or because the mutilation of the relief was part of the ritual that took place in the shrine. The figures were often placed close to modeled bulls' heads. Some people think that the figures were intended to show a goddess giving birth and that the bulls' heads represented male divinities.

Elsewhere a stag was modeled in relief and, at three successive levels, there were pairs of leopards. Each pair was arranged as a heraldic group with the heads close together and the bodies facing in opposite directions. Some had been replastered and repainted many times, each time with a different pattern on the bodies of the animals.

Animal heads, either modeled entirely of plaster or using skulls or horn cores from real animals, were also uncovered on the earlier sites of Ganj Dareh and Nemrik. Bulls were most common but rams and stags were also found. The heads were placed on the walls or on low benches in groups of three, five or seven, or sunk in pillars of mud akin to the horned altars of later periods. The female breasts were usually attached to the wall in groups. Interestingly, they were often built up over the lower jaws of boars, or over the skulls of weasels, foxes or vultures.

Burial customs

People were buried under the living room, but not under the storerooms or beneath open spaces. Often they lay about 60 centimeters below the platforms, contracted and on their left sides with their heads toward the center of the room. In fact, burials were in two stages. After death the bodies were taken away and only later buried under the houses, as was shown by the traces of red ocher found on some skulls and bones, and by the incorrect arrangement of the bones of some of the skeletons. The wall paintings of headless corpses being eaten by vultures perhaps showed how the dead were treated. In one room four detached human skulls had been placed on a platform and elsewhere a female skull had been given cowrie shells for eyes, like an earlier plastered skull from Jericho.

Normally, people were not often buried with their belongings, but there have been exceptional finds including woven textiles and more spectacular items. Male burials were accompanied by weapons, stone mace-heads, daggers with bone or wooden handles, baked clay seals, copper finger rings and S-shaped bone belt hooks (like the one found at Nahal Hemar and others in Greece). Women's graves contained jewelry, stone palettes for grinding up cosmetics and, occasionally, polished obsidian mirrors. Wooden vessels, baskets and food offerings were found buried with both sexes, but no pottery vessels or figurines. Judging by the bones, the people were fairly healthy, though many were anemic, possibly as a result of malaria, and others suffered from arthritis or limb fractures. On average, the men lived to the age of 34 and women to 30. Men were about 170 centimeters (5 feet 7 inches) tall and women about 158 centimeters (5 feet 2 inches).

Artifacts at Chatal Huyuk

The pottery from Chatal Huyuk was rather cumbersome, consisting of bulbous or bag-shaped vessels. The wooden vessels found there—bowls, cups, and boxes—were made from fir and other softwoods. Most of the chipped stone objects were obsidian, which probably came from the Acigol source, 150 kilometers to the northeast. Obsidian was also polished to make beads and mirrors. Some of the finest tools and weapons, particularly daggers and knife blades, were made of flint imported from Syria. Copper and lead were used for beads, pendants and rings from the ninth excavated level and above. Naturally occurring lead is much rarer than copper, and the lead was probably smelted from ore. The discovery of a lump of copper slag, however, suggested that some copper, too, was smelted, even though most of the copper objects from Chatal Huyuk appeared to be made out of hammered native copper.

Of the clay and stone figurines, the fat females were particularly interesting. One represented a woman giving birth, either supported by two cats or seated on a chair with arms in the shape of cats. The animal figurines were mostly of species that were hunted: leopards, cattle, wild boar and wild sheep or goats. Some had stab marks, suggesting that they were used in a hunting ritual. Two clay cattle figurines from Ain Ghazal also displayed a similar feature.

Plants and animals

Nine-tenths of the meat that the people of Chatal Huyuk consumed, as represented by the animal bones found there, probably came from domesticated cattle. Dogs had also been domesticated by that time. Some wild animals were hunted for their skins as well as for their meat. They included wild sheep, deer, wild boar, onager (wild ass), bears and big cats, possibly lions or leopards. Domesticated plants included einkorn and emmer wheat, naked six-row barley and perhaps hexaploid bread wheat. The people of the time also collected other plants native to the area. Some of the varieties found thrive under irrigated conditions, but there is disagreement over how much irrigation was practiced. In general, the scientific evidence for how the people lived differs from the account given by their wall paintings and shows the divergence of reality and ideology in their lives.

After Chatal Huyuk was abandoned toward the end of the seventh millennium, succeeding cultures in Anatolia were distinguished by fine painted pottery from sites such as Hacilar and Can Hasan II. By about 5700 BC, however, both these sites had also been abandoned. At Can Hasan, in a level that had been destroyed by fire, the body of a 45-year-old man was found with a copper bracelet and a copper mace-head in the collapsed debris of one of the houses. This mace, which had a hole for a wooden shaft, had been made by casting into a mold. This is the earliest known example of the use of this technique.

Above A modern village in Iranian Kurdistan shows many of the same features as the early villages of the Near East. The houses are built of mud-bricks and mud mortar and covered with mud plaster. The flat roofs consist of timber beams supporting layers of branches and matting, which have a layer of earth for insulation. The roof is plastered to offer protection against the weather. In winter the roofs have to be cleared of snow, and after rain they must be dried with stone rollers kept on the roof for this purpose. The roofs provide an additional living space and can be used for sleeping or for storage.

By about 6000 BC villages were well established throughout the Near East. The chief varieties of domesticated plants and animals were well known and these still form the main source of food in the region to the present day. The developments that followed did not involve finding a new means of subsistence, as had occurred in the transition from hunter-gatherer to farmer, but lay in changes in social organization and in growing technological competence. These changes were gradual and local, and initially centered on Mesopotamia.

Early Mesopotamian settlements

In the Aceramic Neolithic period settled communities were perched round the edge of the Mesopotamian plains. In a few areas the people were fortunate in being able to exploit the resources outside the region, where rainfed agriculture was possible. In the Pottery Neolithic period settlements were widespread throughout the rainfed agricultural zone. The earliest of such sites in present-day Iraq date to the first half of the seventh millennium BC and are contemporary with Chatal Huyuk. Although often less than a hectare in area, and at first glance showing none of the sophistication of Chatal Huyuk, they perhaps represent a more complex situation with a much greater diversity of activities.

These early Pottery Neolithic sites are sometimes called Proto-Hassuna, as their culture developed into the succeeding Hassuna culture. The pottery was mostly coarse, chaff-tempered ware in simple shapes, open or deep bowls, globular jars with cylindrical necks and flat round or oval dishes. Some of these dishes had rough or corrugated insides and are thought to have been used in cereal preparation. The surface of the bowls was often decorated with appliqué designs in clay, some of which were geometric and others of animals. About one-sixth of the finer pottery was painted with simple red designs. Other pieces of better-fired dark-gray burnished pottery found on the sites may have been imported from the more advanced western regions.

The people of this period lived in rectangular buildings made of packed mud (called in Arabic *tauf*, and sometimes called *pisé*). The houses normally had two or three rooms, probably accommodating a single family. Some of the other buildings had foundations made of rows of parallel walls and these have been called drying racks. Others were grids of small rooms less than 2 meters square which may have been used for storage. At Yarim Tepe I, special round or rectangular structures were sometimes used for the disposal of dead bodies, which showed signs of having been dismembered. A juvenile buried at Tell Sotto had also been treated in this way. The head, arms with shoulder blades, and legs each with half the pelvis, had been cut off and placed on top of the rest of the body before it was buried. Whether this was the standard method of adult burial or whether it was a treatment reserved for special individuals is not known. Infants were normally buried beneath the walls or floors of houses, sometimes inside a pottery vessel.

Most of the sites of this period lie well within the area of rainfed farming. The economy, as shown by plant and animal remains, is typically agricultural.

Einkorn, emmer, bread wheat, club wheat, spelt wheat, six-row naked barley, lentils and peas were all cultivated by the people of the time. They kept domestic cattle, sheep, goats, pigs and dogs, while wild species accounted for less than one-fifth of the animal bones found. Cattle, which compared with sheep and goats were large and fierce, must have been difficult to keep. Perhaps they were used for milk and transportation as well as for meat and hides, or even to pull plows, which might have already been in use to cultivate the wide plains of northern Mesopotamia.

Umm Dabaghiyeh

The small site of Umm Dabaghiyeh lies beyond what is today the dry-farming region. Its four main levels of occupation belonged to the Early Pottery Neolithic period and the lower two levels were well preserved and followed a similar plan. The central feature of the site was three blocks of small rooms, measuring about 1.5 by 1.75 meters, arranged on three sides of an open space. Many of the rooms had no doors and were probably used for storage. Scattered more haphazardly were dwelling houses consisting of one or two rooms. These houses were apparently entered from the roofs: in one corner there were steps and above them toe holes were carved in the walls to serve as ladders. They also had fireplaces with proper chimneys.

Most surprisingly, the stone tools that were found on the site were of a hunting community rather than a farming one. The people ate domesticated plants but these might have been brought there from farther north. Most of the meat consumed was obtained by hunting wild animals. Two-thirds of the bones found on the site belonged to onager, a variety of wild ass, and about 15 percent to gazelles. Only about 10 percent of the bones were from domesticated species, notably sheep. The evidence for hunting and the extensive use of storerooms suggested that the people specialized in the capture of onagers and gazelles for their hides.

Very probably, other sites specialized in other products, such as salt, bitumen or obsidian. How these communities found a market for their products is uncertain, but the fact that they were able to suggests that regular food surpluses were stored and traded for other goods. Such stored wealth was the foundation for the future urban society of Mesopotamia.

Hassuna and Samarra cultures

In the middle of the seventh millennium BC new styles of pottery developed and more elaborate painted and incised pottery replaced the simpler patterns. The Hassuna culture, which was based on the earlier Proto-Hassuna, shared many of its traits. Finds from both Proto-Hassuna and Hassuna levels included clay sling bullets, chipped stone hoes, biconical clay spindle whorls (for spinning thread from flax or wool) and several incised stone beads or pendants, which have been identified as stamp seals. (As at Chatal Huyuk there is no evidence for the stamp seals being used to make impressions on clay.) Copper ores and copper metal were used for tools and jewelry. Lead in a bracelet found at the lowest level at Yarim Tepe I had been smelted from ore, so the people of the later Hassuna culture

Above A painting on a house wall at Umm Dabaghiyeh, in the desert steppe to the west of the Tigris river, showing what might have been an onager hunt. The processing of onager skins was possibly the main economic activity of the settlement. How these animals were captured is not certain, but it has been suggested that they were driven into netted enclosures and that the lines above the onagers in the painting represent the uprights from which netting was hung. The animals are each about 15 cm long and painted in red on a white ground. These simple pictures are contemporary with those of Chatal Huyuk, belonging to the first half of the 7th millennium BC.

Above A painted pottery vessel c. 6000 BC. The style is similar to that of the pottery in the latest level of Hacilar in southwestern Turkey. The potters at Hacilar were very inventive and versatile, producing some vessels shaped like animals or humans, with the eyes inset with pieces of obsidian. Many pots of this type have found their way into European and American museums. Some of the finest ones were taken from cemeteries by modern grave robbers and illegally exported. Others are skillfully-made modern forgeries that can be detected only by scientific analysis.

probably used smelted as well as native copper. However, their large dome kilns, measuring 2 meters across, were most likely used for pottery rather than for metal. Turquoise, rock crystal, obsidian and sea shells from this time were found in northern Iraq, also showing that there was trading throughout the Near East.

Toward the end of the seventh millennium BC, in the later Hassuna levels, a new type of pottery appeared. Well-fired and painted a chocolate brown color, often in stunning patterns, it belonged to the Samarran culture to the south. Samarran sites occupied a band across the center of Iraq. The important site of Tell al-Sawwan, overlooking the river Tigris, has lower levels dating to about 6300 BC according to a radiocarbon determination. Beneath the earliest houses more than one hundred graves were discovered in shallow oval pits. They included adults and juveniles but most were of children. Buried with the bodies were beautifully carved alabaster vessels in the same tradition as those found on Hassuna-period and earlier sites, carved alabaster female statuettes and beads.

Several large, carefully planned buildings of the same period were of rectangular molded mud-bricks, allowing a more regular plan than was normal when using mud alone. The bricks were each about 60 centimeters long, longer than the width of the walls, and at the corners and at the junctions of walls the building had added external buttresses for extra support. This buttressing, which characterized Samarran architecture, later became the hallmark of Mesopotamian religious architecture. The buildings of the earliest two levels each occupied about 150 square meters and contained more than fifteen rooms. The arrangement of the rooms suggested that the two sides of the buildings were used by two groups of people, perhaps males and females. The rooms were less than 3 meters wide, probably the maximum that could safely be spanned with the available timber.

Much of the settlement of the next level, dated to about 6100 BC, has been excavated. Here the houses were smaller, about 70 square meters in area, with two rooms, each 3 meters square, surrounded by smaller rooms. Ten or so of these buildings were situated rather haphazardly in an area of about 45 by 50 meters, which was surrounded by a thick wall and a ditch.

The later levels at Tell al-Sawwan had been eroded. At the site of Choga Mami, however, farther east on the edge of the Mesopotamian plain, excavations have uncovered both classic Samarran occupation and a late phase of the Samarran called Choga Mami Transitional. There the buildings comprised regular rectangular grids of rooms, of a type that has also been found at Songor A in the Hamrin Dam Salvage Project.

The plant remains from Samarran sites included the familiar range of einkorn, emmer, bread wheat, two-row and six-row hulled barley and six-row naked barley. The presence of flax (or linseed), and the size of the seeds, suggested that the people had irrigation. Indeed, water channels found at Choga Mami have been dated to this period. Possibly the inhabitants of Jericho and Chatal Huyuk practiced irrigation on a small scale, but by the Samarran period, people had the technology to build and

Above A painted baked clay head of a female figurine dating to the Samarran period from Choga Mami. The hairstyle is probably a long plait wound over the top of the head, similar to that shown on Sumerian statues 3,000 years later. The coffee-bean eyes were typical of the period. Height 4.8 cm.

Left Beneath the earliest buildings at Tell al-Sawwan, in what is today central Iraq, more than a hundred graves belonging to the Samarran period have been excavated. Most of these were children's graves containing goods such as stone beads, and alabaster statuettes and vessels. The statuettes are female and are thought to represent human rather than divine beings. Some figures have inlaid eyes and features picked out in bitumen (*upper left*). The veined alabaster vessels (*lower left*) were carved in a variety of shapes: jars, bowls and ladles are the most common. Pottery vessels were not buried in the graves at Tell al-Sawwan.

maintain canals stretching for considerable distances. Irrigation brought increased yields to dry-farming areas, so that they could support a greater population, and made agriculture possible for the first time in areas where there was insufficient rainfall. Perhaps reflecting this technical superiority, the Choga Mami Transitional style influenced the local traditions of pottery to the southeast, in the Deh Luran plain and in Susiana.

Halaf culture

In about 6000 BC the Hassuna culture in northern Mesopotamia was replaced by the Halaf culture. Its origins are uncertain, but it seems to have developed in the same area as the Hassuna culture. The Halaf culture survived some 600 years and spread out to cover all of present-day northern Iraq and Syria, exerting an influence that reached as far as

Halaf and other cultures
In the 6th millennium BC the Halaf culture spread in a band across northern and eastern Mesopotamia. Pottery influenced by Halaf styles is found toward the Mediterranean (within the Amuq C culture), to the north and to the east in the Zagros mountains. The distribution of Halaf pottery matches almost exactly the region where dry farming is practiced today, and undoubtedly this was the normal method of farming in the Halaf period. In southern Mesopotamia, where there was too little rainfall for dry farming, the Early Ubaid culture that became established was based on irrigation agriculture. The region around Susa to the east showed a similar development in the Middle Susiana culture, which has parallels with the Early Ubaid pottery styles.

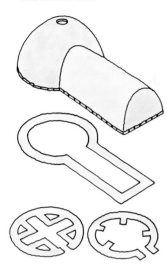

Below The typical Halaf house was a round hut, sometimes with a rectangular entrance chamber or storeroom. The huts may have been roofed with domes or timber beams and often had walls dividing the circular room into smaller units.

the Mediterranean coast and the highlands of the central Zagros. In some ways, however, it was outside the mainstream of development.

The plants grown were the same as in the preceding Hassuna and Samarra periods: einkorn, emmer and hexaploid wheat, two-row hulled and six-row naked and hulled barley, lentils, bitter vetch, chickpeas and flax. The distribution of Halaf settlements lay within the area of dry farming so that most of the agriculture was probably carried out without the aid of large-scale irrigation. Domestic animals included the typical five species—sheep, goats, cattle, pigs and dogs—but also wild animals were hunted.

During the Halaf period people abandoned the rectangular many-roomed houses in favor of a return to round huts, called *tholoi*. These varied in size from about 3 to 7 meters in diameter and are believed to have housed families of one set of parents and their children. The entrance was through a gap in the outer wall, but the design varied. Often a rectangular annex was added to the circular structure. At Arpachiyeh, round buildings with long annexes formed keyhole-shaped structures almost 20 meters long with stone walls over 1.5 meters thick. Originally the Arpachiyeh buildings were believed to be special and used for some religious ritual. However, excavations at Yarim Tepe II have suggested that most of the *tholoi* were used as domestic dwellings, as the rectangular chambers were entered from the circular room and did not serve as an entrance passageway as in an igloo. The *tholoi* were made of mud, mud-brick or stone and possibly had a domed roof. However,

those at Yarim Tepe II had walls that were only 25 centimeters thick and may have been roofed using timber beams.

Tholoi have been found throughout the range of the Halaf culture, from the upper Euphrates near Carchemish to the Hamrin basin on the Iraq–Iran border. As well as having circular dwelling houses, however, the earliest and latest Halaf levels at Arpachiyeh included rectangular architecture. One such building at the latest level had been burned, with its contents left *in situ*. On the floor were numerous pottery vessels, many of them beautifully decorated. There were also stone vessels, jewelry, figurines and amulets as well as thousands of flint and obsidian tools. Much of the pottery and jewelry lay beside the walls, on top of charred wood that had probably been shelves. The building was at first thought to be a potter's workshop, but that did not explain the presence of all the precious materials. It might have been a storeroom for the community's wealth or the treasury of a local chief. In any event, there was a remarkable concentration of wealth in this one building. Yarim Tepe also had some rectangular buildings, some of which were storerooms or houses while others, which had no distinctive plan and contained no domestic debris, had possibly been public buildings.

Little is known about burial customs in the Halaf period. In graves at Yarim Tepe I the burial chamber was off the side of a vertical entrance shaft. Methods of disposing of the dead within the settlement included simple inhumation as well as cremation. There were a few instances, both at

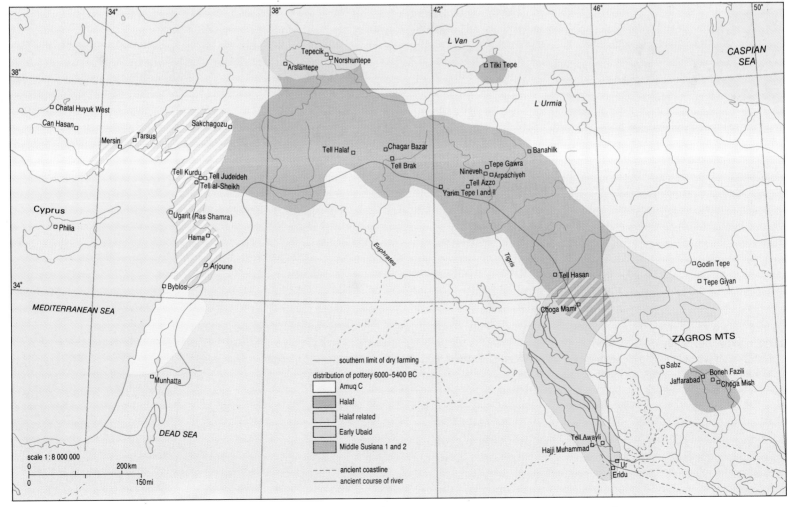

southern limit of dry farming

distribution of pottery 6000–5400 BC

Amuq C

Halaf

Halaf related

Early Ubaid

Middle Susiana 1 and 2

---- ancient coastline

—— ancient course of river

scale 1 : 8 000 000

0   200km

0   150mi

Left and below In the lakes and marshes of southern Iraq live the *Madan* or Marsh Arabs. Their way of life is not based on cereal cultivation but on fishing, herding water buffalo and collecting reeds for making matting. Although the positions of the lakes have shifted over the years, and in the early Islamic period (7th century AD) reached as far north as Nippur, it is likely that there were always marsh dwellers who supported themselves by fishing. (The water buffalo were probably introduced from the east in the 3rd millennium BC.) The canoes in use today are almost identical to models found in the Royal Cemetery at Ur, and reed boats like those depicted on the Assyrian reliefs (c. 700 BC) are still used in the marshes. Reed matting is used in the roofs of traditional mud-brick houses, but reeds are also typical of the buildings of the marshes. Thick pillars of bundles of reeds form the supports for houses made entirely of reeds, very similar to those depicted on cylinder seals and on stone reliefs of the Uruk period more than 5,000 years ago.

Yarim Tepe and at Arpachiyeh, of the separate disposal of the skulls, another trait which, like the round houses, is reminiscent of earlier periods.

The most striking feature of the Halaf culture was its exquisitely painted pottery fired in two-chamber kilns. The clay used was very fine and often salmon pink in color. The earlier pots had simple designs painted on the outside in red or black. The later designs featured elaborate geometric patterns in red and black, overpainted with white, that filled the insides of large shallow bowls. Some painted vessels were made in the shapes of humans or animals. An analysis of the clay of some of the pottery from Halaf sites has shown that pottery vessels were widely traded. Vessels that were probably made at Arpachiyeh have appeared at Tell Brak and Tell Halaf on the Habur, while some from the Habur region have been found to the west on the Euphrates.

Despite changes in the styles of Halaf pottery over time and local differences in style, there is a general uniformity about the culture. Whether, however, the Halaf people formed a separate ethnic group who settled in the dry-farming plains is unclear, as indeed are the boundaries of the Halaf region. The distribution of Halaf sites approached some of the obsidian sources in eastern Anatolia and the copper mines of southeast Turkey.

However, very little metal has been found on Halaf sites and so it is unlikely that copper played an important role in their economy. Thus the view that trade was a major source of Halaf power and influence is probably mistaken.

By the middle of the sixth millennium the Halaf culture had expanded to the southeast where it came into contact with the Ubaid culture. After a transitional phase that combined elements of both, the Ubaid culture became dominant.

The Ubaid period

In the fertile plains built up by silt from the Tigris and Euphrates rivers, the earliest known Ubaid settlements date back to about 5900 BC. However, only a few of them have so far been located. The site of Hajji Muhammad had been buried beneath 3 meters of alluvium and was discovered only because, having been cut by a branch of the Euphrates, it was visible at low water in the fall. Some other early sites have been found beneath the remains of later ones.

One of the sites belonging to the earliest occupation of southern Mesopotamia is Tell Awayli (written by the French excavators as Tell el-Oueili), which had affinities with the Samarran culture of central Mesopotamia. A large building covering more than 200 square meters had rooms of a similar size and shape to those in the early levels at Tell al-Sawwan. Moreover, it had been built of long molded mud-bricks that contained finger impressions like those from Samarran sites. Another building at Awayli consisted of a foundation made of walls at right angles enclosing small, 60-centimeter squares, above which a floor of reed matting had been placed. This structure is thought to have been a storeroom for grain, keeping it away from the damp ground.

Awayli is the earliest excavated site from lower Mesopotamia, but there are undoubtedly still earlier ones buried beneath the alluvial silt. The well-watered river valleys, despite the damaging and unpredictable flooding of the rivers, supported a rich wildlife and natural vegetation. Today, near the mouth of the rivers, the action of the tides irrigates the palm groves, where the palm's wild ancestors once flourished. In places where the rivers flooded and spread out into marshes and lakes, fish would have been abundant. Like the Marsh Arabs of today the ancient inhabitants probably exported dried fish and mats woven from the marsh reeds. Southern Iraq could always have supported hunter-gatherer and fishing communities, as well as shepherds grazing their flocks on the spring steppe vegetation and moving them closer to the rivers in the hot

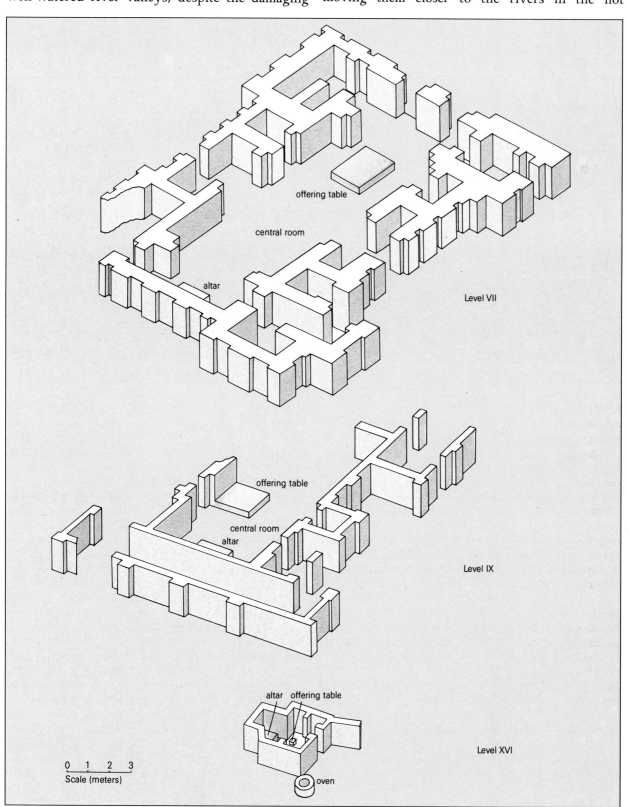

offering table

central room

altar

Level VII

offering table

central room

altar

Level IX

0 1 2 3
Scale (meters)

altar offering table

Level XVI

oven

Left Excavations beside the ziggurat of Ur-Nammu at Eridu have revealed a sequence of superimposed buldings dating to the Ubaid period. The earliest building, belonging to the Ubaid 1 phase, was a small single-roomed structure, which was rebuilt in level XVI with a niche and two platforms. The later levels (XI–VI), from phases 3 and 4 of the Ubaid period, contained buildings that were clearly temples, with elaborate niches and buttresses. They had a tripartite plan, consisting of a long central room with rooms off either side. Inside were offering tables and altars for the statue or emblem of the god, both of which were standard fittings of later Mesopotamian temples.

The extent of the Ubaid culture
In about 5400 BC the Halaf culture, which had dominated northern Mesopotamia, was replaced by the Late Ubaid culture, a development of the Early Ubaid culture of southern Mesopotamia. The Late Ubaid period lasted for more than a thousand years. As in the Halaf period, the peripheral areas show the influence, rather than all the characteristics, of Ubaid culture. However, it is difficult to draw a firm line distinguishing Ubaid from Ubaid-influenced cultures. Ubaid pottery has been found as far down the Gulf as present-day Saudi Arabia, Bahrain and Qatar, and as far east as the United Arab Emirates. Analysis has shown that this pottery was imported from the region of Ur, at the head of the Gulf, but there is otherwise no trace of the presence of Ubaid culture.

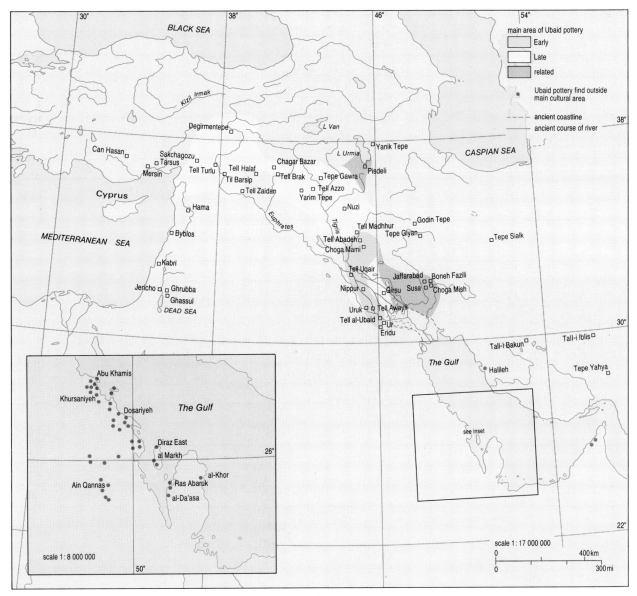

weather. The introduction of canals and irrigation agriculture, however, totally transformed the settlement pattern. .

The pottery from the earliest levels at Tell Awayli also has connections with the later Ubaid pottery. In fact, French archeologists have called the early levels at Awayli Ubaid 0. The dark-painted pale pottery characteristic of the Ubaid period has been found thoughout Mesopotamia. It originated in the south, in the region that later became the country of Sumer, and then spread north and west. The sequence of the whole of the Ubaid period was excavated at Eridu.

Eridu
Eridu now lies in the desert to the south of river Euphrates, but in ancient times a branch of the river flowed past the site. It became an important religious center for the worship of the water god Enki and according to the Babylonian Epic was the first city to be created:

"A reed had not come forth,
A tree had not been created,
A house had not been made,
A city had not been made,
All the lands were sea,
Then Eridu was made."
The Babylonian belief in the antiquity of Eridu was

well founded. The excavation of a deep trench beside the ziggurat, or tower temple, at the site of Eridu revealed some 14 meters of occupation belonging to the Ubaid period. The latest Ubaid level (level VI) was identified as a temple because its plan was similar to those of later Mesopotamian temples. The remains of earlier buildings that were found beneath were divided into four phases, Ubaid 1 to Ubaid 4, each distinguished by different pottery.

The earliest building discovered at Eridu belonging to Ubaid 1 was a small room 2.8 meters square. At the next level was a building that housed a podium in a deep recess and another, with traces of burning on it, in the middle of the room. This building was identified as a temple, as altars and offering tables were standard features of later Mesopotamian temples. The dark painted pottery discovered there, called Eridu ware, has been found on only about ten sites, all in the region around Eridu, Ur and Uruk. However, this does not necessarily mean that it was confined to the area, given the heavy silting in southern Iraq.

The Ubaid 2 phase was marked by the introduction of Hajji Muhammad pottery, in which most of the surface of the vessel was covered in paint, leaving the design in reverse. There were sites at least as far north as the region of Nippur, and possibly

Tell Madhhur

The site of Tell Madhhur was excavated as part of the Hamrin Dam Salvage Project, one of the many projects undertaken to investigate sites threatened by modern development, in this case the construction of a dam across the Diyala river. The site was occupied in the Early Dynastic and Islamic periods, but most of the remains belonged to the Late Ubaid period. In the center of the mound was a large house with walls still standing 2 meters high. The house had been burned and the more valuable items had been removed, but everyday household equipment such as pottery vessels were left in the ruins. The building had a long central room flanked by rows of smaller rooms, and its plan is superficially similar to the temples at Eridu and Tepe Gawra. However, the finds within the building clearly showed that it was a domestic dwelling. After the fire the house had been deliberately leveled, which accounted for its extraordinary state of preservation.

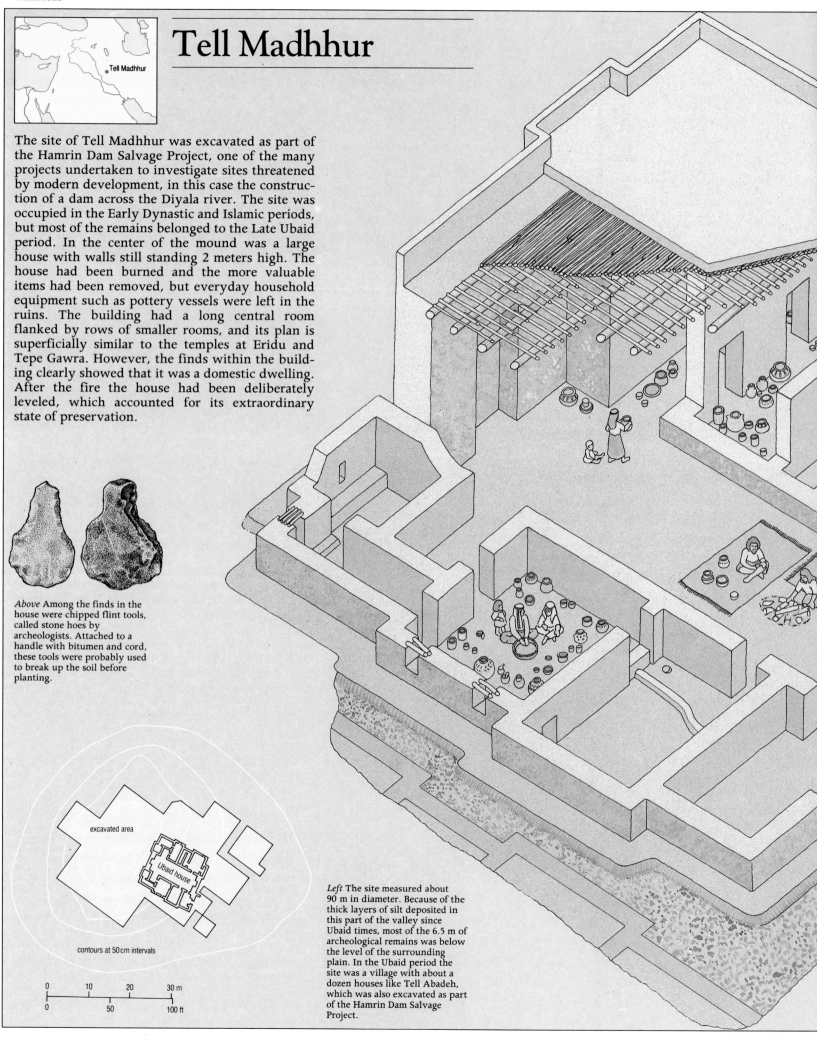

Above Among the finds in the house were chipped flint tools, called stone hoes by archeologists. Attached to a handle with bitumen and cord, these tools were probably used to break up the soil before planting.

excavated area

Ubaid house

contours at 50 cm intervals

0	10	20	30 m

0	50	100 ft

Left The site measured about 90 m in diameter. Because of the thick layers of silt deposited in this part of the valley since Ubaid times, most of the 6.5 m of archeological remains was below the level of the surrounding plain. In the Ubaid period the site was a village with about a dozen houses like Tell Abadeh, which was also excavated as part of the Hamrin Dam Salvage Project.

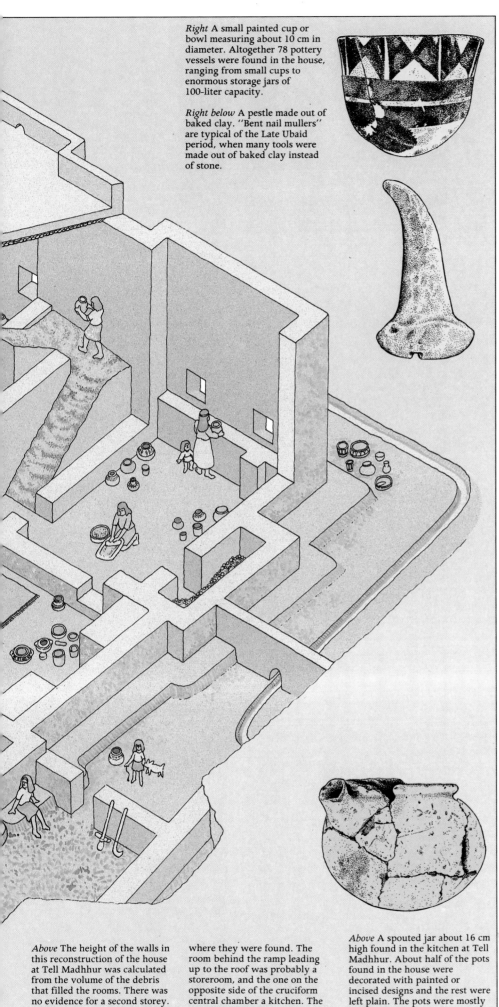

Right A small painted cup or bowl measuring about 10 cm in diameter. Altogether 78 pottery vessels were found in the house, ranging from small cups to enormous storage jars of 100-liter capacity.

Right below A pestle made out of baked clay. "Bent nail mullers" are typical of the Late Ubaid period, when many tools were made out of baked clay instead of stone.

Above The height of the walls in this reconstruction of the house at Tell Madhhur was calculated from the volume of the debris that filled the rooms. There was no evidence for a second storey. In the reconstruction, the objects have been drawn in the rooms where they were found. The room behind the ramp leading up to the roof was probably a storeroom, and the one on the opposite side of the cruciform central chamber a kitchen. The size of the dwelling suggests that it housed an extended family.

Above A spouted jar about 16 cm high found in the kitchen at Tell Madhhur. About half of the pots found in the house were decorated with painted or incised designs and the rest were left plain. The pots were mostly handmade but some show signs of being finished on a wheel.

as far as the Hamrin basin. Hajji Muhammad-style pottery also continued into the Ubaid 3 phase, so its presence is no guarantee of an Ubaid 2 site. Contemporary sites in the lowlands of Iran to the east had pottery similar to the Hajji Muhammad style, which was perhaps due to the influence, dating from the end of the Samarran period, that the more advanced cultures of the west exerted on the villages of the east.

The Ubaid 3 and 4 phases introduced pottery decorated in a new, simple style of painting. In northern Mesopotamia it replaced the Halaf pottery. In the mountains to the east, pottery was similar to the Ubaid style and in Khuzistan the Middle Susiana pottery belonged to the same tradition. Farther south, Ubaid pottery (from Ubaid 3 and later) has been found on some forty sites in eastern Saudi Arabia, two in Bahrain, five in Qatar and even on two as far away as the United Arab Emirates. These were small sites where people lived mainly by fishing and gathering. An analysis of the clays used in the pottery found there showed them to be similar to those in the region of Ur and Eridu, so it is likely that the vessels were imported.

Ubaid temples

The temples at Eridu of the Ubaid 4 period stood on platforms about a meter high. Over the centuries, these platforms grew until they turned into the ziggurats, of which the Tower of Babel is the most famous example.

At the southwest end of the central room of the temple was an altar, while at the northeast end was a freestanding podium on which, at the latest two temples at Eridu, ashes and fishbones were found. These may have been the remains of offerings, as Eridu was the home of the water god Enki. Exactly what these ceremonies involved is not known. Very likely, prayers of some form were said, accompanied by singing and music. It has been suggested that Ubaid temples were used for ceremonial feasting by the elders of the community, but there is little evidence to support this. Eridu was not the only site where religious buildings are in evidence. Uruk, in the Late Ubaid period, had a similar temple and at Tepe Gawra, in the north of Iraq, the inhabitants built a complex of three temples.

Tepe Gawra had been occupied since Halaf times. Six levels belonging to the Ubaid period have been uncovered, each containing buildings that were at first identified as temples, but were probably ordinary village houses. However, in level XIII, the use of the site changed and a carefully planned temple complex was built. Three temple buildings fitted closely together and were all used at the same time, which suggests that the inhabitants worshiped a pantheon of gods. A well in the Northern Temple contained a large collection of impressions of stamp seals on clay bullae, which probably represented ownership or some commercial transaction, and more generally the growth of bureaucracy. In the level above, Tepe Gawra reverted to domestic housing, suggesting that the temple building had been the mark of a foreign power imposing a tyranny of alien beliefs on the local inhabitants. However, this is perhaps reading too much into the evidence.

Ubaid houses

The Ubaid temples at Eridu, Uruk and Gawra all had a similar plan. The layout consisted of a long central hall, with side rooms and with buttressed and recessed facades. A central room flanked by two rows of rooms is called a tripartite plan, and this was typical of temples of later periods. Houses at a number of sites in northern Mesopotamia in the Ubaid 3 and 4 periods also often had a tripartite plan. The layout of houses in the earlier Ubaid periods is not known.

A well-preserved tripartite building dating to the Ubaid 4 period was found at Tell Madhhur in the east of Iraq during the Hamrin Dam Salvage Project. It had caught fire and the ruins had been filled, leaving the walls still standing, in places to a height of 2 meters. Some of the doors and windows were also still intact. The rooms contained grindstones, mullers made out of baked clay for grinding, stone hoes, spindle whorls and numerous pottery vessels for storage, cooking, eating and drinking—indeed, all the equipment needed for everyday life.

More elaborate tripartite houses, from the Ubaid 3 period, have been excavated at Tell Abadeh and Kheit Qasim. Like the house at Madhhur the central rooms were cruciform, not rectangular, but there were also two smaller cruciform rooms on either side of the central room. At Abadeh, eight or nine tripartite houses were arranged fairly haphazardly in the settlement. One of these may have been the residence of the headman of the village and was larger than the rest. It had three parallel tripartite units and a buttressed facade, and was partly protected by a surrounding wall. Another building, which served as a communal storehouse for the village, had a different kind of layout. Tripartite Ubaid buildings are also known from Tepe Gawra and Telul al-Thalathat in northern Iraq. More recently, they have been found at Degirmentepe, a site in southern Turkey, which has Ubaid-related pottery.

Ubaid houses were quite large, occupying about 200 square meters, and probably accommodated an extended family of around twenty people. The tripartite plan (or the triple tripartite plan of Abadeh and Kheit Qasim) must have, in some way, reflected the social structure of the time. It has been suggested that one side of the house was for the men and the other for the women and that they met in the central area, but this is conjecture.

Graves and figurines

At Eridu a cemetery belonging to the same period as the latest temples was found to contain almost two hundred graves. They were dug into the ground and lined and covered with mud-bricks. The bodies had been laid out on their backs with their heads to the northwest. In some cases, a single grave contained two skeletons, believed to be those of a husband and wife. Skeletons of dogs were also found in two of the graves. As well as personal jewelry, a jar, cup and dish had often been placed at the foot of the grave, and sometimes also fish and animal bones, which might indicate some belief in an afterlife.

Near the shoulder of one female skeleton was a terracotta male statuette with a lizard-like head. Other similar figurines, but normally of females,

Left Female figurine of baked clay from Ur dating to the end of the Ubaid period. The heads of the Ubaid figurines were stylized like some of those from Choga Mami and look reptilian. For this reason they are often called lizard-headed, but it is probable that this stylization was intended to represent a human being, not a composite being with a human body and an animal head as in the later Egyptian gods. Stuck on the shoulders of the figure, which stands about 15 cm high, are pellets which may represent decorative scarring. Other figurines have painted decoration, perhaps indicating tattooing.

have been found at Eridu and Ur. They were developments of the Samarra type found at sites such as Choga Mami and Songor A. The quantity and quality of the objects buried varied little between graves, suggesting that there was no great difference in the social status or wealth of those interred. However, it is possible that the ruling elite were buried in a different place, as were infants, who are known from other sites to have been buried in pottery vessels under the floors of the houses.

The end of the Ubaid

Painted Ubaid pottery gradually disappeared, replaced by gray and red burnished pottery. Generally, this signaled the end of Ubaid and the beginning of the Uruk period, but the date of this transition is uncertain. From radiocarbon evidence it probably happened around 4300 BC. The Ubaid culture had lasted for some 1,500 years, exerting its influence from the Mediterranean to the Gulf and even onto the Iranian plateau. Inevitably, a culture that lasted so long and spread so wide was not uniform but exhibited different styles both regionally and across time. Although it is difficult to identify a pottery style with a people, other attributes of the material culture such as the use of tools of baked clay or the distinctive tripartite architecture of the Ubaid period suggest that there was, indeed, a shared cultural tradition.

PART TWO
CITIES

THE URBAN EXPLOSION (4000-3000 BC)

The origin of cities

In the fourth millennium BC remarkable changes took place in southern Mesopotamia, exceeding any expectations that might have been raised by the achievements of the Ubaid period. These innovations, which occurred in the Uruk and Jemdet Nasr periods, constituted what has been called the urban revolution. Like the onset of agriculture, urbanization was a crucial step in human progress. Most obviously, it involved the development of cities and the transition toward a society in which large numbers of people lived in small areas, many of whom did not take part in subsistence farming.

According to the archeologist Gordon Childe (1892–1957), however, this was only one of the characteristics that marked the urban revolution. It also involved the substitution of a society organized politically on territorial principles for one based on ties of kinship. Moreover, this society was divided by class and ruled by a religious, military and political elite, who accumulated wealth through the imposition of tribute and taxes, and erected monumental public buildings. A further feature of urban development was the emergence of full-time professional craftsmen, which, in turn, assisted the growth of long-distance trade. The invention of writing, the beginning of the exact and theoretical sciences and the appearance of representational art were also an integral part of the urban revolution. Indeed, all of these features were present to varying degrees in the towns of the later fourth millennium in southern Mesopotamia.

Clearly, some of the changes that took place depended on others. For example, the erection of public buildings affirmed the existence of a society in which there was a central authority with sufficient resources to carry out the work. Arguably, the basis of the urban revolution was not so much the formation of cities but a change in the nature of society that encouraged larger political and economic groupings of the population. For this reason some archeologists refer to "state formation" rather than to the "growth of cities". This viewpoint emphasizes the interdependence of the cities and the villages, which provided the economic basis for the cities' survival.

Settlements of southern Mesopotamia

The importance of southern Mesopotamia in the development of urban life is generally acknowledged, though some earlier settlements outside Mesopotamia such as Jericho and Chatal Huyuk also had some of the characteristics of cities. The crucial transition from village to city took place in the Early and Middle Uruk periods which, according to radiocarbon dating, probably lasted between 700 and 1,000 years (about 4300–3450 BC). Unfortunately, this period is poorly documented by archeological excavations. Some information can be obtained from archeological surveys, in which sites occupied at a particular period are identified

by the pottery fragments on the surface of the site and the pattern of settlement can be reconstructed. However, problems have arisen in interpreting survey results. For instance, some sites such as Hajji Muhammad lie buried under the alluvial silt, and on sites occupied over a long time the earlier periods are often underrepresented by the pottery sherds found on the surface.

On other sites the later levels are missing. At Choga Mami, for instance, the only evidence of a Halaf-period occupation was a well shaft containing Halaf pottery. Furthermore, many sherds found on the surface of a site cannot be dated reliably, as knowledge of the pottery sequence is still patchy. Some periods are more recognizable by their potsherds than others. Late Uruk sites, with their numerous beveled-rim bowls, have been easy to identify, but sites belonging to the following Jemdet Nasr period are harder to recognize. Sites belonging to a single period are often represented on maps as if they were in use at the same time, when, in reality, this need not have been so. This has presented problems in identifying the smaller settlements, which might have moved more often than the larger towns and cities. Despite these

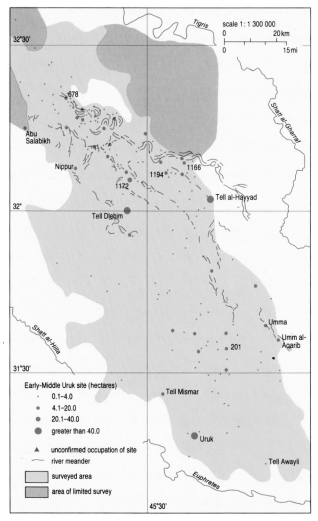

Early urban settlement patterns in southern Mesopotamia
The region to the north and east of Nippur, where there are traces of the meanders left by ancient branches of the rivers flowing through the alluvial plain, was densely settled in the Early to Middle Uruk period at the beginning of the 4th millennium BC. In the Late Uruk period many of these northern sites were abandoned and new settlements were established further south in the neighborhood of Uruk. The city of Uruk itself more than doubled in area. This shift of population from the north to the south continued in the Jemdet Nasr period at the end of the 4th millennium BC.

These maps are based on evidence from an archeological surface survey by the American Robert Adams. He visited all the archeological sites in the area and collected broken pieces of pottery, from which he could recognize the periods when the site was occupied. The distribution of the potsherds suggested the surface area of a given site at a particular period. In this way, Adams has been able to map the size and distribution of sites from the Ubaid period to the present day, showing how the settlement pattern has changed over the millennia.

difficulties it has been possible to build up a general picture of changes in settlement pattern over time. During the Late Ubaid period the surveyed sites were small (very few sites occupied as much as 10 hectares) and fairly evenly distributed. Large parts of the floodplain apparently had no permanent settlements, though they might have been used by nomadic herders or hunters. Possibly, some of the larger Ubaid sites served as focuses for their surrounding areas, acting as market centers, places of pilgrimage, and so on.

The Uruk period

In the Early and Middle Uruk periods there was a vast increase in the number and size of sites. The northern part of the region near Nippur, where meanders of an old river course can still be seen, was particularly well populated. This ancient course was about the same size as the modern Euphrates. It appears that in Early and Middle Uruk times the Tigris and the Euphrates joined farther upstream and then flowed in a number of channels through the alluvial plain. The site of Uruk covered an area of some 70 hectares, while the north had two sites that occupied 50 hectares as well as two 30-hectare sites. Whether this distribution pattern represents the immigration of people from outside or the natural growth of the local population during the period is uncertain.

In the Late Uruk period the pattern changed. Fewer sites were occupied in the north while the number of sites in the south rose. This development might have been due to a change in the river courses between the Middle and Late Uruk periods, forcing the inhabitants of the northern region to migrate. The total area occupied in the Late Uruk period was only slightly larger than that in the earlier period. However, in the earlier period 60 percent of the area was in the region of Nippur, while in the Late Uruk period 60 percent was around Uruk. Uruk grew to be almost twice as big as any other site, occupying about 100 hectares.

In the Jemdet Nasr and Early Dynastic I periods that followed, the same trends continued. By the Early Dynastic I period, the Uruk region had expanded to 850 hectares—more than double the total area occupied in the Late Uruk period—of which the site of Uruk itself accounted for almost half. At the same time, other large centers developed and the number of small villages decreased sharply. In the Early Dynastic period the settlements were arranged in lines like beads on a string, superseding the earlier, more random arrangement. The pattern might have been due in part to the increasing use of long-distance canals.

On the basis of estimates of population, and of land yields, it has been calculated that in the Uruk period the area of agricultural land needed to provide food for the people of Uruk was about 6 kilometers in radius. The farmers cultivating the land might have lived in Uruk itself and then walked for an hour to the fields, as farmers in the Near East do today. In the Jemdet Nasr period, the area needed was about 16 kilometers in radius. By then, and almost certainly before, much of the produce consumed in Uruk came from outside,

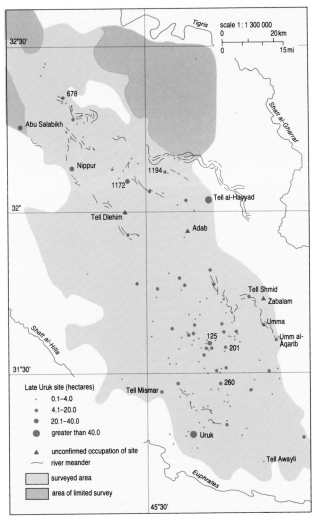

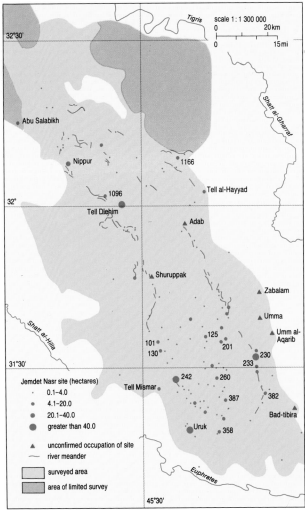

Uruk

Below The ziggurat of the temple of Inanna was built by Ur-Nammu (2112–2095 BC). It originally had a triple staircase and was about 55 m wide. The surviving remains are made of mud-bricks and the layers of reeds and matting between the courses of brickwork can still be seen.

The ancient site of Uruk (now known as Warka) was occupied for 5,000 years from early in the Ubaid period until the 3rd century AD. In the fourth millennium BC Uruk was the most important city in Mesopotamia and included two major religious centers: Kullaba, where there was a temple of An, the god of the sky, and Eanna, where the goddess Inanna (later known as Ishtar) was worshiped. The earliest evidence for writing was also discovered at Eanna. In the Early Dynastic I period the city of Uruk covered an area of 400 hectares and was surrounded by a city wall, which according to later accounts was built by Gilgamesh, Uruk's legendary king. Uruk remained an important religious center and its shrines were embellished by many of the later rulers of Mesopotamia.

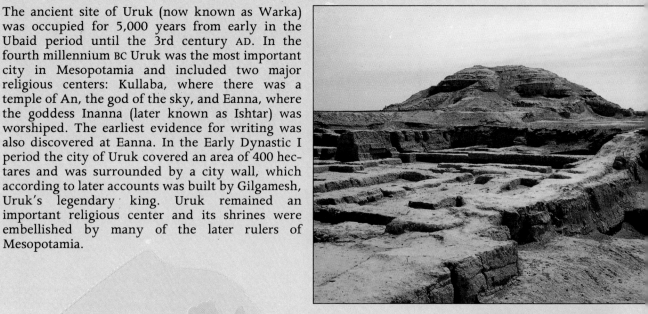

The city wall is about 9.5 km long. According to the Epic of Gilgamesh one-third of the city of Uruk was temples, one-third houses and one-third gardens. The excavations have concentrated on the temple areas, which occupied the center of the city. The temples were extensively rebuilt in the Seleucid and Parthian periods (312 BC–AD 224), including the construction of an *akitu* temple (for the celebration of the New Year festival) to the northeast of the city walls.

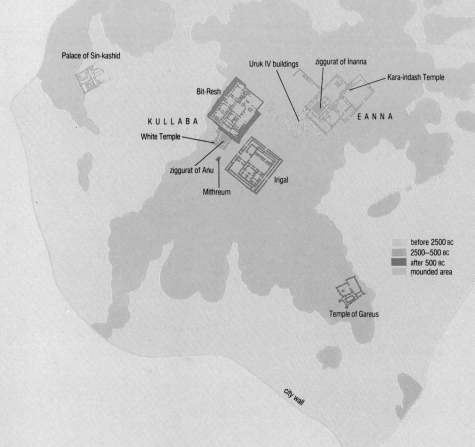

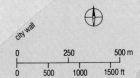

city wall

0	250	500 m
0	500 1000	1500 ft

Akitu Temple

Palace of Sin-kashid

Uruk IV buildings ziggurat of Inanna

Bit-Resh Kara-indash Temple

KULLABA E A N N A

White Temple

ziggurat of Anu

Mithreum Irigal

before 2500 BC
2500–500 BC
after 500 BC
mounded area

Temple of Gareus

Above Life-size limestone mask found in a pit dating to about 3000 BC. It represents a woman and originally had a wig and inlaid eyes and eyebrows. Eyebrows meeting in the middle are still considered a sign of beauty in the Middle East today. The mask was possibly part of a statue of a goddess, perhaps Inanna.

Center right This statuette of a late-4th-millennium ruler of Uruk shows considerable technical skill and, though idealized, it does seem to represent a particular person. Later statues of worshipers intended to be placed in temples hold their hands in front of them. The clenched fists may be an early form of this gesture.

perhaps levied as taxes or tribute, or exchanged for goods that had been made in the city.

The modern name of Uruk is Warka and it was recorded in the Bible as the town of Erech. In the Sumerian period it was called Unu, but here it will be referred to throughout as Uruk. The exceptional character of the site of Uruk revealed by survey has been confirmed by excavations. Two different areas belonging to the early periods have been investigated, one near the Eanna temples of Inanna, the Sumerian version of the goddess Ishtar, goddess of love and of war, and the other about 400 meters to the west, in the area of the temple of An (or Anum), the god of the sky.

Uruk: the Eanna temple complex

Extensive remains of buildings dating to the Late Uruk period have been excavated in the Eanna precinct, but only fragments of the foundations of the original buildings were left, as they had been knocked down and leveled. The main building of the earliest phase (level V) was the Limestone Temple, which was found to continue through two levels. The stone foundations lay on a bed of mud and had originally measured 76 meters long by 30 meters wide. Whether it had, in fact, been a temple is uncertain, but its intricate niching and buttressing, the regular tripartite plan, and its location in a sacred area were strong evidence for supposing that it was.

In the following phase (level IVb), two separate complexes were enclosed by walls, the larger one to the southeast and a smaller one to the northwest. In the southeast area, buildings were approached by a double staircase some 1.7 meters high with two rows of columns (each 2.6 meters wide) at the top. The walls and columns were built of small, square-sectioned bricks (called *riemchen* bricks by the German archeologists who excavated the site), which are characteristic of Late Uruk architecture. They were then coated with a thick layer of mud-plaster in which thousands of small baked clay cones with red, white and black heads were set in a variety of designs—zigzags, lozenges, triangles and diagonal bands—like those found on woven matting. This building is called the Mosaic Court or Pillar Temple, though it was probably not a temple but a monumental entrance to the rest of the sacred precinct. Beyond this were several rectangular tripartite buildings, some with central rooms in a cross-shape and some with elaborate niches and buttresses. These have been identified as temples. The three to the northwest were very similar to houses of the same period that have been found in Syria, and it is possible that they were the residences not of the gods but of their officials.

To the southwest was the Square Building, which had a courtyard with four large rectangular halls each set along one side. The courtyard walls and the outer facade had very elaborate niched brickwork. A square room with a large sunken basin had stood in the north corner. This was not a typical Mesopotamian temple, and its function was unclear, but it clearly had been a major ceremonial public building.

At the west end of the Eanna complex was a separate area that contained the Stone Cone Mosaic Temple. Surrounded by a wall with buttresses on both sides, the temple had been decorated with

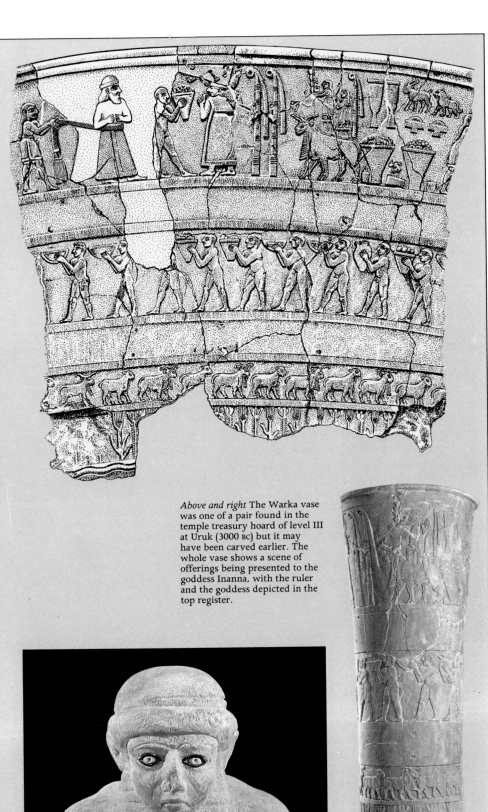

Above and right The Warka vase was one of a pair found in the temple treasury hoard of level III at Uruk (3000 BC) but it may have been carved earlier. The whole vase shows a scene of offerings being presented to the goddess Inanna, with the ruler and the goddess depicted in the top register.

cone mosaics made of red, black and white stone set in gypsum. Only the limestone foundations of the temple, which appeared to follow the plan of the other temples, have survived, but archeologists have found traces of five other buildings which, they believe, may have been earlier versions of this temple.

In the next phase of the Eanna complex (level IVa), the plan of the area changed. The more recent buildings overlaid, or had cut into, the earlier foundations. These changes had taken place over a considerable time, so that some of the buildings attributed to an earlier phase were standing at the same time as some of the later buildings. In both levels the remains were very fragmentry, but a reconstructed plan showed that, once again, the area had been divided into two. The largest building, Temple D, had been built on a terrace by filling in the courtyard and pillared entrance of the earlier phase. The temple measured about 80 by 50 meters and, if the central cruciform hall was roofed (which is probable, as it had the same plan as other temples), the beams would have been more than 10 meters long. These might have been brought overland to the Euphrates from the Amanus mountains and then floated downstream. In the later Sumerian legends there are stories about Gilgamesh and others going on expeditions to the Cedar Mountain and these may have already started in the Uruk period.

To the northwest of this temple was the better preserved, Temple C. (In fact, its clear tripartite plan and cruciform hall served as a basis for reconstructing the plans of other temples.) It measured 54 by 22 meters. A second, smaller tripartite unit at the northwest end was the same size as the largest of the Ubaid temples at Eridu, and of many Late Uruk temples. Contemporary with these two temples were the Pillared Hall, once again with mosaic decoration made out of stone cones, and a squarish area, the Great Court, believed to have been a sunken plaza, with benches round it, measuring almost 50 meters square.

In the separate northwest complex the *Riemchengebäude* (buildings of *riemchen* bricks) replaced the earlier Stone Cone Mosaic Temple. The *Riemchengebäude* consisted of an inner room surrounded by a corridor, with a second room along the southeast side. The corridor surrounding the central room had been filled with stacked pottery flasks and the northeast corridor contained fragments of a statue of a deity about the size of a man. In the middle room there were large quantities of animal bones and the whole area had been burned and filled in while the fire was burning or still smoldering. The remains suggested that some ritual had taken place there. It might, for instance, have been the burial place of the ruler or high priest, but this is uncertain.

Above the later phase of the Eanna complex were signs of extensive burning, which might have been the result of burned offerings. The remains of level III, which belonged to the Jemdet Nasr period, were fragmentary. The principal feature was a raised terrace about 2 meters high, which had remained in use in the following Early Dynastic period. One room contained an important hoard of valuable objects, some of which will be described later.

Left and above A painting of a reconstructed column from the entrance to level IVb in the Eanna precinct at Uruk. The geometric mosaic decoration is composed of the heads of hundreds of painted baked clay cones each about 10 cm long. This type of decoration using either clay cones or colored stone cones stuck into plaster is typical of the Late Uruk period.

Uruk: the Anu temple

About 500 meters west of Eanna was the Anu temple area. Here, a series of temples set on terraces, rather similar to those at Eridu, have been excavated, the earliest dating back to the Ubaid period and the latest probably to the Jemdet Nasr period. The best-preserved among them was the White Temple, so-called because its walls were coated with a thin gypsum plaster. Measuring 17.5 by 22.3 meters (almost the same size as the end part of Temple C at Eanna), it also had a tripartite plan. The walls were niched and the centers of the buttresses were grooved, where poles had originally been set. At the east corner, space had been left in the wall in the lowest course, where the bodies of a leopard and possibly a young lion had been placed. This might have been an early example of a foundation deposit, which in later periods normally included inscriptions identifying the temple and its builder.

The White Temple had an offering table and an altar, the typical furnishings of a Mesopotamian temple, though in this case, the altar had been an afterthought, as it blocked up a doorway in the end wall. The temple had been set on a high platform with a sloping face. Reaching a height of some 13 meters, the platform was significantly higher than those of the Ubaid temples at Eridu. The White Temple was an early predecessor of the ziggurat, which in the following three millennia dominated the skyline of Mesopotamian cities.

Other southern Uruk sites

Elsewhere in southern Mesopotamia there were extensive traces of the Late Uruk period, but those were mostly buried deep beneath the remains of later periods. At the few sites where buildings have been found, the architecture, as at Uruk, was mostly religious. At Eridu the temple platform containing the long sequence of temples of the Ubaid period had been enlarged and decorated with columns. At Tell Uqair, farther north, a temple of the

Above right The inside walls of the Late Uruk period temple at Tell Uqair were decorated with paintings: some geometric with patterns similar to those used in cone mosaic, others of animals. This one shows a spotted animal that has been identified as a leopard of a type still found in the mountains of Iran. Height about 90 cm.

Right Plan of the earlier (IVb) and later (IVa) levels in the Eanna precinct at Uruk in the Late Uruk period. The size, variety and complexity of the architecture shows that the buildings have been carefully designed and intended both for religious ceremonies and to impress the populace with the wealth and power of those who built them.

Late Uruk period stood on a high platform approached by steps. The edge of the platform, which was in two stages, had been decorated with mosaic cones. The upper stage was covered with bitumen and the walls of the temple had been built directly on this. Only half of the temple building was preserved but this showed that it had had a tripartite plan with an altar and offering table, like the White Temple at Uruk. The walls were covered with paintings, which—exceptionally—were preserved because the building had been filled up with mud-bricks as a platform for some later construction. The paintings consisted of geometric and pictorial designs. The altar decoration included the figures of a leopard, a bull and possibly a lion—reminiscent of the burial of a leopard and lion in the lowest course of the White Temple.

Colonies and trade

In the Late Uruk period influence from southern Mesopotamia reached as far as the Mediterranean and the Iranian plateau. Pottery and other objects of southern Mesopotamian styles have been found in regions far away from their place of origin, prompting speculation about how they came there. Some settlements in southwest Iran and in northern Mesopotamia along the Euphrates and Tigris rivers shared so many cultural traits that they probably had had direct contact with lowland Mesopotamia and might even have been colonies. In other cases, links could have arisen through trade or through the local population imitating the

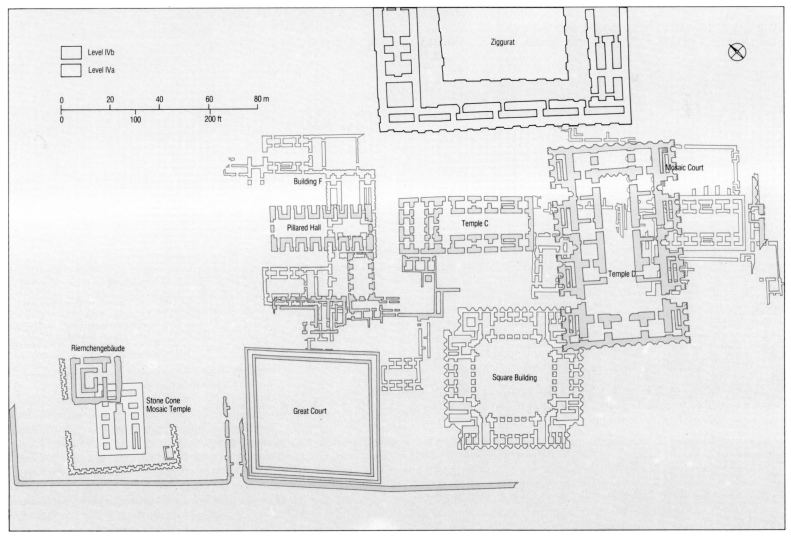

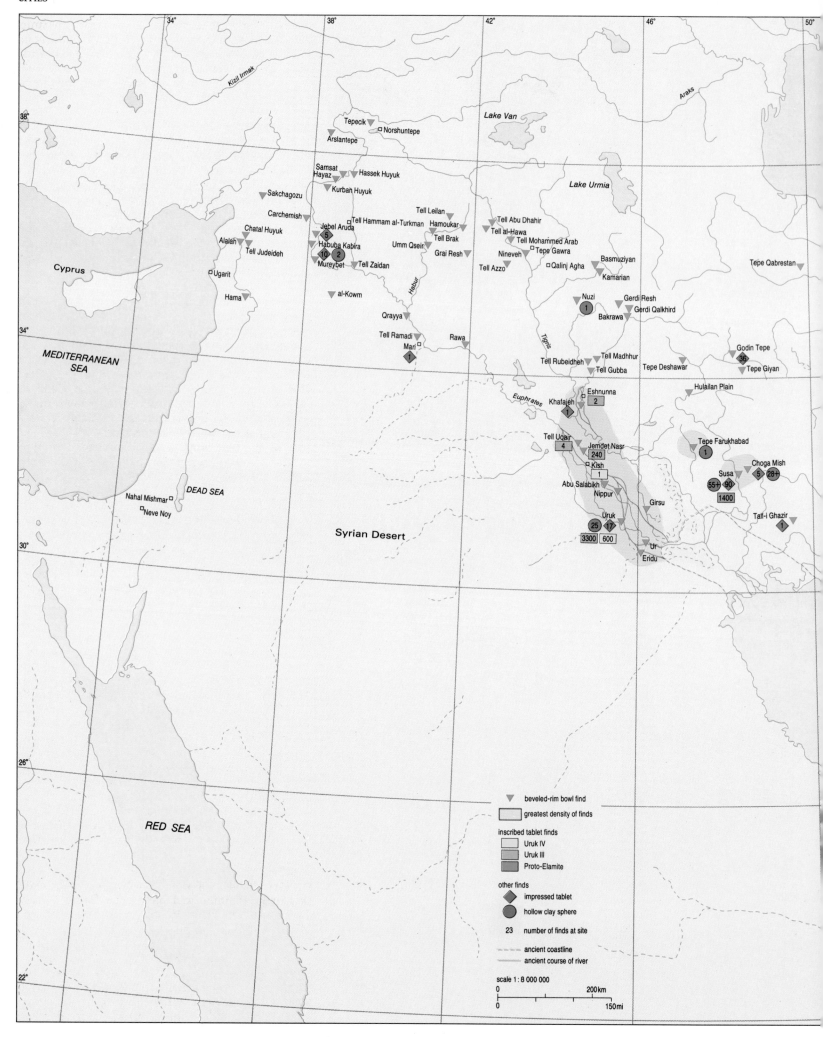

Tepecik □ Norshuntepe

Arslantepe

Samsat
Hayaz   Hassek Huyuk

Sakchagozu   Kurban Huyuk

Carchemish   Tell Leilan

Chatal Huyuk   Jebel Aruda   Tell Hammam al-Turkman   Hamoukar   Tell Abu Dhahir

Alalah   Habuba Kabira   Tell al-Hawa

Tell Judeideh   10   2   Umm Qseir   Tell Brak   Tell Mohammed Arab

Mureybet   Tell Zaidan   Grai Resh   Tepe Gawra

Ugarit   Nineveh   Qalinj Agha   Basmuziyan

Hama   al-Kowm   Tell Azzo   Kamarian

Qrayya   Nuzi   Gerdi Resh

Tell Ramadi   1   Bakrawa   Gerdi Qalkhird

Rawa

Mari   1

Tell Rubeideh   Tell Madhhur   Tepe Deshawar

Tell Gubba

Euphrates   Tepe Qabrestan

Khafajeh   Eshnunna
1   2

Tell Uqair   Tepe Farukhabad
4   1

Jemdet Nasr
240

Kish
1

Abu Salabikh   Choga Mish
5   28+

Nippur   Susa
55+   90

Girsu   1400

Uruk
25   17
3300   600   Tall-i Ghazir
1

Ur

Eridu

Godin Tepe
36

Tepe Giyan

Hulailan Plain

Lake Van

Lake Urmia

Araks

MEDITERRANEAN
SEA

Cyprus

Kizil Irmak

Habur

Tigris

Syrian Desert

DEAD SEA

Nahal Mishmar
Neve Noy

RED SEA

▼   beveled-rim bowl find

     greatest density of finds

inscribed tablet finds
     Uruk IV
     Uruk III
     Proto-Elamite

other finds
◆   impressed tablet

●   hollow clay sphere

23   number of finds at site

- - - -   ancient coastline
———   ancient course of river

scale 1 : 8 000 000
0   200km
0   150mi

64

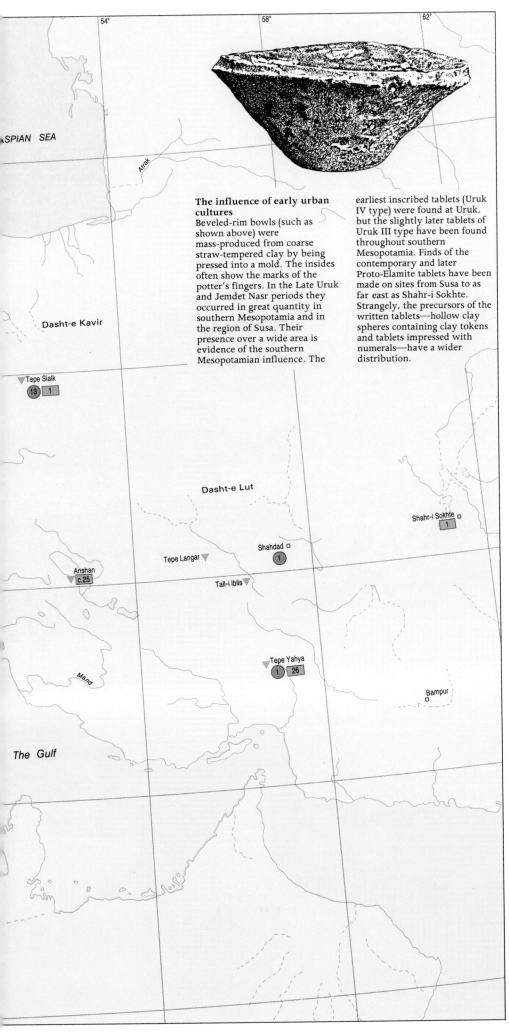

styles of their prosperous neighbors. How much political control the rulers of Uruk exercised is not known, but their reasons for establishing far-flung outposts of Uruk culture might have been related to the control of resources such as timber, metals and precious stones.

Susa and Iran

The alluvial plains region of southwest Iran was called Susiana, after the city of Susa. Susa, founded at the end of the Ubaid period, became the capital of successive kingdoms and was the administrative capital of the Persians in the 4th century BC at the time of Alexander the Great. Susiana's history ran parallel to that of Mesopotamia and in many respects Susiana was an extension of lowland Mesopotamia. In the Late Ubaid period the site of Choga Mish had become a regional center occupying some 15 hectares. Later, in the Susa I (or Susa A) period, corresponding to the earlier part of the Uruk period, the site of Susa grew to the same size.

Excavations at Susa have uncovered the remains of a large mud-brick platform measuring at least 80 by 65 meters and more than 10 meters high, decorated with pottery cylinders stuck into the facade. The top of the platform was badly eroded, but some storage rooms containing jars and carbonized grain remained, as well as parts of buildings that might have belonged to a temple complex. At the base of the platform was a large cemetery which contained more than a thousand graves of adults. Some had been buried whole, but others had been exposed and the bones placed in painted ceramic vessels. Most of the graves also contained pottery, including some of the most elegant painted pottery ever produced. Others held copper objects, flat axes, large and small chisels, pins and pierced disks that possibly served as mirrors.

Very probably, Susa was founded as a religious center. The large platform might have supported an imposing temple as well as storehouses for tithes and would have been visible from afar, above the flat countryside. As with other places of pilgrimage, the people of the time would have wanted to be buried there. The copper objects in the graves had possibly belonged to the priests who ruled the sanctuary. Throughout the lowland zone similar religious centers acted as focal points for the surrounding regions and concentrated wealth and power through gifts to the temples or through tax. This aspect of urbanization, which was apparent in the fifth millennium BC at Choga Mish, Eridu, Uruk, Nippur and Tell Uqair, became increasingly important in the fourth millennium.

The subsequent period at Susa (Susa II) showed the clear influence of the Late Uruk culture of Sumer. The pottery included typical Late Uruk pottery, such as jars with drooping spouts, four-lugged jars, and beveled-rim bowls. The small, crudely made conical beveled-rim bowls were extremely common and have been found in their thousands on sites in southern Mesopotamia. Exactly what the bowls were used for, however, is not known—whether they were ration bowls for the workforce employed by the state, votive bowls for presenting offerings to the temple, bowls used in official feasts, containers for baking bread or given away with some foodstuff such as yoghurt. In any event, at Susa they were not a development

The influence of early urban cultures
Beveled-rim bowls (such as shown above) were mass-produced from coarse straw-tempered clay by being pressed into a mold. The insides often show the marks of the potter's fingers. In the Late Uruk and Jemdet Nasr periods they occurred in great quantity in southern Mesopotamia and in the region of Susa. Their presence over a wide area is evidence of the southern Mesopotamian influence. The earliest inscribed tablets (Uruk IV type) were found at Uruk, but the slightly later tablets of Uruk III type have been found throughout southern Mesopotamia. Finds of the contemporary and later Proto-Elamite tablets have been made on sites from Susa to as far east as Shahr-i Sokhte. Strangely, the precursors of the written tablets—hollow clay spheres containing clay tokens and tablets impressed with numerals—have a wider distribution.

of earlier local styles but had been introduced from the west. Furthermore, sealed hollow clay spheres and impressed tablets (the early means of recording accounts), have also been found in the latest levels of the Susa II period.

At Godin Tepe, a settlement that lay on the main route from Mesopotamia to Iran, there was a small enclave that may have been a merchant colony from Susiana or Sumer. It contained public buildings and was surrounded by a curving wall. It also shared the culture of lowland Mesopotamia, with pottery as well as seal impressions and impressed tablets typical of Susa and Uruk. Uruk influence in the form of beveled-rim bowls has also been found on the Iranian plateau at Tepe Qabrestan, Tepe Yahya and Tepe Sialk, on the edge of the Dasht-i Kavir desert.

Tepe Gawra and northern Mesopotamia

Northern Mesopotamia developed its own local culture (called the Gawra culture) at the end of the Ubaid period. Tepe Gawra, in the north of what is present-day Iraq, again became the site of a village in the levels above the exceptional Ubaid temples in level XIII. After the next level, level XII, which had been destroyed by a huge fire, the rebuilt settlement was dominated by the large Round House, which was believed to have been the fortified residence of the chief. It contained stores of grain and pear-shaped mace-heads, which were

probably some of the earliest weapons used in warfare.

A new style of temple building with a tripartite plan and an overhanging porch continued in the levels above. Around and beneath the temples were numerous graves, which included 80 mud-brick tombs dating from the Gawra period. Some of the tombs contained beads, the most common ornaments, which were worn on the head, neck, hands, wrists, waist, knees or ankles. Several tombs had thousands of beads, and one in particular had more than 25,000. They were made of a variety of stones including turquoise, jadeite, carnelian, lapis lazuli and diorite, white faience, gold, electrum, shell and ivory. The lapis lazuli beads were the earliest examples of the dark-blue semiprecious stone found in Mesopotamia. As the closest source of lapis lazuli was the Badakhshan province in northern Afghanistan, more than 2,000 kilometers away, the presence of 500 lapis lazuli beads in this tomb is evidence of extensive trading links. Gold rosettes and ivory combs made from boars' tusks were also found in the tombs. Perhaps the most interesting object uncovered was a tiny wolf's head made of electrum, a naturally occurring alloy of gold and silver. It was formed from a single piece of metal except for the ears, which were fixed by copper pins, the lower jaw, jointed and held on by an electrum pin, and the teeth, which were of electrum wire. The eye sockets contained bitumen and had, perhaps, been inlaid with colored stones.

After the Gawra period, northern Mesopotamia—like Susiana—came increasingly under the influence of the southern Late Uruk culture. Nineveh, for instance, which produced pottery that was typical of southern Late Uruk, might have been the site of a southern colony, as it lay near an important crossing of the Tigris.

Tell Brak in the Habur plains also showed close connections with the south. The Eye Temple was a southern temple in a northern setting. Its plan included a cruciform central hall and the walls were decorated with stone rosettes and terracotta cone mosaics. The altar had bands of gold, set between bands of colored stone, that had been fixed in position by gold-headed, silver nails. The temple was given its name after the discovery of the thousands of small stone images, which are sometimes called hut symbols and sometimes eye idols, among the ruins. The size of the site in the Late Uruk period was about 110 hectares, as large as Uruk itself.

The upper Euphrates

Excavations of the Tabqa dam area on the Euphrates in Syria uncovered Late Uruk period sites, which seemed to be colonies from southern Mesopotamia. The site of Habuba Kabira, with its religious acropolis Tell Qannas, stretched for more than a kilometer along the west bank of the Euphrates and was defended by a fortification wall. Both the wall bricks and those used for the buildings were the same *riemchen* bricks characteristic of the Uruk and Jemdet Nasr periods in the south.

At Tell Qannas, the plans of the temples and of the houses were similar to those of Uruk and Tell Uqair. Likewise, the pottery included beveled-rim bowls that had been made in a mold, as in Uruk, and other pottery types characteristic of southern

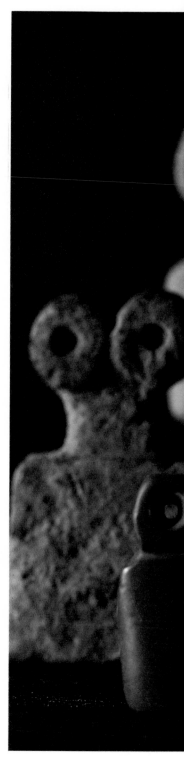

Left A painted pottery beaker dating to about 4000 BC found in the cemetery at Susa. At the top is a row of long-necked birds above a row of long-bodied dogs, perhaps greyhounds. The lower panel shows a bearded goat. The meaning of the symbol between the horns is not known. Height about 25 cm.

Above More than 300 "eye idols" (and thousands of fragments) made of stone or baked clay were found in the 4th-millennium BC temple at Tell Brak. It has been calculated that some 20,000 of these votive symbols measuring between 2 and 11 cm in height were deposited in the temple. Similar objects in smaller numbers have been found on other sites of the period.

Mesopotamia were also common. Tablets impressed with tokens and sealed with cylinder seals have also been found as well as hollow clay balls containing tokens. Very probably, these sites were colonies that had been established by merchants or the government of Sumer.

Late Uruk influence stretched up the Euphrates into Turkey. Cone mosaic has been discovered at Samsat, while Hassek Huyuk, a small fortified site of less than one hectare, included several buildings of typical Late Uruk design, with clay cone mosaic. Further north, at Arslantepe, many typical Late Uruk seal impressions, which probably played a part in the local administration, have been found. Also, beveled-rim bowls have been discovered at Tepecik in the mountains, near the source of the Tigris.

Egypt

The influence of Uruk even reached as far west as Egypt in the Naqada II (or Gerzean) period contemporary wih the Late Uruk and Jemdet Nasr periods. Some pottery types found there, such as ledge-handled jars, derived from the Chalcolithic period of Palestine, but other features, including lugged and spouted jars, were characteristic of Late Uruk pottery. Cylinder seals also first appeared in Egypt at that time. Some were imports from the east, but others had been made locally and used Mesopotamian or Iranian motifs. Also, lapis lazuli from distant Afghanistan has been found in graves there, as in Mesopotamia.

Late Predynastic (before about 2920 BC) art from Egypt also showed some influence from Mesopotamia. In particular, carved ivory knife handles and slate palettes contained Mesopotamian motifs, even though the objects themselves were typically Egyptian. For instance, the "master of animals" on the Gebel el Arak knife handle closely resembles the scene on the Lion Hunt stele from Uruk. Similarly, the elaborately niched mud-brick architecture of early Egypt and the appearance of writing have also been attributed to influence from the east. Naqada II pottery has been found at Habuba Kabira and, very recently, baked clay cones of the kind used in mosaic wall decoration in Late Uruk sites have been discovered at Tell al-Fara'in in the Egyptian delta.

Palestine

During the Uruk period Palestine and Anatolia were largely unaffected by the developments in Mesopotamia. Local cultures based on farming villages thrived wherever the conditions were suitable, and nomadic herdsmen and hunter-gatherers exploited the environments where farming was not possible. Although not urbanized, these cultures were, in some respects, surprisingly advanced. The discovery of a collection of more than four hundred copper objects in the cave of Nahal Mishmar in the Judean hills has transformed our knowledge of early metalworking. Altogether, 240 mace-heads, 138 standards and 10 "crowns" were found there along with eight copper jars and other tools. Similar objects have been uncovered at the Late Chalcolithic settlement and industrial site of Neve Noy, dated to the first half of the fourth millennium BC. It has been suggested that the Nahal Mishmar hoard belonged to a temple treasury, and perhaps came from the small Chalcolithic sanctuary at En-gedi near the Dead Sea.

The Jemdet Nasr period

In southern Mesopotamia the Late Uruk period was followed by the Jemdet Nasr period (about 3100–2900 BC). Uruk remained important but little of its architecture has been preserved. At the site of Jemdet Nasr in Babylonia a large building, believed to have been an administrative building, contained inscribed tablets of the Uruk type as well as elaborate painted pottery. Built of *riemchen* bricks it included a stretch of casemate wall almost 90 meters long with defensive towers set at strategic intervals. A seal impression on a tablet found there bore the symbols of the gods of several towns including Ur, Larsa, Uruk, Zabalam and either Umma or Akshak, suggesting that there might have been a league of city states. The archaic sealings from Ur, which belonged to the slightly later Early Dynastic I period, had similar groupings of city names, but whether these were political or commercial alliances is uncertain.

The painted Jemdet Nasr pottery is found principally in nothern Babylonia, with only occasional finds farther south. However, almost identical pottery has been discovered in tombs of the contemporaneous Hafit culture in Oman at the other end of the Gulf, and an examination of the clay has shown that it probably came from Mesopotamia. Some experts have suggested that the pots might have been brought by Sumerian adventurers who were exploiting the rich Omani copper sources.

Elsewhere in the Jemdet Nasr period the strong

links with Sumer were broken. In Susiana the Late Uruk culture of Susa was replaced by the Proto-Elamite culture, which had closer links with the Iranian plateau. At the same time the city of Anshan (modern Tell Malyan), near Persepolis in Fars, expanded dramatically to occupy 45 hectares. The union of Anshan and Susa formed the basis for the later Elamite state. The rise of the Proto-Elamite culture changed the geography of the Near East. Its influence, seen particularly in seals, extended from the eastern borders of Iran through the Zagros mountains into northern Iraq and continued into the Early Dynastic period.

In northern Mesopotamia some of the southern-influenced settlements were abandoned and others developed their own local independent cultures,

Above right and above Cylinder seal and a drawing of the impression made by it. The scene shows a herd of cattle above with calves and pots in reed huts below. The huts closely resemble those that people still build in the marshes of southern Iraq today. The seal is made of white magnesite and on top is a small figure of a ram, which has been cast out of silver using the lost-wax process. The provenance of the seal is unknown but it probably dates to the Late Uruk period. Height of seal 5.3 cm.

Left This stark, stone head was found beneath the Eye Temple at Tell Brak and probably dates to about 3100 BC. Holes at the top of the headdress and the back of the neck show that it was originally fixed to a wooden backing. The head was probably part of a composite statue, but whether it was of a man or a woman or human or divine is not known. Possibly, it belonged to the cult image of a deity worshiped in the temple. Height 17 cm.

which included traits derived from the Late Uruk culture. In this region urban life seems to have been abandoned and cities became important again only in the middle of the third millennium, again probably as a result of influence from southern Mesopotamia.

Beginnings of a written language

By the Late Uruk period, Uruk was a city. It was a large site, with a concentration of wealth and had monumental public buildings. Uruk was where the earliest known written documents were discovered. The language of these texts is not known and they cannot be "read". However, as the script is largely pictographic (based on recognizable pictures of real objects rather than symbols), they can at least partly be understood.

The early development of the script fell into three stages. In the first, called Uruk IV, signs were drawn with a pointed stylus on clay (or occasionally gypsum plaster) tablets measuring about 5 centimeters across and about half as thick. The script was largely ideographic or logographic, that is, a sign stood for an idea or a word, not a letter or syllable. The numerals can be understood with little difficulty, and some of the signs have been recognized either because they look like the object they represent or because they have been identified with later signs whose meaning is known. Groups of signs were written together in boxes, but appeared to be in no fixed order. Some six hundred tablets belonging to this stage have been found at Uruk and one other at Kish, about 150 kilometers to the northwest.

By the second stage (Uruk III) the signs had become more developed and more abstract, with straighter lines and fewer curves. Also, the arrangement of the signs on the tablets was more complex and the tablets themselves were larger. Once again, most of the texts were economic records. Some were ration lists, recording allocations of goods to different people, while others were records of livestock holdings and the distribution of animals for offering to the gods, in the temples or on festive occasions. Other tablets contained lists of place names, professions and animals. These were early versions of the lists on which the training of scribes was based until the end of the use of cuneiform script.

From the textual variants in these lists, scholars have decided that the language of the Uruk III texts was probably Sumerian, the language spoken in Uruk in the third millennium BC. More than

three thousand tablets have been found at Uruk, 240 from Jemdet Nasr, four from Tell Uqair, and two from Eshnunna. They are believed to date to the Jemdet Nasr period and to have been contemporary with the earliest Proto-Elamite tablets from Iran. These were written in a different script but one that had the same system of number signs and showed a similar level of development.

In the Early Dynastic period (2900–2334 BC) the script became more linear. The lines were formed by pressing an angled instrument on the clay to produce the wedge-shaped marks of the cuneiform script. Few texts have been found belonging to the early part of the Early Dynastic period, but by about the middle of the third millennium BC the cuneiform system of writing had become widespread and was used to record all kinds of textual material—economic and administrative documents, letters, stories, prayers, building inscriptions, and so on.

Whether the elaborate writing system of the early Uruk texts with its large number of signs was the result of a long development or of a rapid breakthrough, perhaps by a single individual, is not known. Already, in earlier periods there had been pointers to suggest that the idea of writing was in the offing. In fact, there were several possible forerunners of the Uruk script. For instance, there were tablets with signs that had been impressed on them rather than written with a stylus. The signs corresponded to the measures of quantity that appeared on the Uruk tablets.

Stamp and cylinder seals for identifying ownership of property, and tokens for recording commodities, were other possible sources. These might have given rise to the hollow clay spheres that contained tokens and were covered with seal impressions. The next stage, recording the contents on the outside, might, in time, have suggested the idea that a tablet impressed with the tokens and bearing seal impressions was as reliable a record as were the clay spheres. The later addition of signs representing things other than numbers could thus have brought about the Uruk script. This scheme seems plausible but doubt remains as to how widely tokens were used to record commodities. Moreover, the impressed tablets and the hollow clay spheres have been found over a greater area and covering a longer period than would have been the case if they had been merely stages toward the texts. Indeed, both impressed tablets and clay spheres apparently had functioned as recording devices at the same time as the more

The Origins of Writing

The earliest known examples of writing are found on clay tablets from Uruk dating to about 3300 BC. Already it was a complete system with more than 700 different signs. There must have been previous stages in the development which are still unknown. The first tablets recorded the transfer of commodities such as grain, beer and livestock or were lists used by scribes learning how to write.

Another system of recording was also practiced at the same time, using small clay tokens of different shapes and sizes—cones, disks, spheres and cylinders and so on. These may have represented different quantities or different commodities, such as grain or sheep. Groups of tokens were placed inside hollow clay spheres which had cylinder seals rolled over them to produce records that could be accessed only by breaking open the sphere. Sometimes tokens were impressed into the surface of the clay spheres or on clay tablets. As the shapes of the signs used in the written script for counting are similar to those of the tokens, it is probable that the written script was based on the token system with the addition of pictographic signs.

The pictographic signs are often simple pictures whose meaning is obvious: the head of a bull stands for cattle, an ear of barley for barley. Sometimes the meaning of the sign was by association: a bowl meant food or bread; a leg meant to stand and to walk. Combinations of signs could express more complex notions, so that a head and a bowl meant to eat. In time the form of the signs was adapted to being written with a rectangular-ended stylus made out of a reed. As a result, all the strokes used were wedge-shaped and hence the script is called cuneiform. In the Early Dynastic period the writing changed from downward to across.

In the developed cuneiform script word signs could stand for their phonetic value (as if in English a picture of a jack could be used for a flag as in Union Jack, the name Jack, or the syllable jac in ejaculate). With the addition of syllable signs to the word signs, the scribes were able to render human speech effectively in their script.

Above Gabled stamp seal and its impression, measuring 4.6 × 3.9 cm and 0.9 cm thick. Seals of this type have been found in northern Mesopotamia and southern Turkey in the 4th millennium BC. From the 6th millennium BC stamp seals were used for marking clay. Their designs probably indicated the owner.

Above Pyramidal stamp seal and its impression: 2.9 × 2.1 cm, height 3.0 cm. Stamp seals have been found from the early Pottery Neolithic period in Anatolia and in Mesopotamia, where patterns of cross-hatched lines were common. The function of these early seals is not known.

Above A hollow clay sphere and tokens from Susa. More than 100 such spheres containing tokens have been found in Elam and Sumer and a few have been discovered in Syria and on the Iranian plateau. One of these clay spheres had clay tokens stuck into the surface while 16 bore marks of either impressed tokens or scratched signs, recording the tokens inside.

Left This clay tablet shows an early form of writing, perhaps earlier than on the tablets from Uruk since the forms of the signs are more naturalistic than those of the Uruk IV tablets. It was not found in an archeological excavation and so its date is uncertain. The signs in the bottom line may be read "en" "nun" and "gal", meaning priest, prince and great, respectively.

Left Impression of a Late Uruk period cylinder seal. Cylinder seals are found earlier than the earliest written tablets but both seem to have been devised for the bureaucracy of the Late Uruk period. The size of the seals (this one is 4 cm high) made it possible to cover large areas with impressions easily. Possibly, seals with different designs were used by different branches of the administration.

Left Table showing the development of the cuneiform script. The later forms of the cuneiform signs appear to be abstract, almost arbitrary, combinations of vertical, horizontal and diagonal wedges. Examination of earlier inscriptions shows that most of the later signs were derived from identifiable pictures of real objects. Over the centuries some of the words and phonetic values represented by the signs changed.

PICTOGRAPHIC SIGN c. 3100 BC									
INTERPRETATION	star	?sun over horizon	?stream	ear of barley	bull's head	bowl	head + bowl	lower leg	?shrouded body
CUNEIFORM SIGN c. 2400 BC									
CUNEIFORM SIGN c. 700 BC (turned through 90°)									
PHONETIC VALUE*	dingir, an	u_4, ud	a	še	gu_4	nig_2, ninda	ku_2	du, gin, gub	lu_2
MEANING	god, sky	day, sun	water, seed, son	barley	ox	food, bread	to eat	to walk, to stand	man

* Some signs have more than one phonetic value and some sounds are represented by more than one sign. U_4 means the fourth sign with the phonetic value u.

developed texts. Two clay tablets found at Tell Brak, in northeast Syria, containing what appear to be early pictographs, show the whole animal, instead of just the head, as on the Uruk tablets, which suggests that the invention of writing was a complex process. The use of signs to represent objects was an important stage; the later use of signs to represent sounds was perhaps equally important.

Art and propaganda

Before the Uruk period there had been a few examples of naturalistic or representational art, for example, the Late Paleolithic cave art of southwest France, the murals of Chatal Huyuk or, in their modest way, the paintings of onagers at Umm Dabaghiyeh. These were, however, exceptional, and during the previous thousands of years of Near Eastern culture, art had been confined to rather stylized, human and animal figurines. In the north, during the Ubaid period, carvings of scenes of humans and animals had appeared on stamp seals. Now, however, the cylinder seal—a new invention of a peculiarly Mesopotamian kind—gave the opportunity for more ambitious compositions.

In levels IV and III at Uruk, seal impressions were common both on clay jar stoppers and on tablets. In some of the scenes depicted, a bearded man wearing a headband and a skirt was shown feeding the herds, traveling on a boat, threatening naked prisoners with a spear or making offerings. Next to him was an emblem consisting of a bundle of reeds, which later symbolized the goddess Inanna, the chief deity of the city of Uruk. Clearly, the man represented the ruler of Uruk, who was her chief priest. Similar figures have been found on seals from Susa, which might have represented Susa's ruler or perhaps Uruk's if Susa had, at that time, been under the control of Uruk.

Among the earliest pieces of monumental stone sculpture found in Uruk, some are of interest not only for their antiquity but for the emotional response that they can evoke from the modern observer. One of these was a mask-like face of a woman, found discarded in a rubbish pit in the northwest enclosure of Eanna, which probably once had inlaid eyes and a wig. It was approximately life size, with a broken nose, which originally would have been quite prominent. Another impressive piece was the Lion Hunt stele. The edges were broken and the back was rough but it seemed to be a freestanding stele, an art form that continued until the first millennium BC. The stele, now 78 centimeters high, showed two scenes: the upper one was of a bearded man wearing a knee-length skirt who was spearing a lion as it reared up on its hind legs; the lower showed a man, probably the same one, aiming his bow and arrow at a rearing lion.

The most fascinating find of this period from Uruk was the Warka vase. A large vessel, more than a meter tall, it had four bands of relief decoration measuring 92 centimeters in height. At the rim, the vase was 36 centimeters across. It had been damaged and repaired in antiquity. The lower two bands depicted plants and animals. The third showed naked servants, possibly priests, carrying loaded containers, presumably as tribute or offerings.

The top band, which was the most interesting, included a carving of the same man shown on the Lion Hunt stele, making offerings to the goddess Inanna. The tassels of his skirt were held by another man wearing a short skirt, in front of whom a naked man was making an offering to a female figure standing before the reed bundles that were the symbols of the goddess. Her headdress had been damaged when the vase was first repaired, making it impossible to ascertain how she was dressed. Slightly later Mesopotamian gods and goddesses were often shown wearing headdresses with cows' or bulls' horns, so the figure might have represented the goddess herself, or she could have been a priestess. Behind the reed bundles two sheep carried platforms on their backs where figures or statues were standing. The figure on the left carried the sign for *en*, the Sumerian word for the chief priest. Behind the sheep, piled up tribute included two vases of a similar shape to the Warka vase and two animal-shaped vessels.

Other remarkable finds contemporary with the Warka vase included a vessel carved with lions and bulls, with the lions on each side of the spout, and a jar with an elaborate inlay of shell and stone. A stone statuette of a bearded man was found in a vessel dating to the Late Uruk or Jemdet Nasr period under a wall from the later Seleucid period. It had been broken before being buried and the lower half was missing. Made of gray alabaster and standing 18 centimeters high, the statuette represented the same man as on the Warka vase. The eyes were of mother-of-pearl set in bitumen, and possibly the pupils were of the blue semi-precious stone lapis lazuli.

At Uruk, for the first time art was used to illustrate the role of the ruler and to reinforce his position. Art and architecture combined to create an effect of power and wealth to impress the local populace and enhance the stability of the ruling group. Political and religious propaganda expressed in the form of works of art have proved to be potent sources of information about the

Below Part of the remarkable hoard of metal objects from the cave of Nahal Mishmar to the east of the Dead Sea. Dating to the first half of the 4th millennium BC, the collection contained more than 400 objects made of copper alloyed with arsenic. At the back is one of the 10 "crowns" with lost-wax cast figures of animals. It has been suggested that these were used as drums. Also shown are standards or scepters and mace-heads, which would have been fixed to wooden hafts, and a hollow horn-shaped object.

ancient Near East, revealing much about the character of the rulers.

Technology and transportation

During the fourth millennium there were major developments in metallurgy. Some of the objects in the hoard from Nahal Mishmar had been made from smelted copper that possibly came from the mines in the Timna valley, about 150 kilometers to the south. Many were an alloy of copper and arsenic, which was easier to cast and harder than pure copper and was often used before tin bronze (an alloy of copper and tin) became common in the second millennium BC. Some of these objects weighed more than a kilogram and had been made by a method known as lost-wax casting. First, the shape was modeled in wax, then coated in clay and heated to harden the mold and melt the wax. Next, molten metal was poured into the mold, which was broken when the cast metal object was taken out. Small lost-wax castings are known from the considerably later temple treasury hoard found at Uruk and some striking statuettes from western Syria also date to this period.

The people of the time also used other metals besides copper and its alloys. Gold and silver ornaments have been discovered, and silver and lead were used for vessels. Iron fragments have been found at Jebel Aruda and Uruk in the Late Uruk period, and iron objects were listed on Uruk III tablets. (However, this iron might have come from meteorites or been an accidental by-product from smelting copper.) Advances in metalworking might have been promoted by the desire of the ruling groups for rare materials as status symbols.

The first use of the plow in the Near East also dates to the Uruk period. Plow marks in the soil have been found from the Susa I period and plows were represented on Late Uruk seals and among the signs on Uruk IV tablets. These tablets also contained signs for sledges and the first wheeled vehicles (shown as sledges with circles beneath) to appear in the Near East, which were probably heavy, lumbering carts pulled by oxen.

In southern Mesopotamia, which was damp and muddy in winter and crisscrossed by numerous water channels, boats presented a more practical means of transportation. A model of a boat in baked clay from the Ubaid period has been found at the cemetery at Eridu, and in the Uruk and Jemdet Nasr periods boats were among the signs that appeared on tablets and cylinder seals. Overland transport was by animal caravan, which remained the normal method in much of the Near East until the present century. Donkeys were the most useful beasts of burden in the ancient Near East and are still widely used today. Bones of domesticated donkeys have been found in the Uruk levels at Tell Rubeidheh.

Plows, wheels, boats and donkeys were almost certainly in use before the Uruk period. Plow marks found in northern Europe have been dated to about 3500 BC, and models of wheeled carts discovered in Poland and actual carts buried in graves in the southern Soviet Union belonged to approximately the same period. However, the origin of the plow (which some experts believe was invented in northern Mesopotamia before 6000 BC) and the wheel remain uncertain.

Cylinder Seals

As their name implies, cylinder seals are cylinders, generally of stone but also of faience, glass, baked clay, wood, bone, shell, ivory or metal, that were carved with a design so that when they are rolled out on clay a continuous impression in relief is produced. They average about 2.5 centimeters in height and 1.5 centimeters in diameter and were generally pierced lengthwise so that they could be worn on a pin or string, or mounted on a swivel. Cylinder seals were developed during the second half of the fourth millennium BC in southern Mesopotamia (Uruk) and in southwestern Iran (Susa) as a convenient way of covering large areas of clay used for sealing storeroom locks, goods carried in jars, bags, boxes or baskets and—above all—the clay tablets used for about 3,000 years as the main vehicle for cuneiform writing.

When the cuneiform system was adapted for writing the languages of Mesopotamia's neighbors, the cylinder seal was used as a seal form instead of the stamp seal. During the course of the first millennium BC, the alphabet replaced cuneiform and the stamp seal once again replaced the cylinder seal. The designs on cylinder seals are a valuable source of information: they chronicle developments in the iconography of deities, mythology and daily life as well as recording events such as the first domed buildings, the first lute or the introduction of the water buffalo from India. They were frequently inscribed and provide genealogical information concerning their owners.

Cylinder seals were often made of hard stones but, given a good abrasive, these could be cut with flint or copper tools. (*Top and above*) Egyptian tombs from Saqqara (c. 2450 BC) and Thebes (c. 1420 BC) show hand-boring and bow-drilling. The bow-drill enabled greater speeds to be achieved and, when mounted horizontally, greater control.

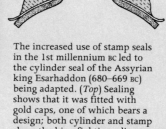

The materials used for cylinder seals varied according to fashion and availability. (*Top*) Cylinder seal from Tell Sleimeh in the Hamrin basin made of royal blue lapis lazuli from Afghanistan. First cut c. 2250 BC, it was inscribed by two later owners. (*Above*) Assyrian chalcedony seals of the 8th century BC.

The increased use of stamp seals in the 1st millennium BC led to the cylinder seal of the Assyrian king Esarhaddon (680–669 BC) being adapted. (*Top*) Sealing shows that it was fitted with gold caps, one of which bears a design; both cylinder and stamp show the king fighting a lion. (*Above*) A piece of leather or cloth, stretched over the mouth of a storage jar, could be secured by strings covered with clay sealed with a cylinder seal.

Below Cylinder seals were used for sealing legal documents such as contracts, sales, ration-lists, treaties, loans and so on. At some periods the tablet itself was sealed; at others the tablet was enclosed in a sealed clay envelope. The seal on this envelope shows the seated water-god with streams flowing from his shoulders; before him stand a naked, bearded hero and a bull-man fighting with an inverted lion. It was found at Kanesh in central Turkey, where Assyrian merchants had established a trading colony.

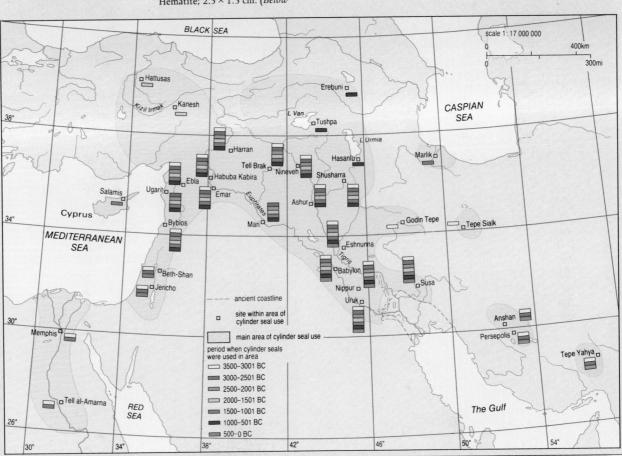

Below As cylinder seals were used to protect property and safeguard legal transactions, they came to be associated with the protection of their owner and were used in rituals against sickness, miscarriage, black magic or slander. The stones from which they were made also had special properties: lapis lazuli, for example, meant power and divine favor. This Kassite seal of the 14th century BC is inscribed with a long prayer to the owner's protective god: *Oh Marduk, sublime lord, prince in whose hands the power of decision in heaven and on earth has been vested; the servant who worships you, by your look may he be happy.* It depicts a god, presumably Marduk, surrounded by symbols. Chalcedony; 3.6 cm high.

The use of cylinder seals
Cylinder seals are mostly found in those regions where the cuneiform script was used for writing on clay tablets.

Above, left to right Many seals were items of jewelry. A shell inlay from Mari, c. 2500 BC, showing a seal hanging from a pin; a Syrian hematite seal (c. 1720 BC), with gold caps and a loop of wire. (*Below*) a green jasper seal from Syria (c. 1800 BC) with gold caps set in a swivel (found in a grave dating to the 7th- or 6th-century BC in Carthage, Tunisia).

Cylinder seals and their impressions. (*Top*) Uruk period (c. 3300 BC), found near Uruk. Marble with a bronze handle shaped like a couchant sheep; 5.4 × 4.5 cm. (*Below top*) Early Dynastic III (c. 2600 BC). Green calcite; 5.0 × 2.6 cm. (*Above*) Akkadian (c. 2250 BC). Rock crystal; 3.2 × 2.2 cm. (*Top right*) Old Babylonian (c. 1750 BC). Hematite; 2.5 × 1.3 cm. (*Below top right*) Middle Assyrian (c. 1300 BC). Chalcedony; 2.8 × 1.2 cm. (*Above right*) Neo-Assyrian (c. 700 BC). Carnelian; 3.65 × 1.7 cm. (*Right*) Achaemenid (c. 450 BC) found at Borsippa, Iraq; detail. Chalcedony; 4.75 × 2.2 cm.

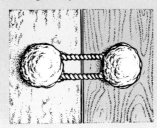

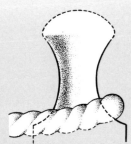

The undersides of clay sealings bear impressions of objects sealed—for instance jars or baskets. Some sealings were used to secure wooden doors fastened with a peg and string (*top*). The flat surface and grain of the wood and the shape of peg and string are found on some sealings (*above*). Whereas sealed jars could be imported, doors were sealed locally. Studying the sealings can give information on different styles and trade patterns.

Map

BLACK SEA

scale 1: 17 000 000

0 — 400km
0 — 300mi

CASPIAN SEA

Hattusas
Kızıl Irmak
Kanesh
Erebuni
L Van
Tushpa
38°
L Urmia
Harran
Marlik
Tell Brak
Nineveh
Hasanlu
Shusharra
Ebla
Habuba Kabira
Salamis
Ugarit
Emar
Ashur
Euphrates
Cyprus
34°
Byblos
Mari
Godin Tepe
Tepe Sialk
MEDITERRANEAN SEA
Eshnunna
Beth-Shan
Babylon
Jericho
Nippur
Susa
Uruk
Tigris
30°
Anshan
Memphis
Persepolis
Tepe Yahya
--- — ancient coastline
□ — site within area of cylinder seal use
▭ — main area of cylinder seal use
period when cylinder seals were used in area
□ 3500–3001 BC
▤ 3000–2501 BC
▥ 2500–2001 BC
▦ 2000–1501 BC
▩ 1500–1001 BC
■ 1000–501 BC
▤ 500–0 BC
Tell al-Amarna
RED SEA
The Gulf
30° 34° 38° 42° 46° 50° 54°

Religion and Ritual

As shown by the religious furnishings of Neolithic houses at Qermez Dere and Chatal Huyuk, religion and ritual, from the earliest times, played a fundamental role in the lives of the inhabitants of the ancient Near East. Indeed some scholars suggest that religion was the motivating force behind the transformation from village to city life.

The rulers of the region all considered themselves to be agents of the gods and an important part of their duties was the performance of ceremonies designed to ward off evil and gain the deities' goodwill. The principal centers for religious activities were the temples, though in certain cultures ceremonies could also take place in sacred groves or on hilltops. The gods were present in the temples in the form of divine statues and the priests were responsible for looking after them. There were different types of priests with different functions including administration, incantations, exorcism, omens, divination and so on. Most of the available information comes from texts dealing with the palace or the temple; little is known about the religion of the ordinary citizens.

Below Drawings of two seal impressions on a tablet of the reign of Tukulti-Ninurta I (1243–1207 BC) found at Ashur. The goatfish was associated with the god Ea and the dog with the goddess Gula.

Below This podium, found in the temple of the goddess Ishtar at Ashur, bears a dedicatory inscription of the Assyrian king Tukulti-Ninurta I to the god Nusku. The king is shown twice, worshiping the tablet and the stylus of the god Nabu set on a similar podium. Height 57.5 cm.

Above Limestone relief from Susa with an inscription in the Linear Elamite script of Puzur-Inshushinak (c. 2200 BC). A god holds a peg to secure the foundations of a temple while an interceding goddess stands behind. Similar figures were used as foundation figures to commemorate the building of slightly later temples by Naram-Sin, the king of Agade, and Gudea, the ruler of Lagash. Driving a peg into the ground probably formed part of an elaborate ceremony connected with the purification of the site before the construction of a temple. Height 52 cm.

Above right A bronze sculpture that was made for the Middle Elamite king Shilhak-Inshushinak (c. 1150 BC). Found at Susa encased in gypsum, it is the only 3-dimensional scene from the ancient Near East to have survived. It shows two naked priests performing a ceremony, perhaps at dawn, as the sculpture is called "sunrise" in the inscription. The setting includes trees, a large vessel and a variety of platforms and altars. It has been suggested that the larger stepped objects represent ziggurats but it is more likely that they were high altars. Length 60 cm, width 40 cm.

Left Sumerian statues found at Eshnunna some of which were part of a cache buried in the Square Temple at Eshnunna. They represent worshipers and were placed in temples to pray perpetually for the life of the donor. The clasped hands are probably a gesture of reverence and prayer.

Below Detail of the stele of king Ur-Nammu (2112–2095 BC) found in pieces at Ur. The scene shows the king making a libation before the moon god Nanna (Sin in Akkadian), the chief god of the city. The god holds the rod and ring, perhaps originally a yardstick and a measuring rope; the other object may be a necklace. Libations were of water, beer, wine, oil or the blood of a sacrificial animal.

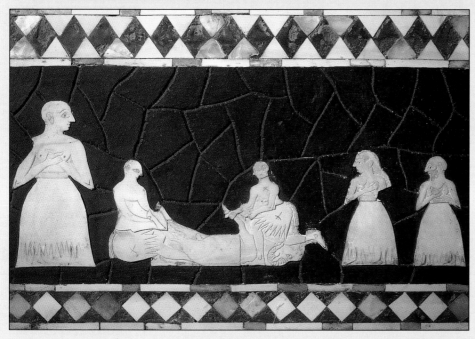

Left Impression from a lapis lazuli cylinder seal found at Uruk in the temple treasury hoard of the late 4th millennium BC. The ruler in a high-prowed boat transports a bull carrying on its back a stepped platform with the emblems of the goddess Inanna (as on the Warka vase found in the same hoard). In later times the statues of the gods were taken in procession from temple to temple on festival days, and at the Babylonian New Year festival the statues of the gods were brought from other cities to Babylon. Height 4.3 cm.

Above Mosaic inlay from the Early Dynastic Temple of Shamash at Mari, possibly showing the sacrifice of a ram. Sacrifices were a regular part of the temple ceremonies and special sacrifices were made on particular days. Animals were also killed for use in divination by consulting the entrails.

Right Statues of the gods being carried off by Assyrian soldiers (c. 730 BC). The statue on the left is of Adad, the storm god, who carries a bolt of lightning. The deportation of the gods of a captured city was standard practice in Mesopotamia.

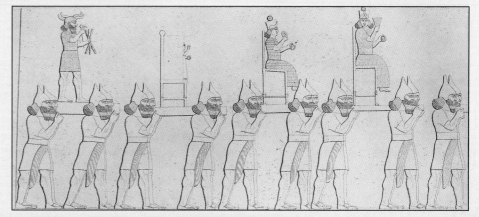

Gods and Demons

Hundreds of gods were worshiped in the ancient Near East, with each ethnic group and even each city having its own gods. In general, there was considerable religious tolerance, and gods of one region were often identified with those of another. The Sumerian and Akkadian pantheons merged at an early date and their divinities cannot be distinguished. Often the prestige of the gods was dependent on the fortunes of their home city: thus Marduk and Ashur rose to prominence as Babylonia and Assyria thrived.

The gods normally took human form and were believed to behave like humans, with the same emotions and the same needs, though they possessed supernatural powers. Alongside the gods were numerous other supernatural beings, both good and bad – demons, spirits, ghosts and so on – that took on a variety of forms, often combining human and animal characteristics. Some demons were thought to be responsible for diseases and other misfortunes and elaborate rituals were undertaken to avert their evil.

Left A naked lady holding lions and lotus flowers was carved on this Phoenician style ivory harness ornament found at Kalhu. Nude goddesses are normally identified with the goddess of love and war known as Inanna to the Sumerians, as Ishtar to the Akkadians and as Astarte in the Levant. Height 16.1 cm.

Right A *kudurru* (boundary stone) of Nebuchadnezzar I (1124–1103 BC) carved with the symbols of the gods. In the top row are the star of Ishtar, the crescent of Sin and the solar disc of Shamash. The three horned crowns on pedestals below may represent Anu, Enlil and Ea. Height c. 60 cm.

Left One popular method of divining the future was to examine the entrails of a sacrificed animal. This Babylonian baked clay plaque from Sippar, dating to about 700 BC, illustrates one such examination and on the other side the interpretation of the omen is recorded. The face is identified as belonging to the demon Humbaba who was slain by the epic hero Gilgamesh. Height 8 cm.

Right The back of this bronze relief plaque (c. 700 BC) shows the demon Pazuzu whose head and hands are visible at the top. It was probably intended as protection against Lamashtu, who attacked pregnant women and newborn children. The plaque shows the symbols of the gods, a row of demons, a sick person attended by two priests in fish cloaks, as well as the demons Pazuzu and the lion-headed Lamashtu beneath. Height 13.3 cm, width 8.4 cm.

Left Winged figure, from the Northwest Palace of Ashurnasirpal II (883–859 BC) at Kalhu, wearing the horned crown that signified divinity in ancient Mesopotamia from the Early Dynastic period on. Many similar figures, some with four wings, some with eagles' heads and some wearing cloaks of fish, carrying a variety of objects – plants, animals, buckets and cones – were carved on the walls of the palace. These supernatural beings are associated with the *apkallu*, or seven sages, whose figurines were buried beneath the floors of the palaces to protect the palace and its occupants from evil.

Below Bronze figure representing the wind demon Pazuzu, who was normally shown with a grotesque face, four wings, bird's legs, animal front paws and a scorpion's tail. It is inscribed "I am Pazuzu, son of Hanbi, king of the evil wind-demons." Although king of the evil demons, Pazuzu was thought of as benevolent. Bronze amulets of Pazuzu's head, worn to protect women in childbirth against the attacks of the she-demon Lamashtu, were very popular in the Late Assyrian and Neo-Babylonian periods.

Right Bronze figure of a god with four faces. It was not found in excavation but may have come from Neribtum (Tell Ishchali) and date to the early 2nd millennium BC. The identity of the god is not known. Height 17 cm.

Below Impression of a greenstone cylinder seal of the Akkadian period (c. 2200 BC) showing the water god Ea with his two-faced vizier Usmu. In front of him the sun god Shamash emerges from between the mountains with Ishtar to his left. Height 3.9 cm.

Right This baked clay plaque from Tutub (Tell Khafajeh) shows a warrior god stabbing a one-eyed solar deity. The identities of the figures are not known. The scene may be from a myth that has not been preserved. Molded plaques depicting gods were popular in the Old Babylonian period (2000–1600 BC) and were found in both temples and houses. They were probably votive offerings or devotional objects. Height 11 cm.

STATES IN CONFLICT (3000-2350 BC)

Recording early history

The invention of writing in the Late Uruk period brought the people of Mesopotamia to the threshold of history. However, it was not until almost a thousand years later that texts were produced that can be used to unravel the history of the region. The contemporary inscriptions of the rulers of the city states from late in the Early Dynastic period are often uninformative, recording only the name of the ruler and a dedication to a god, while information contained in later texts, written in retrospect, tends to be distorted. The chronology, too, is somewhat uncertain. The earliest fairly reliable date is the accession of Sargon of Agade in 2334 BC, which marks the end of the Early Dynastic period in Mesopotamia. This date, however, has been calculated by adding up the lengths of the reigns between Sargon and Ammisaduqa of Babylon, 700 years later, and so may be as much as 200 years adrift.

The decline of the Late Uruk trading empire left a cultural vacuum, which was filled locally: in the east by the Proto-Elamite culture, in southern Mesopotamia by Jemdet Nasr and Early Dynastic I, and in the Diyala and Hamrin by Late Protoliterate and Early Dynastic I. In northern Mesopotamia, the replacement cultures were first a derivative of Late Uruk culture and then Ninevite 5, and in other regions Early Bronze cultures. Southern Mesopotamia remained the focus for civilization, with many cities competing for dominance. Only the little-known Proto-Elamite culture, which included at least one major city, approached the Mesopotamian in terms of its far-flung contacts. Elsewhere the large cities created under Late Uruk influence did not survive. By the end of the Early Dynastic period, however, Sumerian influence was once again being felt throughout Mesopotamia and was affecting the whole of the Near East.

Proto-Elamite culture

At Susa there was a change in the material culture from Susa II, which was similar to the Late Uruk culture of Sumer, to Susa III, which had closer connections with the highland regions of Iran to the east. Much of Susiana was abandoned at this time, including Susa itself. The people might have moved either to southern Mesopotamia or to the Iranian plateau, both of which experienced a growth in population.

The artifacts most characteristic of the Susa III period at Susa are tablets written in the Proto-Elamite A script. This script is generally similar to the Mesopotamian, and the weights and measures systems used are also the same. However, the non-numerical signs differ and presumably were used for writing different languages. In the Uruk III, and probably Uruk IV, texts the language was Sumerian. In the Proto-Elamite texts, it was very likely an early form of Elamite, the spoken language of Susiana and of the mountains to the

east from the third to the first millenium BC. But as the texts have not so far been deciphered, this cannot be proved.

At Susa 1,400 Proto-Elamite tablets have been found and smaller quantities at Tepe Sialk, Tepe Yahya and Tall-i Malyan. A single example was excavated at Shahr-i Sokhte, far in the east of Iran, near the Afghan border. With these tablets were seals and seal impressions relating to Jemdet Nasr and Early Dynastic I types in Mesopotamia. One type of seal was in the shape of a tall, thin cylinder carved out of chlorite (or steatite), which was heated after the design had been cut in order to make the surface harder. The designs on these seals often had rosettes, hatched geometric figures including triangles and circles, as well as arches, arcades and other motifs, all of which were comparable with the signs on Proto-Elamite tablets. These "glazed steatite" seals have been found throughout the Proto-Elamite zone and along the western edge of the Zagros as far as the Ninevite 5 culture of northern Mesopotamia. However, they were quite rare in southern Mesopotamia, which suggests that commercial and political connections ran parallel with the mountains, rather than radiating out from the lowlands (as had been the case in the earlier Late Uruk period).

The largest known Proto-Elamite site was Tall-i Malyan, 450 kilometers eastsoutheast of Susa in the region of Fars. In later periods Malyan was called Anshan, and both Susa and Anshan were included within the boundaries of the kingdom of Elam. In the Banesh period, about 3400–2600 BC, Malyan occupied 50 hectares. Early in the third millennium a defensive wall around the city enclosed an area of some 200 hectares, of which about a quarter consisted of permanent settlements.

In one area excavations have uncovered a well-constructed large building with seventeen or more rooms containing wall paintings in red, white, yellow, gray and black. Other buildings, some of which contained Proto-Elamite tablets and clay sealings, included storerooms and workshops where there were locally available materials such as flint, copper ore and bitumen, as well as imported materials that included obsidian, mother-of-pearl and shells from the Gulf, carnelian and lapis lazuli from Badakhshan in northern Afghanistan. Lapis lazuli could have reached the Near East along two main routes: a southern route passing through Shahr-i Sokhte, then south of the Dasht-i Kavir and the Dasht-i Lut to Kerman and Fars and through Khuzistan; and a northern route, which was followed by the later Silk route, through Khorassan, between the Alborz and the Dasht-i Kavir, and then southwest past Hamadan and Kermanshah to central Mesopotamia. Along both these routes were sites showing evidence for the import and working of semiprecious stones including lapis lazuli. Near Tepe Yahya there are rich deposits of chlorite, which was used for seals and bowls in the

The trade in chlorite vessels of the Intercultural Style
Carved stone vessels made out of chlorite have been found on many Near Eastern sites of the 3rd millennium BC. One of the main sources of chlorite is the region near the site of Tepe Yahya, which was a major production center. In Mesopotamia these luxury vessels have been found in temples, in palaces and in graves. Those from the island of Tarut in the Gulf were probably from graves, but were not recovered in a scientific excavation. The most frequent motifs in the Intercultural Style are a type of building that has not yet been identified with any known architectural style from that region, and animals, most commonly depicting a snake in combat. One of these found in the Inanna Temple at Nippur was labeled in cuneiform script "Inanna and the serpent", but this inscription may have been added after the vessel arrived in Mesopotamia.

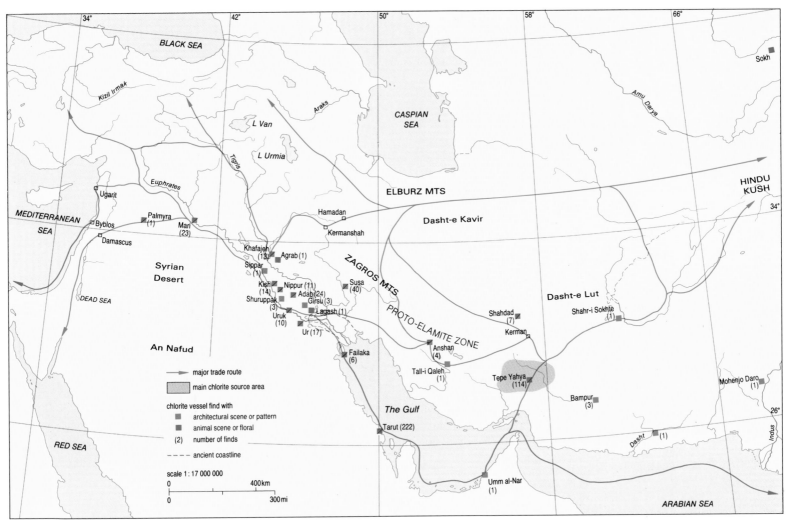

Early Dynastic period. Twenty-six inscribed Proto-Elamite tablets have been found there, together with a further 84 blank tablets. The inscribed tablets recorded small quantities of goods such as grain and beer as well as animals, indicating that their primary use was for local administration, not long-distance trade.

Early Dynastic I

Southern Mesopotamia in the Early Dynastic period was divided up into small city states. Most

of these comprised a single large settlement and the surrounding countryside. From the evidence at Eridu there was a continuity from the Ubaid period into the Uruk. Similarly, there were no major disruptions from the Uruk to the Jemdet Nasr and Early Dynastic periods. In particular, the locations of temples remained the same, and excavations of successive levels have revealed architectural development over hundreds and even thousands of years. During that time there was a gradual evolution in pottery, as new styles were introduced, but the overall impression is one of continuity.

Excavations in the Diyala region, to the east of Baghdad, have established the basic archeological framework. The Early Dynastic period can be divided into an early phase, which is essentially prehistoric, and a later phase, in which historical figures and events can be identified. These phases correspond respectively to Early Dynastic I and Early Dynastic III in the Diyala region, with Early Dynastic II representing a transitional period in between. Early Dynastic I is best known from the Diyala region, and typified by painted pottery known as Scarlet Ware, which is also found in the Hamrin.

Once again, temples have provided a useful source of information. A typical temple had a shrine consisting of a long narrow room, which was entered near the end of one of the long sides from a courtyard, with an altar at the opposite short end. This form of temple, which incorporated a "bent axis" approach, might have developed from the addition of an outer courtyard to the

Right Painted pottery jar from Tell Khafajeh (ancient Tutub) in the Diyala region. This style of painting in black and red paint is called Scarlet Ware and is typical of the Early Dynastic I period. Both geometric and naturalistic motifs were used but scenes showing humans, as on this vessel, were rare. Height c. 30 cm.

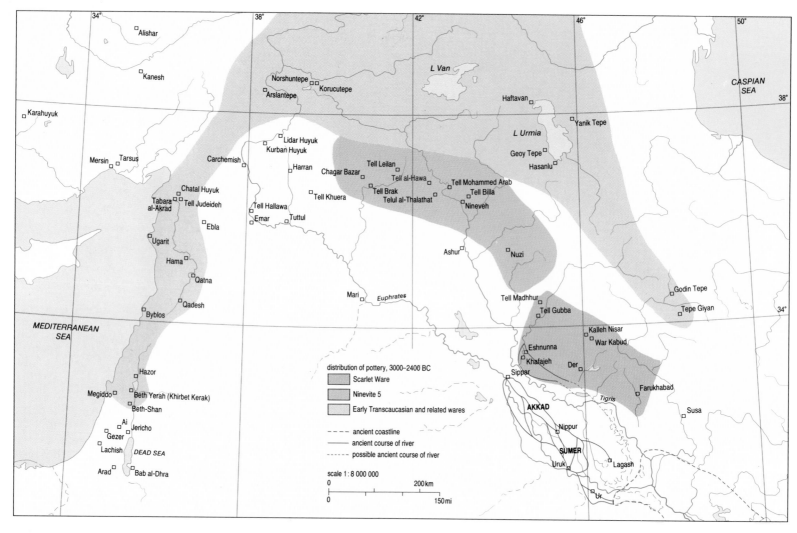

Ubaid and Uruk tripartite temples in the Jemdet Nasr period. Similarly, the tripartite house of the Ubaid period became a courtyard house, with a reception room along one side of the courtyard (an architectural plan that is still in use in Iraq today). Another feature of temples of the Early Dynastic I period, which became very common later, were stone statues that were intended to act as substitutes for the worshiper. A collection of 12 statues has been discovered beside the altar of one of the three shrines in the Square Temple at Eshnunna (modern Tell Asmar). Originally identified as statues of the gods, they were probably meant to represent human beings.

Sites from the Early Dynastic I period in the Hamrin area have shown less evidence for the existence of large cities. Tell Gubba, the earliest and most impressive site, which dates from the end of the Jemdet Nasr period or the beginning of Early Dynastic I, was once a building consisting of a series of eight concentric walls with an outer diameter of about 70 meters. The walls were corbeled with arched corridors between them covered by pointed roofs, and in the thickness of the walls were staircases. The function of this structure, which is unparalleled outside the Hamrin basin, is not known. A pit within contained 16 skeletons, which had been thrown in one after the other. In the corridors, large jars with cereal grains have been found, suggesting that the building had been used for the storage of supplies and treasure.

Another slightly later building, the Round Building at Tell Razuk, also had concentric walls, with a wide open space 10 meters across in the center. The five curving rooms surrounding it had corbeled arches like those at Gubba, but in this case spanning rooms more than 4 meters wide. The building might have been a military outpost established by one of the city states to the southwest. A cemetery found at Kheit Qasim is believed to have been connected with a nearby walled settlement. The brick-built graves were surrounded by rectangular brick platforms, and the larger tombs had long narrow walls projecting from the south side, with a narrow channel between them. The finds in the graves were mainly pottery though some also contained daggers, axes and chisels made from copper mined on the Iranian plateau.

In northern Mesopotamia, a derivative of the Late Uruk culture developed into the Ninevite 5 culture, named after level 5 of the Prehistoric Pit at Nineveh. There, painted pottery has been found as well as the later fine gray ware decorated with elaborate incised patterns. None of the sites dating to this period that have been investigated so far show any urban characteristics. The buildings were all small-scale village buildings, while the graves, though they showed some variation in size and wealth, were quite poor when compared with the riches buried in graves further south. The most elaborate pieces of metalwork known from the Ninevite 5 period are simple copper pins with cast heads. A fragment of an iron knife blade found in a grave at Chagar Bazar is said to have been made from smelted iron ore, perhaps obtained accidentally when using an iron-ore flux to smelt copper.

The distribution of pottery styles in the 3rd millennium Although writing was invented in the 4th millennium BC, written documents cannot be used to reconstruct the history of most of the Near East during the 3rd millennium. As in the study of prehistoric periods, archeologists rely on the distribution of decorated pottery types to define the various cultures in the region. Three main groups can be distinguished. To the northeast of Sumer and Akkad red and black painted Scarlet Ware is found. Northwest of there was Ninevite 5 pottery. The earlier Ninevite 5 decorated pottery was painted but later this was replaced by fine gray pottery, which had incised patterns scratched into the surface of the vessel. In a great arc around Mesopotamia there were groups using black or red burnished pottery, sometimes decorated with white patterns filled in or with raised relief designs. This style was derived from Early Transcaucasian pottery, which spread south from the Caucasus region during the 3rd millennium BC.

Nippur

Below This fragment of a painted and inlaid chlorite vessel made in southern Iran was found in the ruins of the Early Dynastic Temple of Inanna at Nippur. It shows a big cat fighting a snake. The scene is labeled in cuneiform "Inanna and the serpent".

Nippur was the most important religious center of the Sumerians and contained the main temple of the god Enlil, who in the third millennium BC replaced An, the god of the sky, as head of the pantheon. Although in the historical period the city was not the seat of an important dynasty, control of Nippur was thought by rulers of other cities to confer the right to rule the whole of Sumer and Akkad.

Nippur was occupied from the Ubaid period until about AD 800 and the accumulated debris of 5,000 years of settlements has created a vast field of massive mounds covering an area that exceeds 2 by 1.5 kilometers and rises 20 meters above the surrounding plain. There was an important scribal school at Nippur and many thousands of tablets have been recovered from the site. A unique tablet dating to about 1300 BC has a measured drawing of the city showing the Temple of Enlil, the city walls and gates, and the main water courses. The sharp angle of the city walls shown on the tablet has been found in recent excavations at the southern end of the site.

Right Copper statuette, perhaps representing king Ur-Nammu (2112–2095 BC) or Shulgi (2094–2047 BC), found in the foundations of the Temple of Inanna at Nippur. The figure carried a basket on his head and the lower part of the body is shaped like a peg. Height c. 30 cm.

Right Contour plan of the site of Nippur showing the main areas excavated since 1948. Superimposed on this are the main features of the 1300 BC map of Nippur found at the site.

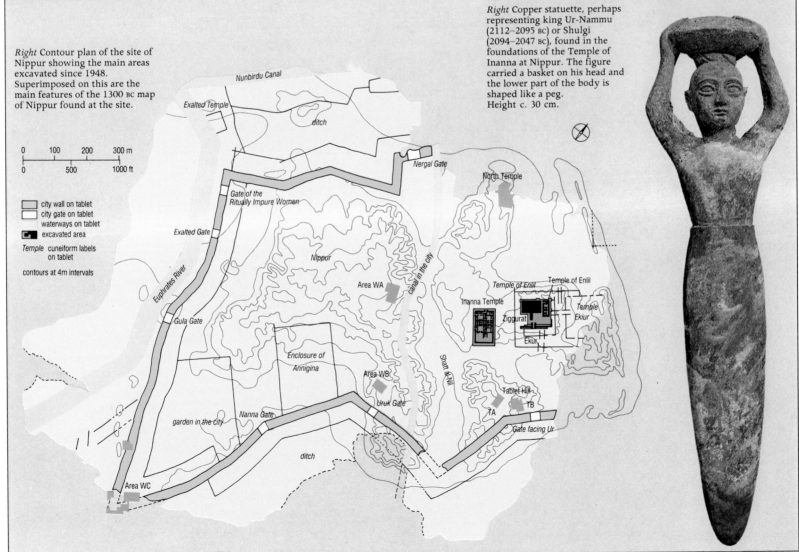

	city wall on tablet
	city gate on tablet
	waterways on tablet
	excavated area
Temple	cuneiform labels on tablet

contours at 4m intervals

Nunbirdu Canal

Exalted Temple

ditch

Nergal Gate

North Temple

Gate of the
Ritually Impure Women

Exalted Gate

Nippur

Euphrates River

Area WA

canal in the city

Temple of Enlil

Temple of Enlil

Inanna Temple

Temple Ekiur

Ziggurat

Ekur

Gula Gate

Enclosure of
Annigina

Area WB

Shatt al-Nil

Tablet Hill

TA

TB

Uruk Gate

garden in the city

Nanna Gate

Gate facing Ur

ditch

Area WC

Early Transcaucasian culture

Farther north, in eastern Turkey, the Early Transcaucasian culture developed. It had probably begun in Armenia along the Araxes valley, but at the end of the fourth millennium it spread. This expansion is thought to have accompanied a movement of people westward and southward to establish settlements in eastern Turkey, in the upper Euphrates valley, and in northern Iran. The characteristic black, brown or red burnished pottery was decorated in relief, sometimes with incised designs filled with a white pigment. It has been found in level IV (dating to about 2700 BC) at Godin, across the main route from Mesopotamia to Iran. Similar pottery from about the same time has been discovered in western Syria as far south as the Sea of Galilee, where it is called Khirbet Kerak ware.

The people who had occupied these sites also shared a liking for round houses and horseshoe-shaped hearths decorated with molded reliefs. They might have been ancestors of the Hurrians, who dominated the northern fringes of Mesopotamia in the late third and second millennia. How far this style of pottery reflected political or commercial links is unknown, but the ring around Mesopotamia could have isolated the lowlands from the rich resources of the mountains, stimulating trade by sea along the Gulf in Early Dynastic times.

The Levant

In the Levant the Khirbet Kerak pottery was only one of a number of local styles prevalent in the Early Bronze Age. These variations were not necessarily due to invasions, but may have resulted from local development and foreign influences by peaceful means over the period.

The Early Bronze Age in the Levant fell into four phases, which corresponded roughly to Late Uruk, the Jemdet Nasr and Early Dynastic I, Early Dynastic III, and the end of the third millennium, respectively. In the first Early Bronze phase the sites were generally small, except for some that spread across 10 hectares or more. One of the most remarkable of these was Jawa, in the rocky basalt desert of northeast Jordan. A fortified town occupying some 12 hectares, it had been built toward the end of the fourth millennium in an area where the annual rainfall was less than 150 millimeters. However, by trapping and storing the runoff from the winter rains the people were able to gather enough water to last them through the hot, dry summer months.

The second phase, Early Bronze 2, was marked by greater contact with the kingdom of Egypt. Palestinian pottery that might have been used for the export of olive oil has been found in tombs of the Egyptian First Dynasty in Abydos. Also, in southern Palestine and northern Sinai some sites have been identified, from the cylinder-seal impressions and mud-brick buildings found there, as having been Egyptian colonies or trading outposts.

Evidence has also been found for the regular fortification of town sites in this period and for the use of gates and towers. Religious buildings, too, have been identified but whether the priests played a prominent part in government is uncertain. Most experts believe that this was a time of city states, with each fortified center controlling the surrounding land. At the end of this phase, many sites were abandoned and the fortifications of those that survived became more massive. In Syria, cities such as Mari, Ebla, Hama, Ugarit and Byblos flourished, and the powerful Egyptian Old Kingdom strongly influenced Palestine and the coastal cities of the Levant during Early Bronze 3.

Sumer and Akkad

Southern Mesopotamia divided into two regions: Sumer in the south, extending from Eridu to Nippur, and Akkad in the north, from Abu Salabikh to the northern edge of the alluvial plains. The names Sumer and Akkad were first recorded at the end of the Early Dynastic period. Apparently, in Sumer most of the population spoke the Sumerian language, which has no known close relatives. In the north most people spoke Akkadian, the ancestor of Babylonian and Assyrian and related to Hebrew and Arabic.

Sumer and Akkad were not countries in the modern sense, but consisted of several city states each of which formed a complete political unit and had its own ruler. Some city states included several towns. For instance, the state of Lagash included Girsu (the home of the state god Ningirsu), Lagash, which gave its name to the state, and Nina, a smaller city to the southeast. Sumer and Akkad were each divided into about a dozen city states. Most of these lay along branches of the Euphrates and were surrounded by uncultivated areas of land (called in Sumerian *edin*) which acted as grazing pastures and as a buffer between the urban settlements. The cities were close together. For example, Umma was only 30 kilometers from Girsu in the state of Lagash, and the inscriptions of the rulers of Lagash described the continual fighting over the land between them. Walled settlements have been found as early as the Aceramic Neolithic period at Jericho and Maghzaliyeh and were common in the Early Bronze 1 period in Palestine. Probably most Sumerian cities were fortified by the beginning of the Early Dynastic period. The earliest evidence for city walls in southern Mesopotamia, however, is from the middle of the Early Dynastic period at Abu Salabikh. Because of shifting alliances and military conquests it is difficult to draw a political map of Sumer. At times the king of Kish was the overlord of the rulers of states as far away as Lagash, and at other times two or more city states were ruled by a single individual.

Rulers and gods

The rulers of the city states had three different titles—*en, ensi* and *lugal*—which, roughly translated are "lord", "governor" and "king" respectively, but what distinguished them from each other is uncertain. Different titles were used in different cities. The *en* had religious duties and originally was probably a priest. *Lugal*, which literally meant "big man", was a more secular role. The title might have originated when a war leader was elected by a council of elders, as in the Babylonian Epic of Creation when the assembly of the gods elected Marduk to wage war against the evil demons. In some cases, a *lugal* had one or more *ensi* subordinate to him. By the end of the Early Dynastic period, secular and religious authorities were distinct in some cities, but until the very end of Mesopotamian civilization the secular rulers held their power only as agents of the gods. The ruler

Below The best-preserved copy of the Sumerian King List is inscribed in cuneiform script on the Weld–Blundell prism. This lists the names of the rulers of Sumer from before the Flood to Sin-magir, king of Isin (1827–1817 BC). More than a dozen copies are known from Babylonia, Susa and the 7th-century BC Assyrian royal library at Nineveh. All of these derived from an original that was probably composed in about 2100 BC in the early part of the Third Dynasty of Ur or a little earlier. The purpose of the Sumerian King List was to show that, from the first time "when kingship was lowered from heaven", a particular city was chosen to exercise dominion over all the other cities. Height 20 m.

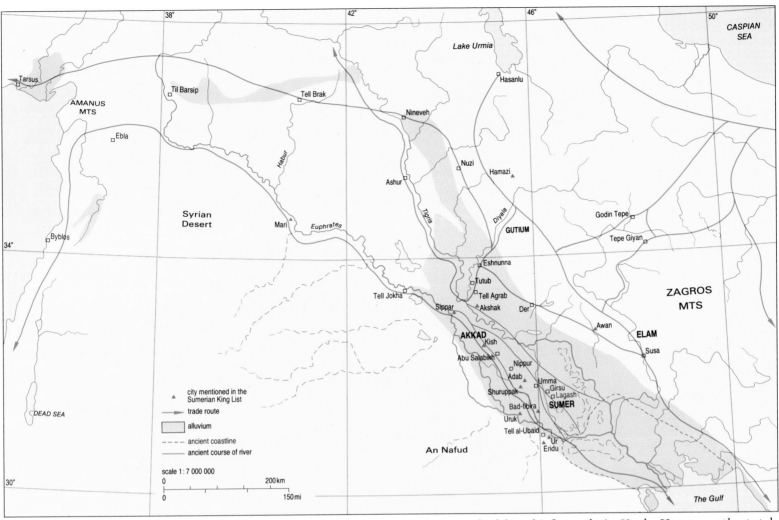

The cities in the Sumerian King List
In the Early Dynastic III period Sumer and Akkad were divided between rival city states. According to the Sumerian King List, at any moment one city held a preeminent position. In fact, this seems to have been a projection into the earlier period in order to legitimize the rule of later dynasties. As in the Bible, early rulers were credited with extremely long reigns of thousands of years. The ruling cities and lengths of dynasty attributed to their kings are recorded in the Sumerian King List.

was the representative of the god and, to a greater or lesser extent, controlled the resources of the main temple of the city. This temple was the city's chief landowner and its richest institution. There was also a thriving private-sector economy, but this is less evident from the tablets, most of which have come from temple archives. The ownership of slaves, some of whom were prisoners of war, was also common in the city states.

Each city had its own guardian god to whom the chief temple was dedicated. Some city gods were only important locally. The god Sud resided in Shuruppak, Bau and her husband Ningirsu were the chief gods of Girsu, and Zababa was the city god of Kish. Other deities exercised a wider dominion, often resulting from the power acquired by their native cities. For example, in later centuries Marduk of Babylon and Ashur of the city Ashur came to dominate the pantheon. The cities also had temples dedicated to gods other than the city god, in particular to Inanna or Enlil.

Sumerian gods, like Greek gods, took human form and often behaved like people. They were subject to the same emotions and jealousies, and the impression given by the myths and legends is that they interfered in human affairs in arbitrary ways. There were gods of the sky and the moon, or who embodied the powers of other natural phenomena, as well as gods of human institutions and artifacts. There was a goddess of writing, a god of the plow, and even bricks had their own god. In fact, hundreds of gods were listed carefully by the Sumerian scribes.

An was the god of the sky and the heavens, who

had his chief temple in Uruk. However, the tutelary deity of the city was not An, but the goddess Inanna. During the Uruk period An might have been the main deity, but by the middle of the third millennium that place had been taken by the god Enlil, or lord of the air, whose wife was called Ninlil. Enlil was the chief god of Nippur, the most northerly of the cities of Sumer and one that had a special role. Any ruler aspiring to control Sumer had a duty to restore the temples of Nippur.

The third of the gods was Enki (Ea, in Akkadian), whose name in Sumerian means lord of the earth, though in fact, he was the god of the sweet waters. He was also the chief god of the city of Eridu and the god of wisdom and magic. The most important goddess was Inanna (or Ishtar), with whom most goddesses in later times were identified. She was the goddess of love and of war (the equivalent of the Greek goddesses Aphrodite and Athena combined) and the city goddess of Uruk and of Agade. Perhaps originally she had been married to An, but in later myths she was the wife of Dumuzi, who went to the Netherworld in exchange for Inanna. In later times, he was called Tammuz or Adonis and was a god who died and revived each year. The sun god, Utu (Shamash), who was also god of justice and of the cities of Sippar and Larsa, and Nanna (Sin) the moon god and chief god of Ur were other important deities.

History and legend
The Early Dynastic period provided the first opportunity to compare archeological findings with historical evidence from the cuneiform texts.

The most important of these was the Sumerian King List, which recorded the dynasties that had ruled over Sumer from earliest times. The oldest copy of this text to have survived dates to the beginning of the second millennium BC, though a version of it was still being used in the time of Berossus, a Babylonian scribe of the 4th century BC. Beginning with the words, "After kingship had descended from heaven Eridu became (the seat) of kingship", the text recounted the four following dynasties of the cities of Bad-tibira, Larak, Sippar and Shuruppak, whose ruler was Ubar-tutu. Finally these entries were summarized as "5 cities, 8 kings reigned 241,200 years. The Flood then swept (over the land)."

A later tradition made Ubar-tutu the father of Ziusudra (or Ut-napishtim), the Babylonian Noah. Ut-napishtim, according to the Epic of Gilgamesh, built a boat on the advice of the god Enki and thus survived the deluge that had been sent by the gods to destroy humankind. Some early archeologists believed that this great flood might have accounted for the layers of waterlaid silt found deep down at sites such as Ur, Kish and Shuruppak, but these were probably due to local inundations at different periods. The antediluvian part of the Sumerian King List has often been identified with the Early Dynastic I period, but as the list is so far the only source of information this cannot be verified. In the period after the great flood it includes names for whom there is some corroborative archeological evidence: "After the Flood had swept [over the land] and kingship had descended from heaven, Kish became [the seat] of kingship." The list gives the names of 23 kings of Kish. The 22nd king was named as Enmebaragesi, "who carried away as spoil the weapons of the land of Elam, became king and reigned 900 years". The scribe probably included the title *en* as part of the name, as two inscriptions of Mebaragesi have been discovered, one on a vase that is now in the Iraq Museum and another in the Oval Temple in Khafajeh, to the east of Baghdad, in a level belonging to the beginning of the Early Dynastic III period.

After Mebaragesi came Aka, his son, according to the chronicle, and the kingship passed from Kish to Uruk. Among the kings of Uruk listed were several who were also mentioned in Sumerian myths and legends—Enmerkar, Lugalbanda, Dumuzi and Gilgamesh. A later Sumerian epic recorded a conflict between Gilgamesh of Uruk and Aka of Kish, the son of Mebaragesi, suggesting that dynasties at Uruk and Kish might have been contemporary rather than sequential, as implied by the king list.

The exploits of the semilegendary kings of the First Dynasty of Uruk were recorded by later Sumerian and Babylonian scribes. In one of these legends Enmerkar was engaged in a struggle with the city state of Aratta, which was separated from Sumer by seven mountains, and thus somewhere on the Iranian plateau. Enmerkar needed gold, silver, lapis lazuli and carnelian to decorate the temples of Sumer. Eventually, by means of trading grain, by negotiation using envoys and written tablets (in this story Enmerkar is credited with the invention of writing) and by armed conflict, he succeeded in securing the precious materials from the *en* of Aratta.

Like the Enmerkar legend, stories about Gilgamesh were reworked in later times but probably contained a kernel of truth. The fullest version of the Epic of Gilgamesh was produced in the early second millennium BC. It combined earlier legends to create a myth whose basic theme concerned human beings' attempts to avoid death. The story told how Gilgamesh, the ruler of Uruk, set out on an expedition to bring back cedars, needed to build temples, from the "land of the living", which possibly referred to the Amanus mountains. There he killed the monster Humbaba and, returning to Uruk, spurned the attentions of the goddess Inanna, as a result of which his friend Enkidu was killed. Frightened by the image of death, Gilgamesh sought out Ut-napishtim who had survived the Flood and been granted eternal life. He lived in Dilmun (which has been identified with the island of Bahrain in the Gulf). Ut-napishtim revealed that the secret of eternal life was to obtain the "plant of life". This may have referred to a pearl, as it was found at the bottom of the sea and Gilgamesh dived for it by tying stones to his feet, in the traditional method of Gulf pearl fishers. On his way back to Uruk, however, a snake (an animal that could be said to renew its life through shedding its skin) stole the "plant of life" and Gilgamesh had to be satisfied with eternal fame. Although not historical, such legends reflect the preoccupations of the Early Dynastic period. These included inter-city rivalries, appeasement and glorification of the gods and their representatives through temple-building and rich offerings, and acquisition of precious and exotic materials by trade or conquest.

The First Dynasty of Ur

The next dynasty in the Sumerian King List was that of Ur, under king Mes-Anepada, who is known from inscriptions at Ur and Tell Ubaid and from an inscribed lapis lazuli bead found at Mari. This bead refers to Mes-Anepada's father as Mes-kalamdug, king of Kish. Inscriptions of Meskalamdug have been discovered in two graves in the Royal Cemetery at Ur, which was excavated by the renowned archeologist Sir Leonard Woolley (1880–1960).

The Royal Cemetery is one of the most spectacular archeological finds to date. In most of the graves, the body had been laid on its side, wrapped in a mat or enclosed in a coffin, at the bottom of a vertical shaft. Alongside each body were personal possessions—jewelry, a dagger, and perhaps a cylinder seal. The grave also contained pottery, stone, or metal vessels, which might have held food and drink, as well as weapons, and makeup paints in cockle shells together with the necessary tools for applying them. Similar graves have also been found at Abu Salabikh, Kish and Khafajeh. However, 17 graves were unusual, both in their construction and in the wealth of goods that they held. Some were of stone or mud-brick, some had several chambers and some had vaults. Most of these graves had been robbed in ancient times, but even so what remained was extraordinary, and particularly so in those tombs that were found intact. In some of the Royal Tombs, the principal occupant had evidently been accompanied to the netherworld by dozens of attendants who had been slaughtered during the funeral rites.

Above The impression of a fine lapis lazuli cylinder seal inscribed "Puabi, queen" found in her tomb in the Royal Cemetery at Ur. In the Early Dynastic period in southern Mesopotamia cylinder seals owned by men normally showed men and animals in combat whereas women's seals often included banquet scenes like this. Feasting was of great importance in Mesopotamian society where ritual banquets reinforced the position of the elite. Perhaps the reason why women were associated with these seals was because the banquet formed part of a sacred marriage ceremony, but this is unproven. Height 4.9 cm.

Above Shell inlay of a warrior found in the Temple of Ishtar at Mari and belonging to the end of the Early Dynastic period. It was part of a larger scene showing warriors and bound, naked prisoners. The man is armed with an axe and wears a flat cap of the kind worn by Early Dynastic kings. Height 11 cm.

Right This lion-headed eagle was found at Mari in the so-called Treasure of Ur, which included a bead inscribed with the name of Mes-Anepada, king of Ur. Whether this was a royal gift or booty from some raid is unknown. The pendant is made out of lapis lazuli, brought from Afghanistan, with the head and tail of gold held on by bitumen and copper pins. Height 12.8 cm.

One Royal Tomb was placed almost exactly above another. The lower one, which Woolley called the King's Grave, had a sloping passageway leading down. At the foot of the ramp were the skeletons of six soldiers wearing copper helmets and armed with copper spears. Farther along were the remains of two four-wheeled wagons each pulled by three oxen. The reins had been made out of lapis lazuli beads and passed through silver rings decorated with statues of oxen. Beyond the wagons there were more than fifty male and female skeletons. The remains of two lyres were found next to a group of women. One of the lyres was decorated with a gold and lapis lazuli bull's head and a shell inlay showing animals playing musical instruments, like an early illustration to one of Aesop's fables.

The tomb chamber had been built of stone with brick vaulting. There the remains of several bodies were found and copper and silver models of boats of the same type as those used by the Marsh Arabs of southern Iraq today. Most of the contents of the tomb chamber, however, had been removed by robbers who had entered through a hole in the roof from a second Royal Tomb directly above. This had a similar layout to that of King's Grave, but the tomb chamber and the outer pit had not been looted. Five bodies lay on the ramp, before a wooden sledge ornamented with gold and silver lions' and bulls' heads with mosaics of lapis lazuli and shell. Attached to the sledge were two oxen whose reins passed through a silver ring decorated with a finely modeled electrum donkey. Near the sledge were a gaming board and vessels made of gold, silver, copper, obsidian, lapis lazuli, alabaster and marble. In the middle of these objects was a large wooden box, decorated with mosaic, that had been placed over the hole in the ceiling of the chamber of the King's Grave. Probably, the builders of the later tomb had found the earlier tomb chamber, and looted it.

In the tomb chamber of the later tomb the body of a woman lay on a wooden bier together with her two servants. Near the woman's right shoulder a lapis lazuli cylinder seal showing a banquet scene bore the inscription "Puabi, queen". Puabi had been buried dressed in all her finery, including a gold headdress. A second headdress, found near the body, consisted of a backing strip onto which had been sewn thousands of tiny lapis lazuli beads, and on top of these were fixed small gold figures of stags, gazelles, bulls and goats, separated by plant motifs.

Another tomb chamber had been robbed, but the outer area, called by Woolley the Great Death Pit, was preserved and in a space measuring less than 9 by 8 meters no fewer than 74 willing victims had been sacrificed. Six soldiers were stationed near the ramp. Four female musicians were found near their lyres, of which one instrument had a gold-bearded bull's head, another a silver cow's head and a third a silver stag's head. A further 64 women lay in orderly rows. About their necks they had chokers of lapis lazuli and gold as well as other jewelry and they wore large, crescent-shaped gold earrings and a simplified version of Puabi's headdress. Twenty-eight of the women had gold hair ribbons, and the rest silver. One unfortunate woman still had her hair ribbon rolled up. Evidently, she had not had time to put on a ribbon, having arrived late at her own funeral.

Two graves in the Royal Cemetery at Ur had inscriptions with the name of Meskalamdug. In one, which contained the remains of a woman, a shell cylinder seal bore the inscription "Meskalamdug, the king", which might have been an offering made on his behalf during the funeral. Another tomb, which has not been classified as a royal tomb as there was no built tomb chamber or evidence of human sacrifice, contained two gold bowls and a shell-shaped gold lamp which all carried the name Meskalamdug, as well as a copper bowl inscribed "Ninbanda the queen". On a cylinder seal found at Ur the same name and title had been recorded for

the wife of Mes-Anepada, who, according to the Mari bead, was the son of Meskalamdug. The most remarkable item found in the grave, however, was a gold helmet in the form of a wig with every strand of the hair carefully engraved. There were also hundreds of beads, many gold vessels, a silver belt, a golden dagger and axes of electrum.

Not everyone agrees with Woolley that his so-called Royal Tombs were the graves of the rulers of Ur and his close family. Some think that they contain the ritually slaughtered victims of some religious ceremony. The custom of royal burial with sacrificial victims is attested in several parts of the world, for example in Early Dynastic Egypt and later in the Sudan, in Shang China, and in Melanesia in the 13th century AD, but in Mesopotamia there is little evidence for it apart from the Royal Cemetery.

Palaces and temples
The Royal Cemetery belonged to the first part of the Early Dynastic III period, as did the earliest palaces found in Mesopotamia. Two of these were in Kish, and one in Eridu, and though the buildings bore no inscriptions to indicate that they had been palaces, several features suggested that this was so. They were large, monumental buildings, not too dissimilar to Early Dynastic temples in their plan, but, unlike temples, after they had been abandoned their sites had not been reused for building.

The plano-convex building at Kish was made out of rectangular bricks with rounded tops typical of the Early Dynastic period, and surrounded by a thick, buttressed wall. Its fifty or more rooms, some of which were for storage and others that might have once contained kilns and bitumen-lined basins, were arranged in units separated by narrow corridors. Another palace at Kish, to the south of the main temple area, comprised three units, the earliest measuring about 70 by 40 meters. This contained a central square courtyard surrounded by rooms and the whole was enclosed by a thick wall, to which had been added a monumental entrance approached by a flight of stairs. To the south of this building had stood a second, consisting of a pillared portico and a large, pillared hall about 25 meters long. Inlaid panels of schist, limestone and mother-of-pearl showed scenes like those

Above A gold necklace from the Tomb of the Lord of the Goats beneath the Western Palace, dating to about 1750 BC. The band in three sections was made by coiling. The disks have six-pointed stars decorated with granulation, a technique developed in Early Dynastic times.

Right Some of the thousands of inscribed tablets found in the archive room in Palace G. The texts are written either in Sumerian or in the local language, using the same cuneiform script.

Left A reconstructed relief from the Temple of Ninhursag, the goddess of childbirth, at Tell Ubaid near Ur. The temple was built by A-Anepada, a king of the First Dynasty of Ur, in about 2500 BC. Its architectural decoration had been dismantled and stacked up next to the staircase of the platform on which the shrine stood. This large panel of beaten copper attached to a wooden backing may have been placed above a door and supported by two columns with colored mosaic. Why the temple was decorated with a lion-headed eagle and two stags is not known. Height 1.07 m, width 2.38 m.

Ebla

In 1968 an Italian expedition excavating Tell Mardikh in Syria showed that it was the site of the ancient city of Ebla. The site was occupied from the fourth millennium BC to the 7th century AD but the most important periods were from the middle of the third to the middle of the second millennium BC. The Early Bronze Age Palace G, whose destruction has been attributed to one of the kings of Agade, has revealed an archive of cuneiform texts as well as numerous fine objects left behind when the palace was destroyed. The finds from the Middle Bronze Age (2000–1600 BC) are no less remarkable. Ebla was sacked in about 1600 BC, perhaps by the Hittite king Mursilis I, who went on to capture Babylon.

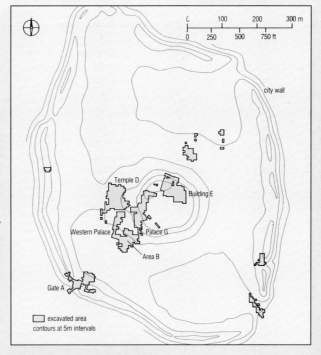

Left Contour plan of site with principal excavated areas. The site covers some 55 ha and has an outer city wall and a central citadel mound more than 15 m high. Much of the city is unexcavated. Apart from Palace G, most of the excavated remains belong to the Middle Bronze Age or later.

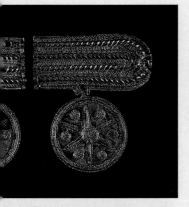

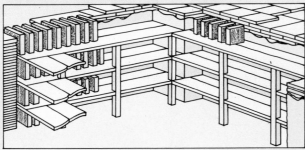

Above left The archive room in Palace G. The tablets lie where they fell from the shelves when the palace was sacked. The presence of a literate civilization in this region at the end of the Early Dynastic period was unsuspected before this discovery.

Left A reconstruction of the shelves of the archive room in Palace G, based on traces left when they burned. The tablets were placed on the shelves like books are today. The texts are mostly economic records.

Above Gold figure of a bull with a human face (5 cm long) found in Palace G. The beard is made of stone (probably chlorite). Its appearance is typically Sumerian: it may have been imported from Sumer or made in Syria in a Sumerian style. The figure probably represents a divine being associated with the sun god Shamash and may be ancestral to the enormous human-headed bulls that were used as guardian figures on much later Assyrian palaces. Length 5 cm.

on the Standard of Ur, and similar inlays have been found at Mari and Ebla. The palace at Eridu included two almost identical buildings side by side, both of which had rooms arranged round courtyards, like later Mesopotamian palaces, and both were surrounded by narrow corridors.

Far more common than palaces were the temples of the Early Dynastic period. Because of the sanctity of the sites and the conservatism of the people, for thousands of years temples were built one above another, and many such sequences have been excavated. In many cases, the earlier, tripartite plan of Ubaid and Uruk temples had been replaced by a courtyard and bent-axis shrine. Another characteristic design was a temple on a platform, such as the one at Ubaid, 4 kilometers

west of Ur. This had been decorated with inlaid mosaic pillars, inlaid friezes showing cows being milked and an elaborate high relief, made of hammered sheet copper, depicting a lion-headed eagle and two stags. The temple, which was enclosed by an oval wall, had been built by A-Anepada, the son of Mes-Anepada, for the goddess Ninhursag.

At Khafajeh a temple on a platform was discovered with a double encircling wall. Before building commenced, the area that the temple would occupy had been dug out to a depth of 4.6 meters and filled with more than 60,000 cubic meters of clean sand. A third oval temple has been found at Lagash. Called the Ibgal of Inanna, it was built by Enanatum I (c. 2410 BC), the ruler of Lagash, though it may have been founded earlier.

Left Stone wall-plaque from Girsu showing Ur-Nanshe the ruler of Lagash (c. 2480 BC) accompanied by his family. In the upper register he is depicted as a builder carrying a basket of bricks. The figure in front may be his wife and behind her are his sons. The lower register shows Ur-Nanshe on the throne. Height 40 cm.

Below Part of the Stele of Eanatum, ruler of Lagash (c. 2440 BC), commemorating his victory over the city state of Umma. The stele was found in fragments at Girsu. On the side shown, Ningirsu, the patron god of the city, uses his mace to crush the skull of one of the enemies he has captured in his net. On the other side the armies are depicted in battle. The bodies of the slain are scavenged by birds and hence the monument is often called the Stele of the Vultures. The long inscription records the details of the border conflict between the two city states of Lagash and Umma. Width of illustrated piece c. 80 cm.

Late Early Dynastic III

Inscriptions from the late Early Dynastic period have shown that the Sumerian King List is incomplete. The rulers of several city states were omitted, including the rulers of Lagash, who are known over more than five generations. Furthermore, inscriptions from Adab and Girsu recorded that Mesalim, the king of Kish, was the overlord of the governors of Adab and Lagash, yet Mesalim does not appear in the king list.

Mesalim had drawn the border between Umma and Lagash, but in the reign of Ur-Nanshe, the ruler of Lagash, border disputes arose and, according to his inscriptions, Ur-Nanshe defeated both Ur and Umma. During this time he built the city wall and temples at Lagash. Ur-Nanshe's grandson Eanatum pursued the conflict with Umma to victory. To celebrate, he erected a monument that bore the inscription "Ningirsu, the lord, crown of Luma is the life of the Pirigedena-canal" and is now known as the Stele of the Vultures, as it shows birds attacking the corpses of the fallen. Eanatum claimed to have defeated Uruk, Ur, Akshak, Mari, Susa, Elam, several districts that were probably in the Iranian Zagros, and even Subartu, believed to have been in northern Mesopotamia. He also stated that Inanna had given him the kingship of Kish. These claims, however, were exaggerated and there is no evidence to suggest that Eanatum made widespread conquests. Perhaps, the truth is that he, like rulers in the Old Babylonian period, sent contingents to distant countries to fight alongside allies in their local disputes. But the perspective of Sumer was widening and the distant contacts that were so important in the Late Uruk period were reawakening.

Sumerian influence abroad

According to the Sumerian King List, dynasties from outside Sumer—Awan and Hamazi in the east and Mari in the west—ruled Sumer, though there is little evidence of this from other sources. However, there was contact between Sumer and the Iranian plateau. At Shahr-i Sokhte, the occupied area grew to more than 45 hectares in Early Dynastic times and had almost doubled before the end of the millennium. At Shahdad, to the east of Kerman, a rich cemetery of the period has yielded metal vessels, sculptures, copper-bronze tools and weapons, as well as stamp and cylinder seals. Metalworking furnaces have also been found, and areas for making objects out of carnelian, agate, chalcedony, calcite, lapis lazuli and chlorite. At Tepe Yahya, farther south, archeologists have uncovered numerous chlorite artifacts, some of them in an unfinished state. Chlorite vessels decorated in the Intercultural Style, like those from Yahya, have been found in the Gulf and at Susa, Sumer and Mari, in levels belonging to the Early Dynastic III period. There has been little evidence for settlement in Fars at this time, and Anshan seems to have been deserted.

In the Zagros region a new style of painted pottery followed the Early Transcaucasian wares found in level IV at Godin Tepe. Known as Godin III, the style survived for more than a thousand years. At Susa the Proto-Elamite culture of Susa III was replaced by a culture using pottery inspired by Godin III, but there was a growing influence from southern Mesopotamia.

In northern Mesopotamia, incised Ninevite 5 pottery was replaced by a hard metallic ware, a development paralleled by the growth of large walled cities in the region. Sumerian-style statues have been found at Ashur and at Tell Khuera, and at Tell Brak and Tell Leilan on the Habur plains southern influence is identifiable in the style of the seal impressions. Mari had long been closely associated with the city states to the south. As well as the evidence of the inscribed bead of Mes-Anepada of Ur found at Mari, two inscriptions from Ur may have been dedicated by a king of Mari. The gods and temples of Mari were in the Mesopotamian tradition and many sculptures found in the temples would not have been out of place farther south.

Interestingly, there was a related literate civilization in western Syria. Halfway between Sumer and Egypt, at Ebla (modern Tell Mardikh), south of Aleppo, some 8,000 clay tablets have been discovered in a royal palace. The tablets, which had been stacked on edge on shelves in an archive room, were in the Sumerian cuneiform script but almost all of them had been written in the local language. At first it was thought that the Eblaite language might have been an early dialect of Hebrew, but it has since been shown that the language was more closely related to Akkadian. More than three-quarters of the texts were to do with administration and the remainder belonged to the traditional field of scribal learning and included lexical texts, as well as some twenty or so literary texts written in the Sumerian and Eblaite languages.

The texts dated to the reigns of three rulers of Ebla who took the title *malikum* and had *lugals* serving beneath them. They were Ar-Ennum, Ibrium and Ibbi-zikir, who probably belonged to the end of the Early Dynastic period. Ibbi-zikir's rule may have been brought to an end by Sargon of Agade, who claimed to have ruled Ebla, or by his grandson Naram-Sin, who claimed to have destroyed Ebla. How far the Eblaite kingdom extended is not certain. It may have reached down to Damascus in the south and certainly had close contact with Mari to the east. The gods mentioned in the texts included some of the Sumero-Akkadian gods, but many of them – including Baal, Lim, Rasap, and El – were known from later periods in the west.

Most of the Ebla texts concerned textiles, especially from wool – the king owned 80,000 sheep – and flax. Barley, olives and grapes were among other crops that were mentioned. Another text indicated how wealthy Ebla had been, by a statement that Ibbi-zikir received each year the weight equivalent of 5 kilograms of gold and 500 kilograms of silver. An alabaster jar lid found in the palace has been important in dating the civilization at Ebla. The lid bore a cartouche of the Egyptian pharaoh Pepi I whose reign is reckoned to have lasted from 2289 to 2255 BC, roughly contemporary with the Mesopotamian kings Sargon (2334–2279 BC) and Naram-Sin (2254–2218 BC). Another important find from the palace was part of a limestone inlay, like those from Kish, with rows of lion-headed eagles between human-headed bulls, alternating with rows of soldiers either carrying weapons, accompanying prisoners, killing prisoners, or carrying the heads of the slain. Such scenes were typical of the Sumerian world and continued into Late Assyrian times. More than 20 kilograms of lapis lazuli have been recovered from the palace, again testifying to the long-distance trade practiced at this time.

The end of the Early Dynastic period

In the last years of the Early Dynastic period Sumer was in ferment. Uruk and Ur were united under Lugalkiginedudu, who took the title King of Kish and formed a pact with the ruler of Lagash. Lagash and Umma continued to fight over the land between them, a conflict dating back to the time of Mesalim. After several changes of ruler in Umma, perhaps brought about by the successes of Lagash, Lugalzagesi followed his father as king of Umma and sacked Lagash. Lugalzagesi also became king of Uruk before he was overthrown by Sargon of Agade in 2334 BC. Lugalzagesi's rule was recorded in the inscriptions on fragments of more than fifty stone vessels found in Nippur, the city of the god Enlil.

"Enlil gave to Lugalzagesi the kingship of the nation, . . . put all the lands at his feet, and from east to west made them subject to him; then from the Lower Sea [the Gulf], (along) the Tigris and Euphrates to the Upper Sea [the Mediterranean], he [Enlil] put their routes in good order for him. From east to west, Enlil permitted him no rival; under him the lands rested contentedly."

Right A silver vase with a copper base dedicated by Entemena, ruler of Lagash (c. 2400 BC), to the god Ningirsu. Ningirsu the city god was later identified with the warrior god Ninurta, the son of Enlil, and may originally have been a storm god. The lion-headed eagle delicately incised on this vase was a common motif in the third millennium and often identified with the Anzu bird (called Imdugud in Sumerian). This thunder bird (with the hindquarters of a lion) may have represented Ningirsu. Later, when gods were depicted only in human form, the association of Ninurta or Ningirsu with the lion-headed eagle was explained in a myth in which Ninurta defeated the Anzu bird.

Sumerian Statues

In Early Dynastic Mesopotamia (c. 2900–2334 BC) it was a common practice for rulers and other citizens to erect statues of themselves in the temples. The statues represented them before the gods in a state of continuous prayer. Examples of such statues have been found at Tell Khuera, Mari, Ashur, Susa and many sites in Sumer and Akkad. The same style of sculpture was popular with both Sumerian and Akkadian speakers.

Art historians have stressed the change from the stylized sculpture of the Early Dynastic Sumerians to the naturalistic art of the dynasty of Agade (2334–2154 BC). However, there is considerable variety within Sumerian art, some of which is very stylized and some quite lifelike, and there is a continuous tradition of sculpture from the Early Dynastic to the Old Babylonian periods.

The bulky rounded shapes that characterized many of the stone statues may have been due to the type of stone available, which was in the form of large river boulders.

Left Statue dedicated by Ebih-il, an official of the Temple of Ishtar in Mari (c. 2400 BC), where it was found. It is made out of white stone (perhaps alabaster) and the eyes are inlaid with bitumen, shell and lapis lazuli. He is shown seated on a stool made out of woven reeds, clasping his hands in a gesture of reverence. Although Mari was 450 km upriver from Sumer on the Euphrates, it shared many of the characteristics of Sumerian civilization. Height 52.5 cm.

Above Small statue of gypsum of a couple, found buried beneath the floor of the shrine of the Inanna Temple at Nippur. The eyes are inlaid with shell and lapis lazuli set in bitumen. A similar group was found in the Temple of Ishtar at Mari.

Left Stone statuette of a human-headed bull wearing a headdress with horns, normally worn by divine beings. Similar carvings are dated to the reign of Gudea, ruler of Lagash (c. 2100 BC). Height 12 cm.

Right This figure of a man carrying a box on his head is made of arsenical copper, the most commonly used alloy in the 3rd millennium BC. Although the statue is of unknown provenance it is similar to a lost-wax casting of a naked priest found in the Early Dynastic Oval Temple at Tell Khafajeh (ancient Tutub). These objects may have been used as stands in the temple ceremonies. Height 38 cm.

Below Limestone statue of a woman found at Girsu. Height 30 cm.

Below A gypsum head of a woman found just outside the Ishtar Temple at Mari. Her headdress is typical of the style worn by women from that city. As several Sumerian statues are of women, it is probable that women enjoyed more equality in early Sumerian society than in later periods. Height 15 cm.

Far right This seated figure from the Temple of Ishtar at Mari is inscribed "Ur-Nanshe the singer". Although the name is of a man, the features of the figure are thought to be feminine. It is possible that Ur-Nanshe was a eunuch in the service of the temple.

The Royal Cemetery of Ur

Sir Leonard Woolley excavated more than a thousand graves in the Royal Cemetery at Ur, most of them dating to the later Early Dynastic period (2600–2400 BC). Seventeen graves were exceptionally rich and have been called Royal Tombs: three have been identified, those of Queen Puabi, Akalamdug and Meskalamdug. The other tombs have either been given names such as the King's Tomb or the Great Death Pit or are known by the numbers given to them by the excavator. In some of the Royal Tombs there was evidence of human sacrifice, with as many as 74 servants being drugged and killed in the Great Death Pit. This practice is almost unparalleled in Mesopotamia, though it has been found in other regions of the world.

The wealth of the graves in the Royal Cemetery and the quality of the workmanship of the objects found there are remarkable. In particular, the metalwork shows complete mastery of the main techniques of jewelry making. The craftsmen often made composite objects using various materials on a wooden backing. Inlays of shell and different-colored stones were common, both as geometric designs and as scenes of people and animals.

Below A cow's head made of gold and lapis lazuli attached to the sounding box of a lyre found in the tomb of Queen Puabi. The lyre was made of wood with inlaid borders. Woolley used plaster of paris and melted paraffin wax to preserve and remove these delicate objects.

Above right The "peace" side of the so-called Standard of Ur, which was probably the sounding box of a musical instrument. The inlay of shell against a background of lapis lazuli set in bitumen shows a banquet with animals and men carrying goods—perhaps the victory celebrations after the successful campaign shown on the "war" side. Length 47 cm, height 20 cm.

Above A gaming board made out of a mosaic of shell, bone, lapis lazuli, red paste and red limestone. The game was played with two sets of seven counters, but the exact rules are not known. Other examples of these gaming boards were found in the Royal Tombs though this came from a private grave. Length 27 cm, width 12 cm.

Left A gold feeding cup with spout from the tomb of Queen Puabi. Numerous fluted and plain gold vessels were found in the Royal Cemetery. Height 12.4 cm.

Right A dagger with a gold blade and a lapis lazuli handle decorated with golden studs. The outside of the sheath was made of exquisite filigree gold work with gold granulation. Length of dagger 37 cm.

Below Queen Puabi was buried in a magnificent gold headdress, decorated with lapis lazuli and carnelian, and with three rows of sheet gold leaves. Crowning the headdress was a tall comb of gold ending in seven rosettes.

Left In a corner of the Great Death Pit two small statues of unequal size were named by Woolley the Rams Caught in the Thicket, though they clearly show goats on their hind legs in front of a golden plant. The face and legs were made of gold, the horns, eyes, and the fleece over the shoulder of lapis lazuli, the belly of silver, and the rest of the fleece of white shell. Height 47 cm.

Below The helmet in the tomb of Meskalamdug was made of electrum (a 15-carat alloy of gold and silver) by hammering from the inside, with the details added later. It had a cloth lining, which was attached to the holes on the lower edge. Height 23 cm.

Overleaf A detail from the "war" side of the Standard of Ur. It shows the victorious troops of the ruler of Ur, who appears larger than the other figures in the top register. The soldiers were either on foot or rode in battle wagons pulled by four onagers. Reproduced at approximately twice actual size.

CHARISMATIC KINGS (2350-2000 BC)

Problems of chronology

The people of ancient Mesopotamia used three different methods to record dates. The simplest was to count regnal years, that is, how long the king had been ruling. This system was adopted in Early Dynastic Lagash and became standard in Babylonia from the middle of the second millennium BC to the Seleucid period (c. 300–150 BC). An alternative way was to name the year after an official who held a particular office at that time. The method was used in Early Dynastic Shuruppak and became the norm in Assyria, where the official was called the *limmu* official and lists of *limmu* names were kept to record the order of the years. A third way was to name a year after an event of the previous year, such as a military victory, the building of a temple or the appointment of a priest. The earliest examples date back to the reigns of Enshakushana and Lugalzagesi and the system became more widespread under the kings of Agade.

These year-names sometimes contain valuable historical information. Unfortunately, complete lists of year-names for the early periods have not so far been found, and the absolute dates of the third-millennium rulers have had to be calculated from the king lists. This can be done by counting backward from the Old Babylonian period, using the fact that Hammurabi, the most important of the Old Babylonian kings, is reckoned to have ruled from 1792 to 1750 BC. Adding up the lengths of the reigns recorded in king lists then shows that the Third Dynasty of Ur lasted from the accession of Ur-Nammu in 2112 BC to the capture of Ur by the Elamites in 2004 BC. According to the Sumerian King List, between Ur-Nammu and the last king of Agade "the kingship was carried to the horde of Gutium". The defeat of one of these Gutian kings is mentioned in a year-name of Shar-kali-sharri, the fifth king of Agade, though it is unclear which year this was within his 25-year reign. Adding up the lengths of the reigns puts Sargon, the first king of Agade, as having become king between about 2340 and 2310 BC. The dates that are usually given for his reign, 2334–2279 BC, might therefore be out by as much as a quarter-century. If the accepted dates for Hammurabi should prove to be too late, as many experts now believe, then Sargon's reign too would have started earlier.

Sumerians and Akkadians

In later Mesopotamian tradition the conquests of the Akkadian kings marked a complete break with the previous Sumerian Early Dynastic period. For the first time in history the whole of Mesopotamia was united under one ruler, and the Akkadian empire was a model that later kings strove to emulate. Furthermore the ruling power passed from Sumerian to Semitic speakers. Until recently this change was seen in racial terms, and changes in the nature of kingship, political organization and even art were attributed to the ethnic background of the rulers. Now, however, it seems that the continuity between the Akkadian rulers and their Sumerian predecessors was greater than had earlier been supposed.

In the Early Dynastic period it is difficult to distinguish Sumerians from Akkadians. For centuries they were in close contact and words borrowed from Akkadian have been recognized in early Sumerian texts. The Akkadians to the north adopted the Sumerian script for their inscriptions, but as logograms (signs representing words) can be read in either Sumerian or Akkadian it has not always proved possible in short inscriptions to tell which language was being used. A few Akkadian suffixes in the inscriptions from Mari suggest that they were read in Akkadian.

In general there are more Sumerian names in the south and more Akkadian names in the north. However, Queen Puabi, who was buried in the Royal Cemetery of Ur, may have had an Akkadian rather than a Sumerian name, while native kings of Kish had both Sumerian and Akkadian names; for example Mebaragesi is Sumerian, but Enbi-Ishtar is Akkadian. As today in the mixed populations of the Near East, many people must have been bilingual, as is shown by the Early Dynastic scribes of Abu Salabikh who had Akkadian names but wrote Sumerian. Although it is generally not wrong to identify the ethnic affiliation of people through the language of their names, in certain cases it may be unjustified. It is, however, almost the only way to estimate the composition of populations of different groups, and so has been used to chart the infiltration of Amorites, Hurrians, Kassites and Aramaeans into the literate part of the Near East in later centuries.

Sargon of Agade

The first ruler of the dynasty of Agade was called Sharrum-kin, which in later times was pronounced Sharken and is preserved in the Bible in the form Sargon. In Akkadian, Sharrum-kin means the true or legitimate king, which is a strong hint that he was a usurper. There were many stories about his origins. According to a later account he was placed in a reed basket sealed with bitumen and, like Moses, allowed to float down the Euphrates. He was rescued and trained as a gardener, and, by winning the love of Ishtar, became king. The

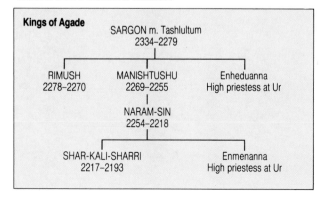

Kings of Agade

SARGON m. Tashlultum
2334–2279

RIMUSH
2278–2270

MANISHTUSHU
2269–2255

Enheduanna
High priestess at Ur

NARAM-SIN
2254–2218

SHAR-KALI-SHARRI
2217–2193

Enmenanna
High priestess at Ur

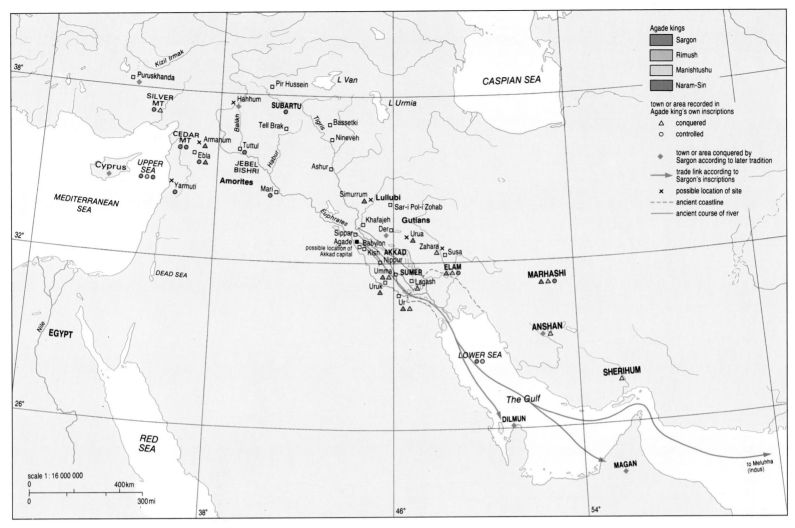

The map legend reads:

Agade kings
- Sargon
- Rimush
- Manishtushu
- Naram-Sin

town or area recorded in Agade king's own inscriptions
- △ conquered
- ○ controlled
- ◆ town or area conquered by Sargon according to later tradition
- → trade link according to Sargon's inscriptions
- × possible location of site
- --- ancient coastline
- — ancient course of river

The conquests of the kings of Agade

The kings of Agade not only established their rule over the cities in Sumer and Akkad but campaigned far to the east and west. According to their own inscriptions, Sargon, Rimush, Manishtushu and Naram-Sin conquered cities from the Mediterranean coast to the other side of the Gulf. Sargon, whose inscriptions and monuments were based on the previous Sumerian styles, is sometimes said to be an Early Dynastic king. However, the breadth of his conquests and his vision of kingship contrast markedly with the parochial concerns of most Early Dynastic rulers. Later traditions and legends credited Sargon with ruling the whole world, from "the sunrise to the sunset", but some of these stories may have been intended to glorify Sargon II of Assyria (721–705 BC) who adopted the name of his illustrious predecessor.

Sumerian king list stated, more simply. "Sharrum-kin, his [father] was a date-grower, cup-bearer of Ur-Zababa, king of Agade, the one who built Agade, became king and reigned 56 years."

An Old Babylonian copy of an inscription found on a monument in the Temple of Enlil at Nippur did not mention Sargon's ancestry, referring to him as King of Agade, King of Kish and King of the Land and recording how, with the assistance of the gods, he defeated Uruk in battle and captured Lugalzagesi, its king. Sargon conquered Ur, Umma and Lagash as far as the sea. A fragment of this monument, or of a similar one, was found at Susa, having been taken there by the Elamites when they conquered Babylonia in the 12th century BC. It showed Sargon, under a sunshade, at the head of his troops. A second fragment, which might also have belonged to the same monument, showed a god holding defeated enemies in a net, as on the Stele of the Vultures found at Girsu.

A second inscription, also known from an Old Babylonian copy, recorded Sargon's contacts with distant countries. The ships of Meluhha, Magan, and Dilmun (which have been identified with the Indus, Oman and Bahrain, respectively) docked at the quay of Agade. In Tuttul (probably Tell Bi'a at the junction of the Balikh and Euphrates rivers) Sargon worshiped the god Dagan who had given him control over the Upper Land (Western Syria), Mari, Ebla and Yarmuti (probably on the Mediterranean coast), as far as the Cedar Forest and the Silver Mountain.

Disentangling the later stories associated with

the name of Sargon has been difficult, particularly as these were reworked in the Late Assyrian period to glorify Sargon II of Assyria. He is said to have conquered Puruskhanda on the Anatolian plateau and to have attacked and conquered Elam and Marhashi in the mountains of Iran, as well as Dilmun. According to later traditions, Sargon founded a new capital called Agade, where he built a palace, and temples to Ishtar and Zababa, the warrior god of Kish. Agade's precise location is still unknown, but it was probably in the region of Babylon, Kish and Sippar. It was Agade, sometimes transcribed Akkade, that gave its name to the dynasty and to the language.

Sargon appointed his daughter Enheduanna as high priestess of Nanna, the moon god at Ur, and a circular limestone plaque depicting Enheduanna making an offering at an altar was found there. Later rulers continued the custom of appointing their daughters to be high priestesses at Ur until the time of Nabonidus in the 6th century BC. Enheduanna was also credited with composing two hymns in honor of Inanna, making her the earliest of the few authors of Mesopotamian literature whose names have survived.

Sargon's sons

Sargon was succeeded by his son Rimush, who continued his father's military adventures. According to copies of his inscriptions, he put down rebellions in Sumer and Akkad and conquered Elam and Marhashi (also known as Barah-shi). Booty from this campaign has been found in

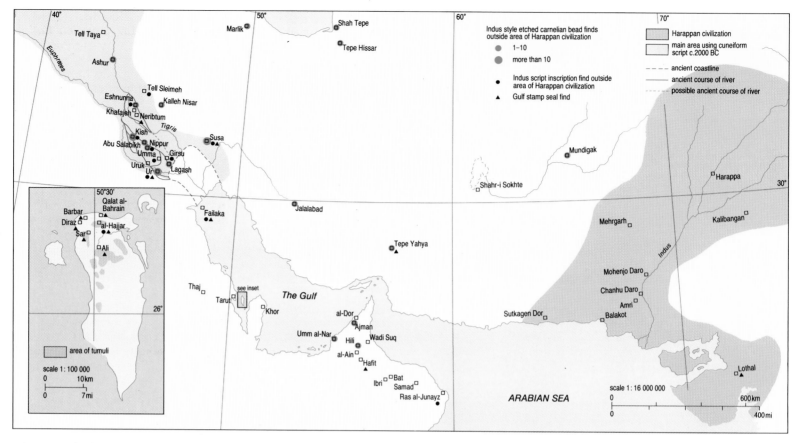

Nippur, Khafajeh, and even as far away as Tell Brak (though in this case it might have been brought there later). Rimush claimed to control the Upper Sea, the Lower Sea, and all the mountains. A later text recorded how Rimush was killed by his servants in a palace conspiracy.

After Rimush, came his brother Manishtushu. His name means "who is with him", suggesting that he might have been Rimush's twin brother. However, according to the Sumerian King List, Manishtushu was the elder brother. In one of his inscriptions he claimed to have led an expedition across the Gulf as far as the silver mines (so far unidentified) and to have brought back stone for making statues. (This stone might have been diorite, which is found in Oman, as diorite was used by the kings of Agade for their sculptures.) He also boasted of his conquest of Anshan and Sherihum, swearing that "these are no lies. It is absolutely true!" Another statue of Manishtushu, found at Susa, had been dedicated to him by Eshpum, the city governor, and showed that Akkadian rule extended to Susa. In the north Manishtushu controlled Ashur and at Nineveh he renovated the Ishtar Temple, as witnessed by the later Assyrian king Shamshi-Adad I, who, in the course of restoring the temples, found statues of Manishtushu.

Naram-Sin the god-king

The 37-year rule of Manishtushu's son Naram-Sin marked the high point of the Akkadian empire. Like his predecessors, Naram-Sin fought to maintain and extend his rule. He also seems to have changed the nature of kingship, by becoming a god himself instead of ruling as an agent of the gods. At some point in his reign Naram-Sin decided to call himself "king of the four quarters, king of the universe", prefixing his name with the sign used to indicate gods. His officials also addressed him as

"god of Agade". Some early kings of Uruk, such as Lugalbanda and Gilgamesh, appeared as divine names in the Early Dynastic texts from Shuruppak, but Naram-Sin was probably the first Mesopotamian monarch to have claimed divine status in his lifetime.

He ruled over a vast empire. In his inscriptions he claimed to have destroyed the city of Ebla, and inscribed bricks found at Susa are evidence of his rule there. At Tell Brak a large building measuring 90 meters by more than 85 meters, with outer walls more than 10 meters thick, was built with bricks bearing his name. This might have been a storehouse, military outpost or administrative center controlling the important trade routes through the Habur. A stone relief of Naram-Sin has even been found at Pir Hussein, north of Diyarbekir in southeast Turkey.

In the Bassetki district, about 50 kilometers north of Nineveh, the base and lower part of a copper statue were discovered, bearing an inscription of Naram-Sin's claiming that he won nine battles in a single year and recording construction work in the city of Agade. The statue represented a male figure wearing a girdle and holding a foundation peg of the sort found in Sumerian foundation deposits. The surviving piece, which weighed 160 kilograms, was made of almost pure copper as a hollow, lost-wax casting.

Another remarkable cast copper object of the Akkadian period—a life-size head—was found in the Late Assyrian destruction level at Nineveh, where it had probably been ritually mutilated by the Median invaders. The detail of the hair is reminiscent of the gold helmet of Meskalamdug at Ur, but the naturalism and fine workmanship show that it belonged to the Akkadian period. The identity of the figure is not certain, but experts consider this head to be a likeness of Naram-Sin.

Trade with the Gulf and the Indus valley
From Early Dynastic times until the Old Babylonian period an important maritime trade was pursued in the Gulf. At one end lay the cities of southern Mesopotamia, from where goods were dispersed to the west and north, and at the other end lay Meluhha, plausibly identified with the Harappan civilization. Two other important regions mentioned in the texts are Dilmun (probably including both the islands of present-day Bahrain and Failaka) and Magan (perhaps Oman). Royal inscriptions and the economic records of the merchants who went by boat from Ur give details of the trade.

Excavations in the Gulf are now providing more evidence for this trade. In Bahrain and Failaka there was a flourishing civilization which buried its dead in tumuli. The number of these burial mounds on the island of Bahrain has been estimated as 150,000. Gulf-style stamp seals of the sort probably manufactured in Dilmun have been found both in Mesopotamia and in India. Harappan types of weights were in use in Bahrain, and Indus inscriptions, seals, beads (including etched carnelian beads) and pottery have been found in Oman, Bahrain, Failaka and Mesopotamia. The end of the Gulf trade coincided with the collapse of Old Babylonian control of southern Mesopotamia and the demise of the Harappan civilization itself.

wooded terrain. Victorious Akkadian standard-bearers and defeated and dying pigtailed Lullubi warriors were carved in such a way as to move the viewer's eye triumphantly upward. As in the Bassetki statue and the Nineveh head, there is a naturalism in the representation of the human form that was missing in earlier works. This relief, apparently, exercised a fascination on later rulers, as versions of it were carved in rock reliefs in the western Zagros at Derbend-i Gawr, at Shaikhan, and at Sar-i Pol-i Zohab, though none of them matched the quality of the original.

Like Sargon, Naram-Sin became the subject of later stories. He was portrayed as a tragic figure, the victim of his own pride, which brought about rebellion, invasion by tribes from the east and the destruction of Agade. However, there is no evidence from Naram-Sin's reign to support these stories. The year-names of Naram-Sin's son and successor, Shar-kali-sharri, suggest that his realm was under pressure both from the Amorite tribes in the west and the Gutians from the eastern mountains. In the Sumerian King List, Shar-kali-sharri was followed by what amounts to a description of anarchy: "Who was king? Who was not king? Was Igigi king? Was Nanum king? Was Imi king? Was Elulu king? The four of them were kings and reigned three years." The last two kings of Agade were Dudu and Shu-durul, by whose time the realm had been reduced to the region round Agade and in the Diyala plains to the north, while other city states in the south, among them Lagash, had gained their independence.

The Neo-Sumerian revival

After the collapse of the Akkadian empire, the most famous member of the dynasty that ruled Lagash was Gudea. He rebuilt 15 temples in Girsu, which became the administrative center of the state of Lagash. The most important of these was the temple of the city god, Ningirsu. In two long texts inscribed on large clay cylinders, Gudea described how it was built. First, he had a dream in which the god Ningirsu revealed to him that the temple should be rebuilt and showed him the building plan. Gudea purified the site, surrounded it with fires, and then, according to the inscriptions, brought craftsmen and materials from distant lands to build the temple.

"From Elam came the Elamites, from Susa the Susians. Magan and Meluhha collected timber from their mountains . . . Gudea brought them together in his town Girsu . . . Gudea, the great *en*-priest of Ningirsu, made a path into the Cedar mountains that nobody had ever entered before; he cut its cedars with great axes . . . Like great snakes, cedars were floating down the water [of the river] from the Cedar Mountain, pine rafts from the Pine Mountain . . . In the quarries, which nobody had entered before, Gudea, the great *en*-priest of Ningirsu, made a path and then the stones were delivered in large blocks . . . Many other precious metals were carried to the governor, the builder of the Ninnu Temple. From the copper mountain of Kimash . . . gold was delivered from its mountain as dust . . . For Gudea, they mined silver from its mountains, delivered red stones from Meluhha in great amounts."

Above Cast copper head found in the area of the Ishtar Temple at Nineveh. The head is hollow and was cast using the lost-wax method. The figure is that of a ruler and was first identified as Sargon, the founder of the dynasty of Agade, but from the style it is more likely to have represented his grandson Naram-Sin. Height 36.6 cm.

Naram-Sin's most famous monument is his Victory Stele, which was found at Susa. Like the Sargon Stele and the Law Code of Hammurabi, it had been taken to Susa as booty by the Elamites. It recorded the victory of Naram-Sin over Satuni, the king of the Lullubi tribe, which had inhabited the central part of western Iran. The stele presented a new approach to the portrayal of historical events, abandoning the old scheme of registers found on Early Dynastic wall plaques and on the stelae of Eanatum and Sargon, in favor of a single coherent composition. The stone has been damaged at the base and at the top, but originally there might have been seven stars at the top, presumably representing the gods. The main focus of the relief, however, was the figure of Naram-Sin carrying a bow and an axe and wearing a headdress with horns, like those worn by gods in Mesopotamia. The setting – the earliest example in Mesopotamian art of a background landscape being shown – was a hilly and

The remains of the temples have not been identified in the excavations at Girsu, but diorite statues of Gudea and other rulers of Lagash have survived to attest both to the wealth of the state and to the artistic ability of its craftsmen.

How far Gudea's kingdom stretched is not known. His only claim to military success was a victory over Anshan and Elam, and he might have exercised some influence in Ur. The dates of his reign are also uncertain but he was probably a contemporary of Utuhegal and of Ur-Nammu. Utuhegal (2019–2013 BC) was the king of Uruk who ended the rule of the Gutians. He appointed Ur-Nammu, who some scholars think may have been his son, military governor (*shagin*) of Ur. Ur-

Nammu succeeded Utuhegal and founded the Third Dynasty of Ur, calling himself Mighty Man, Lord of Uruk, Lord of Ur, King of Sumer and Akkad, but later dropped the title Lord of Uruk.

The Third Dynasty of Ur

Ur-Nammu controlled Ur, Eridu and Uruk and erected buildings at Nippur, Larsa, Kesh, Adab and Umma. According to an inscription found at Nippur, he arbitrated in disputes between the city states of Girtab, Abiak, Marad and Akshak in northern Akkad. At Ur he appointed his daughter Ennirgalanna *entu*-priestess of Nanna, and one of his sons became *en*-priest of Inanna at Uruk. Another son (possibly his successor, Shulgi) had an arranged marriage to a daughter of the king of Mari. There is little evidence to suggest that Ur-Nammu waged war on his neighbors, but it seems that he gradually absorbed them into his sphere of influence by the use of diplomatic alliances and religious influence.

The most impressive monument of his reign was the ziggurat at Ur. Since Ubaid times the temples of lower Mesopotamia had been built on platforms, which over the centuries had increased in height until the platform dwarfed the shrine at the top. The ziggurats built by Ur-Nammu at Ur, Eridu, Uruk and Nippur were the first certain examples of this type of structure. The evidence for their existence in the Early Dynastic period and under the Agade dynasty is doubtful.

Ur-Nammu also constructed other temples at Ur as well as a residence for the *entu*-priestess and a palace. He rebuilt the city walls and dug canals. Fragments of a large round-topped stele about 3 meters tall have been found, on which some of Ur-Nammu's building projects were recorded. The top registers on both sides of the stele show the king twice, on the right in front of the moon god Nanna, the city god of Ur, and on the left in front of a goddess, probably Ningal, Nanna's consort. In the second register, on one side, the king, accompanied by a second goddess, is pouring a libation. This scene resembles the most common design found on cylinder seals of the period. The lower registers of the stele are poorly preserved but fragments show the king holding the tools needed for rebuilding the temple, and below that there are traces of a high wall with ladders and workmen carrying baskets. The other side of the stele has scenes of what might have been religious ceremonies. The overall balanced, static composition lacks the dynamism of the victory stele of Naram-Sin, exemplifying the contrast between the two dynasties – the Neo-Sumerian staid and pedantic, the Akkadian vibrant and adventurous.

Left According to the inscription this statue was made by Gudea, ruler of Lagash (c. 2100 BC), for the temple of the goddess Geshtinanna. Gudea refurbished the temples at Girsu and 11 statues of him have been found in excavations at the site. Nine others including this one were sold on the art market. It has been suggested that this statue is a forgery. Unlike the hard diorite of the excavated statues, it is made of soft calcite, and shows a ruler with a flowing vase which elsewhere in Mesopotamian art is only held by gods. It also differs stylistically from the excavated statues. On the other hand, the Sumerian inscription appears to be genuine and would be very difficult to fake.

Statues of Gudea show him standing or sitting. In one, he rests on his knee a plan of the temple that he is building. On some statues Gudea has a shaven head, while on others like this one he wears a headdress covered with spirals, probably indicating that it was made out of fur. Height 61 cm.

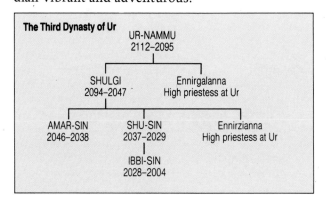

The Third Dynasty of Ur

UR-NAMMU
2112–2095

SHULGI
2094–2047

Ennirgalanna
High priestess at Ur

AMAR-SIN
2046–2038

SHU-SIN
2037–2029

Ennirzianna
High priestess at Ur

IBBI-SIN
2028–2004

Ur

The ancient city of Ur (modern Tell al-Muqayyar) was founded early in the Ubaid period. The prehistoric levels are buried deep beneath the later deposits but have been excavated in a series of trenches, including one that was called the Flood Pit because the excavators thought they had found evidence for the Biblical Flood (though now this appears to have been a local inundation). The extraordinary wealth of the city in the Early Dynastic period was revealed in the Royal Cemetery, where the rulers of Ur were buried.

As the capital of the Third Dynasty of Ur (2112–2004 BC), the city was completely rebuilt by its rulers, Ur-Nammu, Shulgi and Amar-Sin. Ur was the port city for Mesopotamian trade with the countries in the Gulf and beyond until the 18th century BC, when it came under the control of the Dynasty of the Sealand. In the second and first millennia Ur remained an important center for the worship of the moon god Nanna (Sin) and the restoration of the temples of Ur was undertaken by many Babylonian kings. Ur was probably abandoned in the 4th century BC, perhaps because of a change in the course of the rivers.

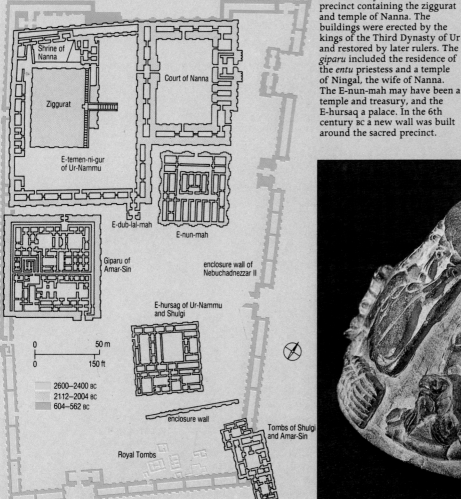

Left The city of Ur was dominated by the sacred precinct containing the ziggurat and temple of Nanna. The buildings were erected by the kings of the Third Dynasty of Ur and restored by later rulers. The *giparu* included the residence of the *entu* priestess and a temple of Ningal, the wife of Nanna. The E-nun-mah may have been a temple and treasury, and the E-hursaq a palace. In the 6th century BC a new wall was built around the sacred precinct.

Above The restored remains of the ziggurat dominate the skyline at Ur. Started by Ur-Nammu and completed by his son Shulgi on the site of an earlier temple, it probably had three stages, on top of which was placed the shrine. It was restored 1,500 years later by Nabonidus, who had a particular reverence for the moon god. Nabonidus' ziggurat may have had as many as seven stages.

Below This decorated stone bowl was found in the ruins of an Achaemenian (5th-century BC) house at Ur but belongs to the late 4th millennium BC. The motifs of the bull and an ear of barley are found on other works of the period and may symbolize the wealth of the land. Height 5.5 cm.

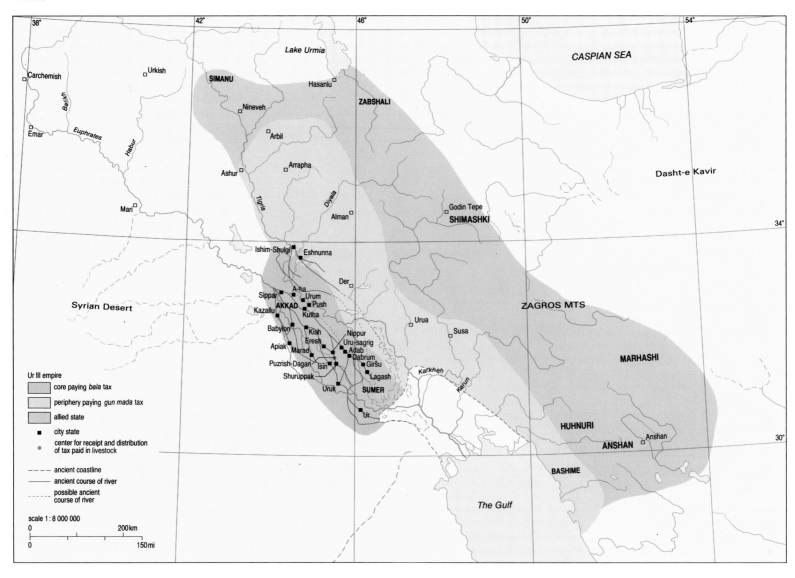

38° 42° 46° 50° 54°

CASPIAN SEA

Lake Urmia

Carchemish
Urkish
SIMANU
Hasanlu
ZABSHALI
Nineveh
Arbil
Dasht-e Kavir
Emar
Euphrates
Habur
Ashur
Arrapha
Mari
Tigris
Diyala
Alman
Godin Tepe
SHIMASHKI
34°
Syrian Desert
Ishim-Shulgi
Eshnunna
Der
ZAGROS MTS
A-ha
Sippar
Urum
Kazallu
AKKAD
Push
Kutha
Urua
Babylon
Kish
Susa
Apiak
Eresh
Nippur
Marad
Uru-sagrig
MARHASHI
Puzrish-Dagan
Adab
Dabrum
Isin
Girsu
Shuruppak
Lagash
Karkheh
Uruk
SUMER
Ur
HUHNURI
Anshan
ANSHAN
30°
BASHIME
The Gulf

Ur III empire
core paying *bala* tax
periphery paying *gun mada* tax
allied state
■ city state
● center for receipt and distribution of tax paid in livestock
--- ancient coastline
— ancient course of river
····· possible ancient course of river

scale 1 : 8 000 000
0   200km
0   150mi

Shulgi the reformer

Ur-Nammu was succeeded by his son Shulgi. Most of the year-names of the first half of his 47-year reign recorded acts of piety, as did those of his father. In about his 20th year, however, Shulgi embarked on a major reorganization of the Ur III state and expanded his empire. Like Naram-Sin, he claimed divine status and many hymns were composed in his honor. Through conquest and diplomacy he extended his kingdom to the north and east of Sumer to include the region between Ashur and Susa. He created a unified administration for Sumer and Akkad – the core of his empire – with *ensi*s (governors), who were often from the local ruling family, and *shagin*s (military commanders), who reported directly to the king. The periphery beyond was administered by military personnel. He also took direct control of the temple lands and introduced new systems of taxation. The *bala* was a tax paid by the provinces of the core of the Ur III state, while the *gun mada* was paid in livestock by the military personnel in the periphery.

To collect, process and distribute the state revenues he established redistribution centers, such as Puzrish-Dagan (Drehem, 10 kilometers south of Nippur), which specialized in livestock. In one year alone 28,000 cattle and 350,000 sheep passed through Puzrish-Dagan, coming as tax from the provinces before being redistributed to the major temples of the land as well as to officials and the

royal household. Another center, Dusabara, specialized in agricultural products.

The administration of these taxes necessitated the training of more scribes, leading to improvements in writing methods and the introduction of new recording practices. Shulgi was one of the few rulers who is believed to have mastered the cuneiform script. He also reorganized the systems of weights and measures and introduced a new calendar that was used throughout the Ur III state. Moreover, Shulgi is now thought to have been the author of the oldest surviving law code, which had previously been attributed to Ur-Nammu.

The dispensation of justice was one of the prime duties of all Mesopotamian rulers. Some hint of this is found in the reforms established by the last Early Dynastic ruler of Lagash, Uruinimgina, who sought to correct abuses in the traditional legal system. Records of court proceedings dating to the time of the Dynasty of Agade have survived, but these became more common in the reign of Shulgi. Although Shulgi's law code is very incomplete, its form is the same as the later, better preserved law codes of Lipit-Ishtar and Hammurabi and for the first time it prescribed fixed penalties for specific crimes.

Shulgi continued and completed the construction work begun by his father. A building just outside the religious precinct at Ur was made from bricks bearing his name, and attached to it were

The empire of the Third Dynasty of Ur
Twenty-three city states in Sumer and Akkad formed the heart of the empire of the Third Dynasty of Ur. These states were ruled by civil and military governors appointed by the king and they paid the monthly *bala* tax. The 90 or more settlements in the region to the north and east were under the control of military officers who had to pay an annual tax in livestock (the *gun mada* tax). Many of these settlements cannot yet be identified. Beyond this region, which was under the rule of the king of Ur, the local states were often allied to Ur through dynastic marriages or treaties.

two smaller structures with bricks inscribed with the name of his son, Amar-Sin. This building is thought to have been the burial place of the kings of Ur, whose bodies were interred in the vaults below, where fragments of human bones have been found. The contents and fittings of the buildings had been plundered in antiquity but surviving fragments indicated that the doors had been covered with gold leaf, the walls decorated with sheet gold inlaid with agate and lapis lazuli, and the ceilings adorned with tiny stars and the sun's rays in gold and lapis lazuli. In one room were benches and channels covered in bitumen and gold leaf, which might have been used for libations, suggesting that the upper rooms served as mortuary temples for the cult of the dead king.

Shulgi had at least twelve sons and eight daughters, one of whom became *entu*-priestess in Ur. Three of the other daughters were married to rulers of the Iranian principalities Marhashi, Anshan and Bashime. Shulgi was succeeded by two of his sons, first Amar-Sin and then Shu-Sin. From early on in Shu-Sin's reign there were signs that all was not well in the empire. In Shu-Sin's fourth year he built a wall between the Tigris and the Euphrates to keep out the marauding Amorites, a Semitic tribe or group of tribes who had infiltrated into Mesopotamia from the southwest. Under Shu-Sin's son, Ibbi-Sin, the empire collapsed. In the second year of his reign, Eshnunna rebelled and in the third year Ibbi-Sin lost control of Susa. The collapse of the empire has been traced in the year-names used to date documents in different cities. Ibbi-Sin's year-names are not found after his third year at Puzrish-Dagan, fifth year at Umma, sixth year at Girsu and eighth year at Nippur. In his 10th year, Ishbi-Erra, one of his military commanders, seized control of Nippur and northern Babylonia, founding a new dynasty with its capital at Isin. Only at Ur itself did Ibbi-Sin retain control for the full 24 years of his reign until, in 2004 BC, the Elamites invaded Ur, sacked and looted the city and took away Ibbi-Sin as a captive to Anshan.

The rise of the Elamites

During the period when Susa was subservient to the kings of Agade, the kingdom of Awan had retained its independence. Awan's exact location is not known, but it probably lay to the north of Susa. In about 2200 BC Puzur-Inshushinak, the king of Awan, established control over Susa and, in inscriptions found at Susa, claimed to have made extensive conquests. Some of these inscriptions were in the Linear Elamite script, a simplified syllabic script for writing Elamite. Very few inscriptions written in this script have been found. Seventeen came from Susa, one from the cemetery at Shahdad and one is said to have been found in Fars.

Shulgi of Ur had annexed Susa and the lowlands, but the highland areas, though linked through royal marriages, remained independent. In the reign of Ibbi-Sin, the ruler of Shimashki, who already controlled Anshan, seized power in Susa. In 2004 BC Kindattu, king of Shimashki, Susa and Anshan, invaded and destroyed Ur. The Elamites were expelled from Ur in about 1995 BC, but the Shimashki dynasty continued to rule Susa for another hundred years.

Anatolia and the west

One of the resources that had been desired by the Agade kings was silver from the mines of Anatolia. Two fragments of an alabaster relief acquired in Nasiriyeh perhaps illustrated one of these forays. On one fragment naked prisoners are being paraded while the other shows soldiers carrying booty, including what has been identified as a metal vessel of an Anatolian Early Bronze Age 2 type.

At Alaca Huyuk, in central Anatolia, 13 rich tombs have been excavated. Although referred to as royal graves, as with the Royal Cemetery at Ur their royal status has not been proved. The tombs were large rectangular pits, up to 8 meters long and 3.5 meters wide, that held the bodies of both men and women. The body was placed in the northwest corner and is thought to have been buried together with wooden furniture. The finest objects found there were of metal, gold, electrum, silver and copper and included vessels, pins and weapons. Two iron daggers with gold-plated handles showed the precocity of Anatolian metalworkers. The most impressive objects were the so-called standards, ending in cast bulls or geometrical shapes. They were made of copper and overlaid or inlaid with electrum, but their function is not known. They had massive dowels that attached to some wooden framework, perhaps a canopy over each tomb. Probably, the tombs were roughly contemporary with the Agade kings, but the chronology is uncertain. Further west, the destruction levels on Early Bronze 2 sites in Anatolia have been attributed to the arrival of the Luwians and the Hittites, who dominated Anatolia in the second millennium BC, but there has so far been no proof of this.

In northern Mesopotamia, Mari had probably come under the rule of the early Agade kings. However, apart from the discovery of two bronzes dedicated by daughters of Naram-Sin, there is little evidence to suggest interference in the affairs of the city by the kings of Agade. In the time of the Third Dynasty at Ur, the rulers of Mari took the title *shaknu*, the Akkadian equivalent of *shagin*, but Mari did not, apparently, participate in the economic structure of the Ur III empire. The famous palace of the rulers of Mari was built over several centuries and some fine wall paintings have been dated to the period of the Third Dynasty of Ur because of their similarity to the stele of Ur-Nammu.

The destruction of Ebla coincided with a decline in the settlement of the Levant. Further south, the Early Bronze 3 period gave way to Early Bronze 4 (c.2350–2000), and most of the urban centers of the earlier period were abandoned. The agricultural and urban way of life, it seems, yielded to a pastoral existence that might have been connected with movements of nomadic groups such as the Amorites further to the east. Toward the end of the Egyptian Old Kingdom the Egyptians mounted expeditions against the Asiatics and perhaps penetrated as far north as Mount Carmel. Their chief interest, however, lay farther north in the Lebanon where Byblos acted as their main port for trade in resin, timber and other goods. With the end of the Old Kingdom in about 2150 BC, contact between the Levant and Egypt ceased and decline set in for the next 150 years.

Below Black stone weight in the shape of a duck found at Ur. The inscription states that Shulgi "established [its weight as] 5 minas for Nanna", the moon god. Nanna's crescent is visible on the other side. Length 14 cm.

Bottom Cast silver figure of a bull inlaid with gold. Similar figures were found in the rich tombs at Alaca Huyuk in central Anatolia. These tombs probably belong to the later 2nd millennium BC, though some scholars have suggested an earlier date. The metalwork from Alaca shows great competence though techniques such as granulation and filigree, which were used with such skill in the Royal Cemetery at Ur, were not found in the tombs at Alaca Huyuk. Height 24 cm.

Ziggurats

Ziggurats were one of the most typical features of ancient Mesopotamia. In many cities the temple of the city god contained a ziggurat, consisting of a series of superimposed platforms on top of which was a temple. Temples set on platforms are found as early as the Ubaid period at Eridu, around 5000 BC. The first proper ziggurats were built by Ur-Nammu (2112–2095 BC), the first king of the Third Dynasty of Ur, at Ur, Eridu, Uruk and Nippur. They were all similar in design, with a rectangular base and three staircases, meeting at right-angles, that led up to the high temple. The same plan was used for the most famous ziggurat of all, that of the god Marduk at Babylon, which gave rise to the story of the Tower of Babel. Begun in the 18th century BC, it was called Etemenanki, meaning "the temple of the foundation of heaven and earth".

The exact nature of the ceremonies that took place in the high sanctuary is not known. The Greek historian Herodotus, who gave a detailed description of the ziggurat at Babylon, suggested that a sacred marriage between a priestess and the god (who was possibly represented in the person of the king) was enacted there in a ritual designed to ensure the future prosperity of the country.

Left A reconstructed drawing of the temple and ziggurat at Tell al-Rimah, probably ancient Qatara. This may have been built in the time of Shamshi-Adad I (c. 1800 BC). Unlike the earlier southern type, with three staircases, the ziggurat was part of the temple building and the upper shrine was probably reached from the roof of the courtyard temple.

Right A drawing of the ziggurat at Ur built by Ur-Nammu. Made out of sun-dried mud-brick, it had a thick outer coating of baked brick. Parts of the lower two stages were preserved. The appearance can be reconstructed from pictures on reliefs and on seals.

Ziggurats were similar in shape to the pyramids of Egypt such as the stepped pyramid at Saqqara (*below, upper picture*), but their function was different. The pyramids were tombs with the tomb chambers concealed in the center of the monument and no structure on the top. Ziggurats, being made of solid brickwork with a temple on top, are more similar to the temples of Central America such as the one at Chichen Itza (*bottom*). However, the concept of a massive pyramid-shaped structure possibly came from Egypt.

Overleaf A view of the reconstructed remains of the ziggurat at Ur.

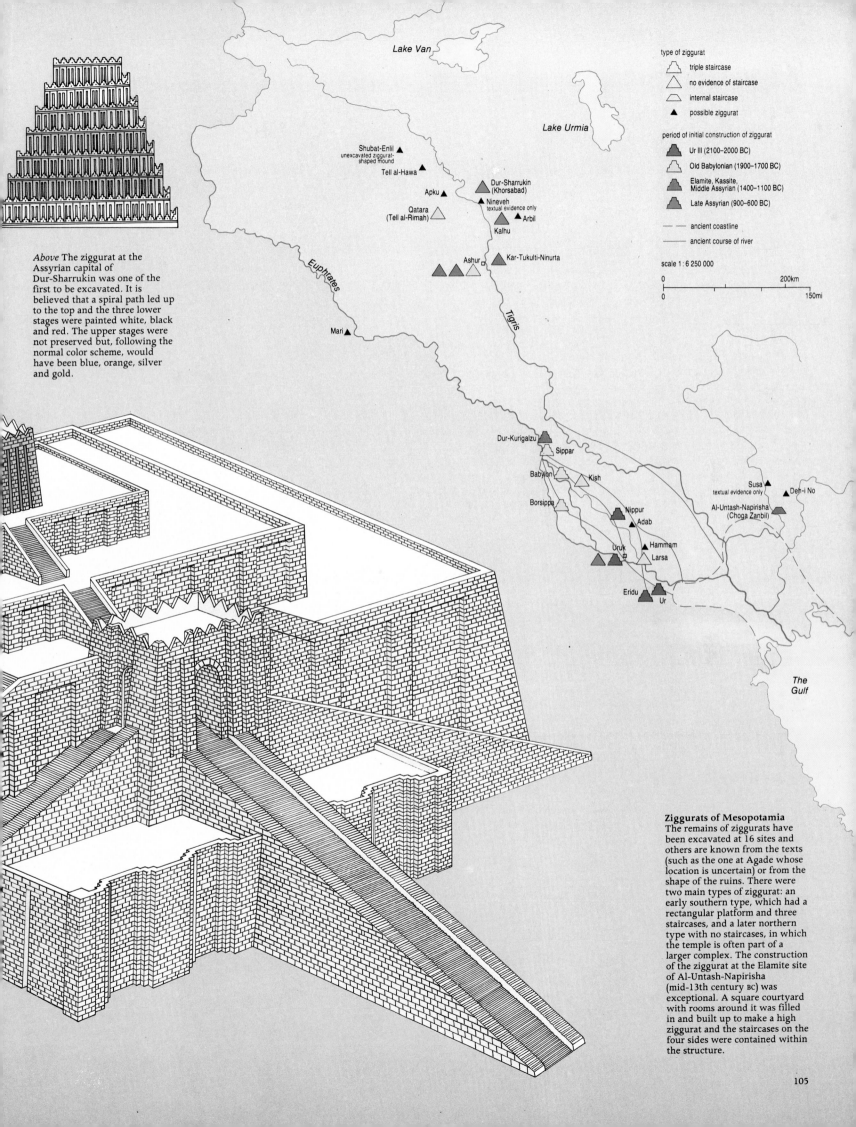

Above The ziggurat at the Assyrian capital of Dur-Sharrukin was one of the first to be excavated. It is believed that a spiral path led up to the top and the three lower stages were painted white, black and red. The upper stages were not preserved but, following the normal color scheme, would have been blue, orange, silver and gold.

type of ziggurat

△ triple staircase

△ no evidence of staircase

⌂ internal staircase

▲ possible ziggurat

period of initial construction of ziggurat

Ur III (2100–2000 BC)

Old Babylonian (1900–1700 BC)

Elamite, Kassite, Middle Assyrian (1400–1100 BC)

Late Assyrian (900–600 BC)

-- -- ancient coastline

—— ancient course of river

scale 1 : 6 250 000

0   200km

0   150mi

Lake Van

Lake Urmia

Shubat-Enlil
unexcavated ziggurat-shaped mound
Tell al-Hawa

Apku

Dur-Sharrukin (Khorsabad)

Nineveh
textual evidence only

Qatara (Tell al-Rimah)

Kalhu

Arbil

Euphrates

Ashur

Kar-Tukulti-Ninurta

Tigris

Mari

Dur-Kurigalzu

Sippar

Babylon

Kish

Borsippa

Nippur

Adab

Susa
textual evidence only

Deh-i No

Al-Untash-Napirisha (Choga Zanbil)

Uruk

Hammam

Larsa

Eridu

Ur

The Gulf

Ziggurats of Mesopotamia
The remains of ziggurats have been excavated at 16 sites and others are known from the texts (such as the one at Agade whose location is uncertain) or from the shape of the ruins. There were two main types of ziggurat: an early southern type, which had a rectangular platform and three staircases, and a later northern type with no staircases, in which the temple is often part of a larger complex. The construction of the ziggurat at the Elamite site of Al-Untash-Napirisha (mid-13th century BC) was exceptional. A square courtyard with rooms around it was filled in and built up to make a high ziggurat and the staircases on the four sides were contained within the structure.

105

TRADE AND WARFARE (2000-1600 BC)

Rival city states

The unification of Sumer and Akkad, first under the Agade kings and then under the kings of the Third Dynasty of Ur, had been exceptional. Although there were no major geographical barriers, only rarely did the alluvial plains of Mesopotamia come under the control of a single ruler and even more rarely could a monarch claim that his realm stretched "from the Upper to the Lower Sea" [the Mediterranean to the Gulf]. Yet many later Mesopotamian rulers strove to emulate the achievement of the Agade kings. At the end of the third millennium BC, as the grip of Ur loosened, its empire split into several kingdoms, with Ashur, Eshnunna, Der and Susa becoming independent.

Ishbi-Erra, a former officer of Ibbi-Sin, founded a new dynasty based at Isin in 2017 BC and controlled most of what had been the core of the empire of Ur. For the next two centuries the dynasty of Isin attempted to retain its territory against encroachment from the north and south. Isin's principal rival was the state of Larsa, and the period is called the Isin–Larsa period. However, there were other, equally powerful states in the Near East including Yamhad (with its capital at Aleppo), Eshnunna, Susa and Babylon.

The textual documentation for this period is particularly rich. The archives of Mari, containing more than 20,000 tablets, covered all aspects of palace life. Records of merchants who traded with Assyria have been unearthed at Kanesh, in central Anatolia. Already more than 4,000 of these tablets have been published and twice as many texts from recent excavations have still to be examined. Smaller collections have been found at Qatna, Alalah, Terqa, Haridum, Chagar Bazar, Kahat, Shubat-Enlil, Qatara, Nineveh, Ashur, Shusharra, Susa, Anshan, as well as towns in the kingdom of Eshnunna and numerous sites in Sumer and Akkad. These texts covered politics, administration, economics, religious practices, theology, trade, law and science. The world that they have revealed extended from Anatolia to the Gulf, and was linked by merchants with donkey caravans on expeditions to exchange goods from distant lands. To the south and west, nomadic pastoralists threatened the settled populations while to the north and east the fierce mountain tribes raided the cities of the plains.

Amorites and Hurrians

The last centuries of the third millennium were a time when new peoples made contact with the settled regions of the Near East. Among them were the Amorites (Amurru in Akkadian), who spoke a west Semitic dialect, and the Hurrians, who spoke a language unrelated to any known in the Near East at this time. The Amorites—like the later Aramaeans and Arabs—first appeared on the fringes of the Arabian desert. They were defeated by Shar-kalı-sharri (2217–2193 BC) in Basar (believed to be Jebel Bishri to the west of Mari), but this did not

hold them back for ever. In the last years of the Third Dynasty of Ur, Shu-Sin's fourth year (2034) was named "the year when the wall of Amurru was built". Another text gave more information about this fortification, which was constructed by digging a dike from the Euphrates to the Tigris in the northern part of the alluvial plain. At first there was some antagonism between the city dwellers and the nomads. The Amorites were accused of not knowing grain, not burying their dead, and being generally uncivilized. However, they could not be restrained and, within a few years Amorites had settled in many of the cities of Mesopotamia. They even took over the government, and many of the rulers of the early second millennium had Amorite names.

The Hurrians have been associated with the Early Transcaucasian culture. The mentions of Subartu in texts of the Akkadian period have referred to a Hurrian state in northern Mesopotamia. Moreover, a Hurrian name has been identified on a tablet of this period from Nippur. During the time of the Third Dynasty of Ur, rulers with Hurrian names, such as Atal-Sin, king of Urkish and Nawar, and Tish-atal, king of Karahar, were found in northern Mesopotamia and in the regions to the east of the Tigris. Another (or the same) Tish-atal, king of Urkish, left an inscription in the Hurrian language on a stone tablet commemorating the construction of a temple of Nergal. In the early second millennium Hurrians (or, at least, kings with Hurrian names) ruled the states around the northern fringe of Mesopotamia from Simurru, Tukrish and Shusharra in the Zagros mountains, to Hassum and Urshum to the northwest of the Euphrates. Hurrian names were found among the populations of Nuzi, Ekallatum (near Ashur), Qatara (Tell Rimah), Chagar Bazar, where at least one-fifth of the people had Hurrian names, and Alalah, on the Orontes in western Syria, where almost half of the names in the texts have been identified as Hurrian. Hurrians traded on equal terms with Assyrian merchants in Anatolia, and their deities were adopted by other peoples. The goddess Hepa was invoked by the king of Yamhad, and the head of the Hurrian pantheon—the weather god Teshup—was adopted under the name Tishpak, as the chief god of Eshnunna.

The struggle for power in Mesopotamia

The population of the heartlands of Mesopotamia remained mostly Sumerian and Akkadian even though many of the rulers had Amorite names. This was a period when political fortunes fluctuated widly. A charismatic leader might exercise control over many other states, but when he was succeeded by a less able ruler these vassal states chose another leader. The chaotic situation was summed up in a letter from about 1770 BC reporting a speech aimed at persuading the nomadic tribes to acknowledge the authority of Zimri-Lim of Mari.

The city states of the Isin–Larsa period
The cities of southern Mesopotamia competed with each other after the fall of the Third Dynasty of Ur. First, Isin was successful and then Larsa and finally Babylon. The maps shown here are based on the work of Douglas Frayne who has deduced from the year-names used in different cities the areas controlled by different city states. Those cities for which there is insufficient evidence to ascertain their status are not included within the shaded areas and to that extent the maps are incomplete. Even so, they give a vivid impression of the constant struggle between the rival states of the time.

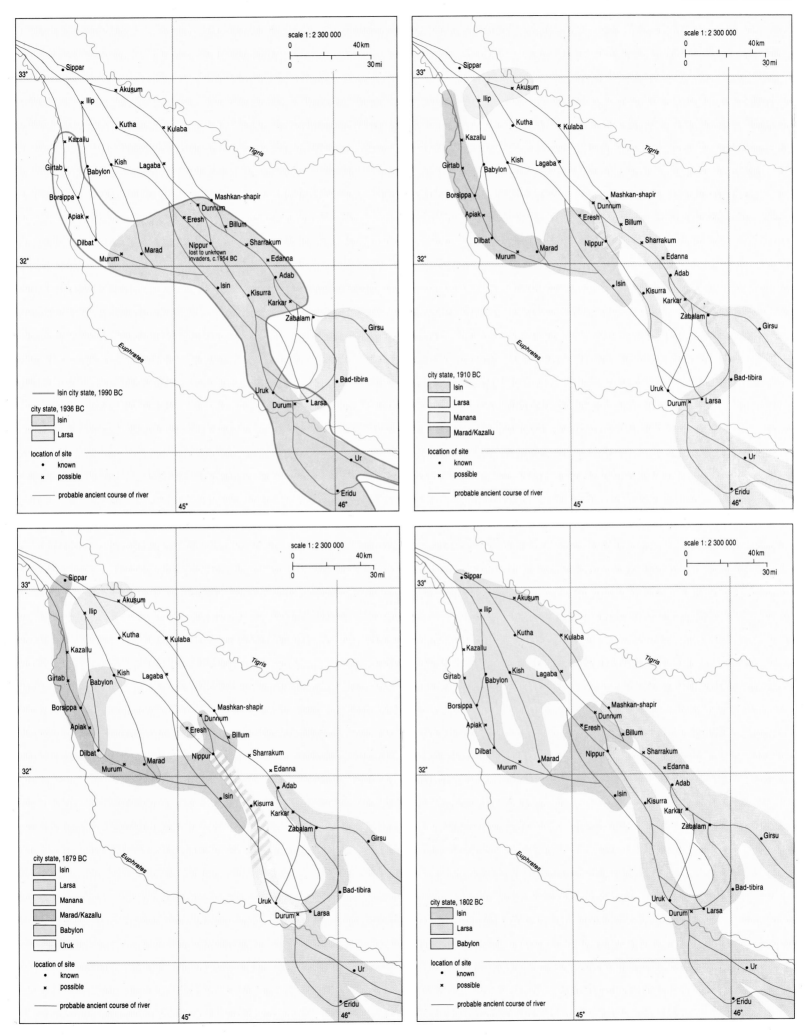

scale 1 : 2 300 000

0   40 km
0   30 mi

33°   Sippar
    Akusum
    Ilip
    Kutha   Kulaba
    Kazallu   Tigris
    Kish
Girtab   Babylon   Lagaba
    Borsippa
    Apiak   Mashkan-shapir
    Dilbat   Dunnum
    Murum   Eresh   Billum
32°   Marad   Sharrakum
        Nippur   Edanna
    lost to unknown   Adab
    invaders, c.1954 BC
        Isin   Kisurra
        Karkar
        Zabalam
    Euphrates   Girsu

        Bad-tibira
        Uruk
        Durum   Larsa

—— Isin city state, 1990 BC

city state, 1936 BC
    Isin
    Larsa

location of site
• known
× possible
    Ur
—— probable ancient course of river   Eridu

45°   46°

scale 1 : 2 300 000

0   40 km
0   30 mi

33°   Sippar
    Akusum
    Ilip
    Kutha   Kulaba
    Kazallu   Tigris
    Kish
Girtab   Babylon   Lagaba
    Borsippa
    Apiak   Mashkan-shapir
    Dilbat   Dunnum
    Murum   Eresh   Billum
        Marad   Nippur   Sharrakum
32°   Edanna
            Adab
        Isin   Kisurra
        Karkar
        Zabalam   Girsu

    Euphrates
        Bad-tibira
        Uruk
        Durum   Larsa

city state, 1910 BC
    Isin
    Larsa
    Manana
    Marad/Kazallu

location of site
• known
× possible
    Ur
—— probable ancient course of river   Eridu

45°   46°

scale 1 : 2 300 000

0   40 km
0   30 mi

33°   Sippar
    Akusum
    Ilip
    Kutha   Kulaba
    Kazallu   Tigris
    Kish
Girtab   Babylon   Lagaba
    Borsippa
    Apiak   Mashkan-shapir
    Dilbat   Dunnum
    Murum   Eresh   Billum
        Marad   Nippur   Sharrakum
            Edanna
            Adab
        Isin   Kisurra
        Karkar
        Zabalam   Girsu

city state, 1879 BC   Euphrates
    Isin
    Larsa   Bad-tibira
    Manana   Uruk
    Marad/Kazallu   Durum   Larsa
    Babylon
    Uruk

location of site
• known
× possible   Ur
—— probable ancient course of river   Eridu

45°   46°

scale 1 : 2 300 000

0   40 km
0   30 mi

33°   Sippar
    Akusum
    Ilip
    Kutha   Kulaba
    Kazallu   Tigris
    Kish
Girtab   Babylon   Lagaba
    Borsippa
    Apiak   Mashkan-shapir
    Dilbat   Dunnum
    Murum   Eresh   Billum
        Marad   Nippur   Sharrakum
32°   Edanna
            Adab
        Isin   Kisurra
        Karkar
        Zabalam   Girsu

city state, 1802 BC   Euphrates
    Isin
    Larsa   Bad-tibira
    Babylon   Uruk
        Durum   Larsa

location of site
• known
× possible   Ur
—— probable ancient course of river   Eridu

45°   46°

"There is no king who can be mighty alone.
Ten or fifteen kings follow Hammurabi, the
man of Babylon; as many follow Rim-Sin, the
man of Larsa, Ibal-pi-El, the man of Eshnunna,
and Amut-pi-El, the man of Qatna, and twenty
kings follow Yarim-Lim, the man of Yamhad."

The struggle for control of southern Mesopotamia
was reflected in the year-names of the period.
When a year-name issued by the ruler of one city
was used in another, it signaled the subordinate
status of that city. Similarly, a king who restored a
temple, or appointed a priest or priestess, in
another city demonstrated his control over the
second city. However, though this was the general
pattern, the evidence is often incomplete and the
location of some of the cities uncertain. For
example, some experts have identified the city of
Eresh with the site of Abu Salabikh, while others
place Eresh about 90 kilometers farther south.
Furthermore, battles recorded as victories might, in
reality, have been inconclusive, or the capture of a
city might not have been followed by a period of
rule, or the sovereignty claims in the royal inscriptions might have been exaggerated.

The prosperity of the cities of the south
depended not only on their rulers' military or diplomatic prowess but also on their economic
strength. Trade and industry were important, but
less vital to a city than an abundant and reliable
water supply. Most of the water came from the
Euphrates, which flowed along interconnecting
channels, as it does today. Over the centuries, the
course of the Euphrates has changed greatly, but
its ancient channels can be partly traced from the
locations of ancient settlements.

The rise of Isin

For the first 70 years of the 20th century BC Isin
dominated the south. Ishbi-Erra (2017–1985 BC)
founded the dynasty out of the remnants of the
kingdom of Ur. Late in his reign he drove the Elamites out of Ur, while his son Shu-ilishu (1984–
1975 BC), who followed him, recovered the statue
of Nanna, the chief god of Ur, which had been
removed by the Elamites and taken to Anshan.
Shu-ilishu took the title King of Ur and claimed
divine status.

As an important religious center lying between
several kingdoms, Nippur was always the subject
of contention. For some years in the middle of the
19th century Nippur was lost by Isin after falling
to some unknown invaders. In the southeast,
Zabaya (1941–1933 BC), who described himself as
an Amorite chief, rebuilt the temple of Shamash at
Larsa. In the king lists the dynasty of Larsa went
back to the Third Dynasty of Ur, but Zabaya (or
perhaps his father) was the first of the dynasty to
have left evidence of their rule. Zabaya was succeeded by his brother Gungunum (1932–1906 BC),
who extended the kingdom of Larsa, campaigned
against Susa, where a tablet bearing one of his
year-names has been found, and possibly controlled Nippur.

Trade in the Gulf

In the eighth year of his reign Gungunum captured
Ur and gained control of the valuable trade with
the Gulf that had begun in the Early Dynastic
period. Situated on the maritime trade route

Kings of Mesopotamia and Elam c.2000–1600 BC		
ISIN	**LARSA**	
Ishbi-Erra 2017–1985	Naplanum 2025–2005	
2000	Emisum 2004–1977	
Shu-ilishu 1984–1975		
Iddin-Dagan 1974–1954	Samium 1967–1942	
Ishme-Dagan 1953–1935	Zabaya 1941–1933	
Lipit-Ishtar 1934–1924	Gungunum 1932–1906	
Ur-Ninurta 1923–1896		
1900 Bur-Sin 1895–1874	Abisare 1905–1895	**URUK**
Lipit-Enlil 1873–1869	Sumuel 1894–1866	
Erra-imitti 1868–1861	Nur-Adad 1865–1850	Sin-kashid
Enlil-bani 1860–1837	Sin-iddinam 1849–1843	Sin-eribam
Zambiya 1836–1834	Sin-eribam 1842–1841	Sin-gamil
Iter-pisha 1833–1831	Sin-iqisham 1840–1836	Anam
Urdukuga 1830–1828	Silli-Adad 1835	Irdanene
Sin-magir 1827–1817	Warad-Sin 1834–1823	Rim-Anum
1800 Damiq-ilishu 1816–1794	Rim-Sin I 1822–1763	Nabi-ilishu
1794	1763	1802
	Rim-Sin II 1740–1736	
1700		
1600		

through the Gulf were the states of Dilmun, Magan
and Meluhha. Dilmun probably included the
islands of Failaka (at the head of the Gulf) and Bahrain (two days' sailing farther down the Gulf) as
well as the eastern coast of Saudi Arabia. Magan,
on the evidence of third-millennium copper-work-
ing sites, has been identified with Oman, while
Meluhha was part of the Harappan or Indus valley
civilization. In the Early Dynastic period Dilmun
supplied timber to Ur-Nanshe of Lagash, and later
texts from Lagash mention the import of copper ore
and exports of wool, cloth, silver, fat and resin.
Sargon (2334–2279 BC) boasted that ships of Dilmun, Magan and Meluhha moored at the docks of
Agade, and his son Manishtushu (2269–2255 BC)
and grandson Naram-Sin (2254–2218 BC) both
claimed to have conquered Magan and brought
back precious stones. The diorite statues of
Manishtushu and of Gudea, the ruler of Lagash,
indicated contact between Mesopotamia and
Oman. Gudea's inscriptions also recorded copper,
diorite and wood from Magan as well as timber,
gold, tin, lapis lazuli and red stone (probably carnelian) from Meluhha. Inscriptions from Ur
showed that trade with the Gulf was conducted by
merchants who were financed by the Temple of
Nanna in Ur, and that the trade was mostly with
Magan, which also served as an entrepôt for goods
from Meluhha.

After the collapse of the Third Dynasty of Ur,
tablets from Ur dating to the reigns of Gungunum
and his two successors (1932–1866 BC) recorded
how trade, instead of being under centralized
bureaucratic control, as it had been earlier, was
now in the hands of wealthy citizens who received
a fixed interest on the capital they supplied. The

Below A pottery vase from Larsa
dating to early in the 2nd
millennium BC. It is decorated
with incised figures and with
smaller reliefs of a naked
goddess, Inanna/Ishtar. The
figures are probably symbols of
the gods. The turtle and the fish
may be associated with the water
god Enki/Ea, the bearded bull
with the weather god Adad, and
the birds with the messenger god
Papsukkal. Height 26.3 cm.

	Not all the rulers are included. The order and dates of many are not certain. The dates at the end of the columns indicate when the dynasty came to an end.	

ESHNUNNA

Ituriya
Ilshu-iliya
Nur-ahum
Kirikiri
Bilalama
Azuzum
Ipiq-Adad I
Shiqlanum
Abdi-Erah
Belakum
Warassa
Ibal-pi-El I
Ipiq-Adad II
Naram-Sin
Dadusha
Ibal-pi-El II
1762

ELAM

Kindattu
Idaddu
Tan-Ruhuratir
Ebarti
Idattu
Ebarat
Shilhaha
Addahushu

Shiruktuh
Shimut-wartash
Siwepalarhuhpak
Kuduzulush

Kuk-nashur

BABYLON

Sumu-abum 1894–1881
Sumu-la-El 1880–1845

Sabium 1844–1831

Apil-Sin 1830–1813

Sin-muballit 1812–1793
Hammurabi 1792–1750
Samsu-iluna 1749–1712
Abi-eshuh 1711––1684
Ammiditana 1683–1647
Ammisaduqa 1646–1626
Samsuditana 1625–1595
1595

ASHUR

Puzur-Ashur I
Shalimahu
Ilu-shumma
Erishum I

Ikunum
Sargon I
Puzur-Ashur II
Erishum II
Shamshi-Adad I c.1813–1781
Ishme-Dagan

MARI

Yaggid-Lim
Yahdun-Lim
Yasmah-Adad 1796–1780
Zimri-Lim 1779–1757
1757

2000
1900
1800
1700
1600

Above This fine alabaster statuette of a monkey was found in the temple of Ishtar Kititum, from the Isin–Larsa period, at Neribtum (Tell Ishchali) to the east of the Diyala river. Monkeys were not native to the Near East but were common in India and in Egypt. The figure combines human and monkey characteristics, as might be expected from an artist who had little first-hand knowledge of the animal. Height 8 cm.

Above right A necklace from a grave in the late Early Dynastic cemetery at Kish. The lapis lazuli came from northern Afghanistan. The long barrel-shaped carnelian beads and etched carnelian beads decorated with white bands were typical of the Harappan civilization.

city temple and the palace also exacted a tithe. The merchants were known as *alik Dilmun*, after the name of the main trading port, which also handled the transshipment of goods from farther east. The importation of copper was the main concern of the Mesopotamian merchants. In one text the equivalent of more than 18 tonnes of copper were received in Dilmun. Other imports included luxury items such as gold, lapis lazuli, beads, ivory and "fish eyes", which have been identified as pearls, for which the Gulf is famous. In return, the merchants exported silver, oil, textiles and barley.

Excavations in Bahrain and Failaka have uncovered evidence of a flourishing civilization during the first centuries of the second millennium. Red Barbar pottery, numerous burial tumuli and distinctive stamp seals characterized this culture. Barbar pottery has also been found in eastern Saudi Arabia and Qatar, perhaps demonstrating the extent of ancient Dilmun. There were about 200,000 tumuli on the island of Bahrain, as well as others on the Arabian mainland. Some recently excavated tumuli contained, as well as the local Barbar pottery, pottery of the types found in the Harappan culture in the Indus valley. Other sites with Harappan imports have been found in Oman and in the United Arab Emirates. The stamp seals that were discovered had rounded or conical backs and were carved in a particular style. Known as Gulf seals, they were typical of the Barbar culture but have also been found at Susa, on the Iranian plateau and in southern Mesopotamia. One has even been discovered at the Harappan site of Lothal in India. The style of carving has also been identified on a cylinder seal from Susa and on stamp seal impressions from Acemhuyuk in

Turkey at the other end of the silver-trade route. Harappan-style weights were used in Bahrain and seals in the Indus style have been found in Bahrain, Failaka, Ur and Eshnunna. Also, typically Harappan beads dating to as early as the Agade period have been discovered in southern Mesopotamia.

The chronological relationship between India and Mesopotamia is uncertain. The end of the Harappan culture has been dated at between 2000 and 1700 BC, but it is not yet known how the changing patterns in the Gulf trade from the Mesopotamian perspective related to events some 2,500 kilometers away in the Indus valley.

Decline of Isin

As Gungunum was encroaching on Isin from the south, other Amorite rulers took control of Babylon, Kish, Kazallu, Marad and Malgium in southern Mesopotamia. Even Uruk, only 20 kilometers from Larsa, became the seat of an Amorite dynasty that controlled Nippur briefly in about 1880 BC. Hemmed in to the north and south, the kingdom of Isin was restricted to the central area of the alluvial plain, though it managed to survive for more than a century. The line of Ishbi-Erra was ousted by a usurper and 60 years later another king of Isin was replaced in circumstances that were described in a later Babylonian chronicle.

"Erra-imitti, the king, installed Enlil-bani, the gardener, as substitute king on his throne. He placed the royal tiara on his head. Erra-imitti [died] in his palace when he sipped a hot broth. Enlil-bani, who occupied the throne, did not give it up [and] so became king."

As is known from the Late Assyrian period, if an omen foretold disaster for the king, a substitute king was appointed who was subsequently killed. In this way the omen proved correct and the true king could stay on the throne. Here, however, it did not work out as Erra-imitti had planned, for, far from being killed, Enlil-bani (1860–1837 BC) stayed on the throne for 24 years and even had himself deified.

Larsa, Isin's great rival

In Larsa, Nur-Adad, a commoner, seized the throne in 1865 in the wake of growing discontent, perhaps fostered by problems with the city's water supply. Sin-kashid, the king of Uruk, who was married to the daughter of Sumu-la-El, king of Babylon, and had remained independent of Larsa, blocked direct passage up the Euphrates from Larsa to Nippur. Control of Nippur shifted back and forth continually from Isin to Larsa, as indicated by year-name changes. Documents from Nippur were dated with Larsa year-names in 1838, 1835, 1832 and 1828 and Isin year-names in 1836, 1833, 1830 and for a few years between 1813 and 1802.

During this period Kudur-Mabuk, the ruler of Emutbal (the region east of the Tigris between Eshnunna and Elam), appointed his son Warad-Sin (1834–1823 BC) king of Larsa and his daughter entu-priestess of Nanna at Ur (normally the prerogative of the king of Sumer and Akkad). Kudur-Mabuk and Warad-Sin embarked on an ambitious program of restoring the temples of Ur, Larsa, Zabalam, Mashkan-shapir, Nippur and others. Kudur-Mabuk called himself father of Emutbal and father of Amurru, both of which were names of Amorite tribal groups (though he and his father had Elamite names). His two sons, Warad-Sin and Rim-Sin, had Akkadian names but his daughter's name was Sumerian. The mixture reflected the composition of the population in Mesopotamia (as well as the difficulty of determining ethnic background on the evidence of name alone).

Rim-Sin (1822–1763 BC), who succeeded his brother Warad-Sin, had one of the longest reigns in Mesopotamian history. In 1804 Rim-Sin defeated a coalition army of men from Uruk, Isin, Babylon and Rapiqum, and of Sutu nomads, and ended the independence of Uruk. In 1794, the 29th year of his reign, he conquered Isin and brought to an end the First Dynasty of Isin. So impressed was he with this victory, that he called the remaining years of his long reign "Year one: Isin conquered" up to "year 30: Isin conquered", until Larsa itself was defeated by Hammurabi, a Babylonian king whose fame eclipsed that even of Rim-Sin.

Left A painted pottery vase in the shape of a lion from the trading colony at Kanesh in Turkey. Painted vessels of this sort were probably used for pouring libations to the gods. The vessel was filled through the large aperture in the back, the liquid emerging through a hole in the nose of the lion. The merchants living at Kanesh came from Ashur and other cities but their houses and the pottery and other equipment that they used were the same as those of the local people.

Below A bronze figure, found at Girsu, of Warad-Sin, king of Larsa, carrying a basket on his head. Although his ancestors were not native to southern Mesopotamia, he, like other rulers of the period, adopted the traditions of Sumer and Akkad and restored the ancient temples. This figure is almost identical to those buried as foundation deposits by the kings of the Third Dynasty of Ur almost 300 years earlier.

The changing fortunes of Ashur

Farther north, the site of Ashur lay on a rocky promontory overlooking an important crossing of the Tigris at the edge of the dry-farming zone. Its position had always made it vulnerable to incursions from the pastoral nomads living in the steppe. Moreover, it lay on important trade routes beside the Tigris and along the line of the hills of Jebel Hamrin and Jebel Sinjar. But Ashur was not an obvious capital for an empire, as it lacked reserves of cultivable land and human resources. When the rulers of Ashur controlled a larger empire, the seat of power moved to areas of greater wealth, either in the Habur plains (under Shamshi-Adad I) or in the area around Nineveh (in the Late Assyrian period of the 9th–7th centuries BC).

In the early periods, Ashur had been an outpost of southern influence, as shown by the Early Dynastic statues and inscriptions of Agade kings found there. One of the early levels of the Ishtar temple contained an inscription of Zariqum, who was governor of Ashur under Shulgi and Amar-Sin, and another an inscription of a native ruler called Ilu-shumma. Ilu-shumma also appeared in the Assyrian King List composed in the first millennium BC. After 29 names including those of kings who are said to have lived in tents, and the Amorite ancestors of Shamshi-Adad, came rulers with Akkadian names: Puzur-Ashur I, Shalimahu, Ilu-shumma, Erishum I, Ikunum, Sharrum-ken [Sargon I] and Puzur-Ashur II. Their dates, however, are uncertain. A later chronicle made Ilu-shumma a contemporary of Sumu-abum (c. 1894–1881 BC) the first king of Babylon, and according to the Assyrian King List Puzur-Ashur II was the king of Ashur before Naram-Sin of Eshnunna. From Ashur itself there has been little archeological evidence for this period, as it is buried deep below the ruins of later buildings. Some 800 kilometers away, in central Anatolia, a copy of a building inscription of Erishum I, and a court decision with the imprint of the seal of Sargon I were among the thousands of

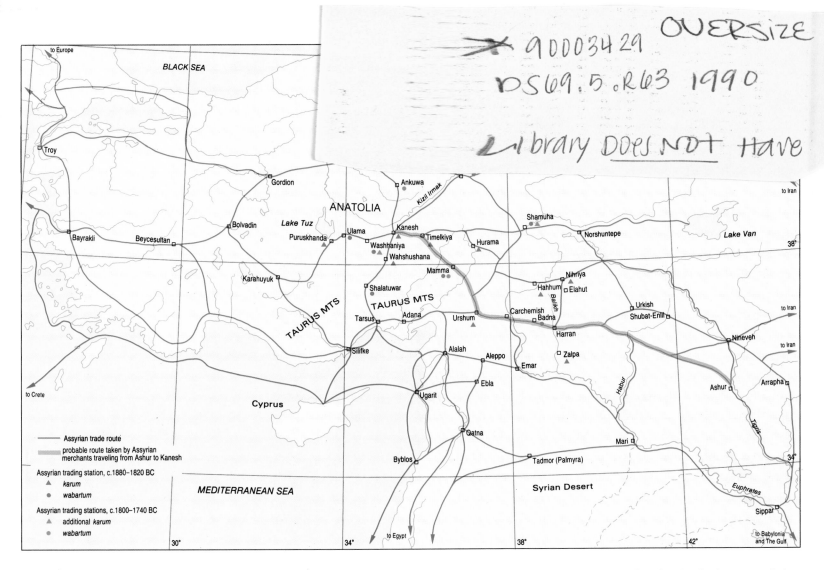

Anatolia and the Old Assyrian trade

The tablets found at Kanesh (modern Kultepe) in Anatolia describe an extensive trading network, which started at Ashur and led through the Taurus mountains to Kanesh, where an important *karum* or trading colony was established. There were other *karum*s and smaller establishments called *wabartum* on the Anatolian plateau and in northern Mesopotamia. Most of the tablets were written between about 1880 and 1820 BC and a much smaller number between about 1800 and 1740 BC. In the later period some additional settlements were classified as *karum*s and fewer *wabartum*s were mentioned. Kanesh and Hattusas are the only trading stations that can be located with confidence. The locations of other *karum*s and *wabartum*s suggested on the map are not certain.

tablets found that had belonged to an Assyrian merchant colony based at the city of Kanesh.

Assyrian trade with Anatolia

Excavations in the *karum*, the merchant suburb outside the wall of the city of Kanesh, revealed evidence for trade with Ashur over a period of three generations (about sixty years), from Erishum to Puzur-Ashur II (c. 1880–1820 BC), and then contemporaneously with Shamshi-Adad and Samsuiluna (c. 1800–1740 BC). More than 10,000 tablets have been discovered from the earlier period but less than 200 from the later.

From Ashur woollen textiles and a metal called *annakum* were carried by donkey across the broad plains of northern Mesopotamia, through the steep passes of the Taurus mountains, to Kanesh, and from there distributed to other trading outposts. *Annakum* was undoubtedly tin, a vital ingredient of bronze, which now replaced the arsenical copper used in earlier centuries. In slightly later texts from Mari and Sippar, *annakum* was brought from Elam to Mari and then traded on to the west. As no evidence has been found for tin mining or tin sources in Elam, the Elamites probably brought the tin from farther east. The goods recorded in the Gulf trade between Dilmun and Ur did not include *annakum*. However, texts found at Shusharra in the mountains to the east of Assyria have suggested that *annakum* was brought from the Iranian plateau or beyond, perhaps from Afghanistan, where tin ores are thought to have been exploited since the third millennium BC.

Each donkey carried a load of about 90 kilograms, made up of either 30 textiles (pieces of cloth) or 10 textiles and 130 *minas* (65 kilograms) of tin as well as 10 *minas* of loose tin for incidental expenses and taxes on the journey. On leaving Ashur a tax of 1/120 of the value of the goods was payable to the *limmu* official (after whom years were named in Assyria). The entry tax in Kanesh was 2/65, paid to the local ruler. One unusually large consignment of goods included 350 textiles carried by 14 donkeys, but normally the quantities recorded were much smaller. The larger quantities might have resulted from merchants banding together in long caravans.

Whereas smuggling was a recognized activity, robbery did not seem to have been a problem on the long journeys. In the published texts (about a third of those known) some 13.5 tonnes of tin and 17,500 textiles, roughly 800 donkey loads, were taken from Ashur to Kanesh—probably no more than one-tenth of the real total. In return, silver and gold were brought back to Ashur, but as there was no mention of the use of donkeys as pack animals on the return journey, perhaps most of them were sold on arrival in Anatolia. This Assyrian trade was undertaken by family firms. The head of the family lived in Ashur while a junior member of the family would act as the resident agent in the *karum* at Kanesh. The venture was normally funded by the family, but sometimes partnerships were formed to raise the necessary capital.

Kanesh was the center of the trade, but there were *karum*s at nine other cities including Hattusas

113

(Boghazkoy), Alishar (possibly Ankuwa), and Acemhuyuk (Purukshanda?) as well as ten or more smaller Assyrian trading establishments in Anatolia. These were self-governing settlements, subject to the local princes to whom they paid taxes.

Government and trade in Anatolia

Among the local populations living in Anatolia, Assyrians were not the only inhabitants of the *karum*. They lived in the north and center of the part that has been excavated, separated from native Anatolians to the south by industrial regions. In addition to importing and exporting goods Assyrian merchants also engaged in local trade. Copper was an important commodity: quantities of the order of 30,000 *minas* (15 tonnes) were mentioned in one of the texts from Kanesh. The people with whom the Assyrians did business included Hattians (the indigenous inhabitants of Anatolia), Hurrians and Indo-Europeans, among whom were Hittites who spoke a dialect later called *neshili* (perhaps derived from the city of Kanesh) and Luwians, whose language, called *luili* by the Hittites, was written in a hieroglyphic script.

The Anatolian cities were ruled by princes whose names were normally Indo-European and who, as in Mesopotamia, fought among themselves. The earlier city and *karum* of Kanesh (level II) were destroyed by fire in about 1820. An unusual Hittite text written about 500 years later described how Pitkhana, king of Kussara, with his son Anitta, conquered the city of Nesa, which was perhaps Kanesh, and adopted it as his capital. He also defeated Zalpa, Puruskhanda, Shalatuwar and Hatti (perhaps Hattusas, the later Hittite capital). Pitkhana and Anitta were possibly responsible for destroying the *karum* at level II, as both were mentioned in tablets from the later period (level Ib), and a dagger inscribed "palace of Anitta, the prince" was found at Kanesh.

Between the time of Anitta and the Hittite kings little is known of the situation in Anatolia. The Hittite rulers traced their descent back to Labarnas I, king of Kussara (c. 1650 BC). His son, who was also called Labarnas, moved the capital from Kussara to Hattusas and himself took the name Hattusilis. His grandson and successor, Mursilis, led the Hittite army through the Taurus mountains, along the route trodden by the Assyrian donkey caravans 300 years earlier, to destroy the remnants of Hammurabi's once great kingdom of Babylon.

The palace at Eshnunna

Eshnunna, under its governor Ituriya, had been the first province to cast off the yoke of the Third Dynasty of Ur. Ituriya's son Ilshu-iliya, who had been a scribe of Ibbi-Sin, incorporated the temple built for the worship of Shu-Sin (the divine king of Ur) into a new palace for the rulers of Eshnunna. The palace was a classic example of Old Babylonian architecture. It included a temple with a courtyard leading into a wide anteroom and *cella* (room where the image of the god was placed) and displayed the typical Mesopotamian palace plan. Along one side of the outer courtyard was a large reception room, and beyond this an inner courtyard with the private rooms of the ruler. This design was found in the palaces of the Late Assyrian kings, a thousand years later.

Toward the end of the 19th century BC, after some 15 little-known rulers, Naram-Sin, the son of Ipiq-Adad II, conquered Ashur and pushed west into the Habur plains. Naram-Sin was included in the Assyrian King List as if he were a native Assyrian ruler.

The conqueror Shamshi-Adad

According to the Assyrian King List,
> "Shamshi-Adad, son of Ila-kabkabi, went to Babylon in the time of Naram-Sin. In the *limmu* of Ibni-Adad, Shamshi-Adad came up from Babylon and seized Ekallatum, and resided for three years in Ekallatum. In the *limmu* of Atamar-Ishtar, Shamshi-Adad came up from Ekallatum. He deposed Erishum, son of Naram-Sin, from the throne, he seized the throne, and ruled for thirty-three years."

Shamshi-Adad's origins are uncertain, but possibly he was an Amorite from the middle Euphrates, for according to texts from Mari, an Amorite chief called Ila-kabkabuhu was active in the region of Terqa to the west of Mari in the time of Yaggid-Lim and Yahdun-Lim. How Shamshi-Adad's conquest of Ashur came about is not known, but he might have taken advantage of the confusion resulting from Naram-Sin's invasion. Shamshi-Adad also seized control of Mari, perhaps from a usurper who had ousted Yahdun-Lim. Yahdun-Lim's son Zimri-Lim sought refuge with his father-in-law Yarim-Lim, king of Yamhad, and returned to rule Mari after the death of Shamshi-Adad. Shamshi-Adad did not make Ashur his capital but resided in a city that he named Shubat-Enlil, which has recently been identified as the site of Tell Leilan. He installed his elder son, Ishme-Dagan, at Ekallatum and his younger son, Yasmah-Addu, at Mari.

According to his inscriptions, Shamshi-Adad conquered as far as the Mediterranean:
> "a stele inscribed with my great name I set up in the country of Laban [Lebanon] on the shores of the Great Sea."

He does not seem to have exercised direct control over the west though he married his son Yasmah-Addu to the king of Qatna's daughter. A cuneiform text listed their wedding gifts, which included four or five talents of silver (about 200 kilograms).

Shamshi-Adad's rule, which stretched from the Euphrates to the Zagros and, by a network of alliances, still farther, was, in effect, controlled by his two sons, whom he installed at Ekallatum and Mari. The elder, Ishme-Dagan, inherited his father's talents, but the younger brother, Yasmah-Addu, seems to have been a weak, ineffectual ruler. Letters between the three of them have been found at Mari, including this one from Yasmah-Addu to his father:
> "I read the letter that [you] sent me, Daddy, in which you said: *How much longer must we keep you on a leading rein? You are a child, you are not a grown man, you have no hair on your cheek. How much longer will you fail to direct your own household properly? Don't you see that your own brother is directing vast armies? You just direct your own palace and household properly!* That is what [you] Daddy wrote to me. Now how can I be like a child and incapable of directing affairs when [you] Daddy promoted me? How can it be, that though I have grown up with [you]

Right The merchant colony, or *karum*, at Kanesh was situated outside the walls of the city. Here, traders from Assyria lived in houses of local design and used the local pottery. Were it not for the thousands of clay tablets recording details of commercial dealings by the Assyrians, their presence would not have been suspected so far from their native city. Besides Assyrians, merchants from other cities of Mesopotamia and Anatolia also lived in the *karum*. The stone foundations of the houses of the *karum* and the alleyways between them can still be seen even though they were excavated some years ago.

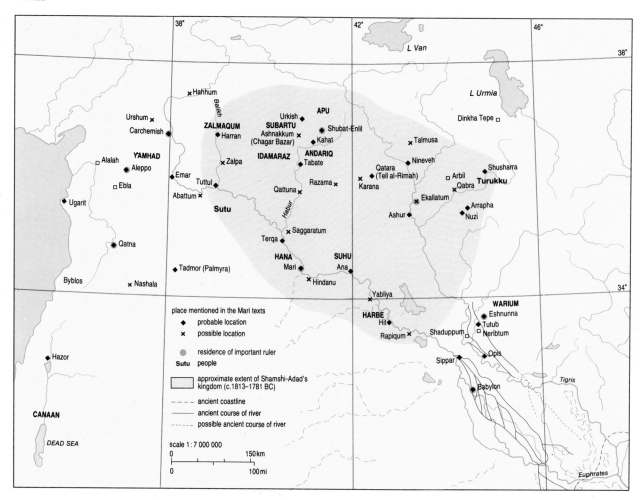

The world of the Mari letters
The clay tablets found at Mari give a remarkably detailed picture of life in the palace and elsewhere in the 19th and 18th centuries BC. In the published texts more than 400 place names were recorded, but only a fraction of them can be identified with confidence. This was the period when, from nothing, Shamshi-Adad I (c. 1813–1781) created a kingdom that included most of northern Mesopotamia. From his capital at Shubat-Enlil, he installed one of his sons at Ekallatum to rule the east and the other to rule the southwest from Mari. After Shamshi-Adad's death his kingdom collapsed. Mari was destroyed by Hammurabi in 1757 BC and little information has emerged about northern Mesopotamia over the next 300 years or so.

Daddy ever since I was little, now some servant or other has succeeded in ousting me from my Daddy's affections? So I am coming to you right now, to have it out with [you] Daddy about my unhappiness.''

On Shamshi-Adad's eastern flank, the rulers of Eshnunna and the Elamites were active. A letter to Shamshi-Adad from his vassal at Shusharra reported the presence of an army of 12,000 troops belonging to the Elamite ruler Shiruktuh. Dadusha, who succeeded his brother Naram-Sin as king of Eshnunna, claimed a victory over Ishme-Dagan as well as conquest of Arbil and of other towns in the region. After the death of his father, Shamshi-Adad, Ishme-Dagan was defeated despite assurances he had given to his brother that he had the Elamites and their ally Ibal-pi-El, king of Eshnunna, ''on a leash''. Shubat-Enlil fell to the Elamites, and the armies of Elam and Eshnunna campaigned in the land of Idamaraz (northern Syria). At this time Zimri-Lim regained the throne of Mari, which he kept until shortly before Mari was finally destroyed by Hammurabi in 1757 BC.

Mari in the reign of Zimri-Lim

Paradoxically, the destruction of Mari by Hammurabi preserved it for future archeologists. The city was abandoned and the ruins of the palace of Zimri-Lim, encased by the collapse of the upper storey, were saved from disturbance by later builders. The entrance to the palace at Mari was from the north. A wide gate led through a small courtyard into a second, much larger courtyard with a room which might have been a shrine or a throne room, approached by a semicircular flight

of steps. Wall paintings in this room showed by their style that this part of the palace had been built before 2000 BC and had remained in use for more than 250 years. Beneath the palace of Zimri-Lim were earlier palaces belonging to the Early Dynastic rulers of Mari. To the west was another large courtyard, which had also been decorated with wall paintings. Its centerpiece panel showed the king receiving the insignia of kingship from the goddess Ishtar, with, on either side, tall trees, divine figures and magical beasts. On the south side of the courtyard were two large rooms, each about 25 meters long. The outer room contained a large statue of a goddess holding a vase, which received water through a hole in the base of the statue. At the west end of the second room a platform might have supported the king's throne, and at the opposite end steps led up to a small *cella*. A fallen statue of an earlier ruler of Mari was found at the foot of these stairs. Around these official chambers were storerooms, workshops, kitchens, and living rooms.

More than 20,000 tablets have been found at Mari, of which about a quarter have been published, providing a detailed picture of life at the time. The settlements were under constant threat from unruly nomadic tribesmen, some of whom were conscripted into the army, while others were offered bribe or had to be kept at bay by force. The Yaminites (sometimes referred to as Benjaminites, which literally means sons of the south) and the Sutu gave the most trouble. Also prominent were the Hapiru, a group of outlaws. (When the texts were first deciphered it was suggested that the Hapiru were ancestors of the Hebrews, but this suggestion was probably wrong.)

Opposing armies fought each other frequently. Siege warfare was common and armies ten or twenty thousand strong were mentioned in the texts. The horse-drawn chariot, which dominated warfare for the next thousand years made its appearance for the first time in the early second millennium BC. The horse had been domesticated more than two thousand years before in Russia, and horse bones have been found in Chalcolithic and Early Bronze Age levels in Israel and Turkey. There were occasional references to horses in texts written before 2000 BC but horses only became common in the following centuries, when they were found not only in the Near East but also in Egypt and in Europe. Initially, horses were ridden like donkeys and were yoked and controlled with nose rings like oxen. However, the development of the bit (at some time before 1700 BC) and the introduction of light but strong spoked wheels made the horse-drawn chariot a formidable weapon of war.

Life in Zimri-Lim's palace was recorded in great detail, as the king engaged in long correspondence with his officials on all manner of subjects: a lion was captured on the roof of a house and sent in a wooden cage to Zimri-Lim; the banks of a canal were in need of repair; a horde of locusts arrived in Terqa and the local governor collected them and sent them to the king. In another letter, Zimri-Lim wrote to his wife, warning of an illness in the family.

"I have been told that Nanna has an infection and that, as she is often at the palace, it will infect the many women who are with her. Now,

Left Baked clay model of a chariot which may have come from northern Syria. It is similar to the chariots depicted on cylinder-seal impressions from Kanesh and probably dates to about the 19th century BC. The introduction of the light chariot drawn by a pair of horses transformed warfare in the Near East. The marks on the wheels of the model may represent spokes. Earlier chariots drawn by asses had solid wooden wheels. Height 19.6 cm.

Right This silver statuette of a woman has head, neck and breasts of gold with gold bands across her upper body. It is said to have come from a grave at Hasanoglan, not far from Ankara in Turkey, and may date to about 2000 BC. Height 20.4 cm.

give strict orders. No one is to drink from the cup she uses; no one is to sit on the seat she takes; no one is to lie on the bed she uses, lest it infect the many women who are with her. This is a very contagious disease.''

The king had an ice house where ice brought down from the mountains was stored to be used for cooling drinks in the summer months. The tablets also recorded the food and drink that were served at the king's table and work carried out by the palace servants, including weaving, carpentry and metalworking. Among the professions practiced by women were spinning, weaving, cooking, singing and playing musical instruments, but there were also female scribes and even a female doctor.

Not surprisingly, religion played an important role. Religious rituals, such as feeding the gods, recitations and incantations for festivals, and appeasing the spirits of the dead, were celebrated regularly. Omens were consulted before taking any decision of consequence, the most usual method being to sacrifice a sheep and examine its liver. This was a highly developed science with thousands of different features of the liver suggesting different prognostications. Model livers made of clay, and labeled with such predictions, that may have been used for instruction and reference have been found at Mari. A well-preserved temple and ziggurat at Tell al-Rimah, perhaps built under Shamshi-Adad, gives an idea of the prominence of religion at this time. The temple and ziggurat of the god dominate the site while the palace nestles below.

The Levant and Palestine
The Mari tablets and, to a lesser extent, the tablets found at Qatna and Alalah on the Orontes have shed light on events in the west. The two main kingdoms were Yamhad, with its capital Aleppo, and Qatna, but other smaller cities such as Ugarit and Hazor were also mentioned. At the end of the

third millennium there was a decline in urban settlement in the Levant and Palestine, but in about 2000 BC, which has been taken to be the beginning of the Middle Bronze period, this trend was reversed. According to Egyptian sources of the time, in the reign of Amenemhet I (1991–1962 BC) the Egyptian traveler Sinuhe visited Asiatic territory, which was mostly populated by nomadic tribes. However, the Twelfth Dynasty "execration texts" tell a different story. These clay figurines or vessels were inscribed with the names of rebels and enemies of Egypt and were then ritually smashed. An earlier group, dated to about 1900 BC, included the names of Jerusalem, Ashkelon, Beth-Shan and Byblos. A group dated about a hundred years later showed that almost all the major Canaanite cities were flourishing. (A surprising omission was the city of Megiddo, but perhaps this was because Megiddo maintained a loyal relationship with Egypt.) The names of the rulers of these cities were all West Semitic. The earlier group listed more than one ruler for each city, but the later group only one, which might have reflected a change from tribal organization to urban.

Archeological evidence has helped to complete the picture. After about 1800 BC, almost all Middle Bronze Age sites in the Levant—including not only the larger towns, but also villages of less than a hectare—were fortified. The "Cyclopean" masonry, made out of huge stones 2 to 3 meters long and each weighing as much as a tonne, was typical of the fortification style. Outside the wall was a steep slope, called a *glacis*, made out of earth or stones and covered with a layer of smooth hard plaster. This feature was probably designed as a defence against the walls being undermined, but it also offered protection against battering rams and scaling ladders. The walls of Qatna once enclosed a square about a kilometer across and still stand between 12 and 20 meters high. Casemate walls and triple-chamber gates added extra protection.

Left The Semitic rulers of Byblos had a close relationship with the pharaohs of the 12th Dynasty of Egypt, receiving precious gifts and adopting the refinements of Egyptian culture. The rock-cut tombs of the rulers were dug into the cliffs on the shore at Byblos. Three were found intact with a great wealth of precious objects, others had been robbed. This golden pectoral (chest ornament) came from one of the intact tombs. It is decorated with the images of the Egyptian hawk-god Horus but details show that it was probably made locally. Width 20.5 cm.

Mari

The ruins of Mari (modern Tell Hariri) lie on the west side of the river Euphrates. The city was founded in the early third millennium BC. In the Early Dynastic period Mari was an important city state and was included as one of the ruling dynasties in the Sumerian King List. Many fine Sumerian-style statues were found in the Ishtar temple. The palace of the third-millennium Semitic rulers of Mari lies under the palace of the early second millennium BC, which was rebuilt according to the earlier plan and remained in use for several centuries. Benefiting from the trade that passed along the Euphrates, the rulers of Mari acquired considerable wealth. In the 19th century BC the city's Amorite rulers were expelled by Shamshi-Adad of Assyria, who installed his younger son Yasmah-Adad as king. After Shamshi-Adad died in about 1780 BC, Zimri-Lim, the son of the previous Amorite ruler, regained control of the city. Excavations of the palace of Zimri-Lim uncovered among the ruins extensive and informative archives of the rulers. Some 20 years later Zimri-Lim was defeated by his erstwhile ally Hammurabi, king of Babylon, who destroyed the palace and the city in 1757 BC. The site remained deserted though it was used as a cemetery in the Middle Assyrian period.

entrance

courtyard 131

courtyard 106

?throne room or shrine 132

64

throne room 65

before 2100 BC
2100–2000 BC
2000–1850 BC
1850–1780 BC
1780–1760 BC

0   25   50 m
0   50   100   150 ft

Above left The black stone statue of Ishtup-ilum, governor of Mari, was found in the throne room (65). It had fallen down the stairs at the east end of the room. Ishtup-ilum probably ruled Mari c. 2100 BC. Height 1.52 m.

Left The river valley near Mari.

Right The body of this goddess holding a vase was found in the antechamber (64) to the throne room and its head in the courtyard. A channel led from the vase to the base of the statue to allow water to flow out of the vase. Height 1.4 m.

Below Fallen near the southern wall of the courtyard (106) were painted fragments of plaster which showed the ruler towering over other figures who may be leading bulls for sacrifice. The paintings probably date to the reigns of Shamshi-Adad or of Zimri-Lim. Width c. 1.35 m.

Excavations at Ebla, Shechem and Hazor have uncovered tower-fortress temples (Migdal temples) that were the prototypes for the Late Bronze Age temples, which in turn provided the model for Solomon's Temple.

The Levant was the meeting place for Egyptian and Mesopotamian influences, though evidence correlating the reigns of individual rulers of Egypt and Mesopotamia has so far been lacking. Inscriptions of Middle Kingdom Egyptian rulers have been found on statues at Megiddo, Qatna and Ugarit. The people of Byblos too had close links with the Egyptians, writing the Semitic names of their rulers in Egyptian hieroglyphs and adopting the Egyptian title "governor". With the collapse of the Middle Kingdom at the beginning of the 18th century BC, the influences from the north and east became more important. A century later northern Egypt was ruled by the Hyksos, described as "chieftains of a foreign hill country", who had close connections with the Middle Bronze III inhabitants of Palestine. Perhaps the most surprising and most enduring of the achievements of Middle Bronze Age Palestine was the invention of the alphabet, whose use became widespread during the Late Bronze Age.

Left A diorite head found in Susa, where it had probably been taken in the 12th century BC. This kind of headdress was worn by rulers of Mesopotamian cities between 2100 and 1700 BC. Hammurabi, king of Babylon, was carved on his Law Code stele wearing an identical headdress, and so this head has been identified as that of the great Babylonian ruler. However, it is equally likely that it represents another ruler of the period, perhaps of Eshnunna, as several finely carved statues of rulers from Eshnunna were taken to Susa. Height 15 cm.

Right The inscription on this bronze and gold figure records that Lu-Nanna, for his god Martu and for the life of Hammurabi, king of Babylon, made a praying statue of copper with its face plated in gold, and dedicated it to be the servant of the god. Believed to have been found at Larsa, it may date from the end of Hammurabi's reign (1750 BC). Height 19.5 cm.

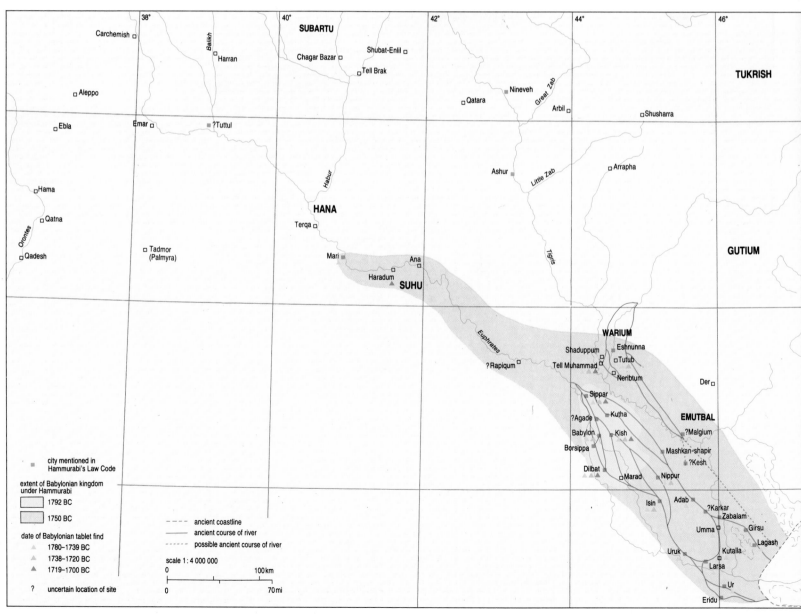

city mentioned in Hammurabi's Law Code

extent of Babylonian kingdom under Hammurabi
- 1792 BC
- 1750 BC

date of Babylonian tablet find
- 1780–1739 BC
- 1738–1720 BC
- 1719–1700 BC

? uncertain location of site

---- ancient coastline
— ancient course of river
···· possible ancient course of river

scale 1:4 000 000
0 ———— 100km
0 ———— 70mi

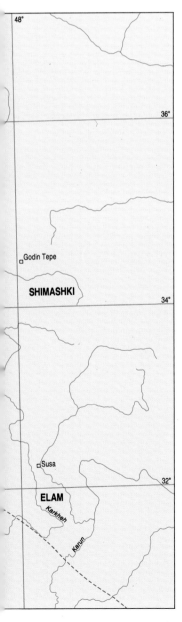

Hammurabi's kingdom
Hammurabi (1792–1750 BC), in the course of the second half of his reign, established control over much of Mesopotamia and ended the independence of many cities. In the prologue to his Law Code he claimed to have restored the temples in many Mesopotamian cities, including Mari and Eshnunna, which he had destroyed, as well as Tuttul, Nineveh and Ashur.

Hammurabi's son Samsu-iluna suppressed the rebellious Rim-Sin II of Larsa, after which the south of Babylonia appears to have been abandoned. There is little evidence for any occupation of Ur, Larsa, Kutalla, Uruk, Umma, Adab or Lagash (the southernmost cities of Babylonia) after 1739. In 1721 tablets dated to the reign of Iluma-ilu, king of the Sealand, were written in Nippur but no texts dated to the 200 years following have been found at Isin or Nippur. This lack of evidence in the south may have resulted from a catastrophic alteration of the courses of the rivers, from conquest by the rulers of the Sealand, from changes in bureaucratic practices, or from a combination of all three.

Hammurabi, king of Babylon

The outstanding figure of the early second millennium was Hammurabi, king of Babylon, who ruled between 1792 and 1750 BC. Patient but ambitious, cautious but resolute, he created an empire which, albeit short-lived, transformed the historical perspective of Mesopotamia. Babylon became its political, cultural and religious center. According to Hammurabi's year-names he captured Uruk and Isin in 1787 and campaigned against Rapiqum and Malgium in 1784. A contract from 1783 suggests that at that time Hammurabi may have been a vassal of Shamshi-Adad.

For the next 20 years Hammurabi devoted himself (according to his year-names) to building temples and canals, but in the 29th year of his reign he claimed victory over an alliance of Elam, Subartu, Gutium, Eshnunna and Malgium. The following year, 1763, with the aid of Mari and Eshnunna he conquered Larsa, putting an end to the long reign of Rim-Sin I. Two years later he defeated Mari itself and destroyed it in 1757. In 1755 he captured Eshnunna by diverting the waters around the city, so disposing of the last of his Mesopotamian rivals. In the prologue to his Law Code, Hammurabi listed the gods and their cities that supported him, from Mari and Tuttul in the west, to Ashur and Nineveh on the Tigris, and down to Ur, Eridu and Girsu in the south.

The 150 or so letters dealing with Hammurabi's administration of Larsa that have been preserved show that he took great interest in the day-to-day running of the captured state and delegated very little responsibility. Hammurabi is best remembered for his Law Code. Earlier codes of law following a very similar pattern were promulgated by Shulgi of Ur, Lipit-Ishtar of Isin, and Dadusha of Eshnunna. Hammurabi defined the purpose of his Law Code as "to cause justice to prevail in the land, to destroy the wicked and the evil, that the strong may not oppress the weak". He further advised those seeking justice to examine the Law Code and find the legal decision appropriate to the case. In fact, there is little evidence to suggest that the Law Code was used to redress injustice, except for the occasional mention in legal documents of a stele that might have been Hammurabi's. The 282 sections of the Law Code dealt with many subjects, including commercial law, family law, property law, slavery regulations and fees, prices and wages, but as a code in itself it is neither complete nor comprehensive.

The laws of Hammurabi presented an idealized view of Old Babylonian society. At the top was the king, who could and did intervene in all the affairs of his kingdom. Below him there were three social classes: the *awilum* (Akkadian for "man"), or freeman, the *mushkenum*, whose exact status is uncertain but who was in some way a dependent of the state, and the *wardum*, or slave. Slaves could, however, own property in their own right and often appear to have led a better life than some members of the *awilum* class who had to sell themselves or their children into slavery to pay off their debts. The standard interest on loans was 33 percent for barley and 20 percent for silver. The *awilum* also had responsibilities to the state and may have had to pay taxes and perform military service in the royal army. On the death of an *awilum*, his property was divided between the sons, resulting in ever smaller holdings of land.

The exact balance of the economy between the temple, the palace and the private citizens has so far been difficult to gauge from the available sources. Generally, however, palaces became more important features of Old Babylonian cities and the power of the kings over the temples did not derive from the king's being the high priest of the city god, but from the increased secular power he enjoyed. This was also reflected in the adoption of more secular titles even though kings still claimed that they had been divinely ordained and were supported by the gods.

As the power of the palace increased, so the private sector in agriculture, in industry and in commerce expanded, as is shown by the increasing numbers of contracts, loans, and property sales between private individuals in the Isin–Larsa and Old Babylonian periods.

Hammurabi's successors

Hammurabi's throne passed without incident to his son Samsu-iluna. However, in 1742, the ninth year of Samsu-iluna's reign, a rival from the south, Rim-Sin II of Larsa, occupied Nippur, though this triumph was only short-lived as by the following year Samsu-iluna had reestablished his control of the city. Two years later, in 1739, disaster struck southern Mesopotamia. Tablets from Nippur showed that there had been an economic crisis at that time. Prices for land plummeted and the number of land sales and sales of priestly offices soared. One possible cause was that Samsu-iluna might have diverted the waters of the Euphrates south of Babylon in order to starve Rim-Sin into surrender. Samsu-iluna's 11th year was named after the destruction of the walls of Uruk and Larsa, and excavations at Ur showed that the city was, indeed, destroyed at this time. Rim-Sin was finally defeated in 1737. Nippur survived this

Transportation

Below The same type of boat found in the Royal Cemetery at Ur is still used by the Marsh Arabs of southern Iraq today. Although normally a boat for fishing, it can also serve, as here, for the transportation of goods such as reeds.

The most efficient way of transporting goods was by water, as most places in Mesopotamia could be reached through a network of rivers and canals. Ships also sailed down the Gulf and on the Mediterranean and the Phoenicians may even have circumnavigated Africa. Where travel by water was not possible, normally donkeys or mules served as beasts of burden and sometimes human porters were used. After about 2000 BC the introduction of the horse enabled messengers to travel more quickly. Camels became increasingly important with the rise of the desert tribes in the first millennium BC.

Wheeled vehicles were known in the Near East from about 3500 BC. However, in the muddy conditions of the alluvial plains sledges were often more practical and in the mountains wheeled vehicles were useless before proper roads were built (the earliest of which may have been Urartian c. 800 BC). Local journeys were often made in carts with solid wooden wheels, which are still in use in the Near East today. The Sumerians had four-wheeled battle wagons pulled by asses.

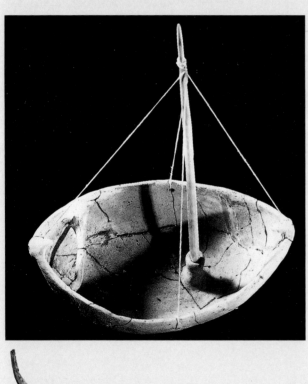

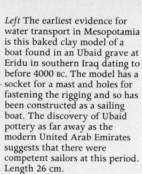

Left The earliest evidence for water transport in Mesopotamia is this baked clay model of a boat found in an Ubaid grave at Eridu in southern Iraq dating to before 4000 BC. The model has a socket for a mast and holes for fastening the rigging and so has been constructed as a sailing boat. The discovery of Ubaid pottery as far away as the modern United Arab Emirates suggests that there were competent sailors at this period. Length 26 cm.

Below A silver boat from the King's Tomb in the Royal Cemetery at Ur (2600–2500 BC). Cylinder seals depict the gods (or their statues) traveling in similar boats, either propelled by paddles or pushed along using a pole.

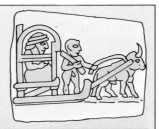

crisis, but 20 years later it too was abandoned and, like the cities farther south, lay desolate for several centuries.

According to a later tradition, the First Dynasty of the Sealand controlled the south, but so far no textual or archeological evidence of their presence in the region at that time has been found. The Amorite dynasty of Babylon, however, survived and continued to exercise its rule over the cities along the Euphrates almost as far as Mari. Farther upstream, the independent kingdom of Hana flourished after the destruction of Mari, under its capital city Terqa, which had previously been ruled from Mari. A pottery jar found at Terqa during excavation of an unpretentious house contained cloves, suggesting that the trading links of Mesopotamia were as distant as the Far East, since the natural habitat of cloves at that time was the East Indies (they were introduced into East Africa only much later).

The final century of Old Babylonian rule made no mention of military campaigns in the year-names. However, two important documents—the Edict of Ammisaduqa and the Venus Tablets—have been attributed to this later period and, in particular, the reign of Ammisaduqa (1646–1626 BC). The first was a royal decreee, issued in the first year of Ammisaduqa's reign, canceling the personal debts of the *awilum* class that had built up during the previous reign. Earlier rulers including Hammurabi had issued similar decrees to assist the state's economic activity.

The Venus Tablets, which included a reference to one of Ammisaduqa's year-names and so were probably produced in his reign, were a collection of observations on the rising and setting of the planet Venus. The sequence described in the observations could have taken place only at certain times as it is repeated at approximately 60-year intervals. This has given rise to systems of dating Ammisaduqa's reign and those of other rulers of the dynasty, with differences of 60 to 120 years. The Middle Chronology (used in this book) has placed Hammurabi's reign at 1792–1750 BC; the High Chronology, which is becoming more popular, puts it at 1848–1806; and the Low Chronology, which was once adopted by many scholars working in Anatolia and the Levant but has fewer followers today, places Hammurabi's reign at 1728–1686. Hopefully, in the future, some reference will be found among the thousands of tablets of the period linking events to a better-dated astronomical phenomenon such as an eclipse, or research in the Levant will succeed in correlating the Mesopotamian sequence with the more reliably dated Egyptian chronology.

The population movements in the Near East that had brought the Amorites and Hurrians into conflict with Mesopotamia continued with the appearance of new peoples, as recorded in the Old Babylonian texts. In the ninth year of Samsuiluna's reign, Kassites were mentioned for the first time, while at the beginning of the 16th century BC the Hittites made their mark in Mesopotamia. In 1595 BC the Hittite king Mursilis marched down the Euphrates and sacked Babylon, putting an end to the First Dynasty of Babylon and ushering in a dark age of some 150 years for which almost no information has so far emerged.

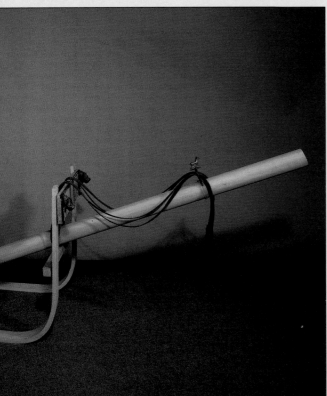

Top The pictographic sign for a cart in Uruk-period tablets was the same as for a sledge but with the addition of two circles for the wheels. This stone plaque, which shows a ruler traveling in a sledge pulled by a bull, probably dates to about 3000 BC.

Below top Baked clay model of a covered wagon from northern Syria dating to the second half of the 3rd millennium BC. Covered wagons were also used by the nomadic Scythians who invaded the Near East in the middle of the 1st millennium BC.

Above Relief showing a chariot brought by the Lydians to the king of Persia at Persepolis c. 485 BC. Chariots were used in battle and in processions as well as by messengers.

Left A reconstruction of the sledge in the tomb of Queen Puabi in the Royal Cemetery of Ur. It was drawn by a pair of cattle. Sledges were also used to transport heavy loads such as the enormous stone winged-bulls in Assyrian palaces.

Science

The invention of writing in the fourth millennium BC allowed the inhabitants of the ancient Near East to record their knowledge of the world around them for posterity. Among the earliest texts were lists of words belonging to certain categories, such as birds, or city names, or professions. They were used primarily to teach apprentice scribes how to write, but the systematic formulation of knowledge contained in them is evidence of an early scientific approach.

The counting systems used in the earliest texts contain elements of the sexagesimal system, that is counting in sixties. As 60 has many divisors, the system makes many calculations quite simple. In fact, it is still used today to measure time and angles. Two kinds of mathematical text have survived from the early second millennium BC: table texts and problem texts. The former include multiplication tables as well as tables of reciprocals, squares, square roots, cubes and even some logarithms to bases 2 and 16. The problem texts covered many topics, including the solutions of linear and quadratic equations, and computing the areas and volumes of different geometric figures. The Babylonian mathematicians reached a remarkable level of achievement. Although they normally reckoned π as 3, they knew its more accurate value of $3\frac{1}{8}$ (3.125, close to the true value, to three figures, 3.142). They calculated the value of $\sqrt{2}$ correct to within 0.000007. One exceptional tablet listed Pythagorean triples of numbers such that the square of the largest number equals the sum of the squares of the other two. These went from 45, 60, 75 up to 12,709, 13,500, 18,541. One of the most amazing features of Babylonian mathematics was that, though expressed in practical terms, it was essentially theoretical.

In the second millennium, omens based on celestial phenomena were recorded and observations of the celestial bodies occasionally made. In the first millennium the science of astrology became extremely impotant. By 700 BC signs of the zodiac had been identified and some of them still bear the same names. Systematic records were kept, and by 500 BC the Babylonians could predict the movements of the moon and the occurrence of eclipses with great accuracy. The earliest surviving horoscope, foretelling someone's future according to the positions of the celestial bodies at the time of their birth, comes from Babylonia and is dated 29 April 410 BC. In the following half-century almanacs predicting the positions of the sun, moon, planets and stars were compiled, one of which, dating to AD 75, is the latest cuneiform tablet to have been preserved.

Another branch of Mesopotamian science for which there is much evidence is medicine. Two kinds of specialist dealt with disease: the *ashipu* practiced magic while the *asu* was a physician who prescribed practical remedies. Hundreds of different diseases were recognized.

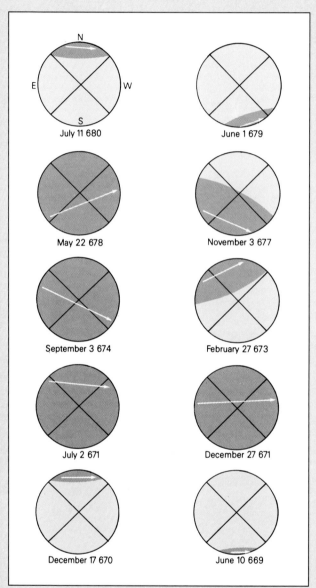

July 11 680   June 1 679

May 22 678   November 3 677

September 3 674   February 27 673

July 2 671   December 27 671

December 17 670   June 10 669

Left and below Under the later Assyrian kings a science for the interpretation of celestial phenomena, especially solar and lunar eclipses, was developed. A prediction based on a lunar eclipse depended on the time of the eclipse, the day of the month, the month, the part of the moon covered by the shadow and the direction in which the shadow moved. The visibility of the planets, particularly Jupiter, also affected the interpretation of the phenomenon. To escape the evil foretold by an eclipse a monarch would sometimes appoint a substitute as king, who was killed after 100 days, when the true king resumed the throne. If the omen referred to both Assyria and Babylonia the substitute was crowned in Nineveh and then again, 50 days later, in Babylon.

For the total eclipse of the moon on the evening of 22 May 678 BC the royal astrologer reported that the month and the day referred to Elam and the direction of the eclipse showed that it foretold bad luck for Elam and Amurru and good luck to Subartu (Assyria) and Akkad (Babylonia). The eclipse of 27 February 673 did not affect Assyria while that of 10 June 669 was a bad omen for Assyria. Clearly astrologers had to exercise their judgment in the interpretation of the eclipses, but the practice of first recording the observations and then applying accepted theories in order to predict the outcome is the basis of modern scientific method.

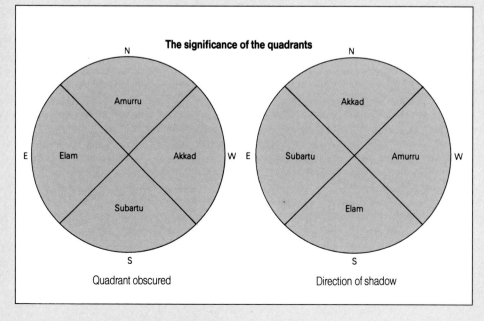

The significance of the quadrants

Quadrant obscured   Direction of shadow

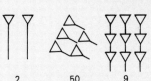

2　　　50　　　9

82
7-14
509

92687

Above In the cuneiform script, numbers were written using vertical wedges for the units from 1 to 9 and diagonal wedges for the tens up to 50; 60 was written with a vertical wedge, which could also represent 1. This is the positional or place-value notation, which was invented before 2000 BC and is still used today. In present terminology, in the number 111.1 the sign 1 stands for 100, 10, 1 and $\frac{1}{10}$. In the cuneiform script the same method was used but with powers of 60 rather than powers of 10 (the sexagesimal rather than the decimal system). The sexagesimal point was not written, nor were zeros until about 300 BC. The number written here could be read $2 \times 60 + 5 \times 10 + 9 \times 1 = 179$ or $2 \times 1 + 59 \times \frac{1}{60} = 2\frac{59}{60}$ or even $2 \times 60^2 + 59 \times 60 = 10,740$, or $2 \times 60^2 + 0 + 59 = 7,259$. In a particular case, it would be easy to tell from the context which was intended.

Left This clay tablet is called the Babylonian Map of the World. It shows a circle labeled the ocean, outside of which are wondrous regions that are described in the text. In the center is the known world oriented with west at the top. The box in the middle top is inscribed with the name of Babylon, and the names of Urartu, Assyria and Der are written on the right-hand side. Susa is placed at the bottom. The vertical lines going through Babylon must represent the Euphrates river. The map was probably composed in about 700 BC, though this copy was made later.

Below Five of a set of 17 bronze weights in the form of lions, found at Kalhu. The largest weighs almost 20 kg and is about 30 cm long; the smallest weighs about 50 g and is only 2 cm long. Some of the lions were inscribed in Akkadian and in Aramaic with the name of the Assyrian

Above A detail from the Rassam Obelisk found at Kalhu showing tribute being weighed in front of Ashurnasirpal II (883–859 BC). Modern science is based on accurate observation and exact measurement. Mesopotamian weights were based on the sexagesimal system. There were 60 shekels to 1 mina and 60 minas to 1 talent. The mina weighed about 0.5 kg. There may have been different weight standards in different cities. A text of about 1900 BC refers to the mina of Dilmun, which weighed the same as the standard unit of weight used in the Harappan civilization of the Indus valley.

king Sennacherib (704–681 BC) and with their weights. The earliest weights identified with certainty belong to the Early Dynastic period in the middle of the 3rd millennium BC. Weights were commonly made in the shapes of ducks and lions or were spherical or barrel-shaped.

Technology

Before the Neolithic revolution there is little evidence for technological expertise. Flint- and obsidian-working was certainly very competent but other, more advanced skills depended on a settled life-style. In the course of the next 6,000 years the inhabitants of the Near East developed almost all the techniques that formed the basis of civilized life before the industrial revolution: architecture, transportation, metalworking, carpentry, potting, glassmaking, textile manufacture and leather-working, as well as the many processes associated with farming and food preparation.

Of fundamental importance were irrigation and flood control, which allowed the development of southern Mesopotamia and gave rise to a number of subsidiary technologies of water management, including canal-building, water storage, drainage and so on.

For some crafts, such as pottery or metalworking, it is possible to determine the processes used from surviving artifacts. A few texts give detailed information on the methods employed in glass manufacture, perfume-making, brewing and tanning, while others contain a wealth of detail on the economics of the industries.

Below This gold vase from the cemetery of Marlik, just southwest of the Caspian Sea, dating to about 1200 BC is a fine example of the goldsmith's craft. The heads of the winged bulls were made as one with the rest of the vessel, and the ears and horns attached separately. Height 18 cm.

Above Glazed vessels, similar to those found in Babylonia and Assyria, from the 1st millennium BC. By 4000 BC faience (an artificial glazed material) was made in Mesopotamia, but glaze was not applied to pottery until the 2nd millennium BC. The problem was to match the glaze to the body so that it did not crack. Height c. 8 cm.

Below Illustration from the walls of the palace of Sennacherib (704–681 BC) at Nineveh showing how the massive stone sculptures that were placed in the doorways of Assyrian palaces were transported. The statues were roughed out in the quarry and placed on a vast sledge resting on wooden rollers. The sledge was pulled to the river by prisoners and floated downstream to the city.

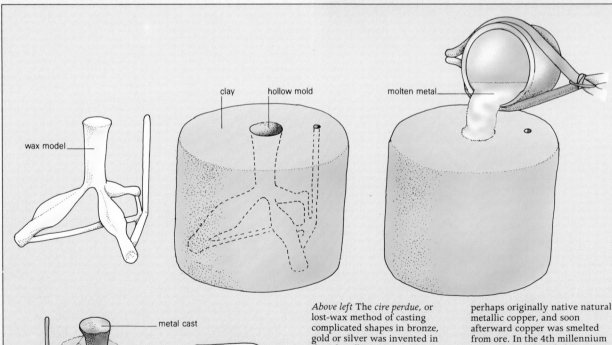

Above left The *cire perdue*, or lost-wax method of casting complicated shapes in bronze, gold or silver was invented in the 4th millennium BC. The earliest examples are from the Nahal Mishmar hoard in Palestine. First, a model was made out of wax. This was covered with fine clay to form a mold, which was then heated so that the wax melted and ran away. Molten metal was poured into the clay mold which would be broken open to release the complete object.

As early as the Aceramic Neolithic period objects were manufactured out of copper,

perhaps originally native natural metallic copper, and soon afterward copper was smelted from ore. In the 4th millennium gold, silver and lead also came into use. The properties of copper were much improved by alloying with other metals: first arsenic, then tin, lead and zinc (c. 700 BC). In the 2nd millennium BC iron and steel were manufactured but they did not become important until the 1st millennium BC.

The earliest objects were shaped by hammering but by the end of the 6th millennium copper artifacts were cast from molten metal.

Below The invention of glass in about 1600 BC was one of the greatest achievements of the Mesopotamian craftsmen. There are a few isolated examples of glass beads from earlier times but these probably arose as vitrified faience beads. The vessel shown was found at Tell al-Rimah and dates to the 15th century BC. The shape imitates that of pottery goblets of the period. It was molded on a core. Rods of colored glass were let into the still plastic surface of the vessel and then dragged up and down to create the zigzag pattern. Height 13.4 cm.

Above The plains of southern Mesopotamia are scarred by the lines of canals and their spoil banks. Some are still in use today, bringing life-giving water to the fertile fields; others have long since been abandoned. Canals had to be carefully designed so that they did not silt up too quickly.

Left Detail from Sennacherib's palace at Nineveh showing a workman using a *shaduf*, or counterbalanced water-lifting device, to raise water into a canal. This simple tool was in use from the 3rd millennium BC though it was seldom depicted on monuments.

Above Molded relief in baked clay from about 1900 BC showing a carpenter working with an adz, like those used in the region today. Except in unusually dry conditions the products of the carpenters' art have not been preserved from the ancient Near East. Height 8 cm, width 7.6 cm.

Right A 9th-century BC relief from Kalhu. The projecting battering ram of an Assyrian siege engine has been caught by a chain held by the defenders of the city. Many technical advances were made in pursuance of warfare.

Everyday Life

In archeological excavations the vast majority of the finds consist of the items discarded by the people of the time—broken pieces of pottery, animal bones, and so on. Most of this waste has resulted from household activities, but there are many aspects of the daily lives of the people that are still unknown. Often the remains of the past can be interpreted by comparing them with contemporary practices, with the caveat that, the daily routines of the inhabitants of the Near East have changed slowly but perceptibly over the millennia and that what is true today was not always so.

Such research has been devoted to the study of the elites of the ancient world—the kings and nobles, priests and generals—who are the subjects of the surviving texts, whereas the lives of the common people have been largely ignored. Far more is known about temples and palaces than about the houses that ordinary people lived in. Most ancient Near Eastern societies were dominated by men and only a handful of women stand out as individuals. The lives of most women and children are only occasionally illustrated by the archeological remains.

Right Impression of a shell cylinder seal of the Akkadian period (c. 2200 BC) showing an ox pulling a seeder plow. The seed was fed through a funnel and dropped directly into the furrow. Height 3.2 cm.

Below Several such pottery molds were found in the kitchen area of the palace at Mari (18th century BC). Some were circular with motifs of animals, others shaped like fishes. The excavator suggested that they were used to prepare dishes for the king's table, perhaps for cheese or bread or some delicacy.

Right Sieve pot, probably from the region to the southwest of the Caspian Sea, dating to the end of the 2nd millennium BC. Pottery vessels were made in a variety of different shapes for different purposes and are the most commonly found objects of daily life. Height c. 11 cm.

Above Metal vessels were normally made by hammering out sheets of metal. As the materials and the manufacture were expensive, they were luxury items and the poorer people had to be content with pottery or leather containers. This bronze vessel with a cast bronze spout ending in a lion's head looks very much like a modern kettle but was probably not used for boiling water. It may have been made in western Iran in early 1st millennium BC. Height 20 cm.

Right Care for the dead was an important duty for the living. This bone or ivory panel was found in the Tomb of the Lord of the Goats in the cemetery beneath the Western Palace at Ebla and dates to about 1750 BC. The scene shows a banquet that was probably part of the funeral rites. The bone or ivory carved figures were fixed onto the backing strip with bronze pegs. Height 4 cm.

Left Relief from the palace of Ashurnasirpal (883–859 BC) at Kalhu showing servants preparing food for the king inside a circular camp.

Bottom left This model of a house made of baked clay is said to have been found near Hama in western Syria and to date to the 3rd millennium BC. Attached to the wall of the house are rows of birds. It was probably a votive offering and so the details may not be accurate. Height 42 cm.

Below In the Ubaid period in southern Mesopotamia sickles were made out of baked clay not flint or obsidian as elsewhere in the Near East. As the price of metals decreased, first bronze and then iron were more generally used for tools and weapons.

Bottom right Seal impression from Susa of a man climbing a ladder and carrying something on his back. It has been identified as a worker filling a grain store. In the 4th and 3rd millennia special rooms resting on parallel sleeper walls were constructed for the storage of grain. Later, large pits dug into the ground were more commonly used. Height 3.4 cm.

Below The women in this relief (c. 630–612 BC) from the Southwest Palace at Nineveh are being deported after a campaign in Babylonia. One woman gives a child a drink from a skin bag.

Above Spinning and weaving were generally done by women in the ancient Near East. As in many parts of the region today, the manufacture of textiles within the house was an important source of income for the family. Here, an Elamite lady accompanied by a servant with a fan is making thread using a spindle. The relief, from the 8th or 7th century BC was found on the Acropolis at Susa. Height 9.3 cm, width 13 cm.

Below Molded relief in baked clay of a naked woman on a bed. Such figures have been associated with a sacred marriage ceremony. This one was possibly made in Elam c. 1750 BC. Length c. 12 cm.

Above Items like this are either classified as toys or as votive objects. The hedgehog is of limestone, and the cart from a bituminous stone. Originally there was a second animal behind the hedgehog. Length of car 6.7 cm.

Left Cosmetics were worn by both men and women in the ancient Near East. This faience vessel may have contained kohl (black eye-paint). Similar vessels have been found at Hasanlu in northwest Iran dating to the early 1st millennium BC. Height c. 7 cm.

PART THREE
EMPIRES

ALLIES AND ENEMIES (1600-1000 BC)

The rise of Egypt

At the beginning of the 16th century, the Hittite king Mursilis destroyed Aleppo and brought Hammurabi's dynasty in Babylon to an end. On his return to Anatolia, Mursilis was murdered by his brother-in-law who seized the throne. Very soon internal dissension and Hurrian encroachment had reduced the Hittites' realm to the neighborhood of their capital. The Near East fell into decline or, at least, obscurity. There are almost no sources of information from the following century in the Near East, and what is known has been derived from later accounts. The ancient Near East was divided between five or six major powers. The sleeping giant Egypt lay to the southwest, while the Hurrian kingdom of Mittani controlled the Levant and northern Mesopotamia including Assyria and the lands to the east of the Tigris. Anatolia was ruled by the Hittites in the center and Arzawans in the west. The Kassites were in charge of southern Mesopotamia, and southwestern Iran was ruled by the Elamites.

The first power to revive was Egypt. While the Egyptian Delta was ruled by the Asiatic dynasty of the Hyksos, control of Upper Egypt lay with the native Egyptian 17th Dynasty. In about 1555 Kamose, the last king of the 17th Dynasty, attacked the Hyksos rulers. His brother Ahmose (1550–1525 BC), who replaced him, continued the struggle and after about twenty years succeeded in driving the Hyksos out. Ahmose, who is reckoned to have been the first king of the 18th Dynasty, restored the boundaries of Egypt both to the south and to the north, creating the New Kingdom.

Under Tuthmosis I (1504–1492 BC), Egypt broke out of its traditional borders. Tuthmosis' armies campaigned 800 kilometers south of Thebes as far as Nubia and 1,200 kilometers north, as far as the Euphrates. The Egyptians, who were used to the Nile flowing from north to south, were amazed at the Euphrates, which they described as "water that goes downstream in going upstream". On his

Left Statue of King Idrimi, the ruler of Alalah, found buried in the temple. It is made of white stone, with eyes and eyebrows inlaid in black stone. The king is seated on a raised throne resting on a basalt base. A long inscription covers the body of the ruler, giving the details of his life. His family came from Aleppo but he fled from there and after many years of wandering became king of Alalah and a vassal of the dynasty of Mittani. Height 1.04 m.

return journey, Tuthmosis took part in an elephant hunt in the swampy region of Niya, perhaps on the Orontes river. The presence of elephants in Syria at this time might be surprising, but elephant bones dating to before Tuthmosis' invasion have been found at Alalah on the Orontes and at Kumidu in the Lebanon. The species that Tuthmosis hunted has been called the Syrian elephant, distinct from both the African and the Indian, but the pictures in the tomb of Rekhmire and a tooth from a later level at the site of Arslantepe (Malatya) have identified the species as the Indian elephant. Whether these elephants were introduced, however, or were survivors from a much earlier time is uncertain. (Interestingly, they received no mention in the Mari texts.)

Tuthmosis did not identify his enemies but called the area he reached Nahrin, meaning the river land. A fragmentary inscription that was probably from his reign included the name Maittani, the country later called Mittani, which rivaled Egypt for control of the Levant until the middle of the 14th century BC.

Mittani and the Hurrian dynasty

The Assyrians called the country of Mittani Hanigalbat, while to the Hittites it was the "land of the Hurrians". The Hurrians had first appeared more than 700 years earlier, and by the early second millennium had formed numerous minor principalities to the north and east of Mesopotamia. By about 1480 BC these had been united under Parrattarna, the overlord of King Idrimi. An autobiographical inscription on the statue of Idrimi found in Alalah

Kings of the Egyptian 18th Dynasty	
Ahmose	1550–1525
Amenophis I	1525–1504
Tuthmosis I	1504–1492
Tuthmosis II	1492–1479
Tuthmosis III	1479–1425
Hatshepsut	1473–1458
Amenophis II	1427–1401
Tuthmosis IV	1401–1391
Amenophis III	1391–1353
Amenophis IV (Akhenaten)	1353–1335
Smenkhkare	1335–1333
Tutankhamun	1333–1323
Aya	1323–1319
Haremhab	1319–1307

Right The valley of Jezreel, known in the Bible as Esdraelon, provides the easiest route from the coast to the Jordan valley. It also lies on the main route from north to south, and so control of the valley was an important goal for the Egyptian invaders. The city of Megiddo lay at the head of the most important pass over the Carmel range, leading from the Jezreel valley to the coastal plain of Sharon.

recounted how he and his elder brothers had fled from Aleppo (Halab), the home of his ancestors, to take refuge with his mother's relatives in Emar. Thinking to himself nothing venture, nothing gain, he took "his horse, his chariot, and his groom" and set out to seek his fortune in Canaan. He spent seven years among the Hapiru before setting sail for the land of Mukish, where he established himself. From there, after a further seven years, Idrimi sent an ambassador with tribute to Parrattarna, the Hurrian king, and having sworn a binding oath as a loyal vassal he became king of Alalah and ruled for 30 years. The death of a king called Parrattarna was also mentioned in a text from Nuzi, to the east

of Mesopotamia, but this Parrattarna might have been a later ruler.

Why Idrimi had fled from Aleppo is not clear, but it was possibly due to an incursion by the Hurrians, following the invasion of Tuthmosis I. The Egyptian king's son Tuthmosis II (1492–1470 BC) campaigned in Nubia and in Palestine, but died when his own son was still a child, and his widow Hatshepsut became the ruler of Egypt and proclaimed herself pharaoh. Soon after her death her stepson Tuthmosis III (1479–1425 BC) embarked on a series of campaigns in the Levant, which were recorded in detail on the walls of the Great Temple of Amun at Thebes.

In the 22nd year of his reign Tuthmosis invaded Palestine. The best route from Egypt to the Levant followed the Roman *Via Maris* along the coast, crossing Mount Carmel into the Jezreel valley (Esdraelon), and then either continued along the coast past Tyre and Sidon to the north or followed the line of the rift valley along the Jordan river, the Beqa' valley and the Orontes river. From the Jordan valley a second route led northeast to Damascus, where it joined the King's Highway running north–south from the Gulf of Aqaba along the edge of the desert. Tuthmosis followed the *Via Maris*, but on receiving news that the ruler of Qadesh and his allies had entered Megiddo in the Jezreel valley, Tuthmosis, according to his inscription, went against the advice of his generals by choosing the most direct but most difficult of the three roads through the mountain to arrive behind the enemy lines. The Egyptians were victorious in the battle that followed and might have captured the city of Megiddo immediately if they had not stopped to loot the belongings of the defeated left on the battlefield. In fact, it took a siege of seven months before the city fell.

Tuthmosis continued to campaign in Palestine and the Levant for the next 20 years of his reign,

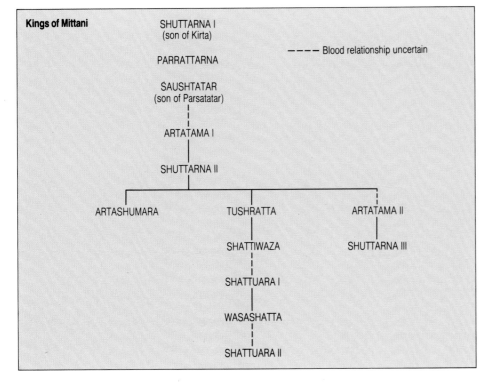

Kings of Mittani

SHUTTARNA I
(son of Kirta)

---- Blood relationship uncertain

PARRATTARNA

SAUSHTATAR
(son of Parsatatar)

ARTATAMA I

SHUTTARNA II

ARTASHUMARA   TUSHRATTA   ARTATAMA II

SHATTIWAZA   SHUTTARNA III

SHATTUARA I

WASASHATTA

SHATTUARA II

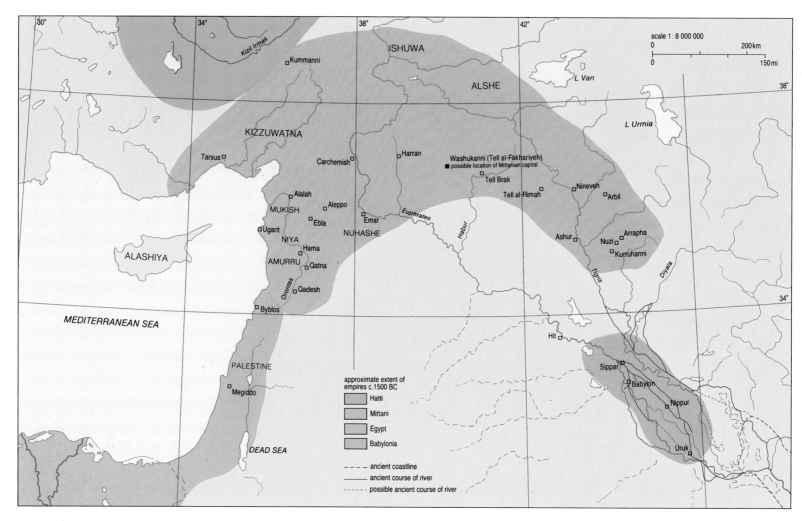

removing rebels and appointing local rulers loyal to Egypt. His greatest success came in his 33rd year as king, when he crossed the Euphrates in the course of his eighth campaign. On his return, he, like his grandfather before him, hunted a herd of elephants in Niya. In these campaigns, Tuthmosis received gifts (from, among others, the Assyrian and Hittite rulers), tribute and booty, which were recorded in great detail. Tuthmosis also recorded his interest in acquiring rare and exotic plants and animals, including a foreign bird that laid eggs every day (probably the domestic chicken). Red jungle fowl was first domesticated in the Far East as early as 6000 BC, but the first reliable discoveries of chicken bones in the Near East date to the last centuries of the second millennium BC (as does one of the first representations, an incised drawing on an ivory comb from a tomb at Ashur).

Tuthmosis listed more than three hundred princes at the battle of Megiddo and more than one hundred places that he had conquered. Most of these were in Palestine, but only about half of them have been identified. Almost all Middle Bronze Age III sites have shown signs of destruction at about this time, most probably attributable to the Egyptian invasions, with later levels being assigned to the Late Bronze Age. Thus, by the end of Tuthmosis' reign, Palestine was divided up into small city states owing allegiance to Egypt. Further north, in the Levant, Egyptian influence was matched by that of the rulers of Mittani.

The conflict continued in the reign of Ameno-phis II (1427–1401 BC), the son of Tuthmosis. In 1421 he crossed the Orontes, captured Niya and

The empire of Mittani *above*
The history of Mittani is not well known. The texts that have been found come mostly from the fringes of the empire, from Alalah in the west and from Nuzi in the east. The heartland of the empire was probably in the upper reaches of the Habur river. The capital was called Washukanni but its location is uncertain. It is often suggested that it was Tell al-Fakhariyeh, to the west of Tell Brak, but this is arguable. Mittani was the principal rival of Egypt for control of the Levant until the rise of the Hittites in the 14th century BC. At this time the Hittites occupied the western half of the former Mittanian empire while the eastern half was held by the newly independent rulers of the city of Ashur. After a century during which there is no information about Babylonia, in the 15th century BC it re-emerged under the rulers of the Kassite dynasty.

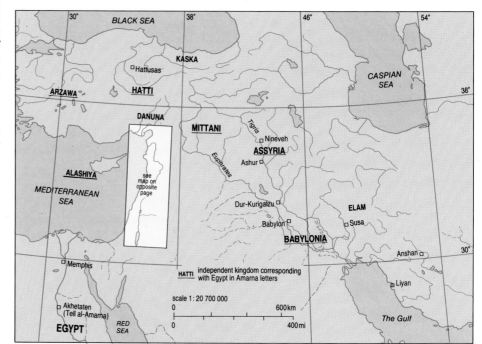

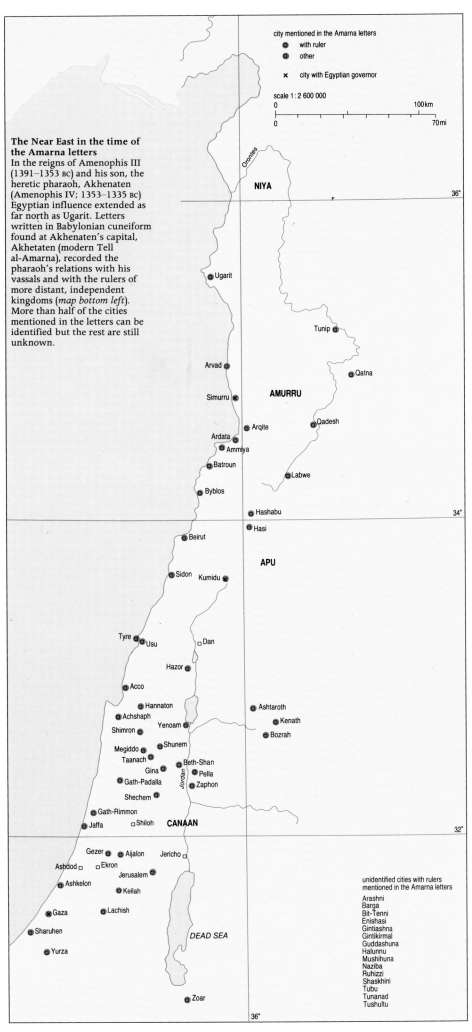

The Near East in the time of the Amarna letters
In the reigns of Amenophis III (1391–1353 BC) and his son, the heretic pharaoh, Akhenaten (Amenophis IV; 1353–1335 BC) Egyptian influence extended as far north as Ugarit. Letters written in Babylonian cuneiform found at Akhenaten's capital, Akhetaten (modern Tell al-Amarna), recorded the pharaoh's relations with his vassals and with the rulers of more distant, independent kingdoms (*map bottom left*). More than half of the cities mentioned in the letters can be identified but the rest are still unknown.

city mentioned in the Amarna letters
● with ruler
● other

✕ city with Egyptian governor

scale 1:2 600 000

unidentified cities with rulers mentioned in the Amarna letters

Arashni
Barga
Bit-Tenni
Enishasi
Gintiashna
Gintikirmal
Guddashuna
Halunnu
Mushihuna
Naziba
Ruhizzi
Shaskhini
Tubu
Tunanad
Tushultu

Qadesh and, on his return journey, in the coastal plain south of Mount Carmel, he "found a messenger of the Prince of Nahrin carrying a clay tablet at his neck and took him prisoner". Amenophis listed the spoils from this campaign as: "*mar-yannu* [nobles] 550, their wives 240, Canaanites 640, children of princes 232, female children of princes 323, female musicians of the princes of foreign lands 270, together with . . . silver and gold . . . horses 820, chariots 730, with all their weapons of war". According to Amenophis' own account, when news of his great victory reached them, the princes of Nahrin, of Hatti and of Sangar all sent tribute. Nahrin has been identified with Mittani, Hatti with the Hittites, and Sangar (somewhat doubtfully) with Babylon.

The ruler of Mittani at this time might have been Saushtatar. Two tablets found at Alalah recorded judgments made by Saushtatar and were impressed with a seal inscribed "Shuttarna, son of Kirta, king of Maitani". This Shuttarna is otherwise unknown, but using the seal of an earlier ruler to give legitimacy to one's own rule was a custom that was practiced by later Mittanian rulers, as well as by Idrimi's son, the ruler of Alalah, and by Assyrian kings. Saushtatar arbitrated between his vassals, Niqmepa of Alalah and Shunashura, king of Kizzuwatna (Cilicia), but probably did not retain control over Kizzuwatna, as a king of Kizzuwatna called Shunashura is known to have made a treaty with the Hittites that invalidated an earlier treaty with Mittani. Saushtatar's seal has been found on tablets at Nuzi and at Tell Brak, where it was used on documents of two later kings of Mittani, Artashumara and Tushratta, the grandsons of Saushtatar's successor. The treaty between Shattiwaza and the Hittite king Suppiluliumas recorded how Saushtatar sacked Ashur and carried off a silver and gold door to his capital Washukanni.

The whereabouts of Washukanni is uncertain. In Middle Assyrian texts, the town was called Ushukani, and because of the similarity of the names it has been tentatively identified with the 9th-century BC town of Sikanu. Sikanu, as a result of the discovery of a statue of its ruler, is now known to to be Tell Fakhariyeh, near Ras al-Ain in northeast Syria. However, excavation has so far failed to show extensive settlement in the Mittanian period. Furthermore, the clay used in the tablets of Tushratta, which were probably produced in Washukanni, has been shown to be different from that used in Middle Assyrian tablets from Tell Fakhariyeh. Information about the Mittanians has come either from foreign archives—Egyptian, Hittite or Assyrian—or from the periphery of the Mittani state, Alalah and Nuzi. Recent excavations at Tell Brak have uncovered a small temple and part of a palace containing texts that included legal depositions made in the presence of the Mittanian ruler, but so far the lack of a major native archive has seriously limited knowledge of the Mittani kingdom.

The Amarna letters
In the reign of Tuthmosis IV (1401–1391 BC) relations between Egypt and Mittani changed from conflict to peaceful alliance, which was cemented by diplomatic marriages. According to a letter written two generations later, the pharaoh had

indication of the extent of Hurrian influence. In fact, Egyptian sources mentioned a tribe called Hurri who lived in Palestine.

Letters from these rulers and governors include professions of loyalty, requests for assistance and accusations against neighboring city rulers. A constant menace to the settled population were nomadic tribes, of whom the two main groups, the Sutu and the Hapiru, had both figured in the earlier Mari letters. Whether there was any connection between the Hapiru and the Hebrew tribes of Israel is doubtful, but very likely the Israelites too were wandering, homeless, dispossessed people.

The Amarna letters also recorded diplomatic exchanges with the rulers of independent countries including Mittani, Hatti, Arzawa in the west of Asia Minor, Alashiya (Cyprus), Assyria and Babylon. These rulers treated with the pharaoh on equal terms, addressing him as their "brother" (whereas a vassal ruler used language such as "the king, my lord, my sun god, I prostrate myself at the feet of my lord, my sun god, seven times and seven times"). Some of the letters were requests for Egypt's assistance against the encroachments of neighboring states; others chronicled the marriages of the pharaohs to Babylonian or Mittanian princesses. Amenophis III's wedding with Kilu-Hepa, daughter of Shuttarna II, the son of Artatama I, was celebrated in his 10th year (1381 BC). He also married Tatu-Hepa, the daughter of Tushratta (Shuttarna's son), who later entered the harem of Amenophis IV (Akhenaten). Often the precisely detailed dowries were matched by requests for gifts from Egypt. For instance, Tushratta, having given away his daughter Tatu-Hepa, suggested that the pharaoh might send him a statue of her cast in gold so that he would not miss her!

Twice, when Amenophis III was ill, Mittanian kings sent the statue of the goddess Ishtar of Nineveh to Egypt. On the first occasion, in the reign of Shuttarna, the goddess seems to have proved an effective remedy, but the second time, in Tushratta's reign, it proved less successful, as Amenophis III died in about 1353 BC. Some scholars have put this event as early as 1379, and others as late as 1340 BC. The disagreement is based on different dating of astronomical observations in the reigns of Tuthmosis III and Ramesses II and on different estimates for the lengths of the co-regencies of the pharaohs. The dates of the non-Egyptian kings are equally uncertain. As far as Assyrian kings are concerned, an eclipse of the sun in 763 BC has provided a fixed point for working out the earlier reigns in conjunction with the lengths of reign recorded in the Assyrian King List. However, two copies of the list give different lengths of reign for one of the kings at the beginning of the 12th century and the dates given here may be 10 years too early. The dating of the Hittite, Mittanian, Babylonian and Elamite kings is based on the Egyptian and Assyrian chronologies and is therefore even more unreliable.

The Indo-Aryan connection

Although most of the names of people from Alalah and at Nuzi were Hurrian, some of their rulers' names were not Hurrian but had possible Indo-Aryan (Vedic Sanskrit) derivations. These included: Tushratta, whose name meant "whose

Above This painted pottery head of a man was found in the palace at Dur-Kurigalzu, the capital of the Babylonian Kassites. Its style is unlike Mesopotamian works of art of the period but is similar to Egyptian figures of the 18th Dynasty. Height 4 cm.

Left One of the letters found at Amarna (ancient Akhetaten) in central Egypt. These letters, written in Akkadian cuneiform on clay tablets, were part of the diplomatic correspondence of the pharaoh. Most of them are concerned with the situation in Palestine. In this letter the ruler of Amurru tried to explain why he himself had not received the pharaoh's envoy though he had received the envoy of the Hittite king. He also sent the king a gift of a ship, oil and timber.

asked Artatama, king of Mittani, seven times for the hand of his daughter before Artatama responded. This alliance, perhaps made to thwart growing Hittite and Assyrian power, brought about a peace between the two kingdoms that lasted for at least forty years during which time two more princesses from Mittani went to join the pharaoh's harem. The period was documented in the diplomatic correspondence of Amenophis III (1391–1353 BC) and Amenophis IV (1353–1335 BC) of Egypt.

Three hundred and fifty letters written in cuneiform on clay tablets have been found at Tell el-Amarna, or Akhetaten, which became Amenophis IV's capital when he changed his name to Akhenaten and embarked on the religious reforms that made him notorious in later Egyptian memory. More than 300 of the letters concerned the government of Palestine and the Levant. The region was divided into three provinces, each with an Egyptian governor: Canaan in the south, with the governor at Gaza, Amurru on the Levantine coast, with the center at Simurru, and Apu in the interior, administered from Kumidu. (There may also have been Egyptian garrisons in Jaffa and in Beth-Shan.)

Other Egyptian officials were responsible to these governors, as were the local rulers of Ashkelon, Lachish, Jerusalem, Gezer, Shechem, Pella, Megiddo, Achshaph, Shimron, Acco, Hazor, Tyre, Sidon, Beirut, Damascus, Byblos, Qadesh, Qatna, Ugarit and other cities, all of whom were subject to the pharaoh. Most of these rulers had Semitic names, but even in Canaan some, such as the ruler of Jerusalem, had Hurrian names—an

The power of the Hittites

One of the Amarna letters was written by the Hittite king Suppiluliumas to preserve the amicable relations between his people and the Egyptians that had been established "in the reign of the pharaoh's father". (The identity of the pharaoh is not certain, but it was probably Amenophis IV.) From the time of the sacking of Babylon in 1595 BC to the middle of the 14th century little information has emerged about the Hittites. They were mentioned in Egyptian records and were rivals of Mittani for the control of Kizzuwatna (Cilicia) and Ishuwa, the region around the upper Euphrates. Their later history is preserved in the 10,000 tablets found in the palace and temple archives of their capital, Hattusas. These contained a variety of texts, written mostly in Hittite and Akkadian, some of which belonged to the Mesopotamian scribal tradition and included word-lists, vocabularies and medical texts as well as lists of omens and clay models of livers used in making prophecies. There were also translations into Hittite (and occasionally into Hurrian) of some of the Baylonian epics, such as the Epic of Gilgamesh, and the tales of Sargon of Agade and of Naram-Sin. Other texts recorded religious ceremonies, prayers, hymns and funeral practices. Copies of royal decrees and treaties between the Hittites and their neighbors were also preserved and, from the reign of Mursilis II (Suppiluliumas' son), royal annals. These included details from the reign of Suppiluliumas, documenting the rise of Hittite power.

Suppiluliumas I succeeded his father, Tudhaliyas III, on the throne and for the first years of his reign established his power in Anatolia. The principal enemies of the Hittites included the independent state of Arzawa to the west, the fierce mountain tribes of the Kaskas to the north and northeast and the states of Kizzuwatna to the south and Ishuwa to the east. Suppiluliumas' victories in Anatolia were followed by campaigns in the Levant and northern Mesopotamia, which resulted in the virtual extinction of Mittani.

During Amenophis III's reign, the king of Mittani, Artashumara (a son of Shuttarna II), had been murdered and succeeded by his brother Tushratta. Tushratta's claim to the throne, however, was disputed by Artatama II, who may have been another brother. Artatama II apparently allied himself with both the Hittites and the Assyrians under Ashuruballit I (1363–1328 BC). When the Hittite king Suppiluliumas I married his daughter to the king of Babylon, and Egypt became preoccupied with its own internal affairs following the reforms of Amenophis IV (Akhenaten) and the succession of the boy king Tutankhamun (1333–1323 BC), Tushratta was left without allies. His kingdom quickly fell apart and he himself was murdered, leaving Artatama II as the ruler of a much reduced Mittani. Tushratta's son Shattiwaza fled first to Babylon and then to the Hittite court, where he signed a vassal treaty with Suppiluliumas whereby he was to be given the throne of Mittani on the death of Artatama II. However, this claim was challenged by Artatama's own son Shuttarna III, who may have had Assyrian support. In effect, the kingdom of Mittani had been divided between the Assyrians and the Hittites, who now controlled the Levant as far south as Qadesh on the Orontes river.

chariot surges forward violently", Artatama ("whose abode is justice") and Shattiwaza ("acquiring booty"). In the treaty between Shattiwaza and the Hittite king Suppiluliumas, the names of some of the gods invoked—Mitrasil, Arunasil, Indar, Nasattyana—were close to those of the Indo-Aryan gods Mitra (Mithras), Varuna, Indra and Nasatyas. Moreover, a text dealing with training horses, written by Kikkuli of Mittani, used numbers that are related to Sanskrit. The term *maryannu*, referring to the chariot-owning nobles of Mittani, is similar to the Sanskrit *marya* meaning a young man or warrior.

The Indo-Aryans are thought to have invaded India from the north in the middle of the second millennium BC. Like the later Saka (Scythians) and Moguls, they might have come, by way of eastern Iran and Afghanistan, from the steppes of Central Asia, from where the Indo-Iranian ancestors of the Medes and Persians might also have originated. Some members of the ruling dynasty of Mittani had typically Hurrian names, including king Shattiwaza, who, before he became king, is believed to have been called Kili-Teshup. The Aryan connections may thus have been established before Mittani dominated northern Mesopotamia.

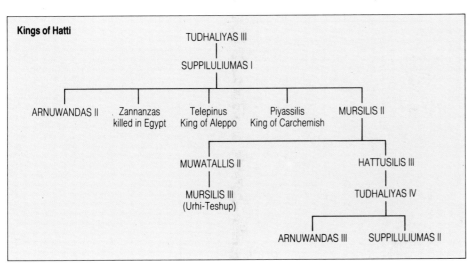

Kings of Hatti

- TUDHALIYAS III
- SUPPILULIUMAS I
  - ARNUWANDAS II
  - Zannanzas killed in Egypt
  - Telepinus King of Aleppo
  - Piyassilis King of Carchemish
  - MURSILIS II
    - MUWATALLIS II
      - MURSILIS III (Urhi-Teshup)
    - HATTUSILIS III
      - TUDHALIYAS IV
        - ARNUWANDAS III
        - SUPPILULIUMAS II

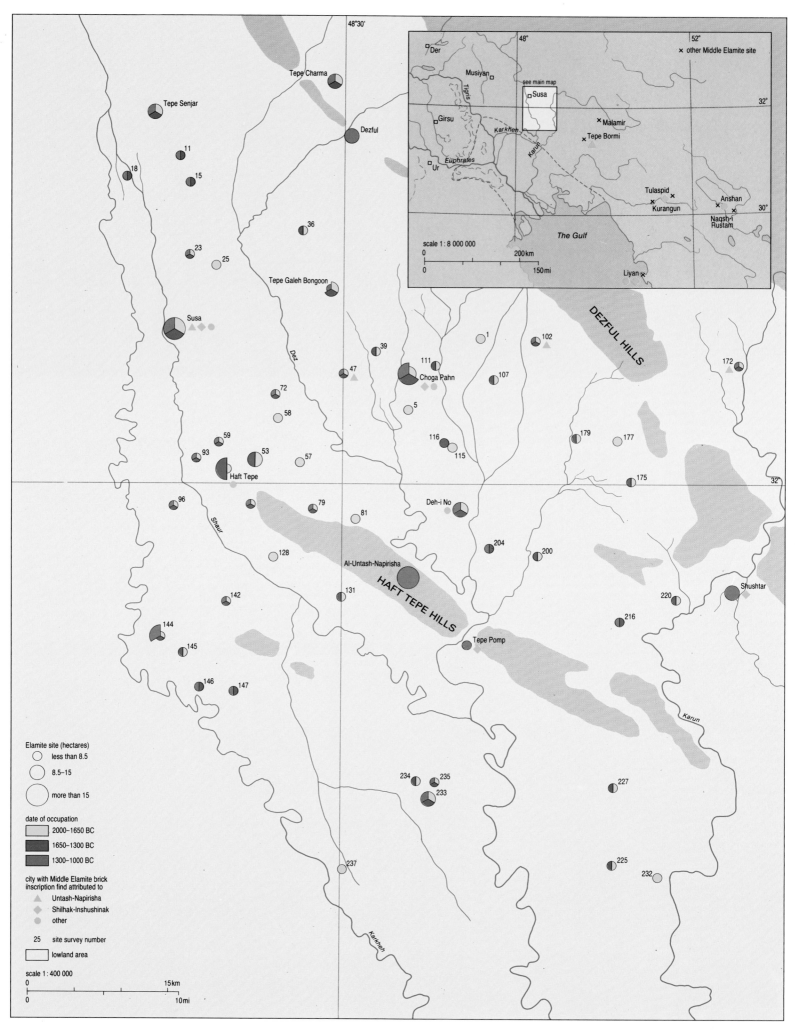

48°30'

Tepe Charma

Tepe Senjar

11

18

15

36

23

25

Tepe Galeh Bongoon

Susa

39

47

72

111

Choga Pahn

58

5

1

102

107

DEZFUL HILLS

172

59

93

53

57

116

115

179

177

Haft Tepe

96

79

81

Deh-i No

175

128

204

200

Al-Untash-Napirisha

HAFT TEPE HILLS

131

Shushtar

142

220

144

216

145

Tepe Pomp

146

147

Karun

Dezful

Dez

Shaur

Karkheh

Inset map (top right):

Der

Musiyan

see main map

Susa

other Middle Elamite site

32°

Girsu

Karkheh

Malamir

Tepe Bormi

Euphrates

Ur

Karun

Tulaspid

Anshan

Kurangun

30°

Naqsh-i Rustam

The Gulf

Liyan

scale 1 : 8 000 000

0   200km

0   150mi

48°

52°

Tigris

Legend:

Elamite site (hectares)

less than 8.5

8.5–15

more than 15

date of occupation

2000–1650 BC

1650–1300 BC

1300–1000 BC

city with Middle Elamite brick inscription find attributed to

Untash-Napirisha

Shilhak-Inshushinak

other

25   site survey number

lowland area

scale 1 : 400 000

0   15km

0   10mi

234

235

233

227

237

225

232

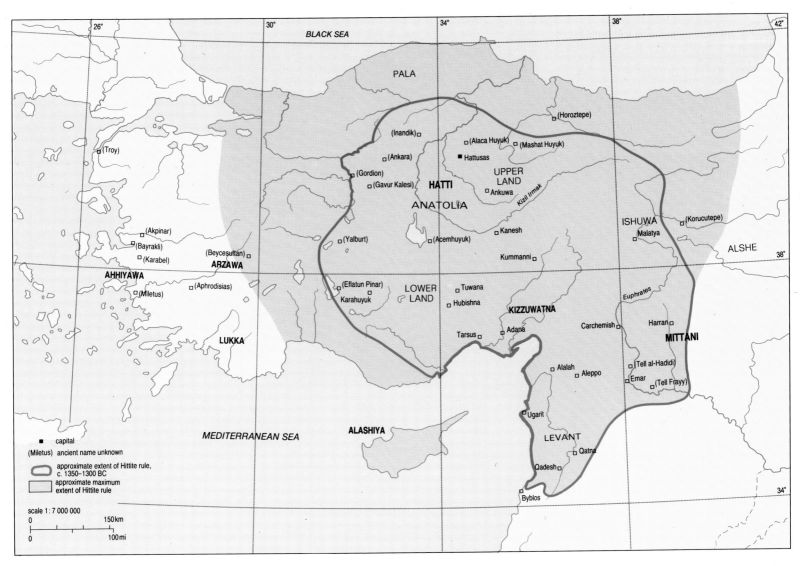

The map shows the Hittite empire with labeled locations including BLACK SEA, PALA, (Horoztepe), (Inandik), (Alaca Huyuk), (Mashat Huyuk), (Ankara), Hattusas, UPPER LAND, (Gordion), Ankuwa, (Gavur Kalesi), HATTI, ANATOLIA, Kizil Irmak, ISHUWA, (Korucutepe), Malatya, (Akpinar), Kanesh, (Bayrakli), (Yalburt), (Acemhuyuk), ALSHE, (Karabel), (Beycesultan), ARZAWA, Kummanni, AHHIYAWA, (Aphrodisias), (Eflatun Pinar), Tuwana, Carchemish, Harran, MITTANI, (Miletus), Karahuyuk, LOWER LAND, Hubishna, KIZZUWATNA, (Troy), LUKKA, Tarsus, Adana, Alalah, Aleppo, Emar (Tell Frayy), Euphrates, (Tell al-Hadidi), Ugarit, MEDITERRANEAN SEA, ALASHIYA, LEVANT, Qatna, Qadesh, Byblos

■ capital
(Miletus) ancient name unknown
approximate extent of Hittite rule, c. 1350–1300 BC
approximate maximum extent of Hittite rule

scale 1 : 7 000 000
0   150km
0   100mi

The Hittite empire (*above*)
The Hittites under Suppiluliumas I and his successors dominated the Anatolian plateau and the northern Levant. The historical geography of Anatolia is still poorly known. There are virtually no fixed points apart from the Hittite capital at Hattusas and the locations of countries such as Arzawa and Ahhiyawa are still uncertain. In the Levant the locations of the main cities, for instance Carchemish and Aleppo, are better known and can for the most part be identified with confidence.

Elam in the 2nd millennium (*left*)
The principal cities of the country of Elam were Susa and Anshan. This dual kingdom survived for some 2,000 years despite the 400 km separating the two centers. The extent of the Elamite kingdom is marked by bricks inscribed with the names of Elamite rulers. As a result of intensive archeological survey in the 1960s and 1970s, the Susiana plain is one of the best-known regions in the Near East and it is possible to reconstruct the changes in settlement patterns over thousands of years.

According to the Hittite account, when Suppiluliumas was besieging Carchemish he received an emissary from the widow of the Egyptian pharaoh saying, "My husband has died, and I have no son. They say that you have many sons. You might give me one of your sons, and he might become my husband." The identity of this queen (and of the pharaoh) is uncertain. Suggestions have included Akhenaten's wife Nefertiti, and their daughters Merytaten, the wife of Smenkhare, and—probably the most likely—Ankhesenamun, the wife of Tutankhamun. (If the woman was Tutankhamun's widow, this would date the capture of Carchemish to 1323.) The Hittite king dispatched an envoy to the queen of Egypt and, after receiving a further letter from her, sent his son. He, however, was murdered on the way and the throne of Egypt was seized by the aged Ay whose wife had been Nefertiti's nurse. Suppiluliumas installed two of his other sons as kings of Carchemish and of Aleppo, and their descendants continued to rule in the Levant after the Hittite kingdom in Anatolia had been destroyed in about 1200 BC.

Suppiluliumas himself died of a plague brought back by the army from Syria, and his eldest son and successor Arnuwandas II died shortly afterward. On Suppiluliumas' death the neighboring peoples of Arzawa, Kizzuwatna, Mittani and the Kaskas attempted to throw off the Hittite yoke. Mursilis II, who succeeded his brother Arnuwandas, crushed Arzawa and installed loyal puppet rulers. Syria too was brought back into the fold but quelling the Kaskas proved more difficult. In his annals covering almost a quarter-century, Mursilis recorded 10 campaigns against the Kaskas.

Assyrians and Kassites
The collapse of the kingdom of Mittani most benefited the Hittites, who took control of the western part of the Mittanian empire, and the Assyrians who, having cast off the Mittanian yoke, established themselves on equal terms with Egypt, Hatti and Babylon. Under the ruler Ashur-uballit I, Assyria extended its control to include the rich farming lands to the north and east of Ashur. This area, often called the Assyrian heartland, which stretched from Nineveh to Arbil, remained under Assyrian control until the demise of the Assyrian empire in 612 BC.

Two missives from Ashur-uballit in the Amarna letters recorded how he had sent a chariot with white horses and a lapis lazuli seal to the pharaoh. In return, he requested gold, which, he said, was "like dust in the land of Egypt", to decorate a new palace. According to later chronicles, Ashur-uballit married his daughter to the Kassite king of Babylon, and when the Babylonians rebelled against her son (or grandson) and killed him, the Assyrian king intervened to depose the usurper and place Kurigalzu II (1332–1308 BC) on the Kassite throne.

Thirty-six Kassite kings ruled Babylonia for 576 years and 9 months, according to the Babylonian

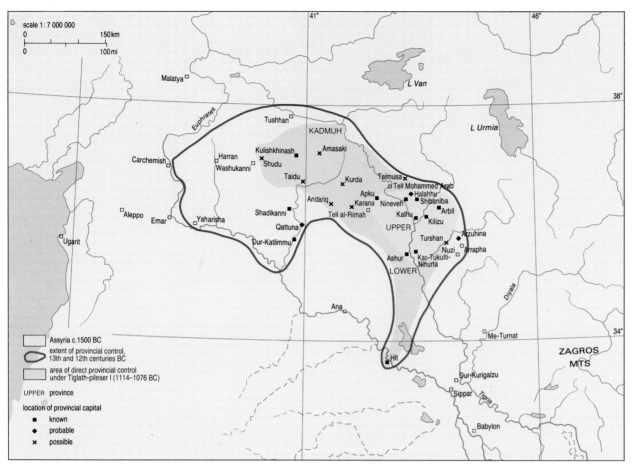

The Middle Assyrian empire
A text from Ashur contains a list of offerings for the Ashur Temple from the provinces of the Assyrian empire in the reign of Tiglath-pileser I (1114–1076 BC). This list is evidence of the extent of territory under direct Assyrian rule at that time. Several centuries earlier the Assyrian kingdom covered little more than from Ashur in the south to Nineveh in the north and Arbil in the east. By the middle of the 13th century, under Shalmaneser I (1273–1244 BC) and Tukulti-Ninurta I (1243–1207 BC), Assyrian provincial control had expanded as far as the western Euphrates and Assyrian conquests ranged even beyond. The farthest boundaries of the Middle Assyrian empire formed the basis for the territorial claims of the Assyrian kings in the 9th century BC.

King List. Comparisons with Assyrian kings imply that the dynasty came to an end in about 1155 BC. But if that were so, the first Kassite king would have been a contemporary of Samsu-iluna (1749–1712 BC), during whose reign dated tablets stopped in southern Babylonia, where the Sealand Dynasty was recorded. Perhaps the early Kassite rulers appearing in the Babylonian King List were ancestors who were not, in fact, kings or perhaps they ruled elsewhere. Indeed, the origin of the Kassites is itself uncertain. They received a first mention in the reign of Samsu-iluna, and at one time, it was thought that they were fierce uncivilized barbarians who invaded from the mountains of Iran. More recent research, however, has indicated a more peaceful immigration from a so-far-unidentified region. What happened after Babylon fell to the Hittites in 1595 BC is shrouded in mystery, but from the end of the 15th until the 12th century BC the rulers of Babylon were Kassite.

Little is known of the language spoken by the Kassites except for a Kassite–Babylonian vocabulary list of 48 words, a list of 19 Kassite names with their Babylonian equivalents, some proper names and occasional Kassite words in Akkadian texts (particularly technical terms to do with horses).

Kassite civilization

The Kassite kings seem to have adopted the Babylonian way of life and built and restored the temples of the traditional Mesopotamian gods. They also had gods of their own. Shuqamuna and his consort Shimaliya were the patrons of the royal family and Kassite kings were crowned in their shrine in Babylon. These gods also figured in Ugaritic literature. Others included Harbe, the chief of the pantheon (also found among the Hurrians),

Mirizir (the equivalent of the Babylonian goddess Beltu), Sah (the sun god), Shipak (or Shihu, the moon god), Shuriash (another solar deity), Maruttash (the god of war) and Buriash (a weather god). These last three have been identified with Indo-Aryan gods Surya and Marutas, and with the Greek god Boreas (god of the north wind), but as with the gods of the Mittani there was not necessarily a close relationship with the Indo-Aryans.

Texts found at Sippar and Tell Muhammad from the Old Babylonian period identified the Kassites as primarily agricultural workers. During the Kassite

Kassite Kings	
Kara-indash	c.1415
Kadashman-Harbe 1	
Kurigalzu I	
Kadashman-Enlil I	1374–1360
Burna-Buriash II	1359–1333
Kara-hardash	1333
Nazi-bugash	1333
Kurigalzu II	1332–1308
Nazi-maruttash	1307–1282
Kadashman-Turgu	1281–1264
Kadashman-Enlil II	1263–1255
Kudur-Enlil	1254–1246
Shagarakti-shuriash	1245–1233
Kashtiliash IV	1232–1225
Tulkulti-Ninurta	1224–1216
Enlil-nadin-shumi	1224
Kadashman-Harbe II	1223–1222
Adad-shuma-iddina	1221–1216
Adad-shuma-usur	1215–1186
Melishipak	1185–1171
Marduk-apla-iddina I	1170–1158
Zababa-shuma-iddina	1157
Enlil-nadin-ahi	1156–1154

Above The twisted, eroded remains of the ziggurat of Dur-Kurigalzu still dominate the flat countryside on the outskirts of modern Baghdad. Early travelers thought that they were the ruins of the Tower of Babel. In fact, the ziggurat was built by the Kassite king Kurigalzu in the 14th century BC. It followed the typical southern plan, with a triple staircase leading up to the temple on the top. The layers of reed inserted every 7 courses of bricks can be seen as horizontal lines at the top. The lower part of the ziggurat is shown in the course of restoration.

dynasty, the Third Dynasty of Babylon, the ruling family had Kassite names but Kassites do not appear to have made up an elite administrative class or indeed a large element of the population. Babylonia and the region along the Diyala into western Iran were the main centers for Kassites. Farther north the population was probably almost entirely Hurrian (2 per cent of the names of people at Nuzi were Kassite but their relatives had Hurrian names). The Kassites had a tribal organization and were grouped into "houses", sometimes named after an eponymous ancestor, for example, the house of Karziabku. The houses were based on male blood relatives and were headed by a "lord of the house" (*bel biti*). In this respect, they were not fully integrated into Babylonian society, and the relationship between these houses and the Kassite ruling family is uncertain.

The Kassite period represented a continuation of the older Babylonian civilization. There were differences from earlier periods but they were probably not attributable to changes in ethnic composition of the population. The inscriptions of the Kassite kings were written mostly in Sumerian and their letters and contracts in Babylonian. Some of the later Kassite kings had Babylonian names.

Kassite kings

The first Kassite king known from contemporary inscriptions was Kara-indash (c. 1415 BC), who built a small temple dedicated to Inanna within the sacred precinct at Uruk. The outer wall of the temple was decorated with baked molded bricks derived from those in Old Babylonian and Old Assyrian temples, but with alternating representations of earth and water deities. The prototypes of these figures also belonged to earlier periods.

Fragmentary examples have been found at other Kassite sites (Ur, Nippur and Dur-Kurigalzu) and the technique was adopted and developed by the Elamites, the Assyrians, the Babylonians and the Persians.

Kara-indash corresponded with the Egyptian pharaoh, as did his successors Kadashman-Enlil I (1374–1360 BC) and Burna-Buriash II (1359–1333 BC). Their chief concerns seem to have been arranged marriages and the exchange of valuable gifts. Burna-Buriash complained that the Egyptians had provided only five carriages to accompany his daughter from Babylonia to her wedding in Egypt; but the marriage went ahead and long lists of precious gifts were recorded as having been exchanged between the Kassites and the Egyptians. Burna-Buriash further claimed to be the overlord of the Assyrians and protested against their negotiating directly with Amenophis IV.

After the death of Burna-Buriash, his son and successor was killed in a rebellion, but the Assyrian king Ashur-uballit I intervened to place Kurigalzu II (1332–1308 BC) on the throne of Babylon (as recorded in the chronicles mentioned earlier). Kurigalzu allegedly carried out extensive rebuilding and restored temples at Ur, Uruk and Isin, though whether this was the work of Kurigalzu I or II is uncertain. A similar doubt hangs over the temple and palace at Dur-Kurigalzu, 90 kilometers north of Babylon, where a well-preserved ziggurat, 57 meters high, still retains the reed matting that had been laid between every seven courses of bricks, as well as the twisted ropes running through the structure. The palace, which lay about 700 meters from the ziggurat and covered an area roughly 300 meters square (9 hectares), consisted of several courtyard blocks. The central block measured about 140 meters square, with a court-yard about 65 meters square surrounded by three parallel rows of rooms. The palace had been rebuilt several times and continued in use until after the end of the Kassite period.

Kurigalzu II was also a successful military leader. According to a later chronicle he defeated Elam, Assyria and perhaps the Sealand (the dynasty that ruled southern Babylonia in the middle of the Old Babylonian period). In his own inscriptions he claimed to have conquered Susa, Elam and Marhashi, and inscriptions bearing his name have been found at Susa.

Kassite cultural achievements

The century from Kurigalzu II to Kashtiliash IV (1232–1225 BC) marked the high point of Kassite rule. Excavations at Nippur, the ancient religious center of Sumer, have revealed 12,000 tablets most of which belonged to this period. The texts, which are mostly economic documents, were dated by the regnal year of the king (the year of his reign), not the year-name, as in earlier periods. The Kassites were responsible for the standardizing of Akkadian and Sumerian texts. The versions of the traditional literature that have been found in the libraries of the first millennium were composed, or at least copied, in the Kassite period, and later Babylonian scribes traced their ancestry back to scribes living at that time.

The Kassites also introduced a new type of document, called a *kudurru*, to commemorate royal grants of land. This was often an elaborately carved stone monument, about one meter high, illustrated with the symbols of the gods who witnessed the transaction. The earliest examples dated to the 14th century BC, but they became common in the 13th and 12th centuries.

The Elamite civilization

Following the collapse of the Third Dynasty of Ur at the end of the second millennium, the rulers of Elam called themselves *sukkalmahs*, or grand viziers, after the title of the official stationed at

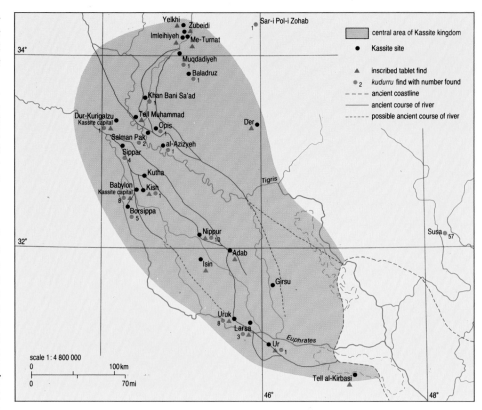

The kingdom of the Kassites
Later tradition connected the Kassites with the mountains of Iran, but the extent of their rule toward the east is debated. Many of the ancient cities of Babylonia revived under the Kassites. *Kudurrus*, sometimes called Babylonian boundary stones, were typical of the Kassites but continued to be made into the 1st millennium BC. Many were found at Susa, where they had been taken by the Elamites who invaded Babylonia.

Below Limestone *kudurru* of Melishipak II (1186–1182 BC) found in Susa. *Kudurrus* were often carved with the symbols and attributes of the gods. Height 68 cm.

Lagash who was responsible for the control of the lands to the east. These *sukkalmah* rulers intervened in Mesopotamia after the collapse of the empire of Shamshi-Adad I (1813–1781 BC). But thereafter, apart from the names of the kings and a few rather uninformative dedicatory inscriptions, nothing is known about them for some 400 years.

Excavations at Haft Tepe, about 15 kilometers south of Susa, have revealed a city built by Tepti-Ahar, King of Susa and Anshan, in the middle of the 14th century BC, which has been identified with ancient Kabnak. The principal monuments on the site, which covered some 30 hectares, were two terraces and a temple with two brick-vaulted tombs. Each of these contained 23 skeletons, some laid out neatly, others gathered up in piles. A stele discovered in the temple listed and recorded the duties of the priests and the disbursement of food-stuffs for sacrifices and funeral offerings. A terrace about 60 meters square and 14 meters high had workrooms where precious items were made for the cult.

Some 600 inscribed tablets found at the site were mostly concerned with the administration of the temple. The year-names on these tablets referred to the construction of the temple and to diplomatic missions between Elam and Babylonia. One inscription perhaps referring to the Kassite king Kadashman-Enlil I was contained on a tablet that bore the seal of Tepti-Ahar.

After the invasion of the Kassite king Kurigalzu II a new dynasty seized power in Elam. The first ruler was Ige-halki, whose inscription has been found at Deh-i No (perhaps ancient Hupshen or Adamdun). Ige-halki's grandson Humban-numena built a temple at Liyan on the Iranian coast of the Gulf, 400 kilometers southeast of Susa.

The Elamite gods were quite different from the Mesopotamian. In the third millennium the goddess Pinikir seems to have been the most important deity; in the second millennium her place was

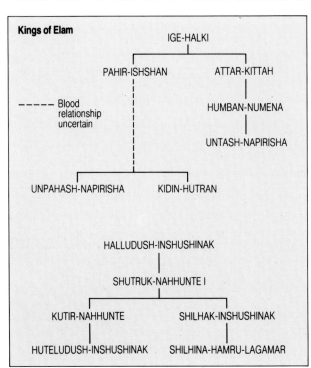

Kings of Elam

Al-Untash-Napirisha

Al-Untash-Napirisha
(Choga Zanbil)

Forty kilometers southeast of Susa are the ruins known as Choga Zanbil. The name means "basket mound" and refers to the eroded remains of the ziggurat in the center of the site which, before excavation, looked like a reed basket turned upside down. This is the site of Al-Untash-Napirisha (sometimes called Dur-Untash-Napirisha or Dur-Untash-Gal), which was the capital city of the Elamite king Untash-Napirisha (c. 1260–1235 BC). Like other rulers in the Late Bronze Age—such as the Egyptian pharaoh Akhenaten, the Kassite king Kurigalzu and the Assyrian king Tukulti-Ninurta I—Untash-Napirisha left the ancient religious capital of his kingdom to found a new city which was intended to replace the former capital. However, in none of these cases was the attempt altogether successful.

The site chosen by Untash-Napirisha lies on the edge of low hills, about 1.5 kilometers from the River Dez. To provide water for the town, the king had a canal, some 50 kilometers long, dug from the River Karkheh north of Susa. The building of the city ceased soon after his death and later Elamite kings ruled from Susa. Al-Untash-Napirisha was not deserted but remained a royal city until it was destroyed in about 640 BC by the Assyrian king Ashurbanipal.

Below Glazed pottery wall-plaque with the inscription, in Elamite cuneiform, "I am Untash-Napirisha". It was stored with hundreds of others in a room in the ziggurat, and was probably intended to decorate the facade of the ziggurat. Similar wall plaques are found in Assyria and their history can be traced back to the Uruk period.

Above The construction of the ziggurat at Al-Untash-Napirisha was most unusual. The first stage of the plan was to construct a large square building about 100 m long with a central courtyard. At a later stage the central courtyard was filled in and the ziggurat built inside it.

Above On all four sides, staircases with arched doorways were built within the structure of the ziggurat.

Left The large city of Al-Untash-Napirisha covered more than 100 ha and was dominated by the ziggurat at the center of the religious quarter. At the base of the ziggurat was a curved enclosure wall and between the ziggurat and a second rectangular wall were numerous temples for the worship of the Elamite gods. A third wall surrounded the whole site. In the eastern corner of the city a large entrance gate led to the king's palaces and his court. There were five underground vaulted chambers in the Funeral Palace, where several cremated bodies and one skeleton were found. It has been suggested that these were burials of members of the Elamite royal family. Much of the area of the city within the walls was never built on.

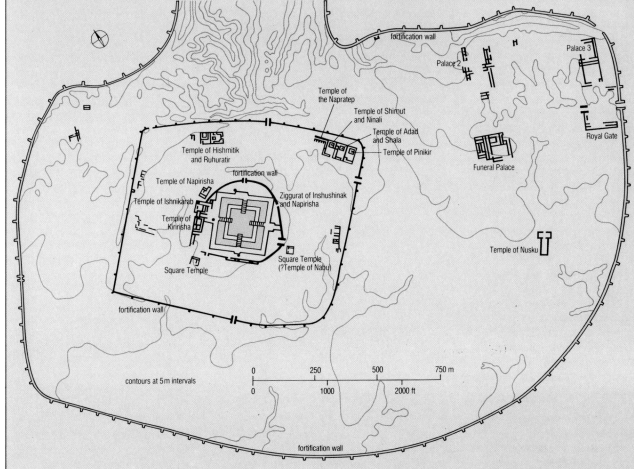

fortification wall

Palace 3

Palace 2

Temple of the Napratep

Temple of Shimut and Ninali

Temple of Adad and Shala

Royal Gate

Temple of Hishmitik and Ruhuratir

Temple of Pinikir

Funeral Palace

fortification wall

Temple of Napirisha

Temple of Ishnikarab

Ziggurat of Inshushinak and Napirisha

Temple of Kiririsha

Square Temple (?Temple of Nabu)

Temple of Nusku

Square Temple

fortification wall

contours at 5m intervals

| 0 | 250 | 500 | 750 m |

| 0 | 1000 | 2000 ft |

fortification wall

taken by the god Humban (also called Napirisha, meaning great god) whose female counterpart was Kiririsha (meaning great goddess), the goddess of Liyan. After these came the city god of Susa, Inshushinak (meaning lord of Susa), who by the end of the second millennium had become preeminent, and the sun god Nahhunte who, like the Babylonian sun god Shamash, was also the god of justice. There were many other Elamite gods, such as Hutran and Shimut, whose names appeared in the names of the Elamite kings. The Elamites also worshiped Babylonian gods such as Adad and his consort Shala, Sin and Nusku, though these may have been identified with local deities.

Humban-numena's son Untash-Napirisha restored many of the temples of Elam including 20 in Susa, but his greatest work was the founding of an entirely new city, Al-Untash-Napirisha, situated about 40 kilometers southeast of Susa and now known as Choga Zanbil. The city was large, with an outer wall enclosing an area of 1,200 by 800 meters. In the east, near the entrance, are the remains of a large gatehouse and three palaces, one of which contained steep staircases leading to barrel-vaulted chambers containing the ashes from cremated burials. These might have been the graves of the Elamite king and his family.

In the center of the city was a large rectangular enclosure which housed temples and a ziggurat. Originally, a square courtyard surrounded by rooms had been constructed and this had then been filled in and successive stages of the temple built. The ziggurat measured 67 meters square at the base and still stood 28 meters high, though once it had probably been more than twice as high, with five or six storeys. The inscribed baked bricks belonging to the first building mentioned only the god Inshushinak, but in the later phase the temple at the top, reached by staircases within the structure, was dedicated to both Inshushinak and the god Napirisha. At the foot of the ziggurat were temples of numerous other gods. The whole complex may have been part of a vast funerary temple, like that built a century earlier at Haft Tepe, and was reminiscent of the palace and ziggurat at Dur-Kurigalzu, which may have performed a similar function for the Kassite kings.

A fragment of a stone stele has been found at Susa showing Untash-Napirisha with his wife Napirasu. The queen's dress and her pose were both repeated in an extraordinary bronze-cast life-size statue of Napirasu that was also found at Susa. Even though the head was missing, the figure weighed 1,750 kilograms and had probably been cast in two stages. A shell about 9 centimeters thick had been cast first and then later filled up with bronze. The technical ability of the metalworkers of the figure was remarkable.

The battle of Qadesh

While Elam and Babylon fought each other, the final acts of the long struggle of Egypt to control the Levant were being played out. Suppiluliumas I had brought the Levant into the Hittite sphere of influence and after his death Hittite control of the Levant remained firm. At the end of the 14th century a new dynasty replaced the ailing 18th Dynasty in Egypt. The second pharaoh of the 19th Dynasty, Sethos I (1306–1290 BC), reestablished

Hattusas

Below View over Temple III, one of the numerous temples built in the Upper Town. Beyond Temple III is Buyukkale, the citadel of Hattusas, and beyond that is the hill of Buyukkaya. In the Hittite period the fortification system included Buyukkaya and the wall was carried across the gorge on a bridge.

Hattusas, now known as Boghazkoy or Boghazkale, was the capital of the Hittite empire. The site was settled at the end of the third millennium BC and in the 19th century, it included a trading colony of Assyrian merchants. In about 1650 BC the Hittite king Labarnas chose it as his capital and took the name Hattusilis after the city.

The city is situated on a promontory formed by the junction of two branches of the Budakozu river. The eastern stream runs through a gorge (*boghaz* in Turkish) between two steep hills called Buyukkaya and Buyukkale. The main citadel of the city was on the top of Buyukkale. Two kilometers to the northeast is the grotto of Yazilikaya, which contains carved images of the Hittite gods. The city was destroyed and abandoned shortly after 1200 BC, but was reoccupied in Phrygian times (c. 7th century BC), when it was called Pteria.

Egyptian control over Canaan and also claimed to have destroyed the states of Qadesh and Amurru. Stelae of Sethos I found at Beth-Shan, Tyre and Qadesh have confirmed some of these exploits. Control of Qadesh, however, did not last. Sethos I's son and successor Ramesses II (1290–1224 BC), the long-lived megalomaniac builder of Abu Simbel, set out to restore Egyptian fortunes in the fourth year of his reign, marching as far north as Nahr-kalb near Beirut where, like many later conquerors, he had an inscription carved.

In the following year he advanced toward Qadesh on the Orontes in a campaign that was described in detail and illustrated on numerous monuments erected by the pharaoh. On the way, according to his account, two tribal chiefs informed him that the Hittites were far away at Aleppo, but as he later found out this was false intelligence planted by the Hittites. Outside Qadesh he captured two Hittite scouts who confessed that the Hittite army, under Muwatallis II, was concealed to the east of Qadesh. By then it was too late to retreat in safety. But, Ramesses II

The Great Temple of the weather god of Hatti (also known as the weather god of heaven) was situated in the Lower Town. The city may have been fortified and extended in the reign of Suppiluliumas I. Some two dozen temples were built in the southern extensions up the hill away from the rivers.

Left Fragment of the rim of a pottery storage jar found at Hattusas, giving an idea of the appearance of a fortified Hittite building. It shows how the ends of the double timber beams protruded from under the parapet.

Below left Not only was the Great Temple at Hattusas a place of worship, it also played an important role in the economy, as is evident from the extensive storerooms.

Below This relief figure of a helmeted warrior was originally identified as a Hittite king and hence the gateway in the city wall where it stood was called the King's Gate. It is now thought that it represents a god.

claimed, though he was "alone, not even supported by a captain, by a charioteer, by a soldier of the army, or by a shield-bearer", he succeeded in defeating the hordes of the Hittites and their allies, including Arzawans and Lukkans from the west of Anatolia, Kaska tribes from the northeast, and troops from Kizzuwatna, Aleppo, Ugarit and Qadesh itself. Timely Egyptian reinforcements arriving from the west then allegedly forced the Hittites to break off the attack and to retreat across the river, and on the following day Ramesses II attacked again and obliged the Hittite king to sue for peace.

However, Ramesses' account of the battle was unreliable, and the Egyptians were almost certainly defeated, as recorded in the Hittite version of events. The Egyptians withdrew and Amurru, Qadesh and Apu, the district around Damascus, fell into the Hittite sphere of influence.

Diplomatic successes and failures
Throughout the period of Egyptian conflict the rulers of Ugarit had survived, and indeed thrived,

by offering their allegiance to Mittani, to Egypt, and to Hatti in turn. Diplomatic marriages and treaties ensured stability, despite the turbulence all around. In the Amarna letters there was a report that Ugarit was destroyed by fire, but whether from the attack of an enemy or natural causes was not stated. Ugarit's prosperity was based on trade, particularly trade in copper with Cyprus, but perfumes, grain, wood, salt and wine were also exported. Agriculture and the local industries of metalworking, textiles and the manufacture of purple dye from the murex shell were other sources of Ugarit's wealth.

The Mittanian kings failed to emulate the diplomatic successes of the rulers of Ugarit in their attempts to play off the Hittites against the rising power of the Assyrians. Adad-nirari I (1305–1274 BC) had extended the borders of Assyria southeast to Lubdu and as far as the Euphrates in the southwest. He captured the Mittanian capital Washukanni, making Shattuara I a vassal of Assyria. When Shattuara's son Wasashatta rebelled and was refused help from the Hittites, Mittani was once again plundered and its king was taken captive to Ashur. Assyrian expansion continued under Adadnirari's son Shalmaneser I (1273–1244 BC). He put down a rebellion by Shattuara II, king of Mittani, and defeated a combined force of Mittanians and Hittites, taking 14,400 prisoners and annexing Hanigalbat (as the Assyrians called Mittani).

The Egyptian–Hittite peace pact

Perhaps as a result of the Assyrian victories, the Hittite ruler Hattusilis allied himself with Kadashman-Turgu, the Kassite king, and in 1296 BC made a treaty with Egypt. Ramesses II was still on the Egyptian throne, where he stayed for almost another half-century, and both he and Hattusilis had fought at Qadesh 16 years earlier. The text of the Egyptian version of the treaty was carved on the walls of the temple at Karnak and the Ramesseum temple and a copy of the Hittite text was preserved in the archives at Hattusas. The original, which was sent to Ramesses, was a silver tablet with the impressions of the stamp seals of Hattusilis and his wife. This nonaggression pact solved the territorial dispute in the Levant and the good relations were cemented some 13 years later by the marriage of Hattusilis' daughter to Ramesses II.

Tudhaliyas IV, the son of Hattusilis, continued the policy of preserving cordial relations in the Levant, but invaded Cyprus (perhaps to compensate for his losses in the southeast). In a treaty made with the King of Amurru, Tudhaliyas listed the kings who he considered were his equals: the kings of Egypt, Babylon, Assyria and Ahhiyawa, though the last-named was later erased. Ahhiyawa was a country to the west of Hatti beyond Arzawa and had appeared in Hittite records from the time of Suppiluliumas I. At one time, it was identified as the country of the Achaeans, that is Mycenaean Greece, but it probably lay on the Asiatic side of the Aegean Sea. Mycenaean pottery of the period has been found at numerous sites along the Aegean coast of Turkey and the Mediterranean coast of the Levant and Palestine —an indication of the importance of maritime trade in the Mediterranean at that time.

The material remains of the Hittites have mostly been discovered by excavating their capital city Hattusas. Here, behind strong fortified walls with a circuit of some 6 kilometers, had been the palace citadel and temples of the Hittite royal family. About 1.5 kilometers outside the walls was the grotto, now known as Yazilkaya, where pictures of the Hittite gods and goddesses were carved in the reign of Tudhaliyas IV. Chief of the deities were the sun goddess Arinna and her consort the weather god of heaven, identified with the respective Hurrian gods Hepa and Teshub. Hittite kings took their religious activities very seriously and several of them were priests before they became kings. They would even interrupt a military campaign if a religious festival required the king's presence.

Tudhaliyas was succeeded by his two sons, Arnuwandas II and Suppiluliumas II, during whose reign disaster struck, in about 1200 BC, when the Hittite cities of Anatolia were burned and abandoned. The end of the Hittite kingdom was part of a much wider phenomenon, the arrival of new entrants into the fray —the "sea peoples".

Movements of new peoples

In the early decades of the 12th century there were widespread movements of people in the Mediterranean region. The Egyptians were threatened on land and on the sea by a coalition of tribes, which they called the "sea peoples". First Merneptah (1244–1214 BC), and then Ramesses III (1194–1163 BC), fought them off. Some of the tribes such as the Meshwesh, the Shardan and the Denyen were already present in the Near East, whereas others were new arrivals. Ramesses III described their attack in his eighth year (1186 BC).

> "The foreign countries made a conspiracy in their islands. All at once the lands were removed and scattered in the fray. No land could stand before their arms, from Hatti, Kode [probably the Orontes valley], Carchemish, Arzawa, and Alashiya [Cyprus], being cut off at one time. A camp was set up in a place in Amurru. They desolated the people, and its land was like that which has never come into being. They were coming toward Egypt, while the flame was prepared before them. Their league was Peleset [Palestine], Tjeker, Shekelesh, Denyen, and Meshwesh, united lands."

Egypt resisted, but Hatti and Ugarit fell, as did many of the cities of the Levant and of Greece. The Hittite kingdom was probably destroyed by the Mushki or Phrygians, who invaded and subsequently occupied the Anatolian plateau. In the Levant the Hittite states of Carchemish and Malatya survived as independent principalities. Egypt's control of Palestine waned, and the people known to the Egyptians as Peleset settled along the Mediterranean coast to the north of Egypt, giving their name to the country as Philistia, or Palestine. By the end of the 12th century Egyptian control was at an end.

The people of Philistia, or Philistines, were not the only ones moving into new regions. At almost exactly the same time, the Israelites appeared in the records. They were first mentioned in a victory stele of Merneptah.

> "Canaan has been plundered into every sort of woe;
> Ashkelon has been overcome;
> Gezer has been captured;
> Yenoam is made non-existent;
> Israel is laid waste."

In this hieroglyphic inscription "Israel" was preceded by the sign for a people, not a city or a country. The details of the Israelites' occupation of Canaan are uncertain. The Biblical story of Joshua's conquests following the Exodus from Egypt has found no support outside the scriptures, and it is possible that the Israelite tribes settled peacefully until they were strong enough to overthrow the local Canaanite rulers.

As well as the Israelites other Semitic people were emerging from the desert steppes. The Sutu and the Ahlamu were regarded in the Amarna letters as barbarous tribes on the edge of the civilized world. The Assyrian king Shalmaneser I fought against the Ahlamu, who in about 1100 BC were associated by contemporaries with the Aramaeans, a group of northwest Semitic people. Like the Amorites a thousand years earlier, the Aramaeans over the next few centuries occupied much

Right During the 60 years of excavating the site of Ugarit, a considerable part of the city has been investigated. The two main areas are the acropolis, where the main temples were situated, and the area of the royal palace to the west. The two main gods worshiped were Baal and his father Dagan. From the myths, it seems that these two deities were introduced into the local pantheon from the east.

Far right The royal palace developed from a small building in the 16th century BC to a large and magnificent structure with some 90 rooms arranged round six large courtyards. In some of the courtyards there were ornamental pools of water.

Ugarit

The ruins of the city of Ugarit comprise the tell known as Ras Shamra and the harbor called Minet al-Beidha. The site was occupied from the Aceramic Neolithic period onward. In the early second millennium it was under Egyptian influence, as is shown by objects bearing the names of Middle Egyptian pharaohs. Ugarit's period of greatest renown was in the second half of that millennium, when it was the capital of a major trading kingdom with commercial links throughout the eastern Mediterranean. The wealth of the city was principally based on trade in copper from Cyprus and timber from the hinterland, as well as grain, wine and salt. Ugarit also had its own industries. Metalworking was of great importance, as was the manufacture of purple dye from the murex shell, the so-called imperial or Tyrian purple, used to color linen or wool. Warehouses near the harbor were stocked with all kinds of goods: one contained 1,000 flasks for perfumed oil from Cyprus.

Perhaps the most significant discovery at the site have been the rich archives of cuneiform tablets. These texts, in several languages and including some written in a cuneiform alphabetic script, are of great importance for the information that they give about the Ugaritic religion and myths. This has, in turn, shed light on contemporary practices described in the Bible.

Ugarit was nominally subject to Egypt but also acknowledged the authority of the Hittites. The rulers of Ugarit were adept at walking diplomatic tightropes. In about 1200 BC Ugarit was sacked, probably by the "sea peoples".

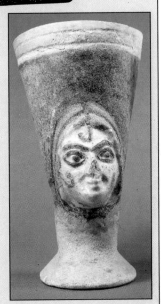

Above This bronze head was found with two scalepans and a set of weights to the northwest of the temple area at Ugarit. The local weight system employed a *shekel* of 9.5 g, with 50 shekels to the *mina*. This head weighs 190 g and so may have been used as a weight of 20 shekels. Height 3.8 cm.

Right Faience vase with the head of a woman dating to the 14th–13th century BC. It was found at Minet al-Beidha in a communal tomb in which at least 28 people were buried. Similar vessels have been found in Cyprus. Height 16 cm.

Left The face and headdress of this 13th-century bronze statuette from Minet al-Beidha are overlaid with gold foil. The silver on the chest, arms and legs may indicate armor. When found, it was identified as the god Reseph but is now thought to be Baal. Height 17.9 cm.

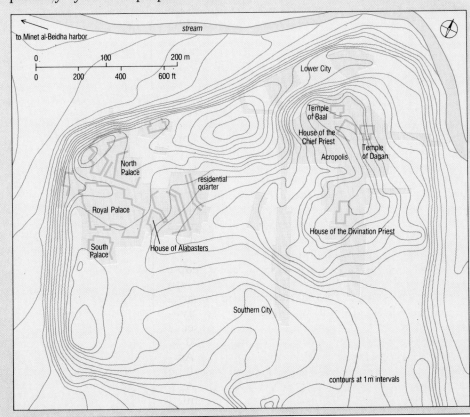

to Minet al-Beidha harbor
stream
Lower City
Temple of Baal
House of the Chief Priest
Acropolis
Temple of Dagan
North Palace
residential quarter
Royal Palace
House of the Divination Priest
South Palace
House of Alabasters
Southern City
contours at 1 m intervals

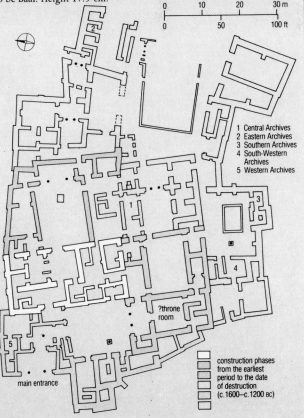

1 Central Archives
2 Eastern Archives
3 Southern Archives
4 South-Western Archives
5 Western Archives

?throne room

main entrance

construction phases from the earliest period to the date of destruction (c.1600–c.1200 BC)

of the Levant and Mesopotamia and eventually their language, written in alphabetic script, replaced Babylonian and Assyrian cuneiform.

To the north, Shalmaneser I defeated the kingdom of Uruadri, mentioned in inscriptions for the first time. Uruadri, later known as Urartu, which has survived in corrupted form in the name of Mount Ararat, proved to be a constant thorn in the side of Assyria. Farther east, on the Iranian plateau, the end of the Godin III culture and the introduction of the gray ware pottery of the Iron Age I period may mark the arrival of Iranian tribes from the north or east. These were the ancestors of the Medes and the Persians, who went on to destroy the Assyrian and Babylonian empires and establish their rule over the whole of the Near East from about the 6th century onward.

Assyria's military might

The Assyrians under their successive rulers Adad-nirari I, Shalmaneser I and Tukulti-Ninurta I (1243–1207) proved to be an irresistible force. Tukulti-Ninurta recounted how he personally attacked the Kassite king Kashtiliash IV.

"I brought about the defeat of his armies, his warriors I overthrew. In the midst of that battle my hand captured Kashtiliash, the Kassite king. I trod on his royal neck with my feet like a footstool. I brought him stripped and bound before Ashur my lord. Sumer and Akkad to its farthest border I brought under my sway. On the lower sea of the rising sun I established the frontier of my land."

Tukulti-Ninurta appointed Enlil-nadin-shumi as king of Nippur. However, according to a later Babylonian chronicle, within a year the Elamite king Kidin-Hutran, who had succeeded Untash-Napirisha, sacked Der, captured Nippur and deposed the Assyrian puppet. Kidin-Hutran attacked Babylonia a second time in the reign of Adad-shuma-iddina, destroying Isin and Marad. Adad-shuma-iddina, who was another Assyrian appointee, was deposed by his nobles in 1216.

As well as campaigning in Babylonia, Tukulti-Ninurta fought in the east, north and west, where he claimed to have crossed the Euphrates and taken 28,800 Hittite prisoners. In an extensive building program at his capital Ashur, Tukulti-Ninurta dug a moat round the city, rebuilt the Ishtar temple and began a new palace in the northwest

Middle Assyrian Kings

Ashur-uballit I	1363–1328
Enlil-nirari	1327–1318
Arik-den-ili	1317–1306
Adad-nirari I	1305–1274
Shalmaneser I	1273–1244
Tukulti-Ninurta I	1243–1207
Ashur-nadin-apli	1206–1203
Ashur-nirari III	1202–1197
Enlil-kudurri-usur	1196–1192
Ninurta-apil-Ekur	1191–1179
Ashur-dan I	1178–1133
Ashur-resh-ishi	1132–1115
Ninurta-tukulti-Ashur	1115
Mutakkil-Nusku	1115
Tilgath-pileser I	1114–1076

Ashur

Below Limestone relief found in the well in the Temple of Ashur. It shows a god carrying plants, which are being nibbled by two goats. The scale pattern on the god's dress and hat may indicate that he was a mountain deity, perhaps Ashur himself. Below are two goddesses with flowing vases. Height 1.36 m.

The city of Ashur was situated on a rocky spur overlooking the Tigris river. The site, now known as Qalat Shergat, was occupied since at least 2400 BC and statues of Early Dynastic style were found in the Ishtar Temple. In the early second millennium the merchants of Ashur established colonies in Anatolia. Ashur was part of the empire of Shamshi-Adad I (c. 1813–1781 BC) and later passed under the control of the rulers of Mittani.

Under Ashur-uballit I (1363–1328 BC) Assyria expanded, after the collapse of the Mittanian empire, and Ashur became the capital of a kingdom that stretched from the Euphrates to the mountains of Iran. Ashurnasirpal II (883–859 BC) chose Kalhu as his capital but he and later Assyrian kings continued to restore the temples and other buildings of Ashur as the religious center of the Assyrian empire. The Assyrian kings were buried in the palace at Ashur.

The city god was also called Ashur and, since the god's fortunes flourished as the Assyrian state prospered, Ashur took the place of Enlil and Marduk in the Assyrian pantheon. The Temple of Ashur was in the city at the end of the promontory. The Assyrian king acquired his authority from the fact that he was the priest of the god Ashur. In 614 and 612 BC Assyria was invaded by the Medes and Babylonians who captured and looted the city, which was later abandoned. The site was resettled in the 1st and 2nd centuries AD when it was known as Labbana.

corner of the city. However, he abandoned this last project after laying the stone foundations and instead founded a new city, which he called Kar-Tukulti-Ninurta, about 3 kilometers north of Ashur on the opposite side of the Tigris river. There, he fortified an area 700 meters square and erected a temple with a ziggurat for the god Ashur. He also built a palace, which was decorated with fine wall-paintings. Perhaps Tukulti-Ninurta built a new city because of his unpopularity in Ashur, following territorial losses toward the end of his reign. In 1207 his son rebelled and, with the backing of the Assyrian nobility, besieged Tukulti-Ninurta in his palace and killed him.

The eclipse of Elam

About forty years later (c. 1165 BC), Shutruk-Nahhunte became king of Elam and, in an age of weak kingdoms, inaugurated a period of Elamite greatness. According to a stele, he crossed the Ulai river, invaded Mesopotamia and captured 700 towns, forcing Dur-Kurigalzu, Eshnunna, Sippar, Opis, Dur-Sharrukin and, perhaps, Agade to pay a heavy tribute. Finds at Susa have testified to the booty of this campaign. They included statues from Eshnunna, the victory stele of Naram-Sin taken from Sippar, a monument of the Kassite king Melishipak from Kara-indash (perhaps modern Karind in the Zagros) and statues from Agade. In

Below The site of Ashur was excavated by a German expedition before World War I. By digging long trenches across the site they established that the major buildings lay in the northern part of the town. These included the temples of Ashur, Ishtar and Nabu, the double temples of Sin and Shamash and of Anu and Adad, and the ziggurat, as well as the palaces of the Assyrian kings. To the north and east the site was protected by steep cliffs. In the early 2nd millennium the city was fortified and was extended to the south in the Middle Assyrian period.

Below View of Ashur from the northwest. On the right can be seen the ruins of the ziggurat, which still dominates the skyline. In the center a 19th-century police-post marks the site of the Temple of Ashur. The Tigris river is visible in the background.

Bottom Five royal tombs were discovered beneath the palace at Ashur. They included those of Ashur-bel-kals (1074–1057 BC), seen in the center of the picture with the stone sarcophagus still in it, Ashurnasirpal II (883–859 BC) and Shamshi-Adad V (823–811 BC).

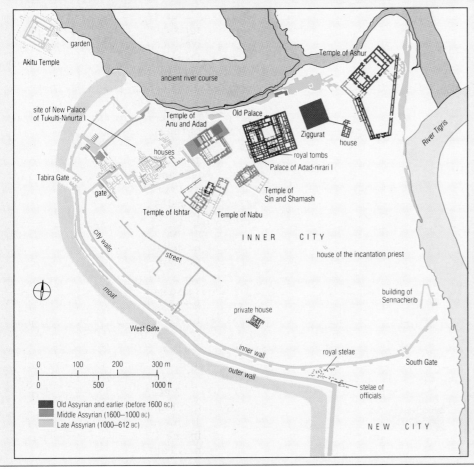

his large realm, Shutruk-Nahhunte restored the temple at Liyan, on the Gulf coast near Bushire, and controlled Anshan in Fars.

When Kutir-Nahhunte, his son, became king, he invaded Babylonia and put an end to the Kassite dynasty, taking the statue of the god Marduk from Babylon, and that of the goddess Inanna from Uruk, back to Elam. His brother Shilhak-Inshushinak, who succeeded him, campaigned along the foothills of the Zagros, reaching as far to the northwest as Arrapha and Nuzi, and including Halman, Me-Turnat, Epih (Hamrin hills)—an encroachment on territory that had been part of Assyria. Shilhak-Inshushinak married his brother's wife and completed the restoration work begun on the Temple of Inshushinak at Susa. He also built at Liyan and Tulaspid, and at about twenty other sites. Among the finds belonging to the reign of Shilhak-Inshushinak was an unusual bronze of a religious scene called sunrise (*sit shamshi*).

Shilhak-Inshushinak was succeeded by his nephew Huteludush-Inshushinak, following the traditional Elamite pattern of succession through the fraternal line. Huteludush-Inshushinak restored the temples of Susa and built at Anshan, where 250 administrative texts written in Elamite that probably belonged to his reign have been found in a public building. Huteludush-Inshushinak came into conflict with Nebuchadnezzar I (1125–1104

BC), a member of the Second Dynasty of Isin, which had seized power when the last Kassite king, Enlil-nadin-ahi (1156–1154 BC) was captured. Nebuchadnezzar's first attempts to invade Elam were unsuccessful, but by a forced march at the height of summer he arrived unexpectedly in the vicinity of Susa and defeated the Elamite army. The Babylonians looted Susa and took back the statue of the god Marduk. The subsequent history of Elam is uncertain, as it was not mentioned in the sources for the next three centuries.

Nebuchadnezzar's successes to the east were not repeated in the north, where he encountered the Assyrians, first under Ashur-resh-ishi I (1132–1115 BC) and then under Tiglath-pileser I (1114–1076 BC). Tiglath-pileser I was a vigorous military campaigner. In the upper Tigris valley he defeated an army of 20,000 Mushki warriors (the same people who are believed to have brought an end to the Hittite kingdom). He attacked Nairi, in the area that was later known as Urartu, and carved a celebratory rock relief to the northwest of Lake Van. In the west he fought against the Ahlamu–Aramaeans, crossing the Euphrates no less than 28 times. In one of these campaigns he reached the Mediterranean at Arvad, where according to Assyrian accounts he took a boat and hunted a beast called a "sea-horse", but which was probably a narwhal or a dolphin. Tiglath-pileser's conquests, however, did not survive his death and in the following centuries Assyrian power was confined to little more than the Assyrian triangle from Ashur to Nineveh to Arbil. However, Tiglath-pileser's campaigns had enabled Assyria to survive the onslaughts of the Mushki and the Aramaeans so that two centuries later Assyria arose to dominate the Near East.

Science and technology

Despite the endless conflicts of the second half of the second millennium it was a time of great prosperity and progress. Trade and industry flourished to provide the luxury goods for the royal courts, each of which attempted to outdo the other in their splendor.

Colored stones have always been valued for jewelry, and from very early on attempts were made to manufacture artificial stones. One of the materials used was faience, made by mixing ground-up quartz pebbles with ashes and copper ore and then heating the mixture to produce objects with a bright-blue glazed surface. Examples of this technique have been dated to as far back as the Ubaid period, but by the end of the third millennium it was commonly used in the making of beads, amulets, seals and inlay. A few vessels also were made of faience at that time and faience bowls became more common in the second millennium. At Susa, in the Middle Elamite period, glazed molded faience bricks were used to decorate the temple of Inshushinak.

The manufacture of glass in the middle of the second millennium was a technological breakthrough. A few early examples of glass might have been produced accidentally in the course of making faience, but there is no evidence for widespread glass-making and certainly not for glass vessels. The first examples of glass vessels, found in sites in northern Mesopotamia, date to the 15th century BC. These had been formed round a core, or made out of short sections of glass rods, to produce a mosaic. Glass was also used for cylinder seals, pendants and plaques. Glazed pottery vessels (covered by a thin layer of glass) from this period have also been found and glazed bricks adorned the palaces of the Middle Assyrian kings.

Some iron objects have been found dating back to the fourth millennium, but they were rare. By the early second millennium iron was mentioned in texts concerned with the Old Assyrian trade with Anatolia, and iron objects have been found from several centuries later, including a dagger in the tomb of Tutankhamun. In some of their texts the Hittites referred to iron weapons, iron writing tablets and iron statues. A letter from the Hittite king Hattusilis III recorded that he had made a gift of an iron dagger to the king of Assyria. At that time iron was more valuable than gold. However, its value lay principally in its scarcity, and it was not until the discovery that iron could be turned into steel by the addition of carbon that it rivaled the usefulness of bronze. The great upheavals of the 12th century BC have normally been regarded as marking the end of the Bronze Age and the beginning of the Iron Age. However, although by this time iron could be smelted, the practice was little understood. Not until the 9th century did steel become common enough to be used for the manufacture of tools and weapons.

Writing

Below The proto-Canaanite alphabet found at sites such as Serabit al-Khadim in Sinai was adapted to form the basis of the alphabet for writing other Semitic languages including Phoenician, Aramaic and, later, Hebrew and Arabic. It was also taken up by the Greeks and was used for European languages. In fact, all the alphabets in use in the world today derive from the one invented in the Near East.

The cuneiform script was invented in the fourth millennium BC in southern Mesopotamia. As there were hundreds of different signs for syllables and for words, scribes took many years to learn to write. The phonetic alphabet, which had fewer than thirty letters was invented by the Canaanites before 1600 BC and effectively replaced the cuneiform script in the following millennium. The shapes of the letters in the earliest alphabet were based on Egyptian hieroglyphs but the sounds were those of the initial consonant of the corresponding Canaanite word. Thus, a picture of a house stood for the sound "b", the first letter of *bet*, the Canaanite word for house. The early alphabets used 27 or 28 letters, but this number was

PROTO-CANAANITE	EARLY LETTER NAMES AND MEANINGS		PHOENICIAN	EARLY GREEK	EARLY MONUMENTAL LATIN	MODERN ENGLISH CAPITALS
	alp	oxhead				A
	bêt	house			B	B
	gaml	throwstick				C
	digg	fish			D	D
	hô(?)	man calling				E
	wô (waw)	mace				F
	zê(n)	?				
	ḥê(t)	fence?			H	H
	ṭê(t)	spindle?				
	yad	arm				I
	kapp	palm			K	K
	lamd	ox-goad				L
	mêm	water				M
	naḥš	snake				N
	cên	eye			O	O
	pi't	corner?				P
	sa(d)	plant				
	qu(p)	?				Q
	ra'š	head of man			R	R
	tann	composite bow				S
	tô (taw)	owner's mark			T	T

reduced to 22 in the 13th century BC. When the Greeks adopted the alphabet early in the first millennium BC, they used some of the letters to represent vowel sounds instead of consonants.

The cuneiform script was adapted for writing many languages, but other scripts were also used in the ancient Near East such as Hittite hieroglyphic and Linear Elamite. At Ugarit and other sites in the Levant, the Canaanite alphabet was converted into cuneiform signs and texts in the local Semitic language called Ugaritic were written in this script. The Old Persian script, invented for writing the royal inscriptions of the Achaemenid kings, was also essentially an alphabet written with cuneiform letters.

Left Cuneiform signs were made by impressing a reed stylus onto clay, leaving a mark shaped like a wedge, from which cuneiform takes its name.

Far left An 18th-century BC school exercise tablet from Sippar. The education of a cuneiform scribe was a long process. The scribes learned to write on round tablets that could be reused.

Above A list of synonyms from Ashurbanipal's library at Nineveh. Lists formed the basis of the Mesopotamian scribal tradition. These were often bilingual, most commonly in Sumerian and Akkadian.

Below Drawing of a folded-up writing board, from a well in the Northwest Palace at Kalhu. The boards were covered with colored wax, on which the text was written. An example from the 11th century was found in a shipwreck off southern Turkey.

Above Assyrian scribes recording the loot from a victorious campaign in Babylonia on a relief from the Southwest Palace at Nineveh (c. 630–620 BC). One scribe is writing in Akkadian cuneiform on a hinged tablet and the other is writing in Aramaic on a papyrus or leather scroll. By the 7th century the Aramaic script and language were widely used in the Assyrian empire, but few documents have survived because papyrus and parchment decay (unlike clay tablets).

Left To ensure that no one tampered with a text, tablets were inserted inside clay envelopes that had the same text written on the outside as on the tablet. This example comes from Alalah in the 18th century BC.

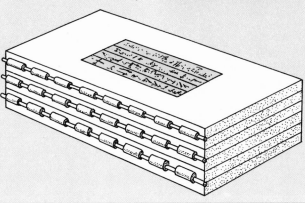

Cuneiform, the most widely preserved script of the ancient Near East, was impressed on clay, scratched on metal or (*above left*) carved in stone. In the 1st millennium BC alphabetic scripts became widespread. These were written in ink with a brush on papyrus or parchment or occasionally on broken pieces of pottery (*above right*). A pictorial hieroglyphic script was used by the Hittites and their successors in the Levant and Anatolia for monumental royal inscriptions (*center right*).

The Discovery of Mesopotamia

The later empires of Assyria, Babylonia and Persia were remembered in the Bible and by Greek authors, but nothing was preserved of the earlier history of Mesopotamia. In the 17th and 18th centuries AD European travelers described the remains at Persepolis, the citadel built by the Persian king Darius I (521–486 BC), and made copies of the cuneiform inscriptions that they found there. A German scholar, Georg Grotefend (1175–1853), succeeded in 1802 in deciphering part of the Old Persian script. Between 1835 and 1837 Henry Rawlinson (1810–1895) copied the long Old Persian inscription of Darius I on the rock of Bisutun and managed to complete the decipherment. Ten years later, with the help of a Kurdish boy, Rawlinson copied the Babylonian version and in 1850 published his decoding of the cuneiform script.

Meanwhile, Mesopotamian sites were yielding their secrets to archeologists. Claudius James Rich (1787–1820), the Resident of the British East India Company in Baghdad, made the first detailed study of the site of Babylon, which was published in 1815. In the 1840s the principal palaces of the Assyrian kings were discovered and in the following decades sites throughout the Near East were dug into in the search for objects to display or study in museums. The 19th-century scramble for antiquities ended with the meticulous excavations of Robert Koldewey (1855–1925) at Babylon between 1895 and 1917.

Right Wax portrait of Major-General Sir Henry Creswicke Rawlinson, who succeeded in copying the trilingual inscription of Darius at Bisutun and thereby was able to decipher both the Old Persian and the Babylonian cuneiform scripts.

Far right Hormuzd Rassam (1826–1910), a Christian from Mosul, was Layard's chief assistant at Nimrud and Nineveh (see opposite) and continued digging after Layard's return to England. In 1877 Rassam was granted a permit to excavate all the sites from the Gulf to the Anatolian plateau. Among his many discoveries were the North Palace of Ashurbanipal at Nineveh and the Balawat Gates.

Right Sir Leonard Woolley (1880–1960) shared some of the virtues of the best 19th-century excavators. He was a conscientious recorder of what he discovered, and had a gift for publicity and popularization. His excavations at Ur between 1922 and 1934 revealed the history of the city from the Ubaid to the Persian periods and were published in exemplary detail. The excavation of the Royal Cemetery brought out his remarkable technical skill, when, using plaster of paris and melted paraffin wax, he was able to lift and save many priceless objects.

Below and left Two of the lyres discovered by Woolley in the tomb of Queen Puabi. All the wooden elements had decayed and the mosaic inlay was loose in the soil. Woolley was abe to lift the objects and they were restored to their original condition in the laboratory.

Below The colorful account of the travels and discoveries of Sir Austen Henry Layard (1817–1894) captured the imagination of Victorian England and still make riveting reading today. After five years of travel in the Near East, Layard, aged 28, started excavations at the site of Tell Nimrud (ancient Kalhu) in November 1845, where he discovered the palace of Ashurnasirpal II. In 1846 Layard moved his attentions to Nineveh, where he discovered the palace of Sennacherib. He calculated that in this building alone he had unearthed some 3 km of sculptured stone reliefs. In 1851 he left Nimrud for the last time. After writing a detailed report on his excavations, he gave up archeology for politics and eventually became an ambassador in Turkey. This painting shows Layard investigating a chamber cut into a rock relief of Sennacherib at Bavian, near the head of the canal system built for Nineveh.

Above Layard in Persian dress. In his early years in the East Layard traveled widely, including journeys through Luristan, which at that time was a very dangerous place. Layard's understanding of and sympathy with the local people enabled him to cope with many difficult situations.

Above Paul Émile Botta (1802–1870) was a medical doctor and explorer of Arabia and the Yemen. In 1840 he was appointed French consul in Mosul. In December 1842 Botta started to dig on Tell Kuyunjik, the citadel mound of ancient Nineveh, but with little reward. In the following March he transferred his excavations to Khorsabad and uncovered the magnificent remains of Dur-Sharrukin, the capital city of Sargon II of Assyria.

Top This early photograph, taken in 1852–3, shows one of the gates into the city of Dur-Sharrukin excavated by Victor Place (1818–1875) after Botta had returned to France.

The Royal Art of Hunting

Below A shrine at the Neolithic site of Chatal Huyuk (c. 6500 BC) in Anatolia was decorated with wall paintings depicting hunting. In this color reconstruction a wild bull some 2 m in length dominates a horde of small hunters dressed in leopard-skin loincloths and armed with bows.

After the Neolithic revolution hunting was no longer necessary for the provision of food, but wild animals remained as potent symbols, playing an important part in the religious iconography of pre-historical times. With the development of kingship the cultural significance of these animals was used by rulers to legitimize their power: the image of the victorious hunter associated the king both with divine favor and with success in this world.

The royal concern for the killing of fierce beasts, often on a massive scale, is also described in the texts. For example, the Middle Assyrian king Tiglath-pileser I claimed on one occasion to have killed 4 wild bulls, 10 elephants and 920 lions—800 from his chariot and 120 on foot. The hunts were carefully managed. The Mari letters (c. 1800 BC) record the capture of wild lions to be released for the king to kill them, and similar scenes are shown in the Assyrian reliefs. This tradition continued under the Persians. Indeed, the English word "paradise" is derived from a Persian word for the king's game park.

Below One of the earliest depictions of an ancient ruler is this basalt stele from Uruk in southern Iraq (late 4th millennium BC). On it a figure with a headband and wearing a kilt is shown twice: above he kills a lion with a spear, and below he shoots an arrow at another lion. In the field are two more lions, presumably already slain. This figure has been identified with the *en* or priest-king of the city. Height 78 cm.

Above Cylinder seal impression inscribed with the name of the Persian king Darius I (521–486 BC). The king hunts a lion from his chariot, a scene copied from the art of previous dynasties. Height 3.7 cm.

Right Detail from a copy of a wall painting in the Late Assyrian provincial palace at Til Barsip showing a lion hunt.

Below Ashurnasirpal II (883–859 BC) decorated the walls of his throne room in his palace at Kalhu with scenes of religious ritual, warfare and hunting. Here he aims his bow and arrow at a lion from his chariot and, in the normal artistic convention, a second lion lies dead beneath the feet of the horses.

Left A gold plate of the 14th century BC found at Ugarit on the Mediterranean coast shows a charioteer, perhaps the ruler of the city, accompanied by a dog, in pursuit of a goat and a herd of wild cattle. Diameter 18.5 cm.

Right and below The most vivid scenes of hunting in the ancient Near East were carved on the walls of the North Palace of Ashurbanipal (668–c. 627 BC) in Nineveh. The motif of the king stabbing a lion standing on its hind legs was adopted as the royal seal of the Assyrian kings and is also found carved on the doorways of the Persian palaces at Persepolis. Although the slaughter of lions and other animals was to some extent a royal and religious duty, its frequent appearance both in the texts and on reliefs shows that the king also took great pleasure in the sport.

Ivory Carving

Since Paleolithic times, ivory has been a favored luxury material. Combining strength with flexibility, it is both beautiful and practical. Ivory can be carved like a hardwood and larger objects can be made up of a number of pieces fitted together. In antiquity ivory was usually colored, being overlaid with gold foil, stained with dyes or inlaid with semiprecious stones or glass. In the second and first millennia there were elephants living in Syria, but most ivory was imported from Egypt or India.

Despite the frequent references to ivory in the 14th century BC Amarna letters, relatively few ivory objects from the second millennium BC have been found. In the Late Assyrian period, however, there are detailed descriptions of ivory acquired by the Assyrian kings and ivory objects have been found on many sites. In particular, thousands of ivories were discovered in the Assyrian capital Kalhu (modern Nimrud).

Many of the cities in the Levant had their own schools of ivory carving and examples of the different styles can be seen among the ivories from Nimrud. They range from those closely related to the art of Egypt, known as Phoenician ivories, to powerful images like those carved on stone monuments in the Aramaean and Neo-Hittite kingdoms, called Syrian ivories, as well as the distinctive Assyrian style.

Below The two women are shown back to back, naked except for their high crowns, necklaces and long ringlets. They formed the handle of a fan or fly-whisk, an object regularly shown on Assyrian reliefs. Carved in the Syrian style, this piece was found on the citadel of Kalhu. Height 13.2 cm.

Top Found in the last decade in a well in the Northwest Palace at Kalhu, this unique and extraordinary item was carved from a single massive piece of ivory. It is decorated on every available surface. In the center of the top is a small bowl, presumably for cosmetics, with two adjacent slots, perhaps for brushes. Length 24.7 cm, width 12.2 cm, height 9.4 cm.

Above This openwork sphinx shares many features with the elaborately carved cosmetic palette and was found at the bottom of the same well in the Northwest Palace. This is the only known example of a sphinx shown entirely from the front. The face is expressionless while the claws grasp a goat, itself being eaten by vultures. Height 9.9 cm, width 14.6 cm.

Left This openwork panel, carved on both sides, was one of a set of four that probably decorated a chair or bed. It belongs to a large group that is united by style and technique, consisting of both small pieces and furniture panels. It may have been carved at Guzana (Tell Halaf), on the river Habur. Height c. 14 cm.

Below left A lioness killing a Nubian against a background of lilies and papyrus flowers: one of a pair of identical plaques in the classic Phoenician style found in the Northwest Palace at Kalhu. The theme is Egyptian in origin, representing the pharaoh triumphant over his enemies. Inlays of lapis lazuli and carnelian were set within golden walls, and gold highlighted the hair and skirt of the Nubian. Height 10.3 cm, width 9.8 cm.

Below One of a set of six openwork figures carved in the round. They were found at Fort Shalmaneser at Kalhu and show a procession of tribute bearers each leading an animal. Their place of origin is uncertain, but was probably Egypt or Phoenicia. Height 14.4 cm, width 7.7 cm.

Bottom center Stylized figure of a woman, adjusted to the form of the tusk, from the Northwest Palace. The base was closed by a disk. Height 30 cm.

Left One of the ivory chairbacks found stacked in a storage room in Fort Shalmaneser. The decorative panels show men, or occasionally women, grasping the stalks of a sinuous plant. They were probably made in north Syria. Height 67 cm, width 76 cm.

Above The "lady at the window" was a favorite motif of the ancient ivory workers and was carved in a variety of styles. This particular example is one of a set of similar panels found by Austen Henry Layard in the Northwest Palace. Height 10.8 cm.

ASSYRIA AND ITS RIVALS (1000-750 BC)

The end of the Dark Age

Between 1200 and 900 BC a Dark Age covered the Near East, Egypt and Greece. The region did not become deserted but there may have been a movement from settled farmers to nomadic herders in marginal areas. The major cities, however, remained occupied. Later accounts have shown that in cities such as Carchemish, Malatya, Ashur, Babylon and Susa, the major institutions were maintained even though few contemporary records have been found. Nevertheless, there can be little doubt that the Near East was in recession and no longer possessed the wealth from rich harvests to support the luxurious life-style of the royal courts, which had previously been the source of so much information about the past. Perhaps this decline was due to a change in the climate, which reduced agricultural yields, and the resultant political instability encouraged the growth of nomadic pastoralism.

The main contemporary sources from the Near East in the early part of the first millennium BC were the copious inscriptions left by the Assyrian kings, recording, in particular, their military successes over their neighbors. The demise of the Hittite kingdom, the disruption in Assyria following the murder of Tukulti-Ninurta I in 1207, and the collapse of the 20th Dynasty in Egypt in 1070 left no strong external powers to dominate Palestine and the Levant. Apart from texts concerning the campaign of Tiglath-pileser I in about 1100, Assyrian sources are silent on the subject of the west until the reign of Ashurnasirpal II (883–859 BC), by which time the region had been divided up into small city states. Israel and Judah dominated Palestine, with the minor states Edom and Moab and Ammon to the east, while farther north, along the coast, the cities were Phoenician. Inland states were ruled by Aramaeans and stretched from Damascus to Amid (Diyarbakir), and Neo-Hittite kingdoms lay along the Taurus mountains.

The Neo-Hittite rulers, the heirs of the Hittite kings, used the hieroglyphic script, which the Hittites had also used for monumental inscriptions instead of the cuneiform script. More than a hundred Hittite hieroglyphic inscriptions dating from between 1000 and 700 BC have been found. The Aramaeans and Phoenicians used the Aramaic alphabet. At Karatepe, in Cilicia (ancient Azatiwandas), the discovery of a long bilingual Phoenician and Hittite hieroglyphic inscription has assisted in deciphering the hieroglyphic script. Most of the inscriptions in the hieroglyphic and Aramaic scripts were short, with little more information than the name and titles of the person who erected the monument. Only with the later Assyrian conquests did more details of the period emerge.

Israel and Judah

According to the Bible, from about 1000 to 930 BC the united monarchy of Israel and Judah under David and Solomon was the dominant power in Palestine. Very probably, this account is based on historical truth even though excavations and the examination of the thousands of texts from Egypt and the Near East have failed to provide independent confirmation. In a period when the neighboring states were in decline an energetic leader such as David might indeed have carved out a small empire.

Again, according to the Bible, after the conquests of Joshua, the Jews were divided into 12 tribes who were in conflict with the Philistines occupying southwest Palestine. These tribes, in the face of Philistine attacks, united under the leadership of Saul. Saul quarreled with David, his son-in-law, who fled and, after a period as an outlaw, allied himself with the Philistines. When Saul was killed during a battle against the Philistines, David became king of the Jews. David consolidated his kingdom and established Jerusalem as the capital. He won victories over the Aramaeans of Damascus, the Moabites and the Edomites.

In reality, how far David's kingdom extended is uncertain. Solomon, his son, is said to have had dominion over all the kings west of the Euphrates and to have built a fleet of ships that traded down the Red Sea to the land of the Queen of Sheba. This claim was probably exaggerated. Solomon may, however, have ruled a kingdom whose wealth was based on trade. He carried out major building projects at Hazor, Megiddo and Gezer, and at Jerusalem, where he built the city walls, his palace and the Temple of Jehovah. Substantial remains from this period that have been found in these cities have been attributed to the building work of Solomon, in particular, the triple-chambered city gates found at Hazor, Megiddo and Gezer. However, similar gates have also been found at Ashdod and Lachish, which belonged to a later period than the reign of Solomon.

After Solomon's death his kingdom was divided between the northern kingdom of Israel and the southern kingdom of Judah. Five years later, the Egyptian pharaoh Shoshenq I (945–924 BC), the first ruler of the 22nd Dynasty, invaded Palestine. In his inscription at Karnak, he listed 150 conquered places, and fragments of a stele of his were found at Megiddo. According to the Bible, he was the same Egyptian pharaoh called Shishak who attacked Jerusalem and looted the treasures of the palace and the temple.

In the 9th century, after a civil war, Omri (c. 882–871 BC) became king of Israel and moved the capital to Samaria. His son Ahab married Jezebel, the daughter of the king of Tyre, and joined an alliance of local rulers under Hadad-ezer (called Ben-Hadad in the Bible), the king of Damascus. Together, they defeated the Assyrian armies at the battle of Qarqar on the Orontes in 853 BC. From then on, the histories of Israel, Judah and Assyria were all closely interwoven.

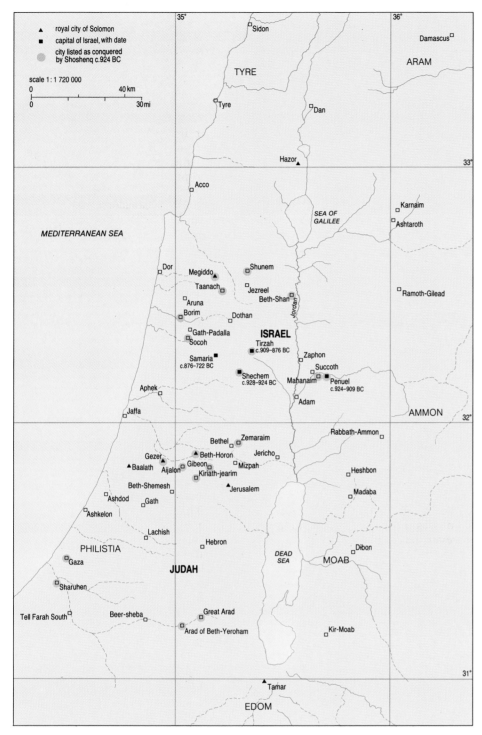

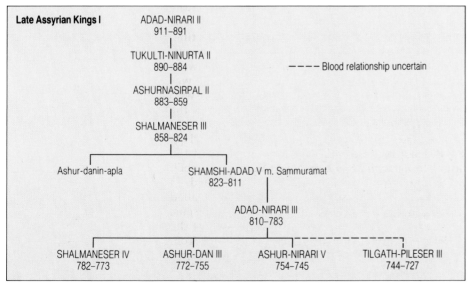

The resurgence of Assyria

Assyria, though weakened, survived the turbulent events of the end of the second millennium and the line of Assyrian rulers was unbroken. The pattern established in the Middle Assyrian period, of strong warrior kings followed by weak kings, was repeated in the Late Assyrian period. The Assyrian kings composed detailed annals of their campaigns. These were included, together with details of the titles of the kings and lists of their building work, in commemorative inscriptions on stelae or rock reliefs or were sometimes deposited as foundation inscriptions. Not surprisingly, these accounts are one-sided and often unreliable. Only Assyrian victories were recorded while Assyrian defeats were either ignored or claimed as victories. Other sources, such as the Bible and Babylonian chronicles, have provided alternative versions of the same events, and letters to Assyrian kings, written from a more practical, less biased viewpoint, have helped to provide more balanced accounts.

Despite the incursions by the Aramaeans all around, the Assyrian heartland had survived more or less intact. Assyrian fortunes began to recover at the end of the 10th century, when Adad-nirari II (911–891 BC) reestablished strong control of their kingdom. He first defeated Babylonia in the south and then, in a series of campaigns, conquered Kadmuh, Nisibin and Hanigalbat and seized control of the Habur region. His victories brought him huge quantities of tribute and booty—gold, silver, precious stones, chariots and horses, male and female prisoners, cattle, sheep and corn. Adad-nirari boasted of his hunting exploits, claiming to have killed six elephants and captured four more, which, following a custom of the Middle Assyrian kings, he put in a zoo that already held lions, wild bulls, deer, ibex, wild asses and ostriches. He also claimed to have plowed more land and piled up more grain than anyone before him. The agricultural prosperity of the Assyrian homeland underpinned its military success and a wise king looked after the fields as well as the armies.

His son Tukulti-Ninurta II (890–884 BC) consolidated his father's successes, launching military campaigns to the east and northwest. In 885 he made a long march south through Babylonian territory (probably with the consent of the Babylonian king, as Assyria did not receive tribute from the cities under Babylonian control) and then up the Euphrates and Habur rivers and back to Assyria. He left a detailed account of this journey, listing the places where he stopped overnight and the tribute that he received from the local rulers.

The reign of Ashurnasirpal II

Ashurnasirpal II (883–859 BC) continued in the footsteps of his father, Tukulti-Ninurta II, and grandfather. In the early years of his reign he carried out campaigns to the north, east and south but, above all, to the west, in Syria and the Levant, where the small city states under the control of a series of local rulers proved no match for the Assyrians. In 877 BC Ashurnasirpal reached Mount Lebanon and the Mediterranean, which he called the Great Sea of the land Amurru. He wrote:

"I washed my weapons in the Great Sea and made sacrifices to the gods. I received tribute from the kings of the sea coast, from the lands

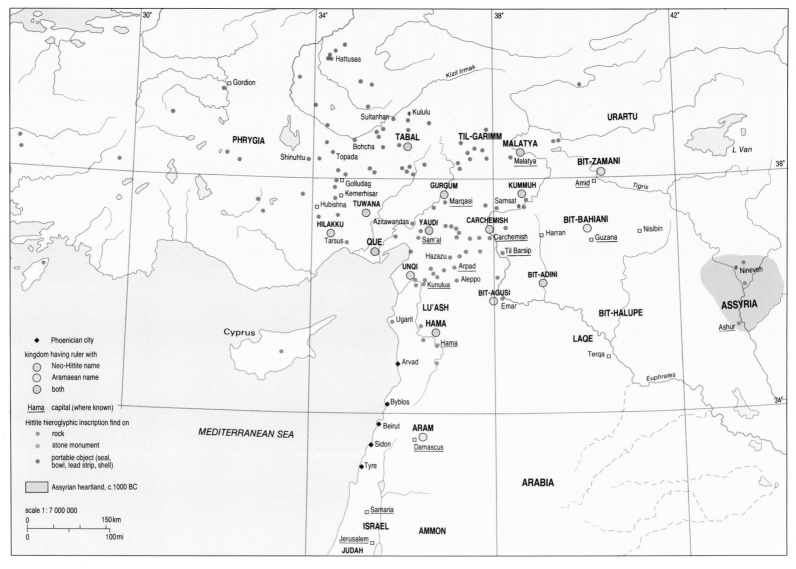

of the men of Tyre, Sidon, Byblos, Mahallata, Maiza, Kaiza, Amurru, and Arvad which is in the sea: gold, silver, tin, bronze, a bronze cauldron, linen garments with multicolored trimmings, a large female ape and a small female ape, ebony, boxwood, ivory, and sea-creatures.''

In fact, this was not a true conquest but was a sign of where the Assyrian sphere of influence extended. Assyria's conquest of its neighbors in the ensuing centuries followed a fixed pattern. First, the Assyrians received gifts from independent rulers, who then assumed client status as vassals of the Assyrians. Later, failure to provide suitable tribute was regarded as rebellion, provoking the mobilization of Assyrian military might and almost certain defeat. After conquest, either a local ruler was appointed as a vassal of Assyria or the country was annexed under a provincial governor appointed by the king.

When Ashurnasirpal attempted to subdue Suhu, the region along the Euphrates with its capital at Ana, even though he claimed a victory he seems to have suffered a defeat. Suhu remained independent until the middle of the 8th century BC, but its rulers still thought it prudent to present gifts to the Assyrian kings.

Kalhu, Ashurnasirpal's new capital
Early in his reign Ashurnasirpal II decided to move his capital from Ashur to the city of Kalhu (modern Tell Nimrud), near the junction of the Tigris and the Greater Zab. By 878 BC work had begun on the city walls, a canal and the palace, but it took about fifteen years before the grand opening ceremony for the palace could be performed.

Ashurnasirpal II transformed Kalhu from a small administrative center to the capital of an empire. (It remained so for 150 years until Sargon II decided to build himself an entirely new royal residence to the north of Nineveh.) The city walls stretched almost 8 kilometers and contained about 70 million bricks, each 40 centimeters square. The walls enclosed an area of 360 hectares including, in the southwest corner, the remains of the old city, which Ashurnasirpal converted into an acropolis with temples and palaces.

Ashurnasirpal's main building, the Northwest Palace, followed the standard Assyrian palace plan. An outer courtyard for public affairs was separated by a large throne room from an inner complex with rooms grouped round courtyards. Entry to the great courtyard had probably been through a gate in the east wall, though all traces have now been eroded away. The south wall had a carved stone facade, which was pierced by three doorways, flanked by enormous stone, human-headed lions, leading into the main throne room. In an alcove to the left of the throne room stood a rectangular block of sandstone, 1.3 meters high. It contained a

The Aramaean and Neo-Hittite kingdoms
During the three centuries after the collapse of the Hittite empire the cities of the Levant formed independent city states. Some of these were ruled by descendants of the Hittites, others by Aramaean tribes which had invaded the region. Some ruling dynasties had both Hittite and Aramaean names. The Neo-Hittite kings left inscriptions in Hittite hieroglyphic script, which had been used under the Hittite empire for display inscriptions and seal legends, but written in the Luwian rather than the Hittite language. Until the reign of Tiglath-pileser III (744–727 BC) the Assyrians did not display territorial ambitions beyond the Euphrates though they did campaign further west.

Right Detail from a relief showing a tributary from the west with a pair of apes, which was part of a composition carved in the main courtyard on the outer facade of the throne room of Ashurnasirpal's palace in Kalhu. The complete scene showed the king accompanied by the members of his court receiving the tribute of the subjects of his empire—an illustration of the authority of the Assyrian king. The tribute given by the cities on the Mediterranean to Ashurnasirpal II when he invaded Phoenicia included two female apes, one large and one small (though the ape, or monkey, shown here is clearly male).

carved picture of the king and a long inscription recording the completion of the Northwest Palace, the rebuilding of Kalhu and the great feast given by Ashurnasirpal to commemorate this event.

The inscription began with Ashurnasirpal's titles and his ancestry and continued with descriptions of his conquests and buildings. He constructed a terrace of bricks 120 courses high on top of which he built a palace with eight wings, each fitted with a different kind of timber. The doors had bronze bands and bolts, and the walls were decorated with paintings and blue glazed bricks. Ashurnasirpal built the temples of Kalhu, his new capital, and according to the inscriptions, restored derelict cities and palaces throughout Assyria. A canal was dug to bring water to the new capital, and trees and plants gathered on Ashurnasirpal's military campaigns were brought back to Kalhu; captives from the north, east and west were also settled there.

The king also recorded his prowess in the chase, claiming to have killed 450 lions and 390 wild bulls from his chariot, as well as trapping elephants, lions, bulls and ostriches. Finally, the text described a feast lasting 10 days to which a total of 69,574 male and female guests were "summoned from all the districts of the land" including 16,000 citizens of Kalhu to celebrate the inauguration of the palace; and how, on that occasion, 14,000 sheep and 10,000 skins of wine were consumed.

Ashurnasirpal's sculptures

The walls of the palace courtyard and of the vast throne room behind it, which measured 47 by 10 meters, were decorated with carved stone panels. This type of decoration probably originated in the west under the Hittites, as in the gates of Hattusas. The tradition was continued in the Neo-Hittite states: buildings at Carchemish, Guzana and Ain Dara were decorated with carved stone panels. Adopting this technique and using the soft local gypsum stone, Ashurnasirpal covered the walls of room after room with carved figures. The themes of the illustrations were either religious or showed the king in the traditional roles of Mesopotamian monarchs—of high priest, warrior and hunter.

In Assyrian sculpture, statues in the round were rare. Almost all of the carvings were essentially paintings in stone—two-dimensional drawings translated into low relief. The freestanding figures tended to be square rather than rounded. The reliefs had originally been colored in black, white, red and blue, with brightly painted murals set above the stone panels. Glazed bricks had added further color to the buildings. The dull appearance of Assyrian monuments today gives a false impression of how they once looked.

In Ashurnasirpal's palace the central of three doorways to the throne room was the main entrance. Walking between the huge stone lions, visitors would have seen ahead of them a stone

Kalhu

In November 1845 Austen Henry Layard began excavations at the site of Tell Nimrud. Although Layard thought that he had found the remains of Nineveh, the decipherment of the Babylonian script showed that he had discovered the city of Kalhu (known in the Bible as Calah). Kalhu had been a provincial capital in the Middle Assyrian period but was chosen by the Assyrian king Ashurnasirpal II (883–859 BC) as his capital. It remained Assyria's capital for over 150 years.

Ashurnasirpal dug a canal from the Upper Zab to irrigate the region and provide water for the inhabitants, and built massive city walls some 8 kilometers long. At the southwest corner of the city was the citadel, with the temples and palaces of the king situated on the city's ancient mound. To the northwest stood the ziggurat and the temples of Ninurta, Ishtar and Kidmuru. South of the ziggurat was the magnificent Northwest Palace. Its doorways were protected by huge stone lions or bulls and the palace walls were lined with stone blocks carved with scenes of the king's military and hunting successes and divine beings. Farther south were palaces built by Shalmaneser III (858–824 BC), Tiglath-pileser III (744–727 BC) and Esarhaddon (680–699 BC). In the southeast of the citadel were the Temple of Nabu and various smaller palaces used by court officials. A large arsenal built by Shalmaneser III lay in the southeast corner of the city. Dubbed Fort Shalmaneser by the British excavators, it had housed booty accumulated by the Assyrians, including carved ivories from the western provinces of the Assyrian empire. Kalhu was destroyed when Assyria was invaded in 612 BC, though a village survived on the citadel until about the middle of the 2nd century BC.

Right A winged, eagle-headed being from the Temple of Ninurta holds a cone-shaped object and a bucket, which were probably used in a purification ritual.

Below The best-preserved and most important building erected by Ashurnasirpal on the citadel at Kalhu was the Northwest Palace. The original entrance, which was probably at the northeast, led into a large outer courtyard flanked by administrative offices. The main throne room, decorated with carved stone reliefs, was situated on the south side of this courtyard, beyond which were other rooms. These were probably used for official functions as they contained carved reliefs that were mostly of a religious character. In the southern part of the palace there were smaller rooms that had probably housed the kitchens and service quarters. It was in this area that the queens of Assyria were buried. Two of their tombs were recently found intact and contained the most fabulous collection of jewelry and other precious objects.

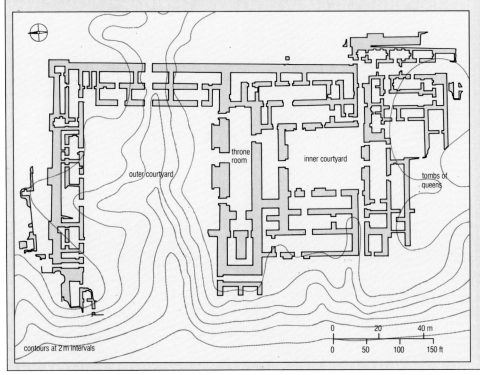

outer courtyard

throne room

inner courtyard

tombs of queens

contours at 2 m intervals

0		20		40 m
0	50	100	150 ft	

Left The principal scene in the throne room of the Northwest Palace was repeated: once opposite the middle entrance from the outer courtyard and once behind the throne at the east end of the room. Ashurnasirpal II is shown twice, on either side of a sacred tree. The god in a winged disk above the tree is possibly Shamash or Ashur. Height 1.78 m.

Right Limestone statue of Ashurnasirpal from the Temple of Ninurta. Despite the quantity of relief carving found in Assyria statues in the round are rare. The shawl worn by the king signifies that he is acting in his role as priest. Height 1.06 m.

Below Detail of a wall decoration from an inner room of the Northwest Palace. The scenes of divine beings or of the king and his attendants are far from the decadent luxury that might have been expected in the harem of an oriental despot. On this relief the black color of the beard and hair is well-preserved.

Bottom Ashurnasirpal II holds a bowl while sitting on a throne. He is flanked by attendant eunuchs.

Right Colossal human-headed winged bull from the south side of the inner courtyard of the Northwest Palace. Five legs were shown so that it could be viewed either from the front or from the side. Height 3.28 m.

Below A painting of the throne room of the Northwest Palace by A.H. Layard. Although some details are incorrect the atmosphere it conveys is accurate.

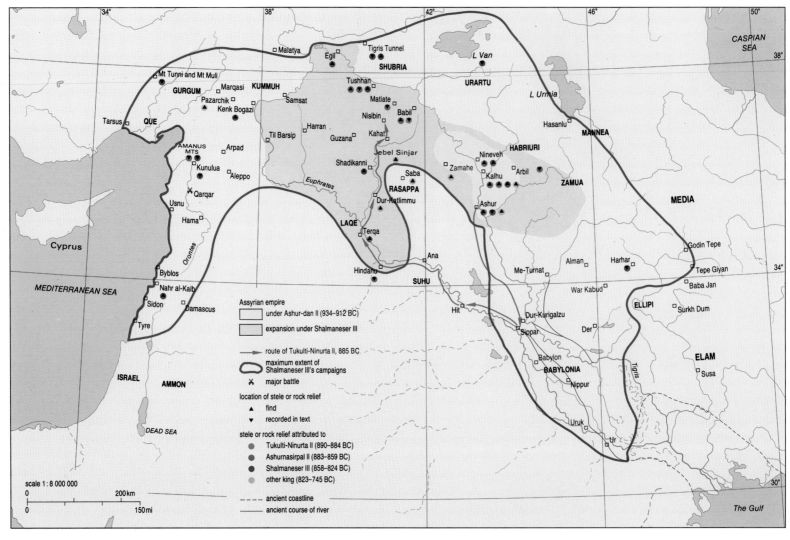

relief of the king on either side of a stylized tree and protected by a pair of guardian genies. To the left was the king's throne and on the wall behind it a similar scene was repeated, flanked by a pair of winged figures wearing the horned cap of the gods. The long side walls were decorated with scenes in two registers. The upper registers show the king in battle or in the hunt. Below the battle scene the king is seen receiving captives and spoils of war. In the lower register of the hunt scene the king is depicted pouring a libation over the bodies of dead animals. The reliefs emphasized the role of the king presented in the inscriptions: as the representative of the gods, as a great warrior and as a great hunter.

The reliefs decorating the wall outside the throne room were visible to people who were on their way to an audience with the king. They showed him victorious, holding his bow and arrow and receiving a procession of foreigners. Their fists were raised in greeting and they carried tribute including jewelry, metal vessels and textiles. One figure was leading a pair of apes, perhaps the same ones mentioned in Ashurnasirpal's description of the tribute he received in Phoenicia. The tributaries were being introduced to the king by two male Assyrian officials in their distinctive long robes, partly covered by a woollen shawl wound over the left shoulder and around the waist. The leading official was bearded, and belonged to the *sha ziqni* group of officials at the Assyrian court, or those "of the beard". The second man was beardless and belonged to another group, known as *sha reshe* or those "of the head". The *sha reshe* did not have children and were probably eunuchs, as "sha reshe" is the origin of the Aramaic and Hebrew words for eunuch.

In the inner part of the palace most of the reliefs showed a combination of the king, his court, winged gods and stylized trees. These rooms were therefore probably not private quarters where the king sought solace in his harem but were used by him for official business.

Ashurnasirpal and other Assyrian kings were buried in the palace at Ashur, but their graves were looted. In the southern part of the Northwest Palace at Kalhu three intact graves, one perhaps of a man and the others of royal queens, have been discovered recently. Both the amount and wealth of the jewelry found there, which included 57 kilograms of gold, was remarkable, though not altogether unexpected, as the texts and reliefs of the time recorded the enormous quantities of precious metals and jewelry brought to Assyria. The reliefs have also provided a valuable record of the changing styles of dress, jewelry, tools and weapons used in Assyria and in the provinces from the 9th to the 7th centuries BC.

Shalmaneser's western campaigns

To the north and east of Assyria, steep, sparsely populated mountain ranges formed an effective barrier to Assyrian conquest of the highland valleys of Iran and eastern Anatolia. Assyrian

The revival of Assyria
The Assyrian kingdom suffered from Aramaean incursions so that in the 10th century BC it had contracted to a point where it was little larger than it had been 400 years earlier. Under Adad-nirari II (911–891 BC) and his successors Assyria expanded, largely toward the west, reaching the Euphrates in the reign of Shalmaneser III. The civil war at the end of Shalmaneser's reign weakened Assyria which still maintained nominal control over the most of the territory gained by the earlier rulers. The annals of the Assyrian kings are invaluable for understanding the historical geography. Occasionally they record itineraries in great detail, as in the case of Tukulti-Ninurta II in 885 BC whose annals recorded the name of each place where he stayed the night during his campaigns. The steles and rock reliefs made to the command of the king also indicate the range of Assyrian military might and often mark the farthest limits of Assyrian conquests.

armies did follow the few difficult routes across these mountains on expeditions to punish and plunder their enemies, but once the mountain-dwellers had been taught a lesson, and a pro-Assyrian ruler installed, the Assyrian armies returned home. Assyria's main territorial ambition was to control the fertile plains to the west and south.

Ashurnasirpal's practice of leading annual campaigns, which featured so prominently in his inscriptions, was repeated in the reign of his son, Shalmaneser III (858–824 BC). As usual, the king always claimed to be victorious, but repeated campaigns against the same region suggest otherwise. The main events of Shalmaneser's reign were outlined in terms of military successes, particularly to the west. The campaigns during the first four years of his reign were directed against Ahuni, the ruler of the Aramaean state of Bit Adini. In Shalmaneser's third year Ahuni abandoned his capital city, Til Barsip, on the east bank of the Euphrates, which the Assyrians quickly occupied and renamed Kar-Shalmaneser. In the following year, Ahuni with his gods, chariots, horses, sons, daughters and armies was captured and taken back to the city of Ashur.

However, this victory brought Shalmaneser only a brief respite, for in 853 BC he led his armies against a coalition of kings, headed by Hadad-ezer, king of Damascus, and including Irhuleni, king of Hamath, and Ahab, king of Israel, as well as Cilicians, Egyptians and Arabs, and other Levantine principalities. The forces met at Qarqar on the Orontes river. Shalmaneser boasted of complete victory, claiming to have killed 14,000 (or 20,500 in a later account) of the enemy, who allegedly numbered more than 60,000. Yet, six years later, Hadad-ezer was still leading an alliance against Shalmaneser, who, as late as 838 BC, was still fighting against the rulers of Damascus. By that time, however, most of the states in the region had decided to pay tribute to the Assyrians rather than risk being attacked by the Assyrian army. After 20

Above A gold wristlet inlaid with stones, part of the immense quantity of precious objects buried in the tombs of queens recently discovered at Kalhu. Similar wristlets were depicted on the reliefs and were worn by the members of the Assyrian court and by divine beings.

Right The front of the throne base in the main throne room in Fort Shalmaneser at Kalhu. In the center Shalmaneser III, who is on the right, and Marduk-zakir-shumi, the Babylonian king, on the left look as if they are shaking hands though this may not be the correct interpretation of the gesture. This representation of a foreign monarch as the equal of the Assyrian king is unique, suggesting a special relationship between Assyria and Babylonia at this time. Height c. 21 cm.

The Balawat Gates

In 1876 some fragments of bronze reliefs were offered for sale in London and Paris. These came from panels belonging to huge doors that had been decorated to the order of Shalmaneser III (858–824 BC). In the following year Hormuzd Rassam, who had been A. H. Layard's assistant and was then in charge of the British Museum's excavations in the Near East, discovered that they had come from the site of Balawat (Imgur-Enlil), 16 kilometers north-east of Kalhu. Rassam's excavations at the site were hampered by the presence of an Islamic graveyard, but he did find the rest of the bronze bands of Shalmaneser's gate and a second set of bronze bands belonging to a gate erected by Shalmaneser's father, Ashurnasirpal II (883–859 BC). He also uncovered the remains of a temple with stone foundation tablets of Ashurnasirpal II.

Subsequently, doubt was cast on Rassam's account of his discoveries, but he was completely vindicated when a third set of bronze strips belonging to a door (again, from the reign of Ashurnasirpal II) was found at Balawat in 1956.

Right Detail from the bronze bands of the Balawat Gates: an Assyrian siege engine attacking a city in northern Syria. Siege warfare was a very important branch of the Assyrian military strategy. The change in design of these machines was recorded in the Assyrian reliefs.

Below left Each gate had eight bronze bands nailed to the door leaves. The bands were decorated in relief by hammering from behind, with the details added from the front. The best-preserved set was that of Shalmaneser III. Each strip was about 27 cm high and had two registers which showed incidents from his campaigns. The doors' leaves were not hinged, but attached to strong vertical posts that turned on pivot-stones sunk beneath the floor. The positions of the bronze strips could be reconstructed from the curvature of the ends of the posts, which tapered toward the top. The gates were probably about 6 m high and 2.3 m wide.

Below Chariots on campaign in Babylonia, as indicated by the palm trees. There were normally three members of a chariot crew, the driver, the warrior and a shieldman. Chariots in the 9th century had wheels with 6 spokes; in the 8th and 7th centuries they were larger and had 8-spoked wheels.

Right Local rulers from the upper reaches of the Tigris are introduced into the presence of Shalmaneser by a beardless official (perhaps a eunuch). They prostrate themselves before the king. The king is depicted as a warrior holding a bow and is accompanied by a servant and his weapons-bearer.

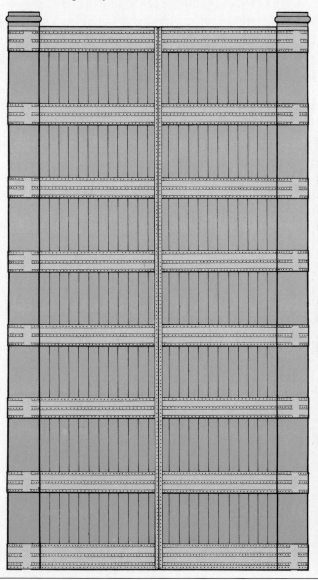

Below Sacrifice in the mountains to the northwest of Assyria. The Assyrian kings were regarded as the earthly representatives of the god Ashur. Important decisions were made with the assistance of the divination priests, who accompanied the army and studied the entrails of sacrificed animals for signs of the future.

Above In his first full year of reign (858 BC) Shalmaneser campaigned in the west and received the tribute of the men of Tyre and Sidon. As Tyre was an island, the tribute was brought in boats to the mainland. The Phoenician navy was used by both its Assyrian and later its Persian overlords.

Left The chariotry was the elite force of the Assyrian army in the time of Shalmaneser. Chariots were also used for hunting and for ceremonial processions. In the late 8th century mounted cavalry became more important, especially for fighting in the mountains.

years on the throne Shalmaneser turned his attentions to the land of Que (classical Cilicia) and the neighboring states in the Taurus, against whom he campaigned for the next decade.

Shalmaneser's reasons for these military ventures are not entirely clear. Apparently, he did not try to impose direct Assyrian rule beyond the Euphrates, and even cities to the east of the Euphrates such as Guzana retained their independence. Tribute might have been important, and control of the trade routes and of resources could also have played their part. Shalmaneser recorded how, on several occasions, he had cut cedar in the Amanus mountains. He also referred to an expedition he had led to Mount Tunni, the silver mountain, and Mount Muli, the marble mountain, both in the Taurus range. Conscripting labor to work the land or to build palaces might also have provided a motive. According to the Assyrian annals, between 881 and 815 BC, 193,000 people were deported to Assyria, 139,000 of whom were Aramaeans.

Assyria's relations with Babylon

The kings of Assyria and Babylon had been allies since Adad-nirari II (911–891 BC) had exchanged daughters in marriage with Nabu-shuma-ukin I, after a battle that Adad-nirari claimed to have won. At that time Assyria and Babylonia agreed on the frontier line between them and later Shalmeneser made a treaty with Nabu-apla-iddina, Nabu-shuma-ukin's son. When Marduk-zakir-shumi, son of Nabu-apla-iddina, became king of Babylon in 851, his younger brother Marduk-bel-usate, rebelled, prompting Marduk-zakir-shumi to call on Shalmaneser for assistance. Shalmaneser captured Me-Turnat on the Diyala River but failed to take the Babylonian rebel captive. Marduk-bel-usate took refuge in Alman (modern Sar-i Pol-i Zohab) in the mountains to the east, but Shalmaneser and Marduk-zakir-shumi together stormed the city and killed him.

Afterward, Shalmaneser visited the important religious centers of Babylonia—the temple of Nergal in Kutha, Marduk's temple in Babylon, and the temple of Nabu in Borsippa. There he made sacrifices and presented gifts. He also held a banquet for the citizens of Babylon and Borsippa. In his account of these events Shalmaneser did not mention the Babylonian king, and so whether Shalmaneser was acting as the overlord of the Babylonian ruler or whether everything was, in fact, arranged by Marduk-zakir-shumi is unclear. Interestingly, in a carving on a throne base at Kalhu from a few years later, Shalmaneser III and Marduk-zakir-shumi were shown as equals shaking or slapping hands—a rarity in Assyrian art, where the Assyrian king was normally depicted as superior to everyone else.

In the southeast Shalmaneser encountered three powerful Chaldean tribes. He defeated one of them, the Bit-Dakkuri, and received tribute from the other two, the Bit-Amukani and the Bit-Yakin. The Chaldeans, like the Aramaeans, who had occupied parts of southern Mesopotamia as early as the 11th century BC, were West Semitic people, whose presence was first noted in the 9th century, about thirty years before Shalmaneser's campaign. How exactly the Chaldeans and the Aramaeans were related is not known. The Chaldeans might have

Urartian Metalwork

Below Solid bronze figurine of a winged bull centaur. Originally its face, divine horns and wings were inlaid, and it was covered with gold leaf, of which some traces still remain. It may have been part of a magnificent inscribed gilded throne that was reported to have been found in the 1870s in Rusahinili (Toprakkale), near Van, where other bronze furniture fittings were discovered in excavations 20 years later. This piece was bought for the British Museum by A. H. Layard who was then British ambassador in Istanbul. Height 20.3 cm, width 16.4 cm.

Between the 9th and the 7th centuries BC the ancient kingdom of Urartu spanned the borders of what are today Turkey, Iran, Iraq and the Soviet Union. Investigation of the Urartian citadels and tombs in this mountainous area has shown that the Urartians were prolific metalworkers, particularly in decorated bronze. When the Assyrian king Sargon II (721–705 BC) captured the Urartian city of Musasir in 714, he brought back quantities of precious stones, ivory, timber, gold, silver and bronze. From the Temple of Haldi he took 3,600 talents (about 108 tonnes) of rough copper, 25,212 bronze shields, 1,514 bronze lances, 305,412 bronze daggers, 607 bronze basins as well as bronze statues of the kings of Urartu and other objects in bronze and more precious materials. In addition, personal jewelry, furniture fittings, armor and horse and chariot trappings have been found in excavations in Urartu.

Although Urartian decorative bronze-work owed much to Assyrian art, it has its own style, as is shown in the details of the motifs and iconography. Some pieces are inscribed with the names of Urartian kings and others attributed to the Urartians because of their style. Many Urartian sites have been looted and much Urartian-style metalwork—which may not all be genuine—has been sold on the antiquities market.

Top Bronze circular sheet decorated with an Urartian god (possibly Teisheba) standing on a bull. The two concentric bands show various mythological beasts. Although some of these are known from Mesopotamian art, others are distinctively Urartian. The object's purpose and where it was found are not known, but the holes round the edge suggest it was sewn onto either cloth or leather. Diameter 25.5 cm.

Above Model of a fortified building made out of bronze, said to come from Rusahinili (Toprakkale). Buttressed facades were typical of Urartian military architecture and similar buildings were shown on the Assyrian reliefs. The ends of the pairs of beams supporting the parapet are visible. Height 28 cm, width 36 cm.

Right This bronze statuette with a face of white stone was part of a larger construction, as is shown by the holes in the side of the figure. The eyes and eyebrows were inlaid as were the necklace and the end of the ribbon that comes over the shoulder and is held by the left hand. There are also traces of gold leaf. The figure was made using the lost-wax process and has been identified as a priest (though it could be a servant). It was sold in the 19th century by a dealer who claimed that the bronze statuette and the face were found together in Rusahinili. Height 36 cm.

been a branch of the Aramaeans, but the ancient sources do consistently distinguish between them.

Shalmaneser's palace

Early in his reign, Shalmaneser III started to build a palace in the southeast corner of the outer town of Kalhu, and by 846 BC, his 13th year, the building was complete. Called Fort Shalmaneser by its excavators, it had served as a royal residence, treasury and fortress. In the 7th century BC it was described as an *ekal masharti*, a display palace, intended "for the ordinance of the camp, the maintenance of the stallions, chariots, weapons, equipment of war, and the spoil of the foe of every kind". Indeed, weapons, armor and other military equipment as well as large quantities of booty taken from the enemy have been discovered there.

Fort Shalmaneser was built within a walled enclosure of about 7.5 hectares. It measured 350 by 250 meters and was divided into two areas: four large courtyards to the north and the palace and residential areas to the south. The outer courtyards contained workshops for the repair and maintenance of military equipment, residential suites for various officials and magazines for storing, among other things, booty. The south side of the southeast courtyard was taken up by the massive rooms of the royal residence, of which the largest was the great throne room. The enormous throne dais was discovered still in its place, set into a niche on the east wall. The dais was made out of two slabs of yellowish limestone. Three sets of symmetrically placed circular indentations showed the positions of three successive thrones, each with its footstool. (When a throne was replaced, the holes in which it had stood were filled with bitumen.)

Most of the upper surface of the dais had been decorated with a geometric floral pattern, originally picked out in white. The edges and two panels at the back bore a long inscription of Shalmaneser III recounting selected events of his reign down to his 13th year (when presumably the dais had been erected). A note on the dais recorded that it had been put up by the govenor of Kalhu, Shamash-bel-usur, for his lord. The sides of the dais were decorated with sculptured friezes, inset in panels varying in heights from 21 to 29 centimeters. The reliefs on the north and south sides of the dais depicted the receipt of the tribute from Syrian and Chaldean rulers that had been mentioned in the texts on the top. Shalmaneser recorded his victory over a coalition led by the king of Damascus and described with satisfaction the reinstatement of his ally Marduk-zakir-shumi on the throne of Babylon. On the front of the throne dais Shalmaneser and Marduk-zakir-shumi were shown greeting each other.

The Balawat Gates

Unlike his father, Shalmaneser did not decorate his palace with stone relief sculptures. He did, however, commission a pair of massive bronze-clad gates, which were erected in Imgur-Enlil (modern Balawat), 16 kilometers north of Kalhu. Each leaf was about 2 meters wide and about 4 meters high, and was fastened to a vertical tree trunk, which turned in a stone socket sunk into the ground. Sixteen embossed bronze bands, nailed to the door leaves, depicted scenes from Shalmaneser's

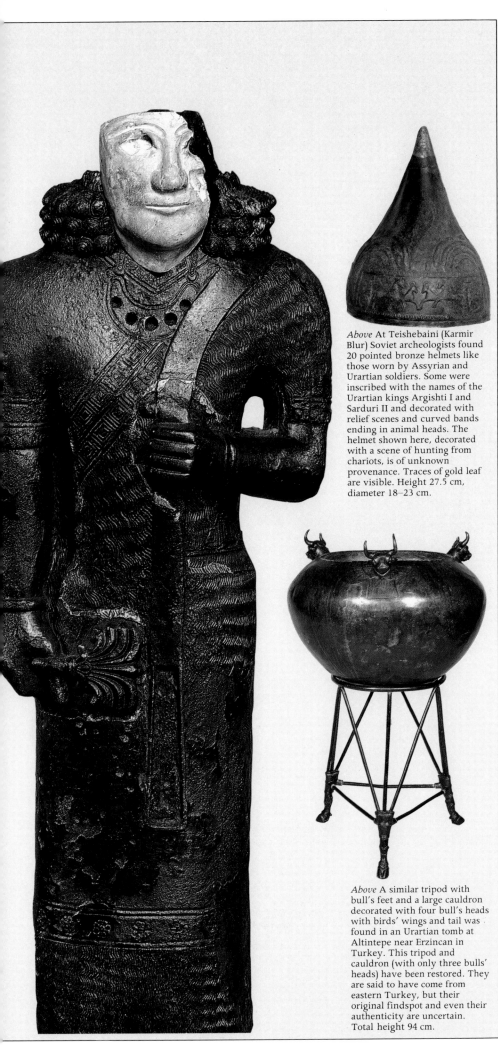

Above At Teishebaini (Karmir Blur) Soviet archeologists found 20 pointed bronze helmets like those worn by Assyrian and Urartian soldiers. Some were inscribed with the names of the Urartian kings Argishti I and Sarduri II and decorated with relief scenes and curved bands ending in animal heads. The helmet shown here, decorated with a scene of hunting from chariots, is of unknown provenance. Traces of gold leaf are visible. Height 27.5 cm, diameter 18–23 cm.

Above A similar tripod with bull's feet and a large cauldron decorated with four bull's heads with birds' wings and tail was found in an Urartian tomb at Altintepe near Erzincan in Turkey. This tripod and cauldron (with only three bulls' heads) have been restored. They are said to have come from eastern Turkey, but their original findspot and even their authenticity are uncertain. Total height 94 cm.

campaigns and expeditions, which were identified by short cuneiform labels. Most of these were accounts of Shalmaneser's conquests and the tribute received from his western campaigns, but his victory over the Chaldeans and various northern campaigns were also recorded. In the north he had visited the source of the Tigris, where he left a rock carving and an inscription and fought against the Urartians. He reached as far as the Sea of Nairi (Lake Van) and there he washed his weapons in the waters and made sacrifices to the gods. Altogether, Shalmaneser undertook five separate campaigns against Urartu.

The kingdom of Urartu

Since the 13th century BC Middle Assyrian kings had fought against Nairi, as the region of Urartu was then called. At that time the region was divided among numerous rulers but in the 9th century it was united under a single ruler. The unification might have been the result of a developing threat from the Assyrian empire. The heartland of Urartu was around Lake Van, and much of the land lay high in the steep mountains and was buried deep under meters of snow for months in winter. The mountains between Lake Van and Assyria proved an obstacle to Assyrian conquest and the Urartian kingdom survived and prospered. Even when Assyrian armies succeeded in reaching the Urartian cities in the highlands, they were unable or unwilling to occupy them.

Much of the history of the Urartians comes from Assyrian sources, but from the 9th century there were inscriptions of Urartian kings. The earliest of these were written in the Assyrian language and the titles of the kings were borrowed from Assyria and echoed the titles of Ashurnasirpal II. Later Urartian kings used the Assyrian script but wrote in their own language, which was related to Hurrian. In Urartian, the land of Urartu was called Biainili, from which the name Lake Van was probably derived. The names and order of the first eight Urartian kings, each of whom succeeded his father on the throne, have been reconstructed from the

Urartian inscriptions and the Assyrian texts, but the order of the last four members of the dynasty is unclear.

An idea of how much territory the Urartian kings controlled can be gained from the distribution of their inscriptions. Shalmaneser III claimed to have destroyed the royal Urartian cities of Sugunia and Arzashkun belonging to Aramu king of Urartu, but the location of these cities and Aramu's relationship to later kings of Urartu are uncertain. Sarduri I, who was king of Urartu in 832 BC according to an inscription of Shalmaneser III, was the first Urartian king to commission inscriptions. These were all found at his capital Tushpa (Van Kale, near the modern city of Van), which may have become the capital after the other centers had been destroyed by the Assyrians.

Sarduri's son Ishpuini left some inscriptions to the north and east of Lake Van and others, in association with his son Menua, 200 kilometers north of Tushpa and 250 kilometers to the southeast at Kelishin as well as at Qalatgah to the southwest of Lake Urmia in Iran. Menua's inscriptions have also been found 300 kilometers west of Tushpa, in the upper reaches of the Euphrates river, to the north, on the Araxes, and south of Lake Urmia. In the middle of the 8th century, Argishti I extended Urartian control as far as Lake Sevan to the north. This period of expansion coincided with a period of Assyrian weakness. Although the territories gained by the Urartians had never been part of the Assyrian empire, the absence of the threat of invasion from the south certainly contributed to the Urartians' success.

Urartian culture

The Urartians owed much to the Assyrians, but their culture was distinct. The most common surviving Urartian sites were placed on the top of steep rocky ridges, and were heavily fortified by stone walls with buttresses and towers. The chief god was Haldi, probably a god of war, whose main temple was at Musasir (called by the Urartians Ardini), between Assyria and Lake Urmia. The Urartian god Teisheba was related to the Hurrian weather god Teshup and had his temple at Qumenu, which has not been located with certainty. The city god of Tushpa was the sun god Shiwine. Urartian texts mentioned a number of religious structures, most of them dedicated to the god Haldi. They were called *susi* ("temples" or "gates") and were often labeled "gates of Haldi". The standard form of temple found on a number of excavated Urartian sites had a square plan with very thick walls. Its inner chamber was about 5 meters by 5 and the whole almost 15 meters square. These temples had plans like those of the tall tower buildings constructed by the Persian kings at the end of the 6th century BC and themselves may have originally been tall towers.

The Urartian kingdom was established by Menua, and more than seventy of his inscriptions have been found referring to almost as many different building projects including palaces, cities, irrigation canals, storehouses and temples. Urartu's wealth was largely agricultural, based on cultivating grain, orchards and vineyards and keeping livestock and horses. The Urartians were also specialists in bronze- and iron-working.

Kings of Urartu		Dates are those when the Urartian king was mentioned in Assyrian records.
SARDURI I 832		The order of the last four rulers is uncertain
ISHPUINI c.818		
MENUA		
ARGISHTI I		
SARDURI II 743		
RUSA I 719–713		
ARGISHTI II 708		
RUSA II 673		
SARDURI III	or	ERIMENA
SARDURI IV		RUSA III
ERIMENA		SARDURI III
RUSA III		SARDURI IV

The destruction of Hasanlu

In the course of Menua's expansion to the southeast, the Urartian armies probably reached the site of Hasanlu, which was destroyed in a huge fire at about the end of the 9th century. Between about 1500 and 1000 BC Hasanlu had been settled by people who used a distinctive burnished gray or black pottery. In the first millennium their buildings consisted of a wide portico, with the lintel supported on columns, leading through an antechamber into a rectangular hall with two rows of wooden columns. A spiral stairway or ramp led off from the antechamber. Four such buildings that were excavated in the southwest part of the town had probably been palaces built by successive rulers. By the time of Hasanlu's destruction some were no longer being used as palaces but as storehouses and, in one case, as a stable. Hasanlu was captured in battle, with the bodies left where they fell, and the city was set on fire before much looting could take place.

The most remarkable find was a decorated gold bowl, beside which were the skeletons of three men. They had probably been on the upper storey of the building when the floor collapsed, killing them and burying the bowl. Whether the men had been guarding the vessel or were invaders plundering the riches of the citadel is not known. The bowl itself probably belonged to a period several hundred years before the destruction of Hasanlu, as it showed scenes of gods, goddesses, animals and chariots that have been associated with the myths of the Hurrians. The wide variety of objects discovered at Hasanlu illustrated many aspects of the life of the town and the palace at this time. Weapons, armor, horse trappings, jewelry, bronze and silver vessels, have all been found in the ruins together with the bodies of those who were killed when the city was sacked.

Although this was probably the work of the Urartians led by Menua, in the absence of inscriptions it is impossible to be certain. Some experts have suggested that the Assyrians, about a century later, were responsible. After a period of abandonment a massive fortification wall of Urartian-style masonry was built on the ruins, which might give further support to the theory that it was the Urartians who captured the city.

Ancient civilizations of Western Iran

Hasanlu was in a region that, according to the Assyrians, was occupied by the Manneans, one of the many peoples encountered by Shalmaneser III in his campaigns to the east. Two other peoples in the region have been identified with the Medes and the Persians, who later dominated the Near East. In 843 BC Shalmaneser marched through the land of Parsua, and in 835 received gifts from 27 kings of Parsua before then continuing on to the land of the Medes. However, although the names of Parsua and Persia (called Parsa in the 6th century BC) are similar, the land of Parsua mentioned by Shalmaneser was far from the later homeland of the Persians, situated to the southeast of Susa. An early theory proposed that the Persians migrated south between the 9th and 6th centuries, but it is more

The kingdom of Urartu
The Urartians lived in the rugged mountains that lie at what is today the junction of Turkey, Iraq, Iran and the Soviet Union. Intensive survey work has revealed many well fortified Urartian sites on rocky outcrops. Urartu was the chief rival of Assyria and its southern borders lay close to the Assyrian heartland. The Urartians used the cuneiform script, first in Assyrian and later in their own language, but very few documents have been found. Most information about the Urartians comes from archeological investigations, monumental rock-cut inscriptions of their kings and Assyrian sources. In the 9th century BC Urartian rule seems to have been confined to the region of Lake Van and the capital Tushpa, but by the middle of the next century it had extended to Lake Sevan, Lake Urmia and the Euphrates river in the west. The Urartian civilization owed much to the Assyrians, but they had a distinctive culture, which is seen in their fortifications, temples, palaces, tombs, pottery and art.

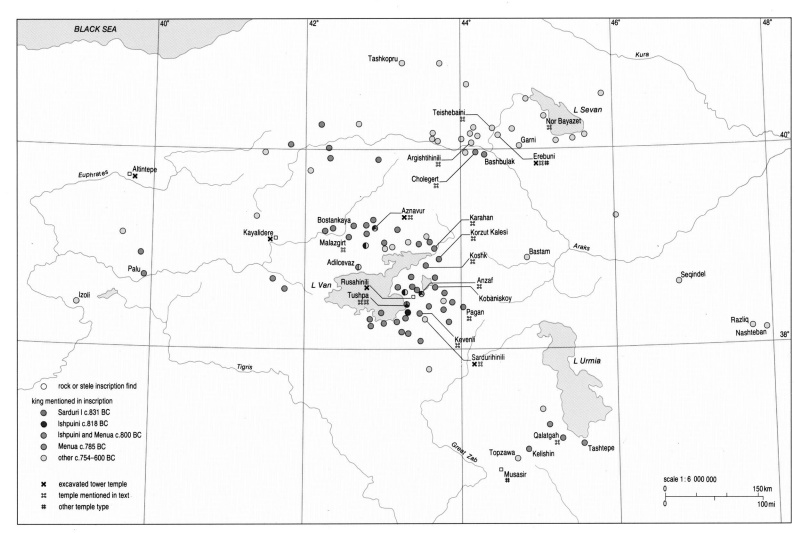

rock or stele inscription find

king mentioned in inscription
- Sarduri I c.831 BC
- Ishpuini c.818 BC
- Ishpuini and Menua c.800 BC
- Menua c.785 BC
- other c.754–600 BC

✕ excavated tower temple
⌘ temple mentioned in text
other temple type

scale 1:6 000 000

0 ____ 150 km

0 ____ 100 mi

probable that there were two regions with similar names. "Parsua" meant borderland in Persian and so could have been given to a number of different regions. The name occurred again some three centuries later as the land of Parthia in the northeast of Iran.

How far Parsua and Media extended is also uncertain, though they must have been near the main route through the mountains from Babylonia to the Iranian plateau, passing Hamadan, which was later the capital of the Medes. As no sites from 1000 to 800 BC have been investigated, the only available information is that contained in the cuneiform texts. These suggest that at this time there were no kingdoms of Media or Parsua as such, but that they were both divided up into many small independent groups.

Farther south the Assyrians encountered the kingdom of Ellipi, which was probably situated in the mountains of modern Luristan. In the first three centuries of the first millennium BC Luristan was the center of a skilled bronze manufacture. Some of the Luristan bronzes were elaborately-wrought, symmetrical castings depicting fantastic beasts, which have been identified as standards. Others were horse trappings or harness ornaments decorated with stylized animal and demon figures. Most of the Luristan bronzes that have survived were looted by tomb robbers and sold on the antiquities market, but a few belonging to this period have been found in the course of archeological excavations.

Shalmaneser's successors

During the reigns of Ashurnasirpal II and Shalmaneser III, Assyria had gradually dominated the lowland areas of the Near East. Its armies had marched with comparative freedom in the highlands to the north and east, but later began to meet greater resistance. According to the annals inscribed on the Black Obelisk found at Kalhu, in 832 BC the Assyrian armies were led by Dayyan-Ashur, Shalmaneser's chief vizier, and for the following four years the king himself stayed in Kalhu. Perhaps, after 30 years on the throne, Shalmaneser was exhausted by his annual campaigns and had chosen Dayyan-Ashur, his chief vizier for more than 20 years, to lead them in his stead. Perhaps, too, Shalmaneser's eldest son, Ashur-danin-apla, felt slighted when he was passed over for this honor.

According to the *limmu* list (the list of Assyrian officials whose names were given to each year), a revolt in 828 led by Ashur-danin-apla broke out, which lasted until well after Shalmaneser's death in 824. Except for Kalhu, all the major cities of Assyria including Imgur-Enlil, Nineveh, Ashur and Arbil joined the rebels. However, it was not Ashur-danin-apla who succeeded to the Assyrian throne but another son of Shalmaneser, who became Shamshi-Adad V (823–811 BC). The circumstances of his victory are not known, but possibly he was helped by Marduk-zakir-shumi, whom Shalmaneser III had assisted in establishing his claim to the throne of Babylon. In fact, Shamshi-Adad had made a treaty with Marduk-zakir-shumi in which the Assyrian was forced to accept a subordinate role, perhaps because, at the time, he was preoccupied by the struggle with his brother.

Left Stele of Shamshi-Adad V (823–811 BC) found at Kalhu and probably erected in the Temple of Nabu. The king is in his court robes with the typical headdress and diadem of the Assyrian monarchy. He holds a scepter and points his right index finger in a gesture of reverence. In front of his face are symbols of the chief gods: the horned headdress probably indicating Ashur, the sun disk of Shamash, the crescent and circle of Sin, the fork of lightning of Adad and the star of Ishtar. The inscription was written after his 4th campaign and gives details of the insurrection throughout Assyria at the end of the reign of his father Shalmaneser III. Height 1.98 m, width 0.94 m.

Right A detail from the Black Obelisk of Shalmaneser III (858–824 BC). The upper register is inscribed "the tribute of Yaua, the son of Humri", who is shown groveling before Shalmaneser. Yaua is identified with the Israelite king Jehu who usurped the throne and put to death the descendants of Omri. The lower register shows the tribute of Musri (possibly Egypt), which curiously includes 2-humped camels of the variety more commonly found in Iran.

A few years later Shamshi-Adad took his revenge for the humiliating terms of the treaty. He captured Marduk-zakir-shumi's son, Marduk-balassu-iqbi, and took him back to Assyria. In a subsequent campaign, Shamshi-Adad deported Marduk-balassu-iqbi's successor and, like Shalmaneser and the kings of Babylon, he worshiped at the shrines of Babylon, Borsippa and Kutha. After Shamshi-Adad's death, his queen, Sammuramat, became the ruler of Assyria for five years while her son Adad-nirari III was still a minor. Little is known about Sammuramat's deeds, but her reputation survived and she entered Greek legend as the beautiful, but cruel, queen Semiramis.

The decline of Assyria

For the next 60 years Assyria experienced a phase of relative weakness. The rule of the monarch was much reduced as provisional governors usurped powers that previously had been the king's. Palil-irish (whose name is sometimes read as Nergal-eresh), the governor of Rasappa, erected stelae and founded cities in his own name, as did the governor Bel-Harran-bel-usur who had his own image, rather than the king's, carved on his monument. The most powerful of these governors, however, was the grand vizier Shamshi-ilu. Ruling the western part of the Assyrian kingdom from Kar-Shalmaneser (formerly Til Barsip) on the Euphrates, he recorded his campaigns in his own name without any mention of the king.

In the middle of the 9th century BC, Suhu, which was situated on the Euphrates, near Ana, and had successfully resisted Ashurnasirpal's attacks, was ruled by Shamash-resh-usur. He recorded his deeds on a carved stele, found in Babylon, where it had probably been taken by a later king. One of his proudest achievements was that he had introduced bees for honey and wax into the land of Suhu.

During this period of Assyrian decline, plagues and rebellions were recorded in the *limmu* list. Against the name of the *limmu* official Bur-sagale, governor of Guzana, there were records of a rebellion in the city of Ashur and, in the month of Simanu, an eclipse of the sun. This has been equated with the almost total eclipse of the sun visible to observers in Nineveh from 9.33 a.m. to 12.19 p.m. on the morning of the 15 June 763 BC. This identification provides the fixed point on which the chronology of the Assyrian and Babylonian kings is based, as far back as the middle of the second millennium BC.

ASSYRIA TRIUMPHANT (750-626 BC)

The resurgence of Assyria

The rapid expansion of Assyria in the 9th century BC was followed by a period of stagnation in the first half of the 8th century. The borders of Assyria remained almost the same but the governors of the provinces acted as if they were independent rulers. Assyria's neighbors such as Urartu and Phoenicia pursued policies that took no account of the interests of the Assyrian king. This period of weakness ended with the accession of Tiglath-pileser III (744–727 BC). The *limmu* list recorded a revolt in the city of Kalhu in 746, shortly before Tiglath-pileser became king. Whether these events were connected is not certain, but very possibly the new king was a usurper. Traditionally, Assyrian kings justified their claim to the throne through the choice of the gods and through descent from a previous king. Tiglath-pileser, however, hardly ever mentioned his parentage in any of his inscriptions, perhaps because of his irregular accession. An inscribed brick from the temple at Ashur called him the son of Adad-nirari, who died almost 40 years before Tiglath-pileser came to the throne.

Tiglath-pileser wasted no time in establishing Assyria once again as the dominant power of the Near East. Early in his reign he led his armies to the south, defeating the Aramaean tribes who had settled in northern and eastern Babylonia. He reached Dur-Kurigalzu and Sippar and received the remains of offerings from the temples of Babylon, Borsippa and Kutha, which normally were given only to the kings of Babylon. He claimed to have conquered as far as the Uknu river (perhaps the Karkheh) on the Lower Sea (the Gulf). Reversing the policy of earlier Assyrian kings, Tiglath-pileser annexed states on the far side of the Euphrates, outside Assyria's traditional boundaries. He appointed a *sha reshe* (eunuch) as governor over the cities of Babylonia and claimed the title King of Sumer and Akkad, but allowed Nabu-nasir, the king of Babylon (747–734 BC) to retain his throne. In 743 BC Tiglath-pileser faced opposition from a coalition of the rulers of Urartu, Arpad, Malatya, Kummuh and Gurgum, led by Sarduri II, king of Urartu. Tiglath-pileser defeated his enemies in a battle in Kummuh (Commagene, in southern Turkey). Sarduri fled into the mountains but Tiglath-pileser pursued him and reached the Urartian capital Tushpa (on Lake Van), where he erected a stele but did not capture the city.

For the next 12 years Tiglath-pileser campaigned in the west, first against Arpad, which fell in 740, then against Unqi (the Amuq plain) and Aram (Damascus). Some of the conquered states were annexed to existing provinces or established as new Assyrian provinces; others were left with pro-Assyrian rulers who delivered an annual tribute to the Assyrian king. By the end of Tiglath-pileser's reign the list of tributary regions included the Aramaean and Neo-Hittite states of Syria and the Taurus, the Phoenician coastal cities, Israel, Judah

and Gaza, the inland states Ammon, Moab and Edom as well as the Arab tribes of the interior including those of Taima and Sab'a (Sheba). In addition to these conquests, the Assyrians were often invited to intervene in the affairs of smaller neighboring states whose rulers were their willing allies. Kilamuwa of Sam'al recorded that he "hired" the king of Assyria (perhaps Shamshi-Adad V, 823–811 BC) to fight against the nearby kingdom of Adana (Danuna). Ahaz of Judah requested assistance from Tiglath-pileser, and Bar-rakib, a later ruler of Sam'al, recorded how his father had "grasped the hem of Tiglath-pileser" and how he and his father "ran at the chariot wheel of the king of Assyria" and as a result his kingdom had prospered.

The Phoenicians

The Phoenicians who lived in the cities on the Mediterranean coast in the first millennium BC were probably the descendants of the Canaanite inhabitants of the Levant in the Bronze Age. The name Phoenician was Greek and it was also applied to the purple dye obtained from the murex shell for which the Phoenicians were famous. The Phoenicians generally referred to themselves by their city of origin. Phoenicians were great sailors and their prosperity came from trade that included timber from the highly valued cedar forests in the mountains that lay behind the coastal cities.

In the last centuries of the second millennium parts of Cyprus came under Phoenician influence and the Phoenicians later established colonies on the island. The trade in Cypriot copper, which in the Bronze Age had passed through Ugarit, was now diverted to the Phoenician cities of Tyre, Sidon, Byblos and Arvad. According to classical authors, the Phoenicians established colonies

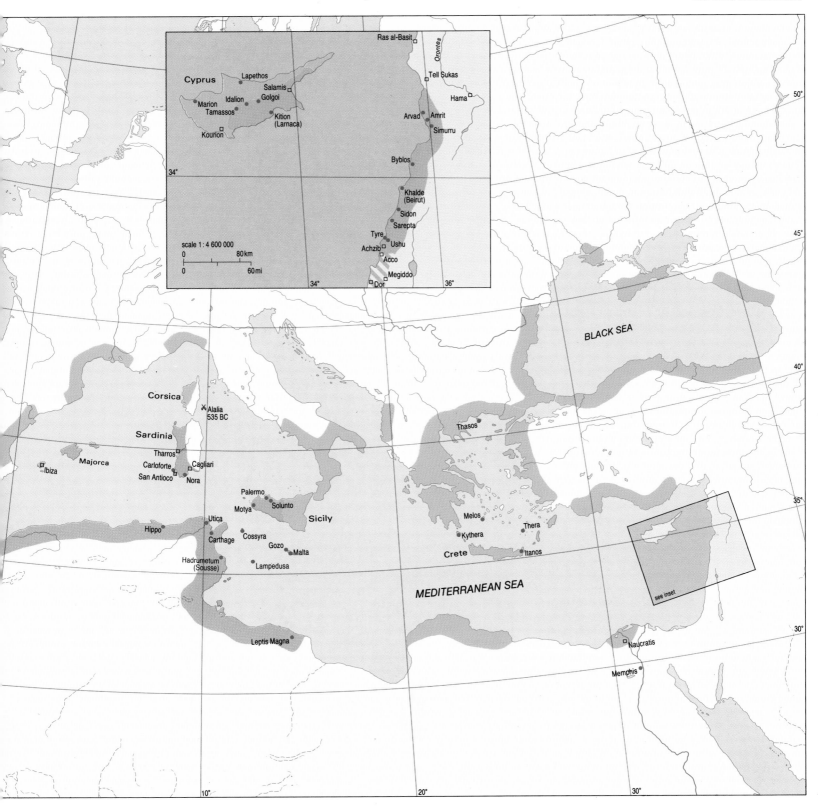

The world of the Phoenicians

scale 1 : 4 600 000

0   80km
0   60mi

Above left Larger than life-size relief of the Assyrian king Tiglath-pileser III found in the Central Palace at Kalhu. Height 1.08 m, width 1.07 m.

Left A coin from Byblos of a type first struck in the early 4th century BC, showing a Phoenician galley above a fabulous sea creature. Phoenician power was based on control of the sea throughout the 1st millennium BC.

The world of the Phoenicians
The Phoenician homeland lay on the eastern coast of the Mediterranean Sea and the principal cities were Tyre, Sidon, Byblos and Arvad. Early in the 1st millennium BC Phoenicians and Greeks established colonies throughout the Mediterranean, the Phoenicians generally occupying the south and the Greeks the north. The most important Phoenician colony was Carthage, which came to dominate the western Mediterranean until its ambitions were curbed by the Romans. The Phoenicians were a major maritime power and

their navy was used by the Assyrians and the Persians. Phoenician ships sailed far beyond the Mediterranean. According to Herodotus, a Phoenician ship commissioned by the Egyptian pharaoh Necho II circumnavigated Africa in 600 BC. It took three years to sail from the Red Sea to the Straits of Gibraltar. The Carthaginians too were great explorers, reaching the coasts of Britain in the 5th century BC.

throughout the Mediterranean and founded Cadiz (Gades) in 1110 BC, Utica in 1101, Lixus a little earlier, Sicily in the 8th century before the Greek colonization, and Carthage in 814. However, these dates have not yet been confirmed by archeological evidence. The earliest Phoenician inscription from Cyprus has been dated to about 850 BC and elsewhere evidence of Phoenician settlement seems to be later than 800. One of the reasons for establishing colonies may have been the growing influence of Assyria, which imposed tribute on the Phoenician cities. In the 7th century the Assyrians conquered Sidon and Tyre, and the western colonies came under the control of Carthage.

177

Assyrian–Babylonian relations

Nabu-nasir the king of Babylon died in 734 BC. Two years later his son was overthrown and, shortly after, the chief of the Bit-Amukani, a Chaldean tribe from the region south of Nippur, seized the throne of Babylon. In response, Tiglath-pileser marched against the Chaldeans and, after a victorious campaign, received the submissions of Aramaean and Chaldean leaders. They included Marduk-apla-iddina, the chief of the Bit-Yakin tribe, who later confronted Tiglath-pileser's successors. In 729 Tiglath-pileser decided to take the throne of Babylon himself rather than appoint a vassal or reduce the holy and venerable city to the status of a province. At the New Year festivals of 728 and 727 he assumed the role of the Babylonian king. The relationship between Babylon and Assyria was one of great significance. Babylon was an important religious and cultural center which, despite its military weakness, affected Assyrian policy. The Assyrians used a Babylonian dialect in literary works and even for royal inscriptions, whereas letters and contracts were written in Assyrian. Assyrian rulers tended to be either pro- or anti-Babylonian and over the next century their policy towards Babylonia shifted violently as they

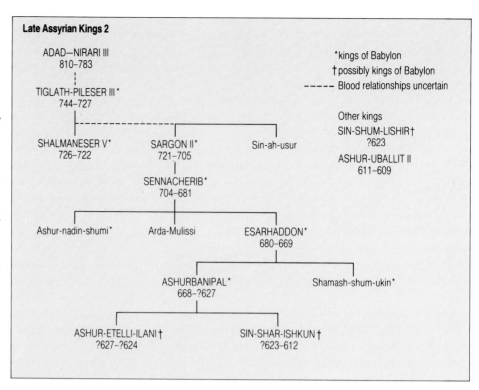

Late Assyrian Kings 2

ADAD—NIRARI III
810–783

TIGLATH-PILESER III*
744–727

SHALMANESER V*
726–722

SARGON II*
721–705

Sin-ah-usur

SENNACHERIB*
704–681

Ashur-nadin-shumi*

Arda-Mulissi

ESARHADDON*
680–669

ASHURBANIPAL*
668–?627

Shamash-shum-ukin*

ASHUR-ETELLI-ILANI †
?627–?624

SIN-SHAR-ISHKUN †
?623–612

*kings of Babylon
†possibly kings of Babylon
----- Blood relationships uncertain

Other kings
SIN-SHUM-LISHIR†
?623

ASHUR-UBALLIT II
611–609

Left Stele found at Sam'al showing Bar-rakib, the pro-Assyrian ruler of the city (Zinjirli), seated on a throne similar to that used by the Assyrian king. Before him stands a scribe with pen-case and writing board, probably used for writing in Aramaic, as in the inscription on the stele. Some rulers of Sam'al had Aramaic names; others had Hittite or Luwian names. Bar-rakib came to the throne in about 732 BC after his father had died fighting as an ally of the Assyrian king Tiglath-pileser III. Despite its rulers' pro-Assyrian stance Sam'al was reduced to provincial status within the Assyrian empire before 681 BC.
Height 1.14 m.

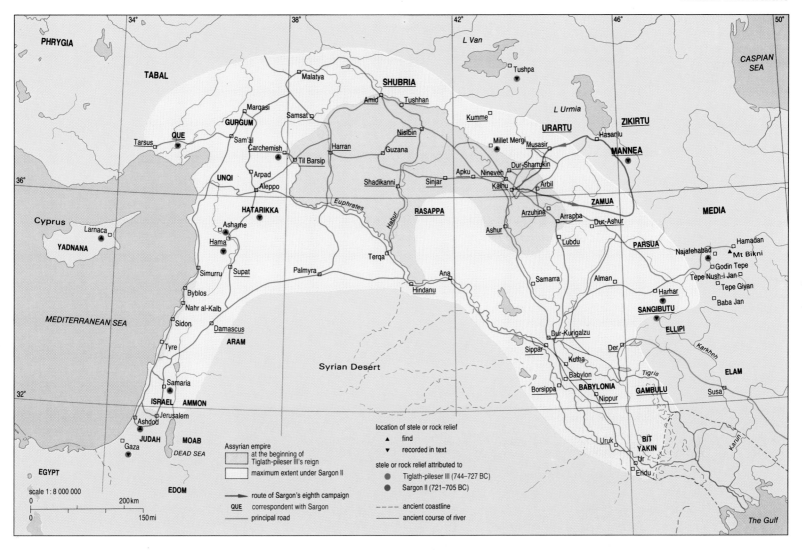

The Assyrian empire in the late 8th century BC
Under Tiglath-pileser III and Sargon II, Assyrian foreign policy changed and large areas of the Near East beyond the earlier borders of Assyria were brought within Assyrian provincial administration. Communication over this vast area was helped by a system of regular staging posts set up on the main roads. The empire created by Tiglath-pileser and Sargon survived for almost another century. The expansion was brought about by continual campaigns, which were recorded in the royal annals, including a detailed description of Sargon's eighth campaign in 714 when Urartu was defeated. However, the route of this campaign, as shown, has been the subject of debate, some authorities believing that the Assyrians went the whole way round Lake Urmia.

tried to achieve a lasting arrangement for governing the south.

Tiglath-pileser's reforms

Tiglath-pileser's military and political successes rested on a fundamental reorganization of the Assyrian state apparatus. He reformed the army, establishing a standing professional force of mercenaries, particularly Aramaeans, as foot soldiers. The mounted forces—chariotry and cavalry—were largely Assyrian but also included some troops of foreign origin. The chariot forces were controlled by the *rab sha reshe*, the chief eunuch. Tiglath-pileser used eunuchs to curb the power of the nobles of Assyria and appointed them provincial governors because, with no descendants of their own, they were loyal to the king. As an instrument of government, Tiglath-pileser pursued large-scale deportations and resettlements of peoples, recording 155,000 Chaldeans and 65,000 Medes as deportees. Many of these were taken to Assyria where they worked in the king's service or as farmers. Sometimes people were moved from one region to another to curb local or nationalistic tendencies.

Tiglath-pileser III's successor was his son Shalmaneser V. During his short reign (726–722 BC) he continued the policies of his father and was also crowned king of Babylon as well as of Assyria. In the Babylonian King List, Shalmaneser and his father were recorded as Ululayu and Pulu respectively and the same names are found in Biblical and Greek sources. These were probably their original names, which they changed to something more suitable on accession to the throne. Shalmaneser's annals have not survived but, according to the Bible, he captured Samaria, the capital of Israel, and deported the Israelites.

The accession of Sargon II

The circumstances in which Shalmaneser V was replaced as king of Assyria by Sargon in 722 are obscure. One of Sargon's inscriptions suggests that he was aided by the citizens of Ashur, who objected to paying taxes that Shalmaneser had imposed. In his inscriptions Sargon did not mention his ancestry and avoided naming his predecessor, whom he called "the prince who went before me". The name Sargon, meaning legitimate king, suggests that he was not Shalmaneser's designated successor.

There are no records of Sargon's campaigns in the first two years of his reign, perhaps because he was fully occupied in establishing his position. However, later versions of Sargon's annals borrowed Shalmaneser's conquest of Samaria, placing it in the early part of Sargon's reign alongside some of Sargon's own later campaigns. In the spring of 720 Sargon marched south, possibly with the aim of recovering Babylonia, which in the turmoil surrounding Sargon's accession had fallen under the control of the Chaldean Marduk-apla-iddina II (called Merodach-baladan in the Bible) of the Bit-Yakin tribe. Having arrived in the neighborhood of Der, the Assyrians fought against the Elamites under their king Humban-nikash I (743–717 BC), but the Babylonians arrived only after the battle was over. Sargon claimed total victory whereas a Babylonian chronicle reported that the Elamites had won. In fact, the result seems to have been a stalemate, with the Assyrians keeping control of the city of Der but avoiding any further military involvement with Elam or Babylon for the next 10 years.

Sargon turned his attention to the west, where the rulers of Hama, Arpad, Simurru, Damascus and Samaria had opportunistically cast off their allegiance to Assyria. They were besieged by Sargon in Qarqar, where in 853 BC a similar coalition had faced Shalmaneser. When Gaza, actively supported by the Egyptians, rebelled, Sargon established Assyrian control right up to the Egyptian border.

The Assyrians also attempted to control the lands to the north and west of the Euphrates, but there they competed with the influence of two major powers on the Anatolian plateau, the Mushki to the northwest and the Urartians to the northeast. Almost 400 years earlier Tiglath-pileser I (1114–1076 BC) had fought against the Mushki. There is no archeological evidence for the occupation of sites in central Anatolia between the 12th and 8th centuries BC, but in the 8th century the Mushki lived in the region that the Greeks called Phrygia. According to Greek legends the Phrygians arrived in Anatolia from Europe at about the time of the Trojan War, at the end of the Late Bronze Age. Some scholars believe that they were responsible for the destruction of Hattusas and the end of the Hittite empire in about 1200 BC, but there is no corroborative evidence for their presence in the region at such an early date. It is possible that Phrygia and Mushki were alternative names for the same people. In any case, by the 8th century they were apparently united under one ruler.

King Midas of Phrygia

Sargon's rival in the area, a ruler whom he called Mita of Mushki, was undoubtedly the same king Midas of Phrygia who in Greek legend had a golden touch and grew ass's ears. Midas' capital was Gordion, named after Midas' father Gordias, who may have refounded the city. From excavations, the buildings at Gordion typically consisted of an antechamber and a rectangular hall (the so-called *megaron* plan), with galleries along each side of the hall supported on wooden columns. Another *megaron* had a mosaic floor comprising geometric patterns made out of colored pebbles.

Seventy-five or so burial mounds surrounded the citadel of Gordion, the largest of which still stands more than 50 meters high and, according to local tradition, was the tomb of Midas. Because of its size the mound had escaped the depredations of tomb robbers and could be excavated only by drilling from the top to locate the tomb chamber and then tunneling in from the side. The chamber was made of large wooden timbers and contained the body of a man about 60 years old and 1.59 meters tall. Inside the tomb were fine inlaid wooden tables and stands, three large bronze cauldrons, more than a hundred bronze fibulae (ornamental safety pins) and more than one hundred and fifty other metal vessels and ladles. One of the bronze vessels ended in a ram's head and another

in a lion's head, similar to those depicted on the reliefs in Sargon II's palace. Oddly, the tomb contained no weapons, no items of precious materials, such as gold, electrum or silver, no ivory or glass or gemstones nor, apart from the fibulae, any jewelry. Some of the fibulae and metal vessels were of brass (an alloy of copper and zinc) and among the earliest examples of its use. Their bright yellow appearance has suggested that the discovery of how to make objects of brass rather than the usual bronze (an alloy of copper and tin) gave rise to the story about Midas' golden touch (though there is some disagreement over whether the occupant of the tomb was Midas or his father). According to a later tradition, Midas committed suicide when his kingdom was overrun in about 695 BC after an invasion by Cimmerians, a people who may have come from Central Asia. The excavations showed that Gordion was destroyed at about this time.

In the first part of Sargon's reign Midas was his enemy. Fears of a conspiracy involving the ruler of Mushki or Urartu sufficed to provoke Assyria's anger, leading to the annexation of Carchemish in 717 BC. When Ambaris of Tabal sent messengers to Rusa of Urartu and Midas of Phrygia, the Assyrians deposed him and in 713 annexed his country. In 709, however, following attacks by the governor of Que (Cilicia), Midas became an ally of Assyria. A

Above In this relief from his newly founded capital Dur-Sharrukin (Khorsabad) Sargon II faces a high official of his court, probably the crown-prince, his son and successor, Sennacherib. The king wears the royal Assyrian crown and a garment decorated with rosettes, possibly of gold and sewn onto the fabric. A similar type of cloth was found covering two skeletons in a stone sarcophagus in a tomb at Kalhu, where Yaba, the queen of Tiglath-pileser III, Baniti, Shalmaneser V's queen and Atalia, the queen of Sargon II, may have been buried. Height 2.90 m, width 2.30 m.

Right Reconstructed head of the man buried in the Tomb of Midas at Gordion. The technique used was the same as that employed to reconstruct the features of unidentified victims of murder or fire. The layers of muscle and skin were built up on a cast of the skull to produce a portrait of the king.

Below A rock relief near a spring at Ivriz shows Warpalawas, the ruler of Tuwana (classical Tyana) in front of a god. Warpalawas or Urbala, as he was called in the Assyrian texts, paid tribute to Tiglath-pileser III and may have been allied to King Midas of Phrygia. When Midas made peace with Sargon II of Assyria Warpalawas returned to the Assyrian fold. The semicircular ornamental safety pin worn by Warpalawas is similar to those used by the Phrygians, of which more than 100 were found in the Tomb of Midas at Gordion. Height of god 4.20 m.

copy of a letter from Sargon to Ashur-sharra-usur, the Assyrian eunuch governor of Que, carried news of the rapprochement between Midas and Sargon and described the consequences for future Assyrian policy. Squeezed between Assyria and Phrygia, the rulers of this region, it said, had no choice but to submit and "polish the sandals of the Assyrian governor with their beards".

The Assyrian royal mail

Not surprisingly, the version of history presented in the Assyrian annals was biased, but sometimes the inscriptions of Assyria's rivals and neighbors provide a corrective. The royal correspondence of the Assyrian court also gives a more objective view. About 1,300 letters between Sargon and officials from all over his empire, and agents living outside the borders of Assyria, have survived. Many of the letters are fragmentary, imprecisely dated and, as much of the background information was omitted because it was familiar to the correspondents, are often difficult to interpret. Still, they reveal the issues with which Assyrian domestic and foreign policy was concerned, which are not evident in the official propaganda. The royal inscriptions create an impression of inevitable success, implying that there was no resistance to the will of the king, before whom, with the gods on his side, all had to submit. The correspondence, in contrast, casts doubt on the outcome of some of the policies, describing how omens and oracles were consulted before any action was taken and recording failures as well as successes.

One of the problems facing the Assyrians was the government of so large an empire. Local administration was under the control of the provincial governor who acted on the orders of the king and who sent reports back to him. Lengthy delays in communication posed the dangers of governors acquiring too much independence or of vital decisions being postponed. To overcome these problems the Assyrians created an efficient road and messenger system. Along the major routes, at regular intervals of about a day's march (30 kilometers), there were road stations where the king's messengers could rest and obtain fresh teams of mules to pull their chariots. In this way, it took only a few days for the king's word to reach the far-flung outposts of the empire. This system formed the basis of the much-admired system of communication used later in the Persian empire.

War with Urartu

The Assyrian war machine needed supplies of men, animals and equipment. These were acquired through taxes, tribute and booty, and the annual campaigns led by the king or his high officials ensured that peoples who were subject or allied to Assyria did not default on their payments. To the north of Assyria the powerful kingdom of Urartu opposed Assyrian designs. As Assyria grew in strength and sought to exert its influence over regions closer to Urartu, conflict between the two became increasingly likely. On the map Assyria and Urartu have a common border, but in reality they were separated by almost impassable mountains, which made a direct military attack impossible. Even if the Assyrians had succeeded in crossing the mountains or in reaching Urartu by the more easily negotiable passes to the east or west, the Urartians could have retreated into their mountain fortresses, leaving the harsh winter conditions to force an Assyrian withdrawal. Annexation of Urartu was not one of Assyria's aims and Sargon avoided direct confrontation with Urartu as he did with Egypt and Mushki. However, conflict arose through their vassal or allied states.

In 716 BC Rusa I, the king of Urartu, overthrew the ruler of Mannea in western Iran, to the south of Lake Urmia, and installed Bagdatti as king in his place. To Sargon, who reckoned that Mannea was within the Assyrian sphere of influence, and to whom Mannea was a vital source of horses for the Assyrian army, Urartu's interference was a provocative act. He invaded Mannea, had Bagdatti flayed and appointed his brother Ullusunu king in his place. In response, Urartu seized 22 Mannean fortresses, but in the following year Sargon came to the assistance of Ullusunu and recaptured them. In 714 Sargon marched to Media and received tribute from the rulers of the central Zagros, before proceeding north into Mannea where Ullusunu persuaded him to march against Rusa I. When the Assyrian and Urartian armies met, somewhere near the southwest corner of Lake Urmia, Sargon was victorious. Having defeated Rusa, he marched into Urartian territory, returning to Assyria by way of Musasir, the city of the god Haldi where the Urartian kings were crowned. Sargon looted the city and brought back huge stores of booty. He provided a detailed account of his campaign in a letter to the god Ashur, which was probably read out aloud at some victory celebration at the city of Ashur. Sargon recorded every step of the campaign, listing all the booty and tribute received and concluding with the casualty figures (which were as implausible as those given out in military press briefings today): only one charioteer, one cavalryman and three foot soldiers in the Assyrian army were alleged to have been killed.

Sargon's victory over Urartu, however, was not as complete or as decisive as his inscriptions suggested. Rusa reestablished his influence over Musasir and probably did not, as stated in Sargon's annals, commit suicide by "stabbing himself with his own iron dagger like a pig". An uneasy truce was established between Assyria and Urartu. Assyrian spies reported on conditions in Urartu and on one occasion said that the Urartians had been defeated by an invasion of Cimmerians. In these circumstances it suited Urartu and Assyria to remain at peace with one another and for the next hundred years no further wars were recorded between them.

The end of Sargon's reign

South of Urartu, astride the main trade route from Mesopotamia, were the people known as the Medes, divided into numerous tribal groups. In Sargon's inscriptions they were called Mighty Medes or Distant Medes on the edge of Mount Bikni, which has been identified with Mount Alvand just south of the later Median capital at Hamadan. According to the 5th century BC Greek historian Herodotus, the Medes were united under Deioces, who built his capital city at Hamadan. Assyrian accounts suggest that it was not until the second half of the 7th century that the Medes were

united. Only a few sites of the Medes have been excavated and these seem to have been founded at the end of the 8th century BC. One of them, Tepe Nush-i Jan, contained the remains of an impressive religious sanctuary. Another was Godin Tepe, where the remains of a fortified palace with columned halls may have once been the residence of a local Median chieftain. A stele erected by Sargon that was found at Najafehabad might have come from Godin Tepe, marking the farthest extent of Assyrian penetration into the Zagros.

Having resolved his problems to the west, north and east, in 710 BC Sargon focused his gaze on the south, where Marduk-apla-iddina II ruled over Babylon. In the course of two campaigns Sargon ousted him, forcing him to take refuge in the marshes in the south, and in 709 Sargon proclaimed himself ruler of Babylon at the New Year festival. In 707 Sargon captured Dur-Yakin, the main city of the Bit-Yakin tribe of which Marduk-apla-iddina II was the chief, but failed to capture Marduk-apla-iddina himself. Sargon brought Babylonia into the Assyrian empire, appointing a governor in Babylon and another in Gambulu, on the border with Elam. More than 108,000 Aramaeans and Chaldeans were deported from Babylonia in an attempt to pacify the country.

As befitted a ruler who denied his ancestry, Sargon decided to build a new capital city. He chose a completely new site and called it Dur-Sharrukin, or Fortress of Sargon. The foundations were laid as early as 717, and in 707 the gods of Dur-Sharrukin entered their temples, a year before the city was inaugurated. In 705 Sargon led his armies to the land of Tabal in the Taurus mountains, where he met his death doing battle against a man called Gurdi (Gordias), a common name among the rulers of the Anatolian principalities. Sargon had been at the height of his power and seemed invincible. He ruled the core of the Near East from the Gulf to the Taurus mountains, from the Zagros mountains to Sinai. He had defeated Urartu and forced other rulers including Midas, king of Phrygia, the pharaoh of Egypt, Uperi, the king of Dilmun, and seven kings of Yadnana (Cyprus) to pay tribute. His death in battle and the loss of his body, so that he could not be buried in his palace, was a great blow to Assyrian morale.

Nineveh, Assyria's natural capital

When Sargon's son and heir Sennacherib became king in 704, he consulted the oracles to find out what had been his father's sins. To dissociate himself from the ill fate of Sargon he omitted his father's name from his inscriptions and moved the capital from the new city of Dur-Sharrukin to the ancient city of Nineveh. Nineveh was the natural center of Assyria. It lay in fertile grain-producing lands, controlled an important crossing of the Tigris and contained the chief temple of the Assyrian cult of the goddess Ishtar. Sennacherib rebuilt Nineveh, constructing a citadel with palaces and temples on the site of the ancient city mound (Tell Kuyunjik). His principal palace was decorated with carved stone reliefs, most of which showed his military victories, and, as at Kalhu and Dur-Sharrukin, an arsenal palace was built away from the citadel (at Tell Nebi Yunus, where according to Muslim tradition the prophet Jonah is buried).

Below The mud-brick buildings at Tepe Nush-i Jan stood on top of a natural rock outcrop in the middle of a flat plain surrounded by mountains. In this photograph, taken at an early stage of the excavation, the walls of the Fort are just visible on the top of the site.

Tepe Nush-i Jan

Below The Central Temple and the Western Temple were the most important structures at Tepe Nush-i Jan. Later the Fort, a square fortified storehouse, and Columned Hall were built. Columned halls were adopted by the Achaemenid Persians for their palaces.

Although the Medes ruled an extensive empire stretching from central Anatolia to Afghanistan, the archeology of the Medes is poorly known. In the 1960s and 1970s Godin Tepe and Tepe Nush-i Jan, two sites not far from the Median capital Hamadan, were excavated and proved to be a large fortified residence occupied from the 8th to the 6th centuries BC and a religious center of the Medes, respectively.

The Medes may have worshiped fire like later Zoroastrians. The Central Temple at Tepe Nush-i Jan, probably built in the 8th century BC, had an unusual stepped plan and contained an altar on which a fire was lit. In about 600 BC the whole building had been carefully filled up with stones, which preserved the walls to a height of some 8 meters, probably as part of a project to renovate the site. However, this was never completed and the monumental buildings were later occupied by villagers squatting in their ruins.

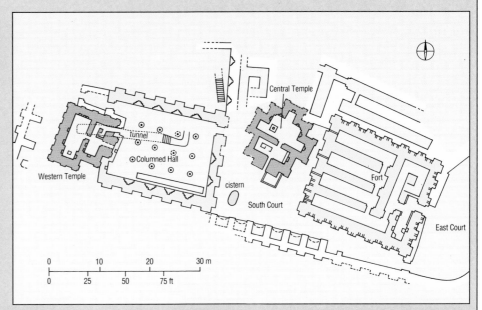

Above The buildings at Tepe Nush-i Jan were exceptionally well preserved with doorways and vaults still surviving. This doorway in the Western Temple was partly blocked when the building was abandoned. The ancient wooden lintel has been replaced with a modern timber beam.

Above center 321 silver objects in a bronze bowl were buried in the Fort in about 600 BC. They included spiral beads and pendants, which date to about 2000 BC, rings, jewelry and silver bars, which may have been an early form of currency. Length of bar in top row, 5.35 cm.

Dur-Sharrukin

In 717 BC Sargon the usurper, who proclaimed himself king of Assyria, king of the world, founded a new capital city. The site that he chose, which lay to the north of the ancient capital Nineveh, he called Dur-Sharrukin, meaning Sargon's Fortress. The gods of Dur-Sharrukin were brought into the new capital's temples in 707, when Sargon with "the princes of all countries, the provincial governors, the overseers and supervisors, nobles and eunuchs and the elders of Assyria took up residence in the palace and held a feast". Two years later, however, Sargon was killed in battle and the court moved to Nineveh.

Approximately rectangular in plan, the city walls at Dur-Sharrukin enclosed an area measuring about 1,600 by 1,750 meters. Seven gates gave access to the city. The great palace of Sargon and the temple area were built on a terrace straddling the northwest wall of the city while the arsenal lay in the southern corner.

The site, which is now called Khorsabad, was excavated by Paul Botta and Victor Place in the 19th century. They discovered a wealth of carved stone reliefs lining the palace walls, but many of these were lost when their boat was sunk.

Left Wall decoration from Residence K of the palace (see site plan). There were no stone reliefs in this hall, which was decorated with a magnificent painting. The much-restored drawing shows the king, perhaps followed by the crown prince, before a god who holds the rod and ring of divine authority. The whole panel is framed by divine beings with buckets and cones, and below are rows of kneeling winged gods and bulls. Height c. 13 m.

Right A painted, sun-dried clay figure found at Dur-Sharrukin. Often wrongly identified as the hero Gilgamesh it is, in fact, the god Lahmu (the hairy one). Figurines like this were buried in the foundations of the building as protection against evil.

Below A 4-winged god with bucket and cone carved on one of the gates at Dur-Sharrukin. Height c. 3.65 m.

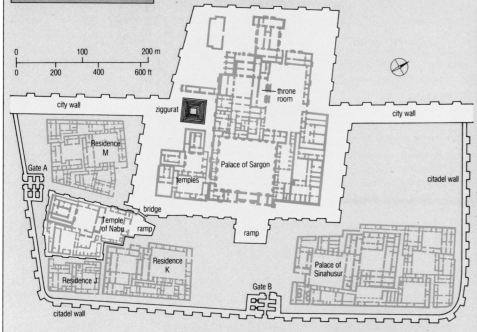

Above The higher part of the citadel consisted of the king's palace and a religious precinct that included a ziggurat. Below were the Temple of Nabu, which could be reached by a bridge, and the residences of the high officials including Sargon's brother Sin-ah-usur, who was the *turtanu*, or chief vizier.

Right This 9-sided baked barrel cylinder from Dur-Sharrukin records the words of Sargon, "Day and night I planned the building of that city."

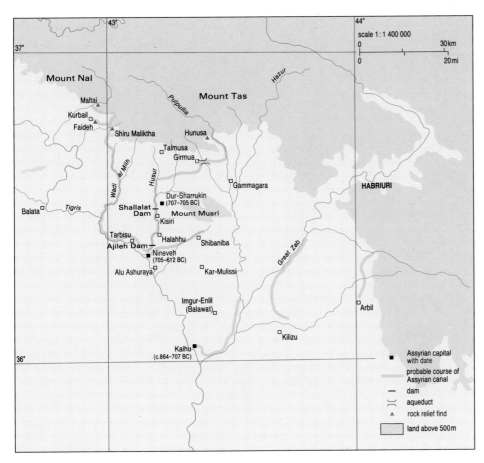

tions with the south dominated Assyrian foreign policy for most of Sennacherib's reign. In 703, the persistent Marduk-apla-iddina II rebelled and seized the throne of Babylon for the second time. Sennacherib marched south to defeat an alliance of Babylonians, Chaldeans, Aramaeans, Elamites and Arabs, near Kutha. He recaptured Babylon and seized members of Marduk-apla-iddina's family and court, though the Chaldean leader himself once more escaped to the marshes. Sennacherib appointed a Babylonian, Bel-ibni, king of Babylon and pursued the campaign into Chaldean country, returning to Assyria with 208,000 captives. The Chaldeans continued to make trouble, and in 700 Sennacherib returned to Babylonia to depose Bel-ibni and appoint his eldest son, Ashur-nadin-shumi, king of Babylon in his stead.

The destruction of Babylon

In 694 Sennacherib mounted another expedition against the Chaldeans and their Elamite allies. This time he launched his attack from boats, built by Phoenicians, after floating down the Tigris and Euphrates and across the marshes into Elamite territory. The Assyrians claimed a great victory, but shortly afterward the Elamites counterattacked against northern Babylonia, capturing Sippar and carrying off Ashur-nadin-shumi.

The events of the next three years were confused. The Assyrians took the Elamite appointee to

Assyrian capitals and irrigation systems
Ashurnasirpal II moved his capital from the city of Ashur to Kalhu in about 864 BC. Sargon II's new capital city Dur-Sharrukin was barely completed before Sargon was killed in battle in 705 BC and his superstitious son Sennacherib moved the capital to Nineveh. The Assyrian kings used existing water courses and constructed canals to provide water for their cities. Sennacherib's schemes were the most ambitious. The canal leading to Arbil ran partly underground, that from Hunusa (Bavian) crossed the valley at Girmua (Jerwan) on an aqueduct, and the one bringing water from the northwest to Nineveh was lined with carved panels of the gods.

Right Judean captives being impaled on stakes outside the walls of Lachish. Although the siege of Lachish was not mentioned in Sennacherib's annals it was recorded on the reliefs in his palace at Nineveh. Excavations at Lachish (Tell al-Duweir) in Israel have confirmed the accuracy of the Assyrian depiction. The city was captured by building a siege ramp, which together with a counter ramp built inside by the defenders, was discovered in the excavations.

A strong wall more than 12 kilometers long surrounded the city, which occupied more than 7 square kilometers.

Sennacherib undertook vast irrigation works to provide water for his greatly enlarged city, as well as for the orchards and fields around Nineveh and a royal park, where he cultivated plants from Chaldea and the Amanus mountains. One exotic species was a "wool-bearing tree", which has been identified as cotton, a plant that had been cultivated since the third millennium BC in India.

Sennacherib's successes and failures

In his inscriptions and on reliefs Sennacherib gave the impression of a successful, invincible monarch. In reality, his reign was marked by a series of uprisings and defeats. In 701 BC Sennacherib marched to the Levant and Palestine to put down a rebellion, and engaged the Egyptian army, which had come to the aid of the rebels, near Eltekeh on the coastal plain of Philistia. Sennacherib's annals claimed that the Assyrians won the battle. However, they did not continue south to the borders of Egypt, but turned inland to besiege Lachish, in a campaign vividly depicted on reliefs in Sennacherib's palace. They then attacked Jerusalem, the seat of Hezekiah the king of Judah, but failed to capture the city. Both the Bible and the Greek historian Herodotus recorded that the Assyrians were defeated by the Egyptians, (though some historians believe the defeat was in a later campaign that received no mention in Sennacherib's annals).

Unlike his father, Sennacherib in his 24-year reign did not embark on territorial conquests but was content to maintain the borders that Sargon had established. Sargon's annexation of Babylonia proved an intractable problem, however, and rela-

Nineveh

The citadel mound of Nineveh, now known as Tell Kuyunjik, was occupied since the Hassuna period (seventh millennium BC) and three-quarters of the mound is made up of prehistoric remains. During the Uruk period (c. 4000–3000 BC) Nineveh was closely related to the developments in southern Mesopotamia. In the second millennium Nineveh, though not the capital of Assyria, was an important city with a prestigious temple of the goddess Ishtar. Sennacherib (704–681 BC) chose it as his capital at the end of the 8th century BC and built the Southwest Palace there, which he called the Palace Without a Rival, decorating it with carved stone reliefs. As at Kalhu and Dur-Sharrukin, an arsenal was also built, which was situated at Tell Nebi Yunus and which later legend claimed as the tomb of the prophet Jonah.

Sennacherib's grandson Ashurbanipal (669–c. 627 BC) built a second palace on Tell Kuyunjik, the North Palace, which contained the famous lion-hunt reliefs. In the summer of 612 BC Nineveh fell to the Medes and Babylonians, who looted and destroyed the Assyrian palaces and temples. The city of Nineveh, however, survived for 1,000 years, before it was eclipsed by the city of Mosul, on the other side of the Tigris.

Above Part of a relief from the Southwest Palace at Nineveh, showing an Assyrian king in his chariot and under a parasol with his driver and eunuch attendant with a fly-whisk. The relief records a campaign in Babylonia and the king is perhaps Sin-shar-ishkun, one of the last kings of Assyria.

Below right This relief from the North Palace at Nineveh was carved in about 645 BC and may show the facade of the Southwest Palace, which was built about 50 years earlier. In his inscriptions Sennacherib boasted that he had built a portico with columns of bronze resting on column bases in the form of solid cast bronze lions and bulls, each weighing some 43 tonnes.

Right Sennacherib constructed the walls of Nineveh and named the 15 gates of the city, which can be identified with mounds on the city wall. Much of the area within the walls was also occupied by buildings, but the city's most important buildings were on Tell Kuyunjik and Tell Nebi Yunus. The earthworks on the east are the spoil banks of a canal, not, as was once believed, a further fortification or siege wall built by the Medes and Babylonians.

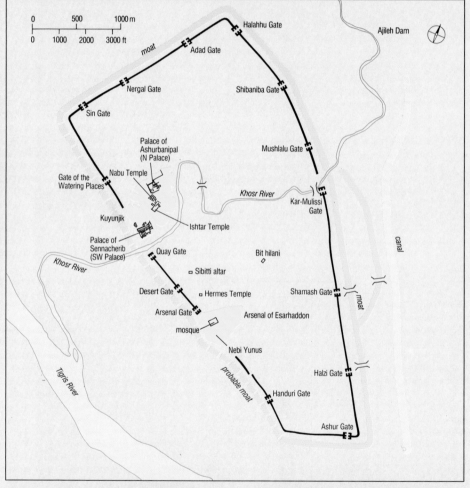

Above Relief carving on Sennacherib's canal. An elaborate system of canals brought water to the city of Nineveh and to the king's nature reserve and game park. The water flowed either in canals or along natural watercourses. The system started in the hills to the north and an aqueduct was constructed at Jerwan which crossed a valley. Along the Jebel Faideh, 45 km north of Nineveh, the line of the canal is clearly visible on the slope of the hill. It is just over 3 m wide and has panels carved with figures of gods spaced at intervals. These are much eroded and partly buried under the ground but can still be recognized.

Above Looking west along the restored northern outer wall of Nineveh toward the Nergal Gate in the distance. The outer part of the wall was stone, defended by a crenellated parapet and interval towers. Behind this was another, much higher wall made of mud-bricks. The circuit of the walls of Nineveh is about 12 km. Sennacherib called it "the wall that terrifies the enemy" and constructed in front of it a deep moat, which is now filled up.

Right A view of a dam on the Khosr river at Shallalat, about 13 km upstream from Nineveh. This was probably part of Sennacherib's canal system. It was restored by the local population in 1970 and still functions as a weir.

the Babylonian throne captive but a Chaldean seized power in Babylonia. The king of Elam was himself deposed in a revolt, as was his successor in the following year. Despite these upheavals, Assyria failed to regain control of Babylon and in 691 a southern coalition marched up the Tigris to attack Assyria. The two armies met at Halule (perhaps near Samarra) and the Assyrians claimed victory, though the more reliable Babylonian Chronicle recorded that the Assyrians had had to retreat. In the next year, however, they regained the initiative and besieged Babylon, which held out for 15 months before it finally surrendered in November 689.

Sennacherib's revenge was harsh, though not unexpected. He carried off the wealth of the city, smashed the statues of the gods, destroyed the city's houses, temples and palaces and dug canals to flood the site. Some of the earth from the ruins was dumped into the Euphrates, which carried it downstream as far as Dilmun, some was sent to the most distant parts of the Assyrian empire and some was placed in the temples at Ashur, which Sennacherib rebuilt in an attempt to replace the religious center of Babylon with that of Ashur.

Although for the rest of Sennacherib's reign Assyria was apparently at peace, he himself met a violent death. He was assassinated by his son Arda-Mulissi in February 680. To the Jews it was just retribution for his attack on Jerusalem; to the Babylonians it represented punishment for his sacrilege against Babylon. Indeed, there might have been some Babylonian involvement in the plot, but it was probably the result of a dynastic quarrel.

The struggle for succession

As Sennacherib's eldest son Ashur-nadin-shumi had disappeared after being carried off to Elam following the Elamite invasion of Babylonia in 694 BC, Arda-Mulissi, who was probably the second eldest son, had doubtless hoped to have been Sennacherib's appointed heir. However, Sennacherib's wife Zakutu (known in Aramaic as Naqia) favored her son Esarhaddon and he was made crown prince in preference to his brothers.

From the time of Sargon II it had been the custom for the king to choose one of his sons (not necessarily the eldest) as his successor. The gods Shamash and Adad were then consulted by oracle and if the response was favorable the crown prince entered into the *bit reduti* (the house of succession or government) to be prepared for kingship. At that stage the heir could decide to take a new name, and in Esarhaddon's case he chose Ashur-etelli-ilani-mukin-apla (though he apparently used this name only occasionally). The method of selection was designed to ensure that the most competent of the king's sons became king, that he had been well schooled in the necessary skills and that there should be no dispute about his succession. However, in Esarhaddon's case things did not work out that way. The slanders and intrigues of his brothers had ousted him from his father's affections, forcing him to flee, or be exiled from the court, in the spring of 681 BC. After the murder of his father, Esarhaddon marched back to Nineveh to defeat his brothers' army, many of whom went over to Esarhaddon's side. Arda-Mulissi and his associates fled.

Above This black stone tablet was inscribed with an account of Esarhaddon's restoration of Babylon. The symbols, including a fine representation of a plow with a seed-drill, shown on this stone may be a way of writing Esarhaddon's name, with each symbol connected with one of the cuneiform signs used in the name.

Left A stele erected by Esarhaddon after 671 BC and found in a gate chamber of an outer tower at Sam'al (Zinjirli). The Assyrian king wearing his religious costume stands in a position of reverence. In front of the king's head are the symbols of the gods. He holds leashes attached to the lips of two defeated enemies, one of whom has negroid features. They have been identified as Taharqa, the king of Egypt and Nubia (or possibly his son Ushanahuru who was captured and taken to Assyria), and either Abdimilqut, king of Sidon, or Ba'lu, king of Tyre. On the sides of the stele were smaller figures of Esarhaddon's heirs: Ashurbanipal dressed as crown prince of Assyria, and Shamash-shum-ukin as king of Babylon. Height 3.18 m, width 1.35 m.

Right The expert astrologers attached to the Assyrian court consulted tablets like this one from the royal library at Nineveh, containing astronomical observations and predictions.

Esarhaddon's superstitions

Esarhaddon (680–669 BC) was not a well man and often consulted his advisers about his periodic illnesses. His symptoms, as he described them, included fever, weakness, loss of appetite, stiffness of the joints, eye infections, earache, chills and skin complaints. Different treatments—lotions, ointments, rest, change of diet, as well as religious rituals—failed to cure him, which no doubt also made him subject to bouts of depression. Diseases, it was believed, were the result of the actions of the gods, and so Esarhaddon was anxious to discover what the gods wanted from him. Before he became king, the court astrologers had sent reports about omens given by the stars. A conjunction of Mercury (the star of the crown prince) and of Saturn (the star of the king) on 18 May 681 BC was interpreted as predicting the murder of the king and the restoration of the temples of the great gods by his successor. As a result of this and other astronomical events, Esarhaddon early in his reign, reversed his father's policy towards Babylon and ordered the rebuilding of Babylon and its temples.

Eclipses of the sun and moon were considered to be times of particular danger for a king and often predicted his death. The science of astrology was well developed and the predictions of its practitioners were based on accurate astronomical observation. If Jupiter was visible the king was safe; if the upper part of the moon were eclipsed then the king of Amurru or of the west would die; if a lower quadrant was obscured the king of Assyria's fate was sealed. However, the king could take evasive action by enthroning a surrogate, who took the ill omens on himself and was killed within 100 days of the eclipse and buried with full royal honors. The earliest instance of a substitute king was the accession of Enlil-bani as king of Isin in 1861 BC, though this was recorded only in a chronicle copied in the Neo-Babylonian period. The Hittites had a similar ritual, which was certainly borrowed from Mesopotamia. Before the reign of Esarhaddon, however, there was only one well-documented case: that of a substitute king, mentioned in texts from Kalhu, who, in about 782 BC, was issued rations. There were six recorded cases of substitute kings in the reign of Esarhaddon and at least two in the reign of his son Ashurbanipal.

Soon after the death of his wife, Esarhaddon chose his sons Ashurbanipal and Shamash-shum-ukin to succeed him: Ashurbanipal as king of Assyria and Shamash-shum-ukin as king of Babylon. In the spring of 672 Esarhaddon, worried by the problems with his own accession and his uncertain health, summoned the officials and vassals of Assyria to Kalhu where he made them swear a loyalty oath agreeing to this inheritance.

The Egyptian campaigns

During Esarhaddon's reign, invading Scythians and Cimmerians curbed the power of Assyria's neighbors to the east and north. They even threatened Assyria itself, prompting Esarhaddon to obey the oracle of Shamash by giving his daughter to the Scythian chief Bartatua (called Protothyes by Herodotus) in pursuit of peace. Whether this gesture achieved the desired result is not known. Esarhaddon claimed to have defeated the Cimmerians and Scythians to the north and east of Assyria, but his greatest success was in the west.

In 679 he captured Arza, on the border of Egypt, but received a setback in 674 when, according to the Babylonian Chronicle, an Assyrian army in Egypt was defeated. In 672 Esarhaddon fell ill but recovered to lead an invasion of Egypt in the following year, this time defeating the Egyptian pharaoh Taharqa (690–664 BC). Taharqa belonged to the 25th dynasty, which came from Napata in Nubia (called Kush by the Egyptians and Meluhha by the Assyrians). A total eclipse of the moon on 2 July 671 predicted the death of the king of Assyria (which was averted by the enthronement of a substitute king) and defeat for the king of Egypt. After three battles the Assyrians captured Taharqa's capital city, Memphis, on 11 July but Taharqa fled to the south, leaving behind his son, his harem and his treasury. Esarhaddon used the booty from Egypt to finance the rebuilding of Babylon. The Assyrians appointed new rulers, governors and officials and imposed taxes on the Egyptians.

124920

By now Esarhaddon's ill health was taking its toll and he faced trouble at home and abroad. In the spring of 670 he uncovered a plot to overthrow him and executed the conspirators. The next month Esarhaddon was again ill but recovered. In the following year, he set out to reconquer a rebellious Egypt, which once again was under the control of Taharqa, but died on 1 November 669 and the expedition was abandoned.

The conquest of Egypt

Following the death of Esarhaddon, his mother Zakutu made her grandsons swear an oath of loyalty to Ashurbanipal, Esarhaddon's appointed heir. His accession presented no problems and he assumed the throne of Assyria before the end of 669. The installation of his brother Shamash-shum-ukin as king of Babylon, however, was delayed until after the Babylonian New Year (in the spring of 668), so that the years of Shamash-shum-ukin's reign in Babylon were one year behind those of his brother in Assyria.

In 667 BC Ashurbanipal embarked on the reconquest of Egypt begun by his father. He defeated King Taharqa outside Memphis, causing him to flee south to Thebes. Ashurbanipal himself had remained in Nineveh but through the efficient messenger service commanded his army to march against Taharqa. Before the command could be obeyed, however, the vassal rulers of Egypt who had been appointed by Esarhaddon rebelled and the Assyrian army first had to put down the revolt. The leaders of the conspiracy were taken prisoner and sent to Nineveh, but one of them, Necho I (the ruler of Sais), succeeded in convincing Ashurbanipal of his loyalty and was confirmed in his kingship and sent back to Egypt.

When Taharqa died in 664, his nephew Tantamani (664–657 BC) became king and invaded Egypt. He made Thebes his capital and marched against the Assyrian garrison in Memphis. There he

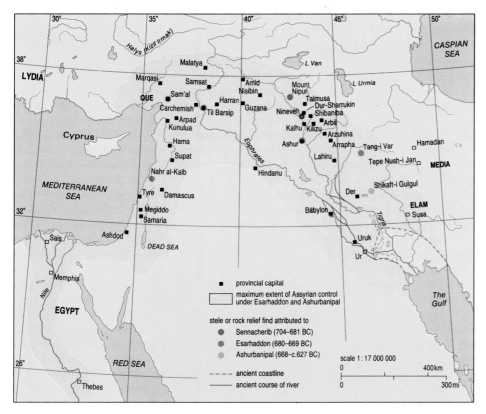

The Assyrian empire in the 7th century BC
The empire created by Tiglath-pileser III and Sargon II remained the basis of the Assyrian empire under their successors. The principal additional conquests were the short-lived invasions of Egypt under Esarhaddon and Ashurbanipal and the destruction of Elam by Ashurbanipal. Two problems plagued the later Assyrian empire: succession to the throne and relations with Babylon. In 652 BC the two came together with the civil war between Ashurbanipal and his brother Shamash-shum-ukin, who was king of Babylon. Ashurbanipal won after a damaging struggle from which Assyria never really recovered. It was destroyed by the Babylonians and Medes in 612 BC.

Above left Relief from the North Palace at Nineveh showing Ashurbanipal and his queen Ashur-sharrat feasting in a garden. The head of Teumman, king of Elam, which was sent to Assyria after the battle of Til-Tuba, hangs from the pine tree on the left.

Left Ashurbanipal defeated the Elamites at the battle of Til-Tuba on the banks of the Ulai river in 653 BC. At the top left an Assyrian soldier cuts off the head of the Elamite king Teumman. Relief from the Southwest Palace at Nineveh.

defeated the armies of the Egyptian princes of the Delta in a battle in which Necho I may have lost his life. On hearing the news, Ashurbanipal sent another army to Egypt with, perhaps, himself at the head, and forced Tantamani to retreat. Ashurbanipal recaptured Memphis and sacked Thebes, returning in triumph to Nineveh with great stores of booty. Assyrian sources are silent about the later relations with Egypt, but it seems clear that Ashurbanipal decided to withdraw while the rulers of Egypt were still bound by oath and friendly to Assyria.

In west Anatolia the Lydians had become the dominant power after the collapse of the Phrygian kingdom at the beginning of the 7th century. According to Herodotus, Gyges (c. 680–c. 650 BC) became king of Lydia by murdering his predecessor and marrying his wife. An inscription of Ashurbanipal's described how the god Ashur caused Gyges to have a dream in which he learned that he would conquer his foes if he submitted to Ashurbanipal. Consequently, Gyges sent an ambassador to Ashurbanipal from his remote country, whose name was unknown to Ashurbanipal's ancestors (or so he claimed), and succeeded in defeating the Cimmerians. But when Gyges supported an Egyptian king's rebellion against Assyria (probably before 665 BC), his kingdom was overrun by the Cimmerians who, under the leadership of Lygdamis (or Dugdamme as he appears in the Assyrian sources), were themselves defeated by the Assyrians in Cilicia in about the year 640.

Ashurbanipal's library
Besides being a military leader, Ashurbanipal was a scholar. In his inscriptions he recorded how he had learned the entire scribal art, could solve complex mathematical problems and could read difficult texts in the Sumerian and Akkadian languages. He even claimed to be able to understand texts from before the Flood.

During his reign he collected a large library of cuneiform texts of all sorts and dispatched agents to search out tablets in the archives and schools of the temples of Babylonia and to bring back copies to Nineveh. Ashurbanipal's library included the reference works and standard lists used by Mesopotamian scribes and scholars, bilingual vocabularies, wordlists and lists of signs and synonyms, lists of medical diagnoses, compendia of omens, rituals and incantations, and works of literature such as the Epic of Creation and the Epic of Gilgamesh. Indeed, the texts from Ashurbanipal's library are the basis of modern knowledge of the scribal traditions of Mesopotamia.

Civil war and the destruction of Susa
For 16 years Esarhaddon's solution for dealing with Babylon had worked well. Shamash-shum-ukin accepted his role as a subordinate monarch despite Ashurbanipal's persistent interference in Babylonian internal affairs. Suddenly, in 652 BC, civil war broke out between the two brothers, though the reasons for the quarrel are not clear. The rebellion lasted four years during which the Babylonians were supported by the Elamites, Arabs and southern tribespeople. The Assyrians held the cities in the south and by the summer of 650 BC Babylon itself was under siege. Shamash-shum-ukin was killed when the city was set on fire and by the end of 648 Ashurbanipal had regained control of Babylonia. He had the other rebels executed in the same temple where Sennacherib had been murdered and their dismembered bodies were fed to the dogs, the pigs, the birds and the fishes.

Shamash-shum-ukin's successor as ruler of Babylon was called Kandalanu. Opinions differ as to whether this was a throne name adopted by Ashurbanipal or whether Kandalanu was the name of Ashurbanipal's appointee. Nothing is known about Kandalanu's deeds, but Babylonia apparently remained at peace throughout the 21 years of his reign.

Before the civil war, Elam had been the object of two Assyrian campaigns, one in 667 and the other in 653 BC. In the second, the Elamite king Teumman (or Tepti-Humban-Inshushinak in Elamite) was killed in a battle on the banks of the river Ulai and his head cut off and brought back to Ashurbanipal, who exhibited it in Arbil and in Nineveh. At the end of the civil war, Ashurbanipal again turned his attention to the Elamites, who had supported his brother's rebellion. In 648 and 647 he led his armies against Ummanaldash (Humban-Haltash III), who had seized the Elamite throne, and eventually defeated him. The Assyrians sacked and looted Susa, destroying the temples, carrying off the gods, desecrating the graves and mutilating the statues of the Elamite kings. They even sowed the land with salt so that nothing would grow. Among the booty from Susa was a statue of the goddess Inanna, which, Ashurbanipal claimed, had been removed from Uruk 1,635 years before.

The later part of Ashurbanipal's reign is not well documented and even the date of his death is uncertain, though it is reckoned to have been in 627. Coincidentally, Kandalanu (who may, in fact, have been Ashurbanipal) also died in that year, and a period of insurrection began in Babylonia which ultimately led to the destruction of Assyria.

Babylon

Babylon, whose name means the gate of the gods, was the cult center of the god Marduk. A provincial capital during the Third Dynasty of Ur, in the 18th century BC it became the temporal and spiritual capital of southern Mesopotamia under the Amorite ruler Hammurabi (1792–1750 BC). The First Dynasty of Babylon ended when the city was sacked by the Hittites in 1595 BC. The Kassite rulers who followed were crowned at Babylon.

In the first millennium BC, Assyrian kings aspired to rule the ancient holy city, while in Babylonia the Aramaean and Chaldean tribes who were settled in the region strove for independence. Sennacherib destroyed the city in 689 BC, but his successor Esarhaddon rebuilt it. Eventually Nabopolassar (625–605 BC) defeated the Assyrians and he and his son Nebuchadnezzar II (604–562 BC) restored the city to its former glory.

Babylon was incorporated into the Persian empire in the 6th century BC and then fell to Alexander the Great and his successors, before eventually losing its preeminent position to the Greek city of Seleucia on the Tigris.

Babylon contained two of the Seven Wonders of the Ancient World, the Hanging Gardens and the city walls. The location of the Hanging Gardens is in doubt but the walls have been traced. The outer wall stretched for more than 8 kilometers and, according to Herodotus, had enough space on top to enable a four-horse chariot to turn around.

Right Stele of Ashurbanipal carrying a basket on his head, a motif dating back to the Early Dynastic period. The Assyrian king returned to Babylon the statue of Marduk removed by his grandfather Sennacherib and restored the Temple of Marduk, as recorded on the stele. Ashurbanipal claimed credit for the restoration even though his brother Shamash-shum-ukin was king of Babylon. Height 36.8 cm.

Top Diorite statue of a god or possibly a deified king (c. 2040 BC). The inscription is a dedication by Puzur-Ishtar, the ruler of Mari, and his brother Milaga. Found in Babylon together with a second almost identical uninscribed statue in the Northern citadel, it probably belonged to the so-called museum. This contained a variety of exotic objects including a huge Neo-Hittite stone lion and the stele of Shamash-resh-usur of Suhu. Height 1.70 m.

Above Under Nebuchadnezzar II the walls of the Processional Way, which ran from the Temple of Marduk through the Ishtar Gate toward the *akitu* temple, were decorated with glazed relief figures of striding lions. Height of lion 1.05 m.

Above right The bulls and dragons on the foundations of the Ishtar Gate were made from molded baked bricks with bitumen mortar and were not glazed.

Right The Euphrates divided the city of Babylon into two parts, connected by a bridge resting on stone, boat-shaped piers. The excavations of Robert Koldewey between 1899 and 1917 revealed much of the plan of the eastern part of the city in the Late Babylonian period. In the center, beside the river, were the Temple of Marduk and the ziggurat. The "Tower of Babel" (Etemenanki) was quarried for its baked bricks and is now a hole in the ground.

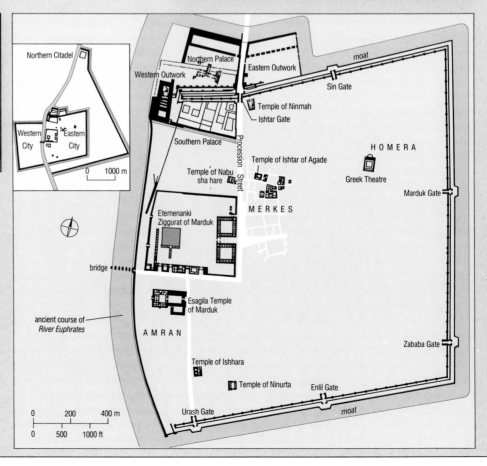

Left and below The Processional Way, called "May the enemy not cross", led from the Temple of Marduk to the *akitu* temple and passed through the Ishtar Gate, one of the eight gates of the inner city. Only the foundations of the gate were found, going down some 15 m, with molded, unglazed figures on them. Above ground level were glazed figures that were not in relief and above them others that were. The gateway has been reconstructed from the glazed bricks found, so its original height is conjectural. Reconstructed height 14.30 m.

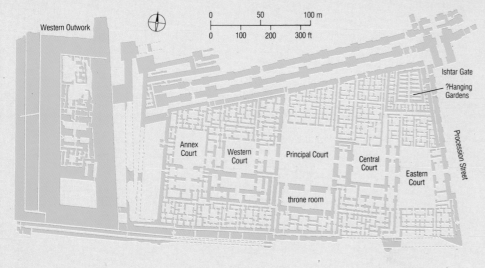

Left The Southern Citadel was built round five courtyards with reception rooms on the south side in the typical Babylonian manner. It was the creation of Nebuchadnezzar II, who called it "the marvel of mankind, the center of the land, the shining residence, the dwelling of majesty", and was later used by the kings of Persia. It was probably the site of Belshazzar's feast and of the writing on the wall, and was the place where Alexander the Great died.

Above The Ishtar Gate was decorated with figures of bulls and dragons, which combined features of snakes, lions and eagles. The bull was associated with the weather god Adad while the dragon was the animal of the god Marduk. The goddess Ishtar's lion was not included though lions did decorate the walls of the Processional Way. The molded and glazed bricks were marked on their upper surface to show where they fitted into the design. Height of bull c. 1.30 m.

Western Outwork

0   50   100 m
0   100   200   300 ft

Ishtar Gate
?Hanging Gardens

Annex Court
Western Court
Principal Court
Central Court
Eastern Court
throne room
Procession Street

Mesopotamian Warfare

The first clear evidence for warfare in the ancient Near East comes from the late fourth millennium BC, when seal impressions found at Uruk and Susa show scenes of fighting and of prisoners. The excavated remains of fortifications from earlier periods may indicate that warfare was prevalent in prehistoric times.

The early weapons were the same as those used in hunting – spears, clubs, bows and arrows, and slings. In the third millennium new weapons, such as copper daggers and axes as well as shields and helmets, came into use. Sumerian armies included battle wagons drawn by wild asses.

Many advances in warfare were made in the second millennium, when armies of 10,000 men or more were recorded. At that time, siege warfare was developed and fortifications were improved. Soldiers wore bronze scale-armor, and horse-drawn chariots were the chosen arm of the military elite.

In the following millennium iron replaced bronze for many weapons and mounted cavalry supplemented the chariot troops. Psychological warfare including religious sanctions and omens as well as threats of deportation or torture was widespread and played an important part in the military successes of the Assyrians.

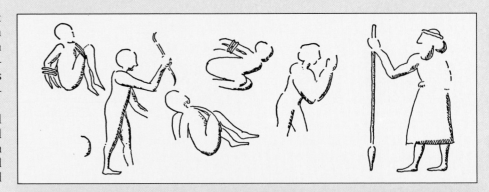

Below A detail from the Stele of the Vultures (c. 2450 BC), found at Girsu. The massed phalanx of the helmeted warriors of Lagash, led by their ruler Eannatum I, trample over the corpses of the soldiers of Umma. In the lower register Eannatum, holding a long spear, attacks from his battle wagon, while his soldiers armed with spears and axes march behind.

Above right On this cylinder seal impression from Uruk (c. 3200 BC) the ruler armed with a spear stands before naked and bound prisoners.

Right A detail from the Standard of Ur (c. 2500 BC), showing a Sumerian battle wagon. The slain enemy shown beneath the animals is a convention found later in Egypt and Assyria.

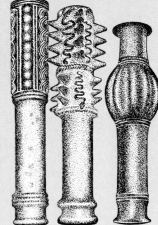

Left In the 9th century BC mounted soldiers rode in pairs so that one could control both horses while the other used his bow. Saddles and stirrups had not yet been invented. Relief from the Northwest Palace at Kalhu.

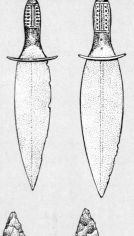

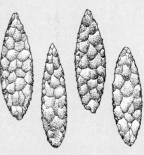

Above After the capture of Hamanu in Elam (c. 647 BC), the city was looted and Ashurbanipal's soldiers set it on fire, demolishing the fortifications with pickaxes and crowbars. The threat of retribution was one of the chief weapons used by the Assyrians. Relief from the North Palace at Nineveh.

Left An Assyrian soldier brings in a severed head to be counted with the rest of the booty after a battle in Babylonia. The royal annals recorded the number of enemy dead but it seems that the figures given were not always based on an accurate head count. From the frieze in the Southwest Palace at Nineveh (c. 630– 612 BC).

Above right A cast bronze crescentic axhead dating to about 2400 BC. Axes were attached to wooden hafts and were fixed into slots (and sometimes riveted, as here) or were cast with a hole to take the haft. Height 14 cm, width 7.3 cm.

Right Relief from the Southwest Palace at Nineveh. An Assyrian soldier tugs at the beard of a captive from the Zagros mountains and threatens him with a dagger. The fate of the prisoners varied. Sometimes they were slaughtered; at other times they were deported to work for the king or resettled in distant regions of the empire.

Top Mace heads, dating from the late 3rd millennium BC. The mace was both a weapon and a symbol of authority. Those shown here were probably ceremonial. Length of largest 20 cm.

Above center Daggers like these were found in the Royal Cemetery of Ur dating to about 2500 BC. The blades and hilts were cast separately and then riveted together. Length of the larger 26.1 cm.

Above Nearly 150 flint arrowheads were found at Tell Brak dating to the late 3rd millennium. Although copper and bronze were used for other weapons and tools, flint was cheaper.

THE LAST EMPIRES (626-330 BC)

The resurgence of Babylonia

Between 900 and 681 BC, the year in which the Assyrian king Sennacherib was murdered, 24 kings had sat on the throne of Babylon. Of these, only six are known to have succeeded their fathers. There were at least 15 (and probably as many as 21) changes of dynasty and the rulers included Assyrians and Chaldean tribal leaders as well as Babylonian nobles and officials. Babylonia suffered during this period of instability, as its prosperity depended on the functioning of the canal system, which required a stable and effective government. Esarhaddon's change of policy toward Babylon, followed by the long reigns of Shamash-shum-ukin and Kandalanu, promoted the economic growth of the Babylonian kingdom. Indeed, in the century that followed, Babylonia overtook Assyria as the main grain-producing area of the Near East.

The deaths of Kandalanu, king of Babylon, and of Ashurbanipal, king of Assyria, in about 627 BC were followed by the rise of a Babylonian leader of uncertain origin who took the name Nabopolassar. He ascended the throne of Babylon on 23 November 626 and became the founder of the Neo-Babylonian or Chaldean dynasty. Later traditions stated that he was a Chaldean who had been a governor of the Sealand under the Assyrians, but in his inscriptions Nabopolassar claimed to be a man of the people, "the son of a nobody".

For 10 years Babylonians and Assyrians fought each other in Babylonia. In a period of intense hardship, cities were besieged and changed hands several times. On one occasion citizens of Nippur sold their children into slavery to avoid starvation during a siege. By 616 BC Nabopolassar had established his rule over Babylonia and was ready to threaten the heartland of Assyria. The Babylonians marched up the Euphrates, where they fought and beat an Assyrian army supported by Egyptian allies. They also defeated an Assyrian army in the vicinity of Arrapha.

In 615 the Babylonians attacked Ashur but failed to capture it. In the following year the Medes, led by Cyaxares, attacked the Assyrian capital Nineveh and captured Tarbisu, about 4 kilometers to the north, before marching on Ashur and sacking the city. Nabopolassar arrived after Ashur had fallen and made a treaty of alliance with the Medes. In 612 the Medes together with the Babylonians marched against Nineveh and, after a siege lasting three months in which the Assyrian king Sin-shar-ishkun died, Nineveh fell. The conquerors destroyed the city and looted the temples. They defaced the carvings of the Assyrian kings in the palaces and mutilated the copper head that possibly represented the Akkadian king Naram-Sin (2254–2218 BC). In the temple of Nabu in Kalhu they smashed copies of the loyalty oath sworn by the vassal rulers of western Iran to Esarhaddon and littered the floor with the fragments.

A group of Assyrians fled to Harran, where they held out for a few years with the assistance of the Egyptians, but after 609 BC Assyrian resistance seems to have ended. Indeed, there is no information about what happened in Assyria after 612. Perhaps this was because the administrative records were written on parchment or papyrus rather than on more durable clay tablets, or it might have been because the administrative structure had broken down completely. It is even uncertain whether it was the Babylonians or the Medes who controlled Assyria at that time.

In the following inscription Nabopolassar graphically described his victory over the hated Assyrian enemy.

"I slaughtered the land of Subartu (Assyria), I turned the hostile land into heaps and ruins. The Assyrian, who since distant days had ruled over all the peoples, and with his heavy yoke had brought injury to the people of the Land, his feet from Akkad I turned back, his yoke I threw off."

In the west the Egyptians, who had been allies of Assyria, attempted to take control. In 610 they had come to the aid of the Assyrians and, having defeated and killed Josiah, king of Judah, at Megiddo (c. 609) when he tried to bar their way, established themselves in Carchemish. The Babylonians succeeded in 605 BC in dislodging the Egyptians and annihilated their army in the region of Hama during a campaign led by Nabopolassar's eldest son, the crown prince Nebuchadnezzar.

Jerusalem's destroyer

When Nabopolassar died on 16 August 605 BC, Nebuchadnezzar (Nabu-kudurri-usur, also called Nebuchadrezzar) immediately returned to Babylon where he was crowned on 7 September. For him to have returned so soon both he and the messenger bringing the news must have averaged a remarkable 50 kilometers a day. After his coronation Nebuchadnezzar II resumed his campaign in the west, returning to Babylon to participate in the important New Year festival, which in the Babylonian calendar was held in the spring. In the following years he continued operations in Syria and Palestine and in 601 he attacked Egypt, where he met with resistance. Describing this action, he wrote "in open battle they smote each other and inflicted a major defeat on each other".

In December 598 Nebuchadnezzar left Babylon once more to campaign in the west. He besieged Jerusalem, which had rebelled three years earlier, and on 16 March 597 it fell. King Jehoiachin and many of his subjects were deported to Babylon and Zedekiah was installed as king of Judah in his place. After some years Zedekiah too rebelled. The Babylonians began a siege of Jerusalem which lasted for more than a year. The walls were finally breached in the summer of 587 (or 586) BC and the city surrendered about a month later. Much of Jerusalem may have been destroyed at this time

Babylonia
In the early 1st millennium BC Babylonia was settled by Aramaean tribes. They were later joined by Chaldean tribes who occupied much of the countryside outside the cities. The prosperity of Babylonia increased in the 7th and 6th centuries BC under Assyrian, Neo-Babylonian and Persian rulers, probably as a result of extensive canal-building. The courses of the rivers are not certain and there were many minor watercourses that are not shown on the map.

The Neo-Babylonian kings devoted much of their wealth to the embellishment of the capital city Babylon and the many other ancient holy cities of Babylonia, such as Borsippa and Kutha. A notable enterprise of Nebuchadnezzar II was the construction of two walls made of baked brick and bitumen running between the Euphrates and the Tigris. One lay just north of Sippar and the other ran between Babylon and Kish. Their purpose was to create artificial lakes so as to strengthen the defences of Babylon.

Previous pages Glazed relief brick panel from the Palace of Darius at Susa showing a horned winged lion with eagle's feet.

and more Jews were deported. Nebuchadnezzar appointed governors, but there were more rebellions, which met with further reprisals from the Babylonians and in 582–581 BC led to more deportations. At that time Judah may have been annexed to the province of Samaria.

Nebuchadnezzar's dealings with the Jews were recorded in the Bible, but the details of his relations with other foreign countries are less certain. Elam may have been defeated in 596 BC, the year before Nebuchadnezzar put down a rebellion in Babylonia. Later in his reign there was apparently less need for campaigning though he may have led one more campaign against Egypt. According to

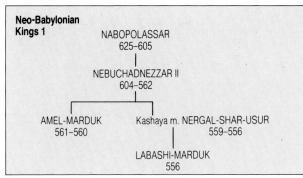

Herodotus, the king of Babylon negotiated a truce between Cyaxares, king of Media, and Alyattes of Lydia in 585. As the Babylonian king was considered a suitable arbitrator, Babylonia probably enjoyed peaceful relations with both Lydia and Media.

Nebuchadnezzar had acquired an empire comparable to that of Assyria and, like the Assyrian kings, he devoted much of the empire's resources to refurbishing his capital city. According to Robert Koldewey (1855–1925), who excavated Babylon before World War I, more than 15 million baked bricks, each about 33 centimeters square and 7 centimeters thick, were used in this venture. Nebuchadnezzar rebuilt Esagila (the Temple of Marduk) and Etemenanki (the ziggurat) as well as many other smaller temples, and he vastly enlarged and refurbished the royal palaces. The famous Hanging Gardens were constructed so that Nebuchadnezzar's wife, the daughter of the Median king Cyaxares, would not miss the mountainous landscape of her homeland. Nebuchadnezzar strengthened the defences of Babylon, surrounding the inner and outer city with walls that enclosed an area of more than 8 square kilometers. He also built two long walls of baked brick with bitumen mortar that stretched between the Euphrates and the Tigris, surrounding the city with water to act as an outer line of defence. The position of the northern wall, later known as the Median wall, has recently been shown to run to the north of Sippar.

Nebuchadnezzar's successors

The succession after the death of Nebuchadnezzar in 562 was a muddled affair. His son Amel-Marduk (called Evil-Merodach in the Bible) ruled only two years, from 561 to 560, and was succeeded by his brother-in-law Nergal-shar-usur (Neriglissar) in 559. He had married a daughter of Nebuchadnezzar and had been present at the destruction of Jerusalem. Nergal-shar-usur ruled for three years (559–556 BC) and was succeeded by his young son Labashi-Marduk, who was murdered in June 556 after only two months on the throne. The conspirators then selected a commoner called Nabonidus to be king of Babylon.

Nabonidus (555–539 BC) was one of the more extraordinary Mesopotamian monarchs—the son of Nabu-balatsu-iqbi, the governor of Harran, and of Adad-guppi, a priestess of the moon god Sin in that city. He loved his mother dearly and when she died in 547 BC, at the age of 104, he had her buried with full royal honors. Nabonidus himself was probably already in his sixties when he came to the throne after years of service to Nebuchadnezzar.

A religious man and great believer in tradition, he appointed his daughter En-nigaldi-Nanna (until

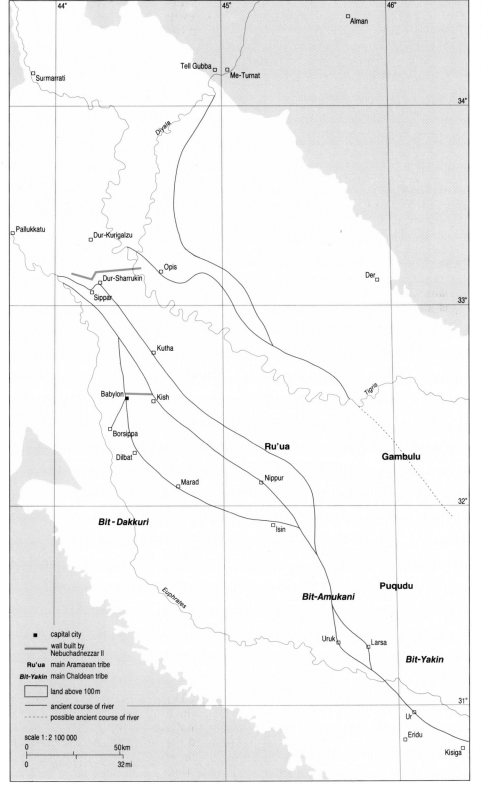

Left Reconstructed glazed brick panel from the façade of the main throne room of the Southern Citadel at Babylon built by Nebuchadnezzar II (604–562 BC). Height 12.4 m.

Right Stele with a relief of a Babylonian king. The inscription records the return of plenty after a drought. The name of the king is missing, but it was probably Nabonidus, as the figure is similar to that of Nabonidus on his stelae found at Harran, with the same symbols carved in front of the king. They are the moon, sun and planet Venus, representing the deities Sin, Shamash and Ishtar, respectively. Height 58 cm, width 46 cm.

recently this name was read as Bel-shalti-Nannar) *entu* priestess of the god Sin in Ur, as Sargon of Agade had done almost 2,000 years earlier. Like his mother he was a devotee of the god Sin, promoting his worship and rebuilding the temples of Sin in Ur and Harran. He also was an antiquarian, who restored the ancient holy places of Sumer and Akkad and, in the course of investigating their foundations, discovered inscriptions and other relics of earlier kings. Nabonidus kept some of the antiquities in a "museum" in the *giparu*, the residence of the *entu* priestess in Ur. These included fragments of a statue of Shulgi (2094–2047 BC), a clay cone of one of the kings of Larsa and a Kassite *kudurru* (stone commemorating a royal land grant).

Early in his reign Nabonidus had a dream in which Marduk or Sin (different gods were mentioned in the inscriptions written by him for Babylonia and for Harran) told him to rebuild the Temple of Sin in Harran which had lain deserted for 54 years. At that time Harran was controlled by the Medes, but, according to Nabonidus, three years later Marduk caused Cyrus, the king of Anshan, or Persia, to defeat the Medes, so that Nabonidus was able to carry out the god's command. Perhaps on account of Nabonidus' preference for Sin of Harran, the priests of Babylonia's holy cities Babylon, Borsippa, Nippur, Uruk, Larsa and Ur objected to Nabonidus' rule and—supposedly, because of their treason—disease and famine struck Babylonia. In response, Nabonidus took himself away from Babylon and went to Taima in northwest Arabia. The precise dates of his

self-imposed exile are not known. In his inscriptions Nabonidus claimed to have been among the Arabs for 10 years, which, according to the Babylonian Chronicle, included the seventh to eleventh years of his reign (549–545 BC).

The reasons for Nabonidus' stay in Taima have been the subject of debate. Later Persian propaganda suggested that Nabonidus was a heretic who ignored the worship of Marduk. In the Bible, according to the Book of Daniel, Nabonidus (called Nebuchadnezzar, perhaps out of a desire that the destroyer of Jerusalem should himself have been destroyed) went mad and ate grass during his seven years of exile. In the Prayer of Nabonidus, found with the Dead Sea Scrolls, he was described as afflicted with malignant boils. Modern scholars have attempted to explain his actions on military, political, commercial, religious or personal grounds. However, it seems equally probable that Nabonidus, as suggested in his own and in Cyrus' inscriptions, and recorded in the Bible, went to Taima because of the interpretation of a dream or omen. Although Nabonidus had left his son Belshar-usur (the Belshazzar of the Bible) as regent in Babylon, the absence of the king meant that the important New Year festival could not be celebrated during the years that he was away.

Babylon's New Year festival

The *akitu* festival, which marked the beginning of the Babylonian year, lasted 11 days. The first five days were spent in preparation, with prayers, incantations, animal sacrifices, and the carving of two small wooden statues decorated with gold and gemstones. On the afternoon of the fourth day there was a recital of the Babylonian Epic of Creation in front of the statue of the god Marduk. It tells the story of the creation of the gods Lahmu and Lahamu from the union of Apsu, the spirit of the fresh waters (male), and Tiamat, the spirit of the salt waters (female). Lahmu and Lahamu, the ancestors of the gods of the Sumero-Babylonian pantheon, disturbed Apsu and Tiamat, who had planned to kill them, but the god Ea put Apsu to sleep and killed him instead. Tiamat, supported by a brood of monsters, attacked the gods, who failed to repulse her until Marduk intervened and agreed to fight her on condition that he was made the gods' leader. When the gods agreed, Marduk, in single combat, killed Tiamat and defeated her army. He split Tiamat's body in two, to form the heavens and the earth and created humankind to do the work that the gods would otherwise have had to do. In gratitude the gods built Babylon and the Temple of Marduk. Based on an earlier myth in which Enlil played the chief role, the epic served to justify Marduk's (and Babylon's) preeminent position. Interestingly, Anu's crown and Enlil's seat were covered during the recitation so as not to offend these gods, whose places had been taken by Marduk.

On the fifth day, the Temple of Marduk underwent a purification ceremony. The god Nabu (represented by his statue) arrived in Babylon from Borsippa and the king entered Esagila, the Temple of Marduk. There, he was stripped of his sword, scepter and other royal insignia. The *urigallu* priest slapped his cheek, pulled his ears and made him prostrate himself before Marduk and swear that he

Neo-Babylonian Kings 2	Nabu-balatsu-iqbi m. Adad-guppi
	NABONIDUS 555–539
Belshazzar	En-nigaldi-Nanna High priestess of Ur

had not sinned or neglected the worship of Marduk or the well-being of Babylon, and had governed justly. The priest then reassured the king before restoring his regalia and slapping him once more. If the king shed tears, it was considered a good omen for the land.

Fewer details are known about the last five days of the festival. On day six the two statuettes that had been made earlier were decapitated in front of Nabu and burned, following which the gods from other cities of Babylonia arrived in Babylon. On the ninth day the king entered Marduk's shrine and "took his hand". The meaning of this phrase is not known, but some scholars think that this was the occasion for a sacred marriage between the king, acting the part of the god, and a priestess. The gods then went by chariot along the Processional Way to the *akitu* temple to the north of the city where, on day 10, they received gifts from the king—Nabonidus claimed to have given more than 5 talents (150 kilograms) of gold and 100 talents of silver (3 tonnes). On the 11th day the gods were taken back to Esagila for a banquet, before returning to their cities.

Nabonidus came back from Taima to Babylon at some time between 544 and 540 BC. During his years of exile the balance of power in the Near East had changed radically. At the beginning of his reign the region was divided between four main powers—the Egyptians, the Lydians, the Babylonians and the Medes—as it had been since the collapse of Assyria. When he returned, the Medes and Lydians had been absorbed into the Persian empire. Within five years, Babylon itself was to fall to the Persians, and Egypt fifteen years later.

The rise and fall of Lydia

After Cyaxares' victory over the Assyrians in 614, the Medes invaded Anatolia. Urartu must have fallen to the Medes by 590 BC, as Cyaxares was by then fighting against Alyattes, king of Lydia. Alyattes was the great-grandson of Gyges and was credited by Herodotus with defeating the Cimmerian tribes who had been ravishing his country for much of the previous century. Fighting between the Medes and the Lydians continued for some five years. On the afternoon of 28 May 585 there was a total eclipse of the sun. According to Herodotus, both armies were so alarmed by this omen that they broke off fighting, which resulted in a peace negotiated between them by Syennesis of Cilicia and Labynetus of Babylon, who acted as mediators. Herodotus referred to both Nabonidus and a previous king of Babylon as Labynetus, but in this account he probably meant Nebuchadnezzar. Alyattes gave his daughter in marriage to Astyages, the son of Cyaxares, and the border between the Lydians and the Medes was established as the Halys river (Kizil Irmak). The burial mound of Alyattes in the royal cemetery, 6 kilometers north of the Lydian capital Sardis, is said to be the largest tumulus from the ancient world.

Part of the prosperity of the Lydians was due to the gold found in the region, giving rise to the proverbial wealth of Alyattes' son Croesus. The Lydians have also been credited with the invention of coinage. Throughout the Near East precious and base metals, particularly silver and copper, had served as currency to facilitate the exchange of

Left Vase with Red Figure painting of Croesus dating to early 5th century. The fate of Croesus is uncertain. He may have committed suicide by being burned on a funeral pyre, but Herodotus recorded that a rainstorm put out the flames and Cyrus spared his life. This painting is attributed to the painter Myson and was found at Vulci in Etruria. Height of vase 58.5 cm.

Below top Silver coin with the heads of a lion and bull, originally thought to have been minted under Croesus. More recently it has been suggested that such coins are from the early years of the reign of Darius I (521–486 BC).

Below bottom A gold *daric* named after Darius I in whose reign these coins were first minted. These "archers" (as the coins were known), paid as bribes, often proved more effective than the Persian army in maintaining the peace and stability of the empire. Darics continued to be minted under Alexander and his successors. This example probably dates to the 4th century BC.

goods. Sometimes metal ingots or rings were made to a standard weight, such as the silver bar ingots found in a 7th-century BC hoard from Tepe Nush-i Jan in Media, or the circular silver ingot inscribed with the name of Bar-rakib, an 8th-century ruler of Sam'al in the Levant, which weighed almost exactly 1 mina (497 grams).

The earliest coins to be stamped with a device to guarantee their quality and weight were found in the foundations of the Temple of Artemis at Ephesus. They were made of electrum (a natural alloy of gold and silver), which occurs in the gravels of the river Pactolus flowing through Sardis. Some of these coins had striated surfaces while others bore emblems such as a lion's head. One carried an inscription in Lydian. There is some disagreement over the date of these coins, and over whether coinage was invented in the middle of the 7th century BC or by Alyattes or Croesus in the 6th century.

Under Croesus Lydia extended its dominion over the Greek cities of the Aegean coast. When Croesus heard of the defeat of the Medes by the Persians, he saw his opportunity to extend his kingdom to the east into territory previously controlled by the Medes. Before setting out he consulted the Oracle at Delphi, which foretold that if he attacked he would destroy a great empire. Croesus, believing that the empire referred to was the Persian empire, not his own, crossed the Halys river to do battle. His army encountered the Persians led by Cyrus at Pteria (Hattusas) but the battle ended in a stalemate. Croesus retired to Sardis, planning to renew the campaign with his allies after the winter, but Cyrus pursued him and captured Sardis (perhaps in the fall of 547 BC) after a short siege.

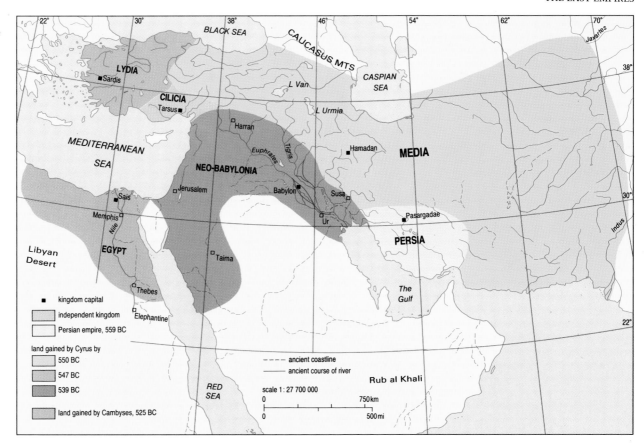

Medes and Persians

In the Biblical and Greek worlds the Medes were closely associated with the Persians, both being tribes of Indo-Iranians who spoke related languages. At the time of the Assyrian empire the Medes were settled in the fertile valleys through which the main route onto the Iranian plateau passed. A group of Persians were neighbors of the Medes in the central Zagros, and another group lived in the area of ancient Anshan in the modern province of Fars. Indeed, a king of Parsuash (Persia) who submitted to Ashurbanipal (668–c. 627 BC) after his victories over Elam had the same name as Cyrus (Kurash), the later king of Persia and Anshan.

The sack of Nineveh in 612 BC brought territorial gains to Cyaxares, the king of the Medes, as well as an immense booty. However, as the Median royal palace at Hamadan has not been excavated and the archives of the Median court still have to be discovered, evidence of how the Medes came to dominate most of Iran and much of Anatolia can be traced only in the occasional references in foreign sources and in later accounts. A fortress at Tell Gubba in the Hamrin region and a building with columned halls at Tille Huyuk on the Euphrates in southern Turkey have been attributed to the Medes, but their precise dates are not known. Soon after the peace treaty with Lydia, Astyages, the son of Cyaxares, became king and ruled for about 35 years. The fact that he is hardly mentioned in western sources may have been because he was occupied with the extensive Median conquests on the Iranian plateau.

The defeat of Babylon

In about 559 BC Cyrus, who was later known as Cyrus the Great, became ruler of the Persians. Many later legends were associated with his birth, but in his inscriptions he claimed that he was the son of Cambyses, the grandson of Cyrus and a descendant of Teispes, all of whom had been kings of Anshan. A seal impression confirming Cyrus' genealogy has been found at Persepolis, inscribed in Elamite with the name Cyrus of Anshan, son of Teispes. According to Herodotus, the Persians were vassals of the Medes until Cyrus persuaded them to rebel. Nabonidus stated that Cyrus defeated the Medes in his third year (553 BC), but, according to the usually reliable Babylonian Chronicle, the Median king Astyages attacked Cyrus in Nabonidus' sixth year (c. 550 BC). Apparently, the Median army refused to fight and handed Astyages over to Cyrus, who then marched to Hamadan where he emptied the treasury and took the contents back to Anshan. Cyrus thus inherited the Median kingdom, which stretched from the borders of Lydia to the Iranian plateau.

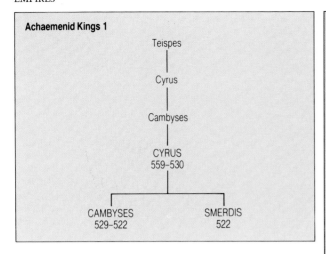

Achaemenid Kings 1

Teispes

Cyrus

Cambyses

CYRUS
559–530

CAMBYSES
529–522

SMERDIS
522

In the years following the defeat of Croesus of Lydia in 547, Median generals appointed by Cyrus led Persian forces to subjugate the coastal cities and islands of Ionia, Caria and Lycia. In 539 Cyrus moved against Babylon and in late September or early October defeated the Babylonian army at Opis. Sippar was captured without a fight on 10 October and two days later the Persian army led by Ugbaru, the governor of Gutium to the east of the Tigris, entered Babylon unopposed. His troops surrounded the Temple of Marduk but ensured that the religious services taking place there were not interrupted. Nabonidus was taken prisoner but, according to a later tradition, Cyrus appointed him governor of Carmania, in southern Iran. Belshazzar's fate is uncertain. Cyrus entered Babylon on 29 October and Ugbaru died a week later. In the following months the gods whom Nabonidus had earlier brought to Babylon from other Babylonian cities were returned to their sanctuaries.

The benevolent conqueror
Cyrus left behind a reputation as a benevolent monarch. Nabonidus early in his reign stated that Cyrus was the servant of Marduk. In his own inscriptions Cyrus claimed that, after the heresy of Nabonidus, Marduk chose him to be ruler of all the world and that, when he entered Babylon,

"all the inhabitants of Babylon, as well as of the entire country of Sumer and Akkad, princes and governors, bowed to him [Cyrus] and kissed his feet, jubilant that he had received the kingship, and with shining faces happily greeted him as a master through whose help they had come to life from death and had all been spared damage and disaster, and they worshiped his name."

Cyrus was considered by the Jews as a savior, an agent of Jehovah, delivering them from captivity and allowing them to rebuild their temple in Jerusalem. Even among the Greeks Cyrus was held up as a model ruler. Cyrus' conquests and reputation were aided by propaganda. The stories about the vicious behavior of Astyages, who was alleged to have first ordered the death of the infant Cyrus and then forced Cyrus' protector Harpagus to eat his own son, of the folly of Croesus in misinterpreting the Delphic oracle, and of the blasphemy of Nabonidus might not have been true but they certainly aided the cause of Cyrus and his supporters. Similarly, the genealogy that made Cyrus' mother the daughter of Astyages and niece of Croesus lent

Pasargadae

After Cyrus the Great (559–530 BC) had conquered Media and Lydia, he founded a new city at Pasargadae where, according to one story, he had fought the final battle against the Medes. As the Persians had no tradition of monumental buildings or of stone sculpture, Cyrus drew on the talents of the peoples he had conquered. Lydian stonemasons, in particular played an important role in the construction of the city.

Over the Morghab plain, Cyrus built a fortified citadel, a sacred precinct with a fire altar, a tower in the form of a double cube, now called Zendan-i Suleiman (the Prison of Solomon), a garden with palaces and pavilions, a gatehouse and his own tomb. When Darius usurped the throne from Cyrus' branch of the Achaemenid clan, he built his palaces at Persepolis, 40 kilometers to the southwest of Pasargadae. He chose Susa as the capital of his world empire and as a result Pasargadae lost its importance.

Below Unlike the earlier architecture of the Near East, the palaces and pavilions built by Cyrus at Pasargadae were structures that were open to the outside. Columned porticoes allowed access into the buildings from all sides, taking maximum advantage of their garden setting. Today all that remains of the garden are the stone channels that led water from one small stone basin to another. Trees and water are still the main feature of Persian gardens.

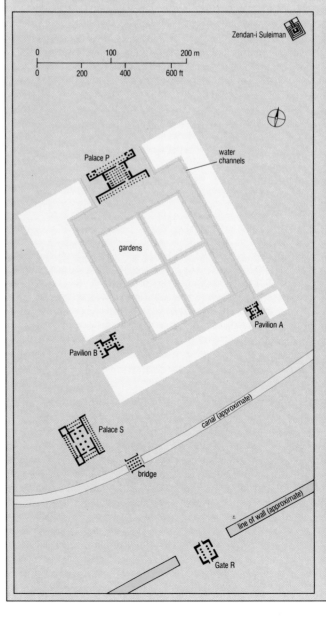

Right Palace P had a rectangular columned hall with finely worked horizontally fluted column bases and plain columns. The upper part of the columns may have been completed in timber covered by painted plaster. The stonework was inspired by the eastern Greek work and has close parallels at Ephesus. A long columned portico looked over the gardens. The columned halls of Pasargadae were derived from Median architecture, but the origin of the porticoes is less certain: they may have come from the Greek world or from a native Iranian tradition. The Pasargadae plan was adapted to form the standard plan for the palaces at Persepolis.

Left Cyrus' tomb is a simple gabled building set on a stepped platform and was once about 10 m high. According to one account, there was an inscription on the tomb that read "O man, I am Cyrus, who founded the empire of the Persians and was king of Asia. Grudge me not therefore this monument."

Above Figure on a side door of Gate R. Above it, "I, Cyrus, an Achaemenid" was carved in three languages. The combination of Assyrian-style wings with an Elamite garment and Egyptian headdress is typical of later Achaemenid art, which borrowed motifs from all over the empire.

legitimacy to his rule over Media and Lydia. Cyrus even managed to find supporters among the ranks of his opponents, and his victories were achieved by diplomacy as often as by military action. Moreover, he allowed considerable religious freedom to his subjects and did not impose unduly harsh taxes or tribute (perhaps the lavish treasures accumulated in Hamadan, Sardis and Babylon sufficed for a ruler who came from a mountain tribe and was unaccustomed to world dominion). Certainly his capital, built at Pasargadae with the use of Lydian craftsmen, was modest when compared with the extravagant edifices of the Babylonian and Assyrian kings. Cyrus died in the summer of 530 BC, possibly while fighting against nomadic tribes in Central Asia, and was buried in a gabled stone tomb at Pasargadae. The vast Persian empire passed peacefully into the hands of his son Cambyses.

The conquest of Egypt

Cambyses had accompanied his father in his conquest of Babylon and participated in the Babylonian New Year festival for 538 BC. For the first 10 months of that year he bore the title King of Babylon, but later did not use the title even though he resided in Babylonia.

As king of Persia (529–522 BC) his greatest military achievement was the conquest of Egypt in 525 BC. When the pharaoh Amasis died in 526, after more than 40 years on the throne, his son who replaced him was defeated in battle at Pelusium, after being betrayed by one of his chief officials, Udjahorresne of Sais. Cambyses was crowned pharaoh and acted like a native-born Egyptian ruler, even undertaking the religious duties of the pharaoh. However, he gained the reputation of being a crazed, tyrannical despot, perhaps as a result of slanders by Egyptian priests who opposed his attempts to reduce the power and wealth of the temples and by his successors who wished to justify their seizure of the throne.

The accession of Darius

Cambyses left Egypt in 522 but died before he reached Persia. Darius, his successor (521–486 BC), gave an account of the circumstances surrounding Cambyses' death, and how he himself assumed the throne, in a long inscription carved in Old Persian, Babylonian, and Elamite cuneiform on the rock of Bisutun overlooking the main route from Babylon to Hamadan. The story was translated and sent all over the empire (copies have been found in Babylon and at Elephantine in southern Egypt) and a version of it was incorporated into Herodotus' *Histories*.

Achaemenid Kings 2

Achaemenes
|
Teispes
|
Ariaramnes
|
Arsames
|
Hystaspes
|
DARIUS I
521–486
|
XERXES I
485–465
|
— ARTAXERXES I   Darius
464–425
|
XERXES II   SOGDIANUS   DARIUS II
424   424   423–405
|
ARTAXERXES II   Cyrus   Ostanes
404–359 |
| Arsanes
ARTAXERXES III |
358–338 |
| |
ARSES   DARIUS III
337–336   335–330

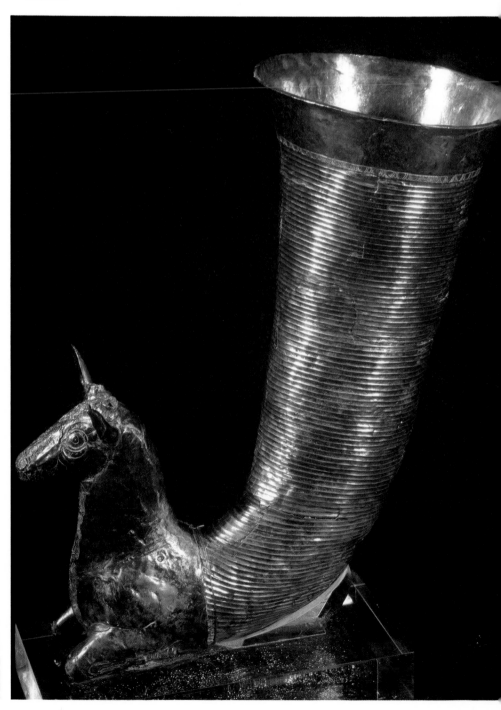

Above The upper section of the column capitals found at Susa consisted of the foreparts of two bulls placed together. The main beam would have rested on the backs of the animals. Below the bulls is a double volute (spiral scroll) loosely based on Ionic columns and beneath this a floral element inspired by Egyptian column capitals.

Left Silver drinking vessel with traces of gold leaf ending in the foreparts of an animal, perhaps a deer. Although vessels of this type (called rhytons) were not depicted on the reliefs of Persepolis, they are shown on Greek vases of the late 5th century BC and continued to be used after the end of the Achaemenid period. Height 20 cm.

According to Darius, Cambyses had secretly murdered his own brother Smerdis (Bardiya) before he went to Egypt. A *magus* (Median priest) called Gaumata, posing as Smerdis, seized the throne in his absence and was acknowledged as king by the people of Persia, Media and the other provinces. Cambyses, Darius claimed, committed suicide and no-one dared resist Gaumata until Darius with six conspirators slew him on 29 September 522. Evidently, Darius' account is fabricated. It is more likely that Smerdis rebelled while his brother was in Egypt and that Cambyses, on his return, died or was killed. Thus it was the real Smerdis, not some impostor, who was murdered by Darius and the other Persian nobles.

Darius, whose father Hystaspes, the governor of Parthia, and grandfather were still alive when he became king was clearly not in the direct line of succession. In the Bisutun inscription he traced his ancestry back through five generations to his great-great-grandfather Teispes and great-great-great-grandfather Achaemenes, asserting that from long ago kings had come from his family. According to Herodotus, the rulers of the Persians came from the Achaemenid clan of the Pasargadae tribe. The inscriptions at Pasargadae in the name of Cyrus (some think they may have been carved by Darius, as he claimed to have invented the Old Persian cuneiform script) confirm that Cyrus was an Achaemenid.

After the death of Smerdis, rebellions had broken out in Persia, Elam, Media, Assyria, Egypt, Parthia, Margiana, Sattagydia and Scythia, but within a year Darius had quelled them all. The relief accompanying the inscription of Bisutun recorded his triumph over Gaumata the impostor and over nine other rebels who claimed to be kings. Thereafter he took steps to eliminate opposition to his rule. Darius was already married to the daughter of Gobryas, one of the seven conspirators, but he also married the daughter of Otanes, like himself an Achaemenid and the most senior of the conspirators. This daughter had been in the harems of both Cambyses and Smerdis, which Darius had taken over. In addition, he married the surviving female descendants of Cyrus—two daughters and a granddaughter—to strengthen his claim to the throne.

Darius' European campaigns

Darius extended Persian conquests into Europe, occupying parts of Thrace and campaigning against the Scythians across the Danube. He also added the

22°   26°   30°   34°   38°   42°

SKUDRA

COLCHIS
gift of 25 boys
and 25 girls

BLACK SEA

□ Dascylium

XII
IONIA
vessels, cloth

2

VI
LYDIA
vessels, arm-rings,
chariot

Sardis □

3

IX
CAPPADOCIA
horse, clothing

Kizil Irmak

13

19

L. Van

18

XXI
CARIA
shield, spear,
chariot

1

4
CILICIA
360 white horses

III
ARMENIA
horse, vessel

L. Urmia

Cyprus

Aleppo □

VIII
ASSYRIA
vessels, ingot/hide,
cloth, rams
250 eunuchs

9

Tigris

Orontes

5

MEDITERRANEAN SEA

Euphrates

Babylon □

XXII
LIBYA
goat, chariot

Jerusalem □

DEAD
SEA

Syrian Desert

V
BABYLONI
vessels, cloth
bull
250 eunuchs

6

Memphis □

XX
ARABIA
cloth, camel

gift of 1000 talents
of frankincense

An Nafud

Nile

X
EGYPT
cloth, bull

Persian heartland

independent kingdom, 500 BC

ELAM   region paying tribute to Darius, 500 BC

delegation number on relief at Persepolis
relating to region

XII   clear identification

VII   probable identification

cloth   gift brought by delegation

tribute paid in talents of silver according to
Herodotus' list

150–349

350–599

600–1000

boys   other tribute

Herodotus' satrapy boundary
(approximate)

12   Herodotus' satrapy number

canal built by Darius, 500 BC

ancient coastline

ancient course of river

scale 1 : 9 200 000

0   300km

0   200mi

XXIII
NUBIA

vessel, elephant tusk,
okapi/giraffe

gifts of unrefined gold,
100 logs of ebony,
10 elephant tusks

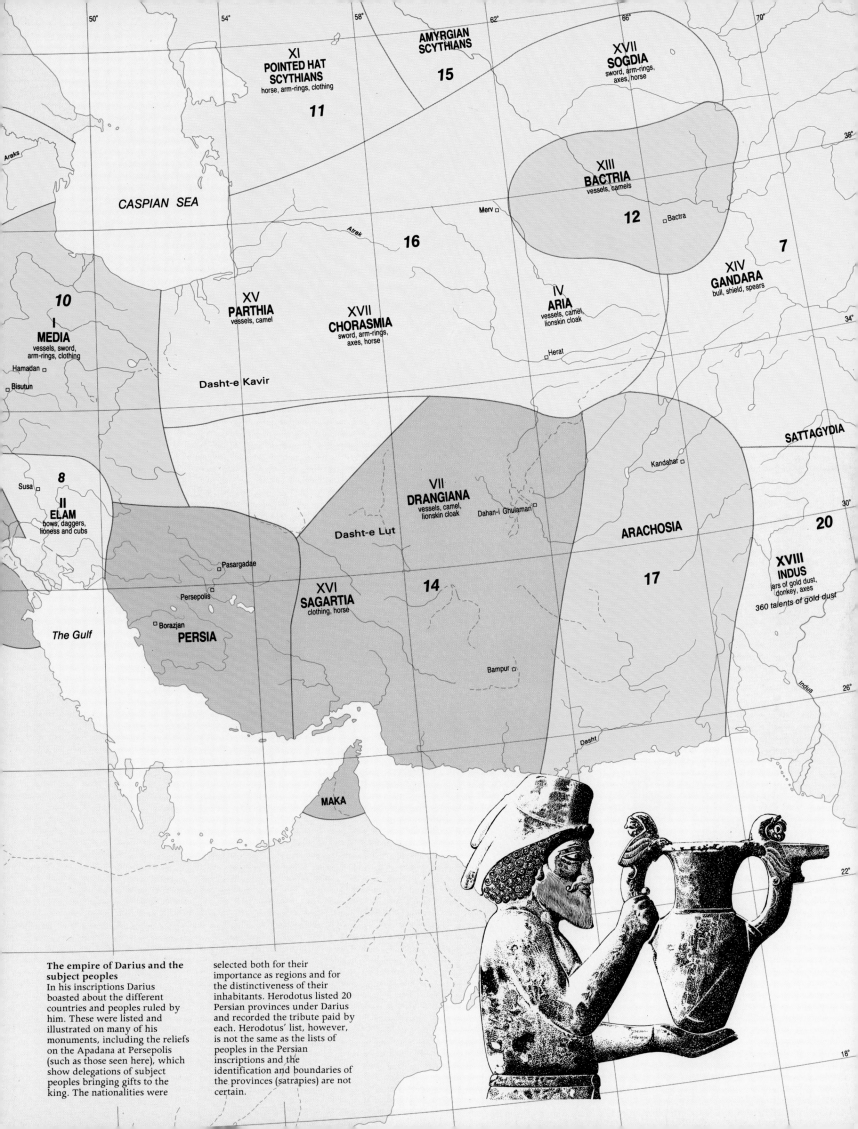

XI
**POINTED HAT
SCYTHIANS**
horse, arm-rings, clothing

11

**AMYRGIAN
SCYTHIANS**

15

XVII
SOGDIA
sword, arm-rings,
axes, horse

XIII
BACTRIA
vessels, camels

12

□ Bactra

7

XIV
GANDARA
bull, shield, spears

CASPIAN SEA

Merv □

Atrak

16

10

I
MEDIA
vessels, sword,
arm-rings, clothing

Hamadan □

□ Bisutun

XV
PARTHIA
vessels, camel

XVII
CHORASMIA
sword, arm-rings,
axes, horse

IV
ARIA
vessels, camel,
lionskin cloak

Herat □

34°

Dasht-e Kavir

SATTAGYDIA

Kandahar □

8

II
ELAM
bows, daggers,
lioness and cubs

Susa □

VII
DRANGIANA
vessels, camel,
lionskin cloak

Dahan-i Ghulaman □

ARACHOSIA

20

Dasht-e Lut

□ Pasargadae

17

XVIII
INDUS
jars of gold dust,
donkey, axes

360 talents of gold dust

□ Persepolis

XVI
SAGARTIA
clothing, horse

14

The Gulf

□ Borazjan

PERSIA

Bampur □

Dasht

MAKA

Indus

Araks

50°   54°   58°   62°   66°   70°
38°
30°
26°
22°
18°

**The empire of Darius and the
subject peoples**
In his inscriptions Darius
boasted about the different
countries and peoples ruled by
him. These were listed and
illustrated on many of his
monuments, including the reliefs
on the Apadana at Persepolis
(such as those seen here), which
show delegations of subject
peoples bringing gifts to the
king. The nationalities were
selected both for their
importance as regions and for
the distinctiveness of their
inhabitants. Herodotus listed 20
Persian provinces under Darius
and recorded the tribute paid by
each. Herodotus' list, however,
is not the same as the lists of
peoples in the Persian
inscriptions and the
identification and boundaries of
the provinces (satrapies) are not
certain.

Susa

The city of Susa was founded in about 4000 BC as a religious center and from at least the third millennium BC it was the capital of Elam. The territory of Elam included the alluvial plains of Khuzistan in southwestern Iran, and sometimes stretched into the mountains to the east to the city of Anshan and beyond. Susa was subject to the kings of Agade (c. 2250) and to the rulers of the Third Dynasty of Ur (c. 2050). In the following millennium, Elamite armies invaded Mesopotamia and ravaged the cities of Babylonia and Assyria, taking some of the finest Mesopotamian monuments back to Susa as trophies of war.

In the first millennium BC Elamite interference in Babylonia angered the Assyrian kings. After many campaigns, Ashurbanipal (668–c. 627 BC) captured Susa in about 647 BC. He burned the city, destroyed the temples and sacred groves, and plowed the fields with salt. In the late 6th century BC Darius I chose Susa as his administrative capital. On the Apadana mound, he built a huge palace which combined the Babylonian courtyard plan with a vast columned hall with porticoes.

Susa was captured by Alexander the Great in 331 BC and it was here, during that campaign, that a mass wedding between Greek soldiers and Persian brides took place in an attempt to merge the Hellenistic and Asiatic cultures. Susa remained an important city long after the fall of the Persian empire, and the Tomb of Daniel, to the west of the Acropolis, is still a major site of pilgrimage.

Above Headless statue of Darius I found in the gatehouse of the Apadana palace. It was carved in Egypt and brought to Susa, probably by boat through the canal, which Darius completed, from the Nile to the Red Sea. The statue is in the Achaemenid court style and has inscriptions in four languages—Old Persian, Babylonian, Elamite and Egyptian—carved on the folds. Surviving height of figure 1.95 m.

Above right Part of the facade, made of molded baked bricks, belonging to a Temple of Inshushinak, the patron deity of Susa. It was built by Kutir-Nahhunte and his son Shilhak-Inshushinak in the mid-12th century BC. The bricks were found reused in a water channel of the Achaemenid period near the palace of Darius. Molded brick panels were used for architectural ornament in the Old Babylonian period and for relief decoration in Kassite times. Reconstructed height 1.37 m.

Below In 1851 W. K. Loftus, a British geologist, explored Susa and identified it with Shushan, the palace mentioned in the Books of Daniel and Esther in the Bible. Since then, French archeologists have excavated at Susa, removing all the later levels of the Acropolis mound, which was the main religious center of the city, and enriching the Louvre Museum and later the Tehran Museum with their finds. The Achaemenid city occupied the three main mounds: the Apadana, the Acropolis and the Royal City. The Artisans' Town mound to the east was the site of the city after the Achaemenid period.

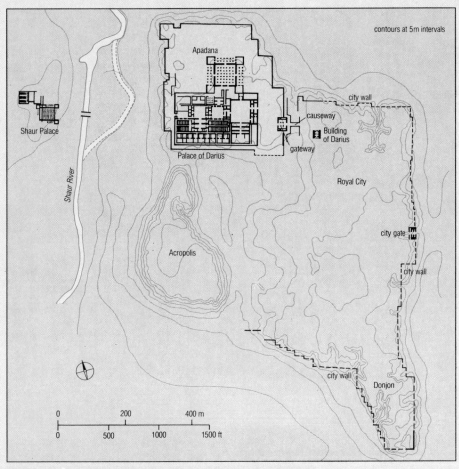

Far left and left Glazed brick reliefs and detail from the palace of Darius. According to one of the foundation inscriptions, the baked bricks were worked by the Babylonians. Glazed brick reliefs were used extensively in Babylon, but they also had a long history in Elam. These archers were probably part of the king's Persian bodyguard. Because the Elamites and Persians wore a similar dress they were sometimes identified as Elamite. Height of archer 1.46 m.

Right This gold figure of a man carrying a baby goat is one of a pair (the other is made of silver) found on the pavement of a ruined tomb near the Temple of Inshushinak on the Acropolis mound and may have been part of a votive offering. It dates to the end of the 2nd millennium BC, perhaps the 12th century. Height 7.5 cm.

211

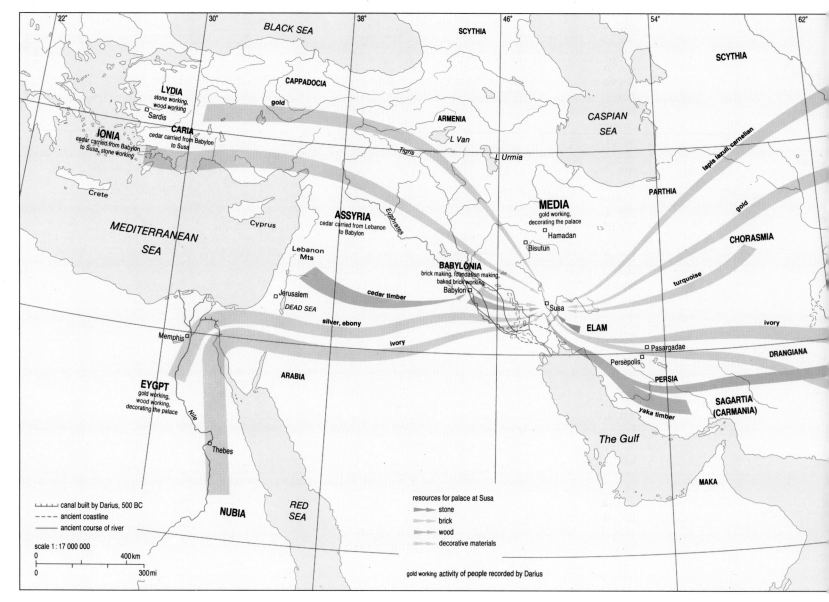

canal built by Darius, 500 BC
ancient coastline
ancient course of river

scale 1:17 000 000

0   400km
0   300mi

resources for palace at Susa
stone
brick
wood
decorative materials

gold working activity of people recorded by Darius

province of the Indus to his empire. Whereas Cyrus had been content to take over the existing administrative structure of the conquered regions, Darius reorganized the empire into a system of provinces, called satrapies, each ruled by a governor, or satrap, who was normally a close associate or a relative of the king. Darius also established a regular system of taxation and tribute and possibly instituted legal and economic reforms, in particular in Egypt.

The successful administration of the empire depended on good communications. Herodotus' description of the Royal Road between Sardis and Susa, with regular relay stations where spare mounts were available, is almost identical to the Assyrian system introduced two centuries earlier. Tablets found at Persepolis and dating to the time of Darius include authorizations issued to travelers on the king's business.

In 499 BC the Greek subjects of the Persian king in Cyprus and along the Aegean coast joined together and rebelled, sacking and burning the satrapal capital of Sardis. Cyprus, which had become subject to the Persians at the time of the conquest of Egypt, was quickly reconquered with the help of the Phoenicians, but the struggle in the Aegean lasted longer. The decisive battle took place off the island of Lade, near Miletus, in the fall

of 494. With 600 ships the Persian fleet, requisitioned from the Phoenicians, Egyptians, Cilicians and Cypriots, easily outnumbered the opposing Greek force made up of contingents from nine cities and containing only 353 ships. Seduced by Persian promises of leniency for those who submitted, some of the Greek ships sailed away, allowing the Persians to inflict a heavy defeat on the remainder.

Once the Greeks in Asia were under their control, the Persians turned their attention to the Greeks on the other side of the Aegean. Persia already controlled the coast of Thrace and its position there was strengthened by a campaign led by Mardonius, the son of Gobryas, in 492. However, after landing successfully the Persians were defeated by the Athenians at Marathon, and failed to take Athens from the sea when the Athenians quickly returned to defend the coast. After that the invasion was called off.

Darius' building program

Darius chose the ancient Elamite city of Susa as his capital, though he had palaces at Babylon, Hamadan and in the Persian homeland. Early in his reign he rebuilt Susa and constructed a palace some 250 meters square. It combined a series of courtyards, similar to the ones at Babylon, with columned halls

The building of the palace at Susa
In the foundation inscriptions for his palace at Susa, Darius listed the people and the materials involved in its construction. The intention of the list was not to provide an accurate record of how the palace was built but to indicate the contribution made by the whole empire and demonstrate the immense resources at the command of the Persian king. The organization of the work is indicated by the tablets from Persepolis, which record contingents of workers under Persian supervisors receiving rations from the royal treasury. Many of the workers were slaves, prisoners of war or deportees. The design and architectural decoration of Persian palaces represented a synthesis of the artistic traditions of different regions of the empire.

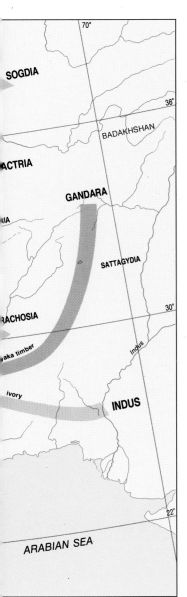

like those at Pasargadae and in Media. This palace became the principal residence of the Persian kings. Forty kilometers southwest of Pasargadae, Darius built a new royal residence, which in Old Persian was called Parsa but it is now known as Persepolis. The high citadel, about 450 meters long by 300 meters wide, formed part of a vast complex commissioned by Darius, which included many small palaces spread across the plain. The construction of Persepolis was not completed during Darius' lifetime but continued into the reigns of his son and grandson.

Darius and his successors were buried in rock-cut tombs some 6 kilometers north of the palace, at Naqsh-i Rustam. Darius' tomb bears a remarkable carved inscription in which he summarized his beliefs: he had been made king by Ahuramazda, the creator of the world; he was a friend to good and an enemy to evil; he protected the weak from the strong and also the strong from the weak; he desired what was right; he was a good horseman, a good archer and a good spearman. Darius further commanded the reader to follow the commands of Ahuramazda, to believe these inscriptions and not to rise in rebellion.

To build Persepolis and Susa Darius brought both materials and workers from all over the empire. As the Persians had no tradition of palace building, he also borrowed motifs and designs from different regions, and the influences of Egypt, Greece and particularly of Mesopotamia are apparent in the buildings and their decoration. Monuments commissioned by Darius in Egypt also had a similar mixture of styles, including a larger than life-size statue of the king found at Susa but which, according to the inscriptions, had been carved in Egypt. It had probably been brought by sea from Egypt through the canal, which Darius completed, leading from the Nile to the Red Sea.

Persian defeats

In 486 BC Egypt rebelled, but Darius died before the rebellion could be put down and the crown prince Xerxes became king. Xerxes was not Darius' eldest son but he was the first son born after Darius had become king. His mother was Atossa, the daughter of Cyrus, who, before becoming Darius' wife, had been married to Cambyses and Smerdis. According to Herodotus, Atossa had exercised great influence over Darius, presaging the harem intrigues that later dogged the succession of Achaemenid rulers, though in Xerxes' case his claim to the throne was not challenged.

Early in Xerxes' reign (485–465 BC) he put down two rebellions in Babylonia and another in Egypt. Most of what is known about Xerxes has come from his enemy, the Greeks, and concerns his unsuccessful invasion of Greece. Herodotus recounts how, after years of preparation, Xerxes led an army numbering almost two million men across the Dardanelles on bridges formed by boats. To avoid a repetition of the disaster of 12 years earlier, when a Persian fleet had sunk in a storm off Mount Athos, Xerxes had a canal dug through the promontory. The Persians marched victoriously south, easily overcoming the brave but ineffectual opposition of the Spartans at the pass of Thermopylae. Xerxes took Athens but while he "looked on from under a golden canopy", the Greek navy

defeated the Persian fleet at the battle of Salamis. With the approach of winter, the Persian army abandoned Athens and went into winter quarters in northern Greece while Xerxes returned to the east, leaving his experienced general Mardonius to carry on the war. The following year Mardonius again marched south and recaptured Athens, but shortly afterward he was killed at the battle of Plataea and his army heavily defeated. In August 479 the Greeks again routed the Persian army, at Mycale on the mainland opposite the island of Samos, causing plans to invade Greece to be abandoned.

These defeats inflicted by the Greeks were no mean achievement even though blunders by the Persian commanders and lack of resolve had been contributory factors. Greece was, in any case, peripheral to Persia's main interests and the rest of the empire remained intact and at peace under the rule of the Persian king. The battles of Salamis, Plataea and Mycale marked a turning point in the relations between the Greeks and the Persians. The Persian army was no longer invincible and the Persian navy no longer ruled the seas. During the next decades Persia lost its territories in Europe and the Greek cities in western Turkey effectively gained their independence.

Palace and harem intrigues

Xerxes died in 465 BC. According to Ctesias, a Greek doctor at the Persian court some 60 years later, he was murdered by three of his courtiers including the *hazarapat*, or grand vizier, and his eunuch chamberlain. After accusing Xerxes' eldest son Darius of the murder, the conspirators persuaded another son, Artaxerxes I, to kill Darius and become king. Twenty years later in 425, when Artaxerxes died, three of his sons occupied the throne in quick succession, as the first two were murdered after only a few months of their reigns. The third son, called Ochus, whose mother was a Babylonian concubine, took the throne name Darius II (423–405 BC). Together with his wife Parysatis, who was a daughter of Artaxerxes by another concubine, he eliminated all opposition within the court. Their eldest son was Arsaces but their favorite son was Cyrus, who was made satrap in Sardis. When Darius died, Arsaces became king, taking the name Artaxerxes II (404–359 BC). At about this time Egypt rebelled and gained its independence. In 401 BC Cyrus, at the head of an army that included 10,000 Greek mercenaries, marched through Turkey and down the Euphrates to challenge Artaxerxes II, but his cause was lost when he was killed at the battle of Cunaxa in northern Babylonia. Cyrus' Greek mercenaries were left stranded in the middle of the Persian empire. The epic story of their march north through Assyria and Armenia to the Black Sea and from there to Greece was recorded by Xenophon, who was one of the leaders of the 10,000.

Artaxerxes II was reputed to have had 360 concubines and to have fathered 115 sons. His eldest son conspired against him and was put to death after being betrayed by a eunuch. The next son was persuaded by his brother Ochus that his father was displeased with him and he committed suicide by drinking poison. Artaxerxes II died in 359 and Ochus became king, taking the name Artaxerxes III

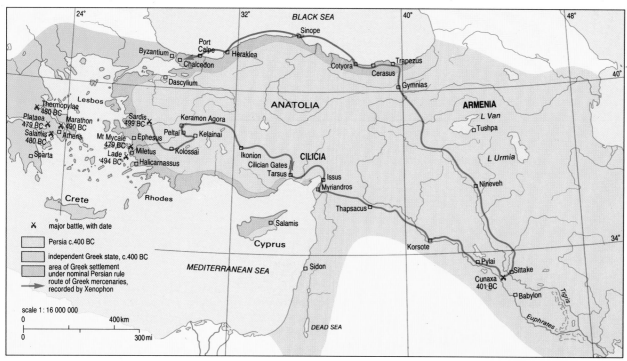

Persia and the Greeks
Under Darius I and Xerxes I the Persians attempted to conquer the independent Greek city states. Yet, despite the overwhelming superiority of Persian land forces, they failed. First at Marathon and then at Salamis and Plataea, the Persians were defeated by a Greek confederation led by the Athenians.

In 401 BC Cyrus the Younger, the satrap (provincial governor) and brother of the Persian king Artaxerxes II, rebelled. Among the troops under Cyrus' command was a contingent of 10,000 Greek foot soldiers. Cyrus marched through Anatolia and Cilicia and then followed the Euphrates down toward Babylon, where he was defeated and killed at the battle of Cunaxa. The Greek mercenaries, rather than surrender, fought their way back to Greek territory by marching almost due north to reach the Black Sea. The details of this march were recorded by Xenophon, who was one of the Greek generals.

(358–338 BC). Immediately, he killed off any of his relatives who might have laid claim to the throne. He faced serious revolts in the west but he survived them and in 343 BC even managed to recapture Egypt. However, five years later, Bagoas, the chief eunuch and commander of the Persian forces in Egypt, murdered Artaxerxes and made his son Arses (337–336 BC) king in his place. Arses attempted to remove Bagoas but he himself was poisoned after less than two years on the throne. Bagoas then made Darius, a second cousin of Arses, king, as all the relatives with a better claim to the throne had already been killed. The new king Darius III (335–330 BC) forced Bagoas to drink poison and then set about restoring the empire.

The end of the ancient Near East
In the first year of his reign, Darius invaded Egypt, which had again rebelled after the death of Arta-

xerxes III, but it was too late to save the Persian empire. Sixty years earlier Xenophon had observed that "whereas the king's empire was strong in that it covered a vast territory with large numbers of people, it also was weak because of the need to travel great distances and the wide distribution of its forces, making it vulnerable to a swift attack". And so it proved to be. In 334 BC, the 22-year-old Alexander, after two years on the throne of Macedon, led his army against Darius III. Alexander had not set out to annex the whole of Darius' empire, but as victory followed victory his aims and ambitions increased. Darius' armies suffered defeat in three major battles, at Granicus in 334, the following year at Issus and then, after Alexander had invaded Egypt, at Gaugamela, near ancient Nineveh, in 331. Darius fled from the battlefield, leaving Alexander to take possession of the palaces and treasuries of Babylon, Susa, Persepolis and

Alexander's conquests
In 343 Artaxerxes III recovered Egypt after 60 years of independence. The geographical extent of the Persian empire was then not much different from what it had been in the time of Darius I, 150 years earlier. Alexander and Darius III both came to their thrones in 336 BC after their predecessors had been murdered. Alexander invaded Asia in 334 and defeated Darius III who died in 330. Alexander spent the next seven years fighting almost entirely within the borders of the Persian empire, carving out a kingdom, which was divided between his generals after his death. Along the course of his route, Alexander founded cities which he named after himself or renamed existing cities in his own honor.

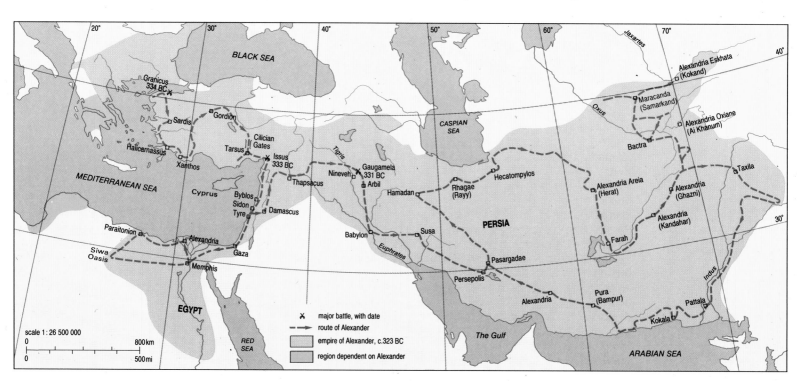

Above The Tomb of Xerxes. Four Persian kings, Darius I, Xerxes, Artaxerxes I and Darius II were buried in almost identical tombs at Naqsh-i Rustam, 6 km north of Persepolis. The king is shown worshiping in front of a fire altar before the god Ahuramazda. He stands on a dais supported by 30 peoples of the empire.

Overleaf The Alexander Mosaic showing the the battle of Gaugamela in 331 BC. It was found in the House of the Faun at Pompeii and is thought to be a mosaic copy made in about 100 BC of a 4th century BC painting by Philoxenos of Eretria. Complete height 3.42 m.

Hamadan. The burning of Persepolis, whether accidental or as a matter of policy, marked the end of the ancient Near East. Darius III was murdered by one of his courtiers and Alexander extended his campaign throughout the eastern provinces of the Persian empire, before returning to Babylon, where he died in 323 BC.

The empire of Cyrus and Darius I had survived for over 150 years until it fell, still almost intact, to Alexander. But within a few years of Alexander's death, the empire had split up. The conquests of Alexander effectively brought to an end the Mesopotamian civilization and the scribal tradition of the previous three millennia. From then on, Europe would play as important a part in world history as the Near East. Over the next thousand years the Near East remained divided between east and west until it was reunited under the banner of Islam. Its distinctive culture faded away under foreign rulers and although Mesopotamian gods continued to be worshiped, they were increasingly assimilated by Greek and Iranian deities. Cuneiform writing lingered on in the temples of Babylonia to the 1st century AD, long after papyrus and parchment had replaced clay tablets elsewhere. During the Babylonian exile of the Jews and the Greek rule over Asia, the accumulated wisdom of the Near East became part of the intellectual heritage of the Jews and the Greeks. Through them it survived and contributed to the development of European civilization.

Persepolis

The citadel of Persepolis is one of the best-preserved of all the ancient Near Eastern sites. Building was started by Darius I (521–486 BC) in about 500 BC, continued under his son Xerxes I (485–465 BC) and was completed by his grandson Artaxerxes I (464–425 BC). The palaces borrowed elements from many traditions—Median, Mesopotamian, Greek and Egyptian. The citadel formed part of a complex including the fortified hill to the east, the buildings at the foot of the citadel platform, the royal tombs in the cliff of Naqsh-i Rustam, where Darius and three of his successors were buried, and a large city where the common people lived but which has not yet been located.

Right Persepolis was one of the first of the ancient sites in the Near East to be recognized by European visitors, but the early reports were somewhat fanciful. By the 18th century quite accurate descriptions of the visible ruins were published such as this drawing by Carsten Niebuhr.

Far right Most of the citadel was excavated by the Oriental Institute of Chicago in the 1930s and this reconstructed plan is based on its work and that of the Iranian Archeological Service since then. The plans of Palace D, Palace G and of the fortification wall are mostly restored, as these structures were almost completely eroded away.

Below Some of the most interesting of the reliefs decorating the palaces show peoples subject to Persian rule, in their distinctive dress, presenting gifts to the king. Here an Armenian wearing the typical hat, tunic and trousers of Iranian horsemen brings a jar, presumably of gold, with the handle and spout decorated with winged griffons.

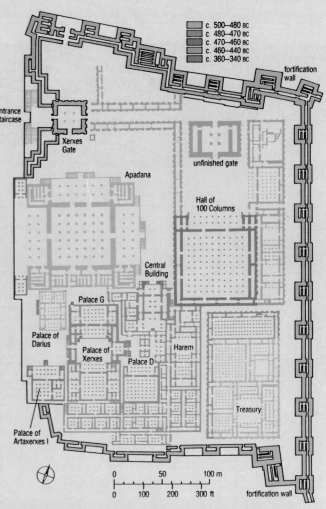

Left Often shown above the king is a figure in a winged disk, probably representing Ahuramazda, the chief god of the Persians. The coloring of this drawing of the figure on a door of the Hall of 100 Columns is based on traces of paint still remaining on the stone.

Below The largest of the buildings on the terrace was the Apadana, probably the main reception hall of the king. It had columns almost 20 m high surmounted by complex capitals in the shape of bulls or lions. From the western portico the king's throne overlooked the Marv Dasht plain.

Bottom right This double griffon capital was found to the northeast of Xerxes Gate; it is not certain to which building it originally belonged. Columned halls were characteristic of Persian architecture and column capitals with lions, bulls or human-headed bulls were most common.

Left The king is the focus of the decoration of the palaces at Persepolis. This carving, between the staircases on the platform of the Apadana, shows the king on his throne receiving gifts from his subjects. He holds a staff and a flower, and in front of him is a censer for burning incense. The inspiration for this relief is probably Assyrian. A similar scene was painted on the walls of the Assyrian palace at Til Barsip 200 years earlier.

Right Behind the carvings of the king were others of soldiers and members of his court. These guards may have belonged to the elite Persian regiment of the Ten Thousand Immortals.

The Oxus Treasure

In May 1880 three merchants in Afghanistan were attacked by robbers. Their servant escaped and alerted the local British political officer, Captain F.C. Burton, who set off in pursuit. At midnight he caught up with the robbers and persuaded them to return more than half of the merchants' goods. One of the bags had been cut open and contained a magnificent gold bracelet, which Burton himself later bought. The merchants told him that they were carrying gold and silver ornaments, gold cups, a silver and a gold idol and a large ornament resembling an anklet, all of which had been found at Takht-i Kuwad on the north bank of the Oxus river.

The merchants eventually sold the treasure in Rawalpindi (today in northeast Pakistan) to Major General Sir Alexander Cunningham, the Director of the Archaeological Survey of India, who sold it to Sir Augustus Franks. On Franks' death in 1897, it passed into the collections of the British Museum.

More than 150 objects and as many as 1,500 coins are said to be part of the Oxus Treasure. Most of the objects are of the Achaemenid period. The coins, however, range from the early 5th century to about 200 BC. While some objects may have been added to the Treasure by astute dealers in Rawalpindi, most of them probably came from a single hoard that may have belonged to a temple treasury.

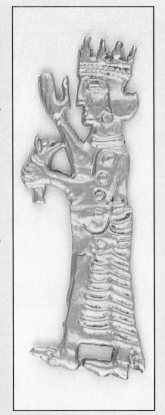

Left Cutout gold figure of the Persian king, in a long robe of the type worn by Elamites and Persians at court. Height 6.15 cm.

Below left Gold roundel of a winged lion griffon with four loops on the back. Garments with gold decorations sewn on them were worn by the Persian and Assyrian kings and by the statues of the gods. Diameter 4.75 cm.

Below Gold sheet showing a man wearing the tight trousers and tunic that are characteristic of the Medes, Armenians and Cappadocians on the reliefs at Persepolis. This dress was also worn by Persians, particularly in the hunt or in warfare. The figure has been identified as a priest. Height 15 cm.

Above A dozen gold signet rings are associated with the Oxus Treasure. Some, like this one, are in the Achaemenid court style; others are Greek in style. The motif may represent the queen or a noblewoman. Diameters of hoop 2.25 cm, of bezel 1.9 cm.

Left Gold model of a chariot drawn by four horses. On the front of the chariot is a head like that of the Egyptian god Bes. A second fragmentary gold chariot was acquired by the Earl of Lytton, the Viceroy of India, at about the same time that the Oxus Treasure was discovered and may have come from that source. Length 18.8 cm.

Below left Hollow head of beaten gold. This is one of the objects that is not in the Achaemenid style. It may be of local manufacture and postdate the Achaemenid period or it may have been added to the Oxus Treasure by dealers in Rawalpindi. Height 11.3 cm.

Below This gold bracelet is the companion to the one bought by Captain Burton, which is now in London's Victoria and Albert Museum. The hollow spaces would have contained inlays of glass or semiprecious stones. The bracelets are typical of the Achaemenid court style and similar to the objects shown as part of the Lydians' tribute on the Persepolis reliefs. Less elaborate bracelets with simpler animal terminals have been found at Pasargadae and Susa. Width 11.5 cm.

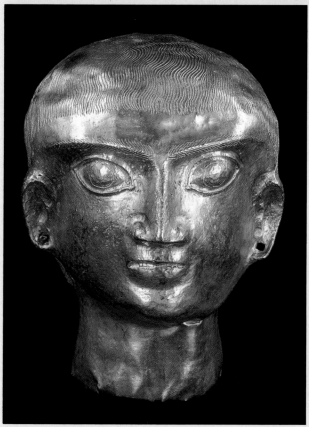

221

Babylon in Western Art

During the 150 years that have passed since Botta and Layard discovered the palaces of the Assyrian kings, Mesopotamian civilization has been rediscovered and its story recounted using the evidence of ancient Mesopotamian monuments and texts. Yet, despite the wealth of information made available by archeological excavation, the art and literature of the Western world have clung to the stereotyped images of the ancient Near East presented in the writings of the Jews and the Greeks. Those images chosen were all drawn from episodes that were made familiar through the Bible and classical authors—the Tower of Babel, the feast of Belshazzar, the death of Sardanapalus, the burning of Babylon. None of them have, however, been corroborated by contemporary Mesopotamian sources and they all display a hostile attitude toward Mesopotamian civilization.

Because of the exile of the Jews the name of Babylon was cursed in the Bible. "Babylon, the glory of kingdoms, . . . shall be as when God overthrew Sodom and Gomorrah", wrote the prophet Isaiah (Isaiah 13:19), and in the New Testament Book of Revelation Babylon was denounced as "the mother of harlots and abominations of the earth" (Revelation 17:5). The Babylon of Western art and literature has been tailored to the expectations and prejudices of the Western public. Although Western paintings may suggest Mesopotamian themes, ofen they allude to contemporary concerns of the artist or they refer to events in the past in an allegorical way.

The most sympathetic treatment of Mesopotamia and the ancient Near East in art today is found in the Arab world, where modern rulers support the work of artists treating traditional themes.

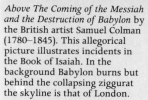

Above The Coming of the Messiah and the Destruction of Babylon by the British artist Samuel Colman (1780–1845). This allegorical picture illustrates incidents in the Book of Isaiah. In the background Babylon burns but behind the collapsing ziggurat the skyline is that of London.

Right A still from *Intolerance* (1916), an epic of the silent cinema directed by the American D.W. Griffiths. Unusually, Cyrus was cast as a tyrannical untrustworthy despot. Griffiths used the most up-to-date knowledge of the culture of Babylon and Persia: the soldiers carved on the sides of the stairs come straight from Persepolis. This scene shows part of the great banqueting hall in Babylon, the set for which stretched for one mile (1.6 km).

Above right Belshazzar's Feast by Rembrandt (1606–1669). The incident of the writing on the wall which was interpreted to mean that the kingdom of Babylon had been weighed and found wanting is dramatically portrayed.

Right A 16th-century German woodcut showing the burning of Babylon, which was a popular topic for Bible illustration. In the vision related in the Book of Revelation, Babylon was destroyed in one hour and those who witnessed the destruction "cried when they saw the smoke of her burning, saying What city is like unto this great city!" (Revelation 18:18). That allusion however, is to the destruction of Rome. The city shown here has been identified as Mainz or Worms. Indeed Babylon was later used as a metaphor for any large, corrupt commercial city.

Above The Tower of Babel by Pieter Bruegel the Elder (c. 1525/30–1569). The magnificent tower owes more to the Colosseum in Rome than to the ziggurats of Mesopotamia.

Left The Tower of Babel by the 20th-century Polish artist Josef Szubert. Like Bruegel, Szubert has made no concessions to historical accuracy, though he has given the scene a Near Eastern, rather than European, setting by including palm trees and camels. Here, however, the Biblical story of the Tower of Babel has been neglected and the Tower acts as a symbol for tyranny from which Mary and Joseph, themselves symbolizing refugees, are fleeing.

BIBLIOGRAPHY

There is an extensive literature on the ancient Near East, but many of the basic tools for research, such as bibliographies, gazetteers, encyclopedias and dictionaries, are still in the course of preparation and it will be many years before these projects are completed. This bibliography includes a small selection of the works that may be of interest to the nonspecialist reader and most of the titles listed are of books in the English language. Much important research is published in other forms—academic journals, symposia, conferences or *festschrifts*—and in other langujages—German, French, Italian, Flemish, Russian, Hebrew and the native languages of the Near East, Arabic, Turkish and Persian.

Reference works
Tübinger Atlas des Vorderen Orients produces excellent maps and other volumes on the ancient Near East including the *Répertoire Géographiques des Textes Cunéiformes* vols. 1–8, Tübingen, 1974–.
R.S. Ellis, *A Bibliography of Mesopotamian Archaeological Sites*, Wiesbaden, 1972.
Atlas of the Archaeological Sites in Iraq, Baghdad, 1979.
Reallexikon für Assyriologie und Vorderasiatische Archäologie, Berlin and New York, 1928–.
The Assyrian Dictionary of the Oriental Institute of the University of Chicago, Chicago, 1956–.
L. Vanden Berghe, *Bibliographie analytique de l'archéologie de l'Iran ancien*, Leiden, 1979 (with additional supplements).
M. Avi-Yonah (ed.), *Encyclopaedia of Archaeological Excavations in the Holy Land* 4 vols., Oxford, 1975–8.
W. Kleiss and H. Hauptmann, *Topographische Karte von Urartu*, Berlin, 1976.

General works and picture books
E. Akurgal, *The Birth of Greek Art, the Mediterranean and the Near East*, London, 1968.
P. Amiet, *Art of the Ancient Near East*, New York, 1980.
J. Baines and J. Málek, *Atlas of Ancient Egypt*, Oxford, 1980.
C.A. Burney, *The Ancient Near East*, Ithaca, 1977.
J.E. Curtis (ed.), *Fifty Years of Mesopotamian Discovery*, London, 1982.
H. Frankfort, *The Art and Architecture of the Ancient Orient*, 4th impression, Harmondsworth and Baltimore, 1970.
R. Ghirshman, *Persia from the Origins to Alexander the Great*, London, 1964.
S. Lloyd, *Art of the Ancient Near East*, London, 1961.
A. Moortgat, *The Art of Ancient Mesopotamia*, London, 1969.
S. Moscati, *The Phoenicians*, Milan, 1988.
H.J. Nissen, *The Early History of the Ancient Near East, 9000–2000 BC*, Chicago, 1988.
D. and J. Oates, *The Rise of Civilization*, Oxford, 1976.
J. Oates, *Babylon*, London and New York, 1979.
A. Parrot, *Nineveh and Babylon*, New York, 1961.
A. Parrot, *Sumer*, London, 1960.
E. Porada, *Ancient Iran: the Art of Pre-Islamic Times*, London, 1965.
J.N. Postgate, *The First Empires*, Oxford, 1977.
J.B. Pritchard (ed.), *The Times Atlas of the Bible*, revised edition, London, 1989.
J. Rogerson, *Atlas of the Bible*, Oxford, 1989.
G. Roux, *Ancient Iraq*, 2nd edition, Harmondsworth, 1980.
H.W.F. Saggs, *The Greatnesss that was Babylon*, London, 1962.
H.W.F. Saggs, *The Might that was Assyria*, London, 1984.
E. Strommenger and M. Hirmer, *The Art of Mesopotamia*, London, 1964.
H. Weiss (ed.), *From Ebla to Damascus: Art and Archaeology of Ancient Syria*, Washington, 1985.

Prehistory
W.C. Brice (ed.), *The Environmental History of the Near East since the Last Ice Age*, London, 1978.
S. Davis, *The Archaeology of Animals*, London, 1987.
D. Frankel, *Archaeologists at Work: Studies on Halaf Pottery*, London, 1979.
A.N. Garrard and H.G. Gebel (eds.), *The Prehistory of Jordan: the State of Research in 1986*, Oxford, 1988.
J. Mellaart, *Çatal Hüyük: a Neolithic Town in Anatolia*, London, 1967.
J. Mellaart, *The Neolithic of the Near East*, London and New York, 1975.
P.R.S. Moorey (ed.), *Origins of Civilization*, Wolfson College Lectures, Oxford, 1979.

A.L. Perkins, *The Comparative Archaeology of Early Mesopotamia*, Chicago, 1949.
J.N. Postgate and M.A. Powell (eds.), *Bulletin on Sumerian Agriculture*, Cambridge, 1984–.
C.L. Redman, *The Rise of Civilization*, San Francisco, 1978.
P. Singh, *Neolithic Cultures of Western Asia*, London, 1975.
P.J. Ucko and G.W. Dimbleby (eds.), *Domestication and Exploitation of Plants and Animals*, London, 1969.
P.J. Ucko, R. Tringham and G.W. Dimbleby (eds.), *Man, Settlement and Urbanism*, London, 1972.
G.A.Wright, *Obsidian Analysis and Prehistoric Near Eastern Trade: 7500 to 3500 BC*, Ann Arbor, 1969.
T.C. Young, P.E.L. Smith and P. Mortensen (eds.), *The Hilly Flanks and Beyond*, Chicago, 1983.

History
J.A. Brinkman, *Prelude to Empire: Babylonian Society and Politics 747–626 BC*, Philadelphia, 1984.
J.A. Brinkman, *Materials and Studies for Kassite History I*, Chicago, 1976.
J.A. Brinkman, *A Political History of Post-Kassite Babylonia*, Rome, 1968.
Cambridge Ancient History, new edition, Cambridge, 1970–1984.
E. Carter and M. Stolper, *Elam: Surveys of Political History and Archaeology*, University of California Publication in Near Eastern Studies 25, Berkeley, 1984.
A.H. Gardiner, *Egypt of the Pharaohs*, Oxford, 1961.
O.R. Gurney, *The Hittites*, revised edition, Harmondsworth, 1980.
W.W. Hallo and W.K. Simpson, *The Ancient Near East: A History*, New York, 1971.
A.T. Olmstead, *History of the Persian Empire*, Chicago, 1948.
D. Oates, *Studies in the Ancient History of Northern Iraq*, London, 1968.
A.L. Oppenheim, *Ancient Mesopotamia*, Chicago, 1964.
N. K. Sandars, *The Sea Peoples: Warriors of the Ancient Mediterranean*, revised edition, London, 1985.

Texts in translation
J.S. Cooper, *Sumerian and Akkadian Royal Inscriptions*, vol. 1, New Haven, Connecticut, 1986.
S. Dalley, *Myths from Mesopotamia: Creation, the Flood, Gilgamesh and Others*, Oxford, 1989.
A.K. Grayson, *Assyrian and Babylonian Chronicles*, New York, 1975.
A.K. Grayson, *Assyrian Royal Inscriptions*, vols. 1 and 2, Wiesbaden, 1972, 1976.
A.K. Grayson and others, *Royal Inscriptions of Mesopotamia*, Toronto, 1987–.
D.D. Luckenbill, *Ancient Records of Assyria and Babylonia*, Chicago, 1926–7.
A.L. Oppenheim, *Letters from Mesopotamia*, Chicago, 1968.
J.B. Pritchard (ed.), *The Ancient Near East: an Anthology of Texts and Pictures*, Princeton University Press, Princeton, 1958.
J.B. Pritchard (ed.), *Ancient Near Eastern Texts Relating to the Old Testament*, Princeton, 3rd edition, 1969.
S. Parpola (ed.), *State Archives of Assyria*, Helsinki, 1987–.
E. Sollberger and J.-R. Kupper, *Inscriptions Royales sumeriennes et akkadiennes*, Paris, 1971.

Places and periods
R.M. Adams, *Heartland of Cities: Surveys of Ancient Settlement and Land Use on the Central Floodplain of the Euphrates*, Chicago, 1981.
R.M. Adams and Hans J. Nissen, *The Uruk Countryside: the Natural Setting of Urban Societies*, Chicago, 1972.
Y. Aharoni, *The Archaeology of the Land of Israel*, London, 1982.
P. Amiet, *L'art d'Agade au Musée du Louvre*, Paris, 1976.
P. Amiet, *Elam*, Auvers-sur-Oise, 1966.
G. Bibby, *Looking for Dilmun*, London, 1970.
K. Bittel, *Hattusha: the Capital of the Hittites*, Oxford, 1970.
C.A. Burney and D. Lang, *Peoples of the Hills, Ancient Ararat and Caucasus*, London, 1971.
A. Curtis, *Ugarit (Ras Shamra)*, Cambridge, 1985.
J.E. Curtis, *Ancient Persia*, London, 1989.
S. Dalley, *Mari and Karana: Two Old Babylonian Cities*, London and New York, 1984.
D. Frankel, *The Ancient Kingdom of Urartu*, London, 1979.
D.B. Harden, *The Phoenicians*, London, 1962.
S.W. Helms, *Jawa: Lost city of the Black Desert*, London, 1981.
F. Hole (ed.), *The Archaeology of Western Iran*, Washington, 1987.

K.M. Kenyon, *Archaeology in the Holy Land*, 4th edition, London, 1979.
K.M. Kenyon, *The Bible and Recent Archaeology*, revised edition by P.R.S. Moorey, London, 1987.
Shaikha Haya Ali Al Khalifa and Michael Rice (eds.), *Bahrain through the Ages: the Archaeology*, London, 1986.
S.N. Kramer, *The Sumerians: their History, Culture and Character*, University of Chicago Press, 1963.
M.T. Larsen, *The Old Assyrian City-State and its Colonies*, Copenhagen, 1976.
S. Lloyd, *Early Highland Peoples of Anatolia*, London, 1967.
S. Lloyd, *The Archaeology of Mesopotamia*, London, 1978.
S. Matheson, *Persia: an Archaeological Guide*, London, 1972.
P. Matthiae, *Ebla: an Empire Rediscovered*, London, 1977.
J. Mellaart, *Archaeology of Ancient Turkey*, London, 1978.
B.B. Piotrovskii, *The Kingdom of Urartu and its Art*, London, 1967.
M.D. Roaf, *Sculptures and Sculptors at Persepolis*, London, 1983.
D.B. Stronach, *Pasargadae*, Oxford, 1978.
G. Wilhelm, *The Hurrians*, Warminster, 1989.
C.L. Woolley, *Excavations at Ur*, revised by P.R.S. Moorey, London, 1982.
J. Yakar, *The Later Prehistory of Anatolia: the Late Chalcolithic and Early Bronze Age*, Oxford, 1985.
T.C. Young and L. Levine (eds.), *Mountains and Lowlands: Essays in the Archaeology of Greater Mesopotamia*, Undena, 1977.

Special studies
R.D. Barnett, *Ancient Ivories in the Middle East*, Jerusalem, 1982.
J.A. Black and A.R. Green, *Gods, Demons and Symbols of Ancient Mesopotamia*, London, 1990.
D. Collon, *First Impressions: Cylinder Seals in the Ancient Near East*, London, 1987.
J.H. Crouwel and M.A. Littauer, *Wheeled Vehicles and Ridden Animals in the Ancient Near East*, Leiden, 1979.
J.E. Curtis (ed.), *Bronze Working Centres of Western Asia c. 1000–539 BC*, London, 1988.
R.W. Ehrich (ed.), *Chronologies of Old World Archaeology*, Chicago, 1965.
H. Frankfort and H.A.G.-Frankfort (eds.), *The Intellectual Adventure of Ancient Man*, Chicago, 1946.
A.M. Gibson and R.D. Biggs (eds.), *Seals and Sealing in the Ancient Near East*, Malibu, 1977.
A.M. Gibson and R.D. Biggs (eds.), *The Organization of Power: Aspects of Bureaucracy in the Ancient Near East*, Chicago, 1987.
C.J. Gadd, *The Stones of ASssyria*, London, 1936.
G. Herrmann, *Ivories from Room SW37 Fort Shalmaneser, Ivories from Nimrud (1949–1963)*, vol. 4, London, 1986.
T. Jacobsen, *The Treasures of Darkness*, New Haven, 1976.
W.G. Lambert, *Babylonian Wisdom Literature*, Oxford, 1960.
M.T. Larsen (ed.), *Power and Propaganda: a Symposium on Ancient Empires*, Copenhagen, 1979.
A.H. Layard, *Nineveh and its Remains*, London, 1849.
S. Lloyd, *Foundations in the Dust*, revised edition, London, 1980.
K.R. Maxwell-Hyslop, *Western Asiatic Jewellery c. 3000–612 BC*, London, 1971.
R.H. Meadow and H.-P. Uerpmann (eds.), *Equids in the Ancient World*, Wiesbaden, 1986.
P.R.S. Moorey, *Materials and Manufacture in Ancient Mesopotamia: the Evidence of Archaeology and Art: Metals, Metalwork, Glazed Materials and Glass*, Oxford, 1985.
J.D. Muhly, *Copper and Tin: the Distribution of Metal Resources and the Nature of the Metals Trade in the Bronze Age*, New Haven, 1973–6.
O. Neugebauer, *The Exact Sciences in Antiquity*, Princeton, 1952.
O. Neugebauer and A. Sachs, *Mathematical Cuneiform Texts*, New Haven, 1945.
S.A. Pallis, *The Antiquity of Iraq*, Copenhagen, 1956.
M.V. Pope, *The Story of Decipherment*, London, 1975.
J.E. Reade, *Assyrian Sculpture*, London, 1983.
B. Teissier, *Ancient Near Eastern Cylinder Seals from the Marcopoli Collection*, University of California, Berkeley, 1984.
G. Waterfield, *Layard of Nineveh*, London, 1963.
T.A. Wertime and J.D. Muhly (eds.), *The Coming of the Age of Iron* (Yale University Press, 1980).
Y. Yadin, *The Art of Warfare in Biblical Lands*, London, 1963.

GLOSSARY

Technical and foreign terms appearing in the book are, for the most part, explained in the contexts where they occur. Such explanations are also included here in the glossary, in some cases in fuller form and with additional information. Headwords and cross-references are given in bold type. The glossary also includes explanatory notes on proper names and on the dating systems employed by the author.

The spelling of words and names belonging to ancient languages, although based on the written forms, is partly a matter of convention. The pronunciation can be guessed at by comparison with words that survive in modern languages such as Persian, Arabic or Aramaic and from names that were also written in other scripts such as Greek. As with all languages, the pronunciation varied according to the dialect and period. In later periods the final m on nouns was dropped, but here the more familiar form has been used: thus *akitu*, not *akitum*, and *awilum*, not *awilu*.

accession year The year in which a ruler became king. See also **regnal year.**

Aceramic Neolithic The early part of the Neolithic period before the widespread use of pottery vessels (c. 8500–7000 BC), including the Pre-Pottery Neolithic B period in the Levant.

Achaemenid dynasty The line of Persian kings (c. 559–330 BC) who ruled the Near East from Cyrus to Darius III.

acropolis The higher part of a town, the citadel where the palaces and temples were situated.

Agade A city in southern Mesopotamia, founded by Sargon (2334–2279 BC) as his capital. Its location is uncertain.

akitu A seasonal festival that took place in the *akitu* temple situated outside the city walls. The most famous was the New Year festival in Babylon but there were also *akitu* temples in Harran, Terqa, Nineveh, Arbil, Ashur, Sippar, Dilbat and Uruk.

Akkad The northern part of the southern Mesopotamian plain named after the city of Agade. See also **Sumer.**

Akkadian language The Semitic language spoken in Mesopotamia from the 3rd to the 1st millennium BC. The principal known dialects were Assyrian and Babylonian.

alluvium Silt brought down by the rivers and deposited as sediment in the floodplain.

Anatolia The plains of highland Turkey.

annakum A metal taken by the Old Assyrian merchants from Ashur to Anatolia, almost certainly tin.

apkallu One of the seven sages from the time before the **Flood.** Clay statuettes of *apkallus* were placed under the floors and doorways of buildings to ward off evil spirits.

ashipu A priest specializing in exorcism.

Assyria The part of northern Mesopotamia that is in present-day Iraq.

Assyriology The study of ancient Mesopotamia, principally through the **cuneiform** texts.

awilum The so-called freemen class in Hammurabi's Law Code. *Awilum* means "man" in Akkadian. See also **mushkenum, wardum.**

Babylonia Southern Mesopotamia.

bala A taxation and redistribution system in operation on the cities of southern Mesopotamia in the time of the Third Dynasty of Ur.

bel Akkadian *bēlu*, meaning master, lord, ruler, owner, and a title of the god Marduk. *Bel biti* was the chief of a tribe.

beveled-rim bowl A crudely-made conical pottery vessel formed in a mold. This widespread type was characteristic of the Late Uruk period.

bit reduti The house of succession, the palace of the Assyrian crown prince.

Bronze Age The period when cutting tools were made of copper alloys. The Bronze Age is often divided into three periods, the Early Bronze Age (c. 4000–2000 BC), the Middle Bronze Age (c. 2000–1600 BC) and the Late Bronze Age (c. 1600–1200 BC) but the chronological limits and the terminology vary from region to region.

bulla A lump of clay bearing seal impressions.

burnish To rub the surface of a pottery vessel before firing to give a smooth shiny surface. This was done to make the vessel less porous and as a decorative technique.

calendar Ancient Near Eastern calendars varied from city to city and from period to period. In most cities the year started in the spring and was divided into 12 or 13 months. In some places the months were of fixed length; in others they were lunar months starting at the first sighting of the crescent of the new moon. As there are more than twelve lunar months in a solar year additional, or intercalary, months were included so that every third year contained thirteen months.

cartouche An oval containing a name, used in Egypt for writing royal names.

casemate wall A defensive wall with chambers in the thickness of the wall. Sometimes these chambers were rooms; sometimes they were filled with debris or left empty.

cella The room in a temple where the statue or symbol of the god was worshiped.

Chalcolithic The period between the Neolithic and the Bronze Age when stone and copper tools were in use. The dating of the period varies from region to region.

chlorite A soft gray or black stone used for seals and vessels, also called steatite (soapstone).

chronology A dating system. Relative chronology is based on the application of the principles of **stratigraphy** and **typology** to determine the timing of a sequence of events. For the early periods the absolute chronology is based on scientific methods such as **radiocarbon determination** and for the later periods on historical evidence. For the period 2600–1500 BC three different schemes have been proposed, called the High, Middle and Low Chronologies, based on different possibilities for the dating of observations of the planet Venus contained in the **Venus tablets of Ammisaduqa.** The Middle Chronology, which gives the dates of Hammurabi's reign as 1792–1750 BC, is still the most widely supported. Dates according to the High Chronology are 56 years earlier and dates according to the Low Chronology are 64 years later. For dates after 1500 BC the absolute chronology is not likely to change by more than about ten years.

cone mosaic A type of wall decoration used in the Uruk and Jemdet Nasr periods in which stone or baked clay cones were stuck into the surface of a wall to produce a colored pattern.

cuneiform The script used in Mesopotamia and neighboring regions for writing on clay tablets. The signs were formed by pressing a rectangular-ended instrument into the plastic clay to leave a wedge-shaped impression. The word is derived from *cuneus*, the Latin for nail (early nails were cut from sheets of metal and had no heads).

cylinder seal A cylinder engraved with a design, which was impressed onto the plastic clay when the cylinder seal was rolled over a clay tablet.

daric A gold coin bearing the design of a royal archer, issued by Darius I (521–486 BC) and later Achaemenid rulers.

dendrochronology A method of dating timber by the patterns of the annual growth rings.

Dilmun A region and island situated in the Gulf, probably to be identified with Bahrain, the western shore of the Gulf and the island of Failaka in Kuwait.

divination Forecasting the future. The principal forms of divination practiced in the ancient Near East included the examination of the internal organs (extispicy)—especially the liver (hepatoscopy)—of animals, the patterns formed by oil in water (lecanomancy) or by smoke (libanomancy), as well as the behavior of animals, freak births, dreams and the movements of celestial bodies.

divine kings In Egypt the pharaoh was accorded divine status, but most rulers in the Near East claimed to be merely the priests or agents of the gods. Some early kings such as Gilgamesh were deified after death and others, particularly in the late 3rd and early 2nd millennia BC claimed to be gods in their lifetimes.

dynasty Line of rulers normally from a single family, but sometimes used for rulers from a single city or ethnic group.

en Sumerian word meaning high priest, ruler, lord, a title used by the rulers of early Sumerian cities, notably Uruk.

ensi Sumerian title used by rulers of some city states, meaning governor.

entu-priestess Akkadian form of the Sumerian term for high priestess.

Epic of Creation A religious poem in praise of the god Marduk which was recited at the Babylonian New Year Festival. It describes the origin of the world and Marduk's rise to power.

epigraphy The study of ancient inscriptions.

Epipaleolithic The continuation of Paleolithic (Old Stone Age) cultures after the end of the last Ice Age. It was followed by the **Neolithic** period.

excration texts Curses written on clay figurines or pottery vessels containing the names of the enemies of Egypt, which were ritually smashed to bring misfortune to the enemies of Middle Kingdom Egypt.

faience An artificial material made of crushed quartz pebbles held together by a glaze.

Flood, the The Bible and Sumerian and Babylonian myths recorded a catastrophic flood sent by the gods to destroy humankind. With the assistance of the gods, one man (variously called Noah, Ziusudra or Ut-napishtim) and his family survived by building a boat. Attempts by archeologists to identify the Flood either with historical events or by means of archeological evidence have not been successful.

flotation The technique of recovering plant material such as carbonized seeds by immersing the soil from an archeological deposit in water and collecting the organic material that floats to the surface.

foundation deposit A collection of objects buried in the walls or beneath the floors of a building to ensure the goodwill of the gods and to perpetuate the fame of the builder.

Gilgamesh Epic An Akkadian poem written on 12 tablets describing the deeds of the legendary Gilgamesh ruler of Uruk and his search for immortality. It includes the story of the **Flood.**

giparu Sumerian term for the residence of the *entu*-priestess, particularly in Ur where at times it also included the temple of the goddess Ningal.

glaçis A smooth, often plastered, slope at the base of a defensive wall, particularly characteristic of the Middle Bronze Age in the Levant.

granulation A metalworking technique for joining tiny droplets of gold together to decorate jewelry. Many examples of the technique were found in the Royal Cemetery at Ur and it is still used in the Near East today.

Great Sea (or Great Sea of Amurru) The Mediterranean Sea.

gun mada An annual tax paid in animals by military personnel in the regions to the north and east of the core of the empire of the Third Dynasty of Ur.

Hammurabi's Code See **law codes.**

Hamrin Dam Salvage project See **rescue projects.**

hazarapat Leader of one thousand, called *chiliarch* by the Greeks, the highest official at the Persian Achaemenid court.

hieroglyphic script Writing system in which the signs for words or syllables are mostly identifiable pictures. The most important were Egyptian and Hittite hieroglyphic.

husking tray A type of pottery dish with a corrugated inside, typical of the Hassuna period.

Ice Age Period of intense cold throughout the world, which resulted in a lower sea level. In the past, there were many Ice Ages, of which the last started to end c. 15,000 BC.

incision A decorative technique in which a design is scratched into the surface, particularly of pottery vessels or metal objects.

Intercultural Style A style of decoration of stone vessels (normally made of **chlorite**) found in Iran, Mesopotamia and the Gulf in the second half of the 3rd millennium BC.

Iron Age The period when iron was used for tools and weapons, starting c. 1400–1200 BC. Iron did not become more widely used than bronze until the 9th century BC.

karum An Akkadian word for quay or market place, especially the trading stations established by Old Assyrian merchants in Anatolia and elsewhere.

Khirbet Kerak ware A type of black or red burnished pottery found in the Levant and related to Early Transcaucasian wares.

king list A text recording the names of kings and the lengths of their reigns. The most important are the Sumerian King List, which recorded the dynasties ruling southern Mesopotamia from the mythical period before the Flood to the Isin–Larsa period, and the Assyrian King List, which listed the rulers of Assyria from before 2000 BC to the Late Assyrian period.

kudurru An Akkadian term for a document recording a royal land grant. It was normally a carved stone stele containing the details of the grant and images of the gods who guaranteed it. *Kudurrus* have been called Babylonian boundary stones, as some were placed in temples and others were possibly used as boundary markers. The word also means son, as in personal names such as Nabu-kudurri-usur (more familiarly, Nebuchadnezzar).

lamassu A guardian figure. This term has been used to describe the colossal, stone, part-human, part-animal figures carved on the doorways of Assyrian and Achaemenid buildings.

law codes Texts written for Mesopotamian and Hittite rulers recording the judgments and appropriate penalties for various crimes. The most famous is Hammurabi's Code.

Levant The lands bordering the eastern Mediterranean.

level (or building level) In archeological excavations the remains are divided into levels that contain the buildings and objects belonging to an architectural phase.

limmu (or *līmu*) The title of an official in Assyria whose term of office lasted for one year. The name of the *limmu* official was used to refer to the year in which he held that office.

Linear Elamite script A syllabic script used in Elam for inscriptions of Kutik-Inshushinak (c. 2200 BC).

logogram A sign standing for a word.

lost-wax casting A method of turning wax models into metal objects by forming an intermediate clay mold. Also called *cire perdue*.

Lower Sea The Gulf.

lugal The Sumerian word for king (literally meaning big man). The *lugal* may originally have been a war leader.

Luwian An Anatolian language spoken in the 2nd and 1st millennia. It was often written down using the Hittite hieroglyphic script.

magus A priest among the Medes and Persians. It is the origin of the word magi (the three kings) and of the English "magic".

malikum The Akkadian word for counsellor, but at Ebla the title of the ruler.

Meluhha In the 3rd and 2nd millennia BC a country to the east of Sumer, which was reached by way of the Gulf, probably the Indus valley. In the 1st millennium BC Meluhha refers to Nubia, to the south of Egypt.

Migdal temples Tower-fortress temples typical of the Middle Bronze Age in the Levant.

mina A weight of about 500 g. There were normally 60 shekels to 1 mina and 60 minas to 1 talent.

mushkenum One of the three classes of people in Hammurabi's Code, probably a servant of the state. See also **awilum** and **wardum.**

Natufian A part of the **Epipaleolithic** period in the Levant which witnessed the development of cereal grain exploitation, c. 11,000–9300 BC.

Neolithic New Stone Age, the period characterized by the use of stone tools and the adooption of agriculture as the principal means of subsistence.

New Year festival See *akitu*.

Ninevite 5 The period from c. 3000–2500 BC in northern Mesopotamia characterized by distinctive painted and incised and excised pottery. The name derives from the site of Nineveh where it was first excavated.

obelisk A form of stele or stone monument that tapers toward the top.

obsidian A naturally-occurring volcanic glass. It was widely used for cutting tools and occasionally for vessels, mirrors and jewelry.

onager A type of wild ass (*Equus hemionus*) which lived in the steppes of the Near East.

papyrus Writing material made from the pith of the papyrus plant. Used first in Egypt, it later replaced clay tablets in the Near East when the Aramaic alphabet replaced the cuneiform script. The English "paper" is derived from papyrus.

pictograph A sign in a script whose picture suggests the meaning.

plano-convex brick A sun-dried or kiln-fired rectangular brick with a flat under surface and a domed upper surface. Such bricks were used extensively in southern Mesopotamia in the Early Dynastic period.

pollen core A stratified sample of soil or sediment that is taken to recover the plant pollen, and hence to discover changes in the local vegetation over time.

potsherd See **sherd.**

processional way A route along which the statues of the gods were carried at festivals, in particular the road leading from the Temple of Marduk to the **akitu** temple in Babylon.

Proto-Elamite The undeciphered script and the civilization of Elam in the late 4th and early 3rd millennia BC.

Proto-Neolithic The transitional period between the hunting and gathering cultures of the **Epipaleolithic** and the farming cultures of the **Aceramic Neolithic** (c. 9300–8500 BC). The term is used differently by different authors, but here it includes the Pre-Pottery Neolithic A of the Levant.

radiocarbon determination The estimation of the date of materials through the measurement of the surviving proportion of the isotope Carbon 14. This may be calibrated to obtain a more accurate value.

regnal year The year of reign. At some periods documents were dated by the king's regnal year. Before the time of Alexander the Great the first regnal year started as the New Year following the king's accession. See also **accession year.**

relief Sculpture in which the design stands out from a flat surface (also called raised bas-relief).

rescue projects In the last 30 years much archeological research has been carried out as part of rescue projects in areas threatened by development, often through flooding behind dams or by large-scale agricultural or urban development schemes. The principal projects in Iraq have been the Dokan Dam, the Derbend-i Khan Dam, and the Eski Mosul (or Saddam) Dam; in Syria the Tabqa Dam and the Lower Habur Dam; and in Turkey the Keban Dam and the Erbaba Dam. But even outside these projects almost all archeological sites are in danger through increasing pressure on the available land.

rhyton A drinking vessel in the shape of an animal head, with a small hole in the base through which the liquid flowed.

riemchen A rectangular, square-sectioned brick used in the Uruk period.

sacred marriage A religious ceremony, performed by the Sumerians and Babylonians, that was intended to ensure the fertility of the land. The groom and the bride were the ruler and a priestess and they represented the city god and his spouse.

sacred tree The notif of a stylized tree in ritual scenes is found in Middle and Late Assyrian art as well as in the Levant. It was probably the result of Egyptian influence in the 15th century BC. The significance of the motif is not clear.

satrapy A province of the Persian empire, ruled by a governor or satrap appointed by the king.

Scarlet ware A type of red and black painted pottery used in the early 3rd millennium BC in the plains of eastern Mesopotamia.

sea peoples Invaders of Egypt in the 13th and 12th centuries BC. They were part of a wider movement of peoples including those responsible for the widespread destruction of settlements in the Aegean, Anatolia and the Levant.

Sealand The area of marshes and lagoons at the head of the Gulf. In the middle of the 2nd millennium BC the dynasty of the Sealand had control of much of southern Mesopotamia, but little is known about its rule.

Semitic A group of languages including Akkadian, Eblaite, Canaanite, Amorite, Ugaritic, Phoenician, Aramaic, Hebrew and Arabic, widely spoken throughout the Near East.

sha reshe An Akkadian term meaning "one of the head" used to refer to a class of people at the Assyrian court, almost certainly consisting of eunuchs.

shaft grave A grave in which the burial chamber was reached by a vertical shaft.

shekel A weight. Normally there were 60 shekels to the mina but sometimes 50.

sherd A broken fragment most commonly of pottery, sometimes written "shard".

sit shamshi Akkadina for sun rise, the name of a remarkable bronze sculpture from Elam.

slip A thin layer of fine liquid clay applied to the surface of a pottery vessel to improve its apearance and to make it less porous.

stamp seal An engraved seal which is pressed into the surface to leave an impression.

stele A stone monument normally erected by a ruler. Stelae (plural) were often inscribed and had sculptured images carved on them.

stratigraphy The principle that, on an archeological site, a deposit overlaying another was therefore laid down later.

sukkulmah A high court official in southern Mesopotamia and the title of the ruler of Elam in the early 2nd millennium BC.

Sumer The part of the southern Mesopotamian plain that lay to the south of Nippur. See also **Akkad**.

susi temple A type of temple found in Urartu, perhaps the square, single-chambered tower-like buildings found in excavations.

talent A weight unit equal to 60 minas, that is, about 30 kg.

tablet A flat, cushion-shaped object on which inscriptions in the **cuneiform** script were written. Tablets were normally of clay but were also made of stone or metal. The shape and size varied according to the the nature of the inscription and the period when the tablet was inscribed.

tauf The Arabic term for building out of mud. Mud mixed with straw is applied to the top of the wall and allowed to dry before a further course is added. Also known as *pisé* (French) and *chineh* (Persian).

tell The Arabic term for a mound consisting of the debris of an ancient settlement. Also called *tel* (Hebrew), *choga* or *tepe* (Persian) and *hüyük* (Turkish).

tholos A round building with a conical or vaulted roof, in particular a circular hut of the Halaf period.

tripartite The architectural plan common to Ubaid houses and early Mesopotamian temples, with a long central room flanked by rows of smaller rooms.

tumulus A mound of earth or stones covering a burial.

turtanu The chief official of the Late Assyrian court, often translated as grand vizier or field marshal.

typology The study and classification of artifacts. In particular, the placing of a group of objects in chronological order on the assumption that similar objects were close in date.

Upper Sea The Mediterranean Sea.

urigallu A standard. The same word refers to a high priest, but this may be read *sheshgallu*.

Venus tablets of Ammisaduqa Records of observations of the planet Venus that may establish the date of the reign of the Babylonian king Ammisaduqa. See **chronology**.

Via Maris Latin for the Way of the Sea, the Roman name for the most important route from Egypt to Syria, which followed the coastal plain before crossing over into the plain of Jezreel and the Jordan valley.

wardum A slave, and hence a servant or official of the king.

winged disk A solar disk with wings, derived from Egypt. Commonly used in the Levant and by the Hittites, in Assyria it represented the sun god Shamash and perhaps Ashur. It was adopted by the Achaemenid Persians to represent their chief god Ahuramazda.

year-name In Mesopotamia, dates were sometimes referred to by an event that occurred in the previous year. Lists of year-names enable the chronology of the period to be determined. See also **regnal year** and *limmu*.

ziggurat The anglicized form of the Akkadian *ziqqurratu*, a high mound on which a temple was situated.

Note on proper names

Most of the names of people and places in the ancient Near East are unfamiliar to the nonspecialist readers. Furthermore there are different versions of names that are accepted by different scholars and this can be confusing. Thus, the name of the Assyrian king who is called Sargon in the Bible is sometimes given as Sharrukin or Sharkēn. One of the reasons for such inconsistencies is that there were many languages spoken in the ancient Near East each of which had its own way of representing names, so that the modern version of a name may depend on which language was being used. In particular, most names written in the cuneiform script could be read either in Sumerian or in Akkadian. Furthermore different versions of the names are used in Hebrew, German, English, Arabic, Turkish, Persian, French and so on. Generally, in this book the most familiar version of a name has been used even if, strictly, this may be less correct: thus Hammurabi is preferred to Hammurapi, and Nineveh to Ninua. Throughout the text the ancient name of places have been used rather than the modern even when the ancient names is not as familiar as the modern. For example, the Assyrian capital city is called Kalhu rathern than Nimrud. When a place changed its name in antiquity, as did the city of Gasur, which became Nuzi in the second millennium, the more familiar ancient name has been used – in this case Nuzi – even when the reference is to an earlier period. When the ancient name of a place is not known the modern name has been used instead. Undoubtedly many new identifications will be made in the future and many now thought to be secure will prove to be erroneous, as happened in the case of Tello, which for many years was thought to be the site of Lagash but is now known to be that of Girsu.

Note on dates

There are still many problems for dating the past in Mesopotamia. In the early periods the dates are based on the calibration of radiocarbon determinations (Carbon 14). However, recent research has shown that these dates are inaccurate and subject to considerable error. Archeologists prefer to cite radiocarbon determinations as time intervals, but in this book, to avoid confusing the reader, dates have been given according to the middle of the range suggested by calibration.

For the historical periods the traditional dating system has been followed even though recent research suggests (though has not yet proved) that earlier dates may satisfy the evidence better. Consequently, for the period 2600–1500 BC, where the so-called Middle Chronology has been adopted, there may be an error of as much as 100 years. Thereafter, historical dates are unlikely to differ by more than about ten years.

In the Near East the year was normally reckoned to start in the spring, and this method has generally been followed in this book. Thus 1792 BC means the year starting in spring 1792 and ending in spring 1791. However, where months are given according to the Julian calendar, the year is reckoned from January to December. Thus January 1792 BC was part of the year 1793 by the old Near East calendar. In Mesopotamia the part of the year after the death of a previous ruler until the following New Year (in the spring) was called the accession year of the new ruler, and the first year of a king's reign was reckoned as the New Year. The convention used by Assyriologists, of dating the reigns of kings from the year after the accession year, has been followed. Thus the dates for Ashurbanipal are given as 669–?627 BC, even though his father died on 1 November 670 and he actually ascended the throne before the end of December 670. If the king ruled for less than one year and died before the next New Year, his accession year is given as his reign. The dates given for kings, unless otherwise specified, refer to the duration of reign and are not from birth to death.

Note on maps

A number of features that *regularly* appear on the maps are not keyed. These include: drainage (coastline, rivers, seasonal rivers, and lakes), boundaries, sea and background colors, and general town/site location symbols. There are many instances where more than one category of symbol occurs at one site. Where possible the symbols are combined, but the different combinations are not keyed. Where the symbols cannot be combined they have been ranged below the name of the site. A separate symbol – usually an open black square – indicates the location of the site. Different typefaces are also used to signify water features, physical features (mountains, deserts etc.) and administrative areas.

LIST OF ILLUSTRATIONS

Whilst every effort has been made by Equinox (Oxford) Ltd to trace the copyright owners of the illustrations in this book, it has not proved possible in every case. Anyone concerned is invited to contact Equinox (Oxford) Ltd.

GAZETTEER

INDEX